Living and Learning in the Least Restrictive Environment

edited by
Robert H. Bruininks
and K. Charlie Lakin

·P·A·U·L·H·
BROOKES
PUBLISHING C<u>O</u>

Baltimore • London

LIVING
AND
LEARNING
IN THE
LEAST RESTRICTIVE
ENVIRONMENT

LIVING
AND
LEARNING
IN THE
LEAST RESTRICTIVE
ENVIRONMENT

---

edited by

Robert H. Bruininks, Ph.D.
and
K. Charlie Lakin, Ph.D.
Department of Educational Psychology
University of Minnesota

·P A U L ·H·
BROOKES
PUBLISHING CO

Baltimore · London

Paul H. Brookes Publishing Co.
Post Office Box 10624
Baltimore, Maryland 21204

Typeset by The Composing Room of Michigan, Inc. (Grand Rapids).
Manufactured in the United States of America by
The Maple Press Company (York, Pennsylvania).

Library of Congress Cataloging in Publication Data
Main entry under title:

Living and learning in the least restrictive environment.

Includes bibliographies and index.
1. Handicapped—Services for—United States—Addresses, essays,
lectures.   2. Handicapped—Civil rights—United States—Addresses, essays,
lectures.   3. Mental retardation facilities—United States—Addresses, essays,
lectures.   4. Group homes for the developmentally disabled—United States—
Addresses, essays, lectures.   5. Handicapped—Education—United States—
Addresses, essays, lectures.   6. Mainstreaming in education—United States—
Addresses, essays, lectures.   I. Bruininks, Robert H.   II. Lakin, K. Charlie.
HV1553.L58   1984   362.4'048'0973   84–12142
ISBN 0–933716–42–7

Contents

Contributors

Leona L. Bachrach, Ph.D., Research Professor of Psychiatry, Maryland Psychiatric Research Center, University of Maryland School of Medicine, Box 3235, Catonsville, Maryland 21228

Leona L. Bachrach, a sociologist, is nationally known for her research and writing on deinstitutionalization, mental health, and rural sociology. She was a research scientist for several years in the Biometry Branch of the National Institute of Mental Health and currently serves on the faculty of the University of Maryland.

Valerie J. Bradley, M.A., Human Services Research Institute, 120 Milk Street, 8th Floor, Boston, Massachusetts 02109

Valerie J. Bradley received her formal training in policy analysis and public policy. Prior to her current position, she served as an analyst for the California legislature. She is currently president of a highly respected consulting and research institute devoted to study of public policy issues in human services. Presently, she is directing a longitudinal analysis of the legal and organizational impact resulting from the court-ordered deinstitutionalization of Pennhurst (Pennsylvania), a case recently adjudicated by the United States Supreme Court.

Mary Jane Brotherson, Ph.D., Kansas University Affiliated Facility at Lawrence, Bureau of Child Research, University of Kansas, Lawrence, Kansas 66045

Mary Jane Brotherson is the coordinator of a family involvement project at the Kansas University Affiliated Facility. She has extensive experience in services and research with families with disabled children and adults. She has also served on several projects to design curriculum and deliver inservice training to service providers.

Robert H. Bruininks, Ph.D., Department of Educational Psychology, University of Minnesota, 204 Burton Hall, 178 Pillsbury Drive, S.E., Minneapolis, Minnesota 55455

Robert H. Bruininks is chairman of the Department of Educational Psychology at the University of Minnesota. He has conducted numerous studies and published extensively on the policy issues of deinstitutionalization and public education.

Janis G. Chadsey-Rusch, Ph.D., Department of Special Education, University of Illinois at Urbana-Champaign, 288 Education Building, Champaign, Illinois 61820

Janis G. Chadsey-Rusch received her Ph.D. degree in speech pathology and audiology at the University of Illinois, and has special interest in developing ecologically valid approaches to the study of mental retardation. She has extensive experience in working with severely and profoundly mentally retarded children in the area of language development. She has also published in this area and on the topics of social integration and language development.

James W. Conroy, M.A., Temple University, Developmental Disabilities Program, 972 Ritter Hall Annex, 13th Street and Columbia Avenue, Philadelphia, Pennsylvania 19122
    James W. Conroy is a research psychologist at the University-Affiliated Center on Developmental Disabilities at Temple University. He serves as project director for a large and complex longitudinal research study of the impact of the court-ordered deinstitutionalization of Pennhurst. He is the author of numerous research publications and is currently conducting a major study of the effects of deinstitutionalization upon family members.

Laird W. Heal, Ph.D., Department of Special Education, University of Illinois, at Urbana-Champaign, 288 Education Building, Champaign, Illinois 61820
    Laird W. Heal is a professor of special education at the University of Illinois. In recent years, he has focused his energies on research dealing with community placement of mentally retarded and other handicapped people. He is particularly interested in evaluation research and issues of cost of care. He has held academic positions at George Peabody College of Vanderbilt University and the University of Texas at Dallas, and served as Director of Research for the National Association of Retarded Citizens.

Julie Gorder Holman, M.A., Department of Educational Psychology, University of Minnesota, 206e Burton Hall, 178 Pillsbury Drive, S.E., Minneapolis, Minnesota 55455
    Julie Gorder Holman is an advanced degree student in educational psychology at the University of Minnesota. She has extensive background as a teacher and program director in public school programs and in institutional settings. The major concentration of her doctoral study is on the assessment and training of adaptive behaviors in handicapped individuals.

K. Charlie Lakin, Ph.D., Department of Educational Psychology, University of Minnesota, 218 Pattee Hall, 150 Pillsbury Drive, S.E., Minneapolis, Minnesota 55455
    K. Charlie Lakin is a research scientist at the University of Minnesota. In recent years, his work has focused on national studies of residential services for mentally retarded and other handicapped citizens.

Sharon Landesman-Dwyer, Ph.D., Department of Psychiatry and Behavioral Sciences, Child Development and Mental Retardation Center, University of Washington, WJ-10, Seattle, Washington 98195
    Sharon Landesman-Dwyer is a research psychologist at the University of Washington, Seattle, and holds a joint appointment in the Department of Social Service in the state of Washington. She has extensively researched a wide range of issues on the impact of environmental qualities on the development of handicapped people, and is widely recognized for her scholarly accomplishments in this area of emphasis. Recently she coordinated a national conference devoted to discussion of research on the impact of environmental qualities on the behavior of handicapped people; the proceedings from this conference have been published. Her work on the influence of environmental factors upon the development of people clearly stands out for its major impact on practice and research.

Frank J. Laski, Ph.D., Project Director, Disability Projects, Public Interest Law Center of Philadelphia, 1315 Walnut Street, Philadelphia, Pennsylvania 19107
    Frank J. Laski is a prominent lawyer who has participated directly in many landmark judicial cases concerned with deinstitutionalization and educational services for handicapped citizens. He is a practicing attorney with the Public Interest Law Center of Philadelphia and a recognized author of many publications in this area.

Lisa L. Rotegard, M.A., Department of Educational Psychology, University of Minnesota, 210 Pattee Hall, 150 Pillsbury Drive, S.E., Minneapolis, Minnesota 55455

Lisa L. Rotegard is a research scientist with the Center for Residential and Community Services at the University of Minnesota. Her work at the center has focused on research studies of residential services for mentally retarded and other handicapped citizens.

Robert L. Schalock, Ph.D., Chairman, Department of Psychology, Hastings College, Program Consultant–Mid-Nebraska MR Services, 522 East Side Boulevard, Hastings, Nebraska 68901

Robert L. Schalock chairs the Department of Psychology at Hastings College, Nebraska. He has conducted research and written extensively in the areas of deinstitutionalization, rehabilitation, and human services. Author of numerous books and articles, he has published extensively on the longitudinal impact of deinstitutionalization on clients and the issues of managing complex service programs.

Marsha Mailick Seltzer, Ph.D., Boston University, School of Social Work, 264 Bay State Road, Boston, Massachusetts 02215

Marsha Mailick Seltzer, a research psychologist, has conducted a number of nationally recognized studies on deinstitutionalization. One of her early studies was summarized recently in book form. Her recent work has focused on community impact issues and strategies for achieving integration of individuals perceived as deviant in neighborhoods and communities. She currently serves on the faculty of Boston University.

Jean Ann Summers, B.G.S., Kansas University Affiliated Facility at Lawrence, Bureau of Child Research, University of Kansas, Lawrence, Kansas 66045

Jean Ann Summers is the Acting Director of the Kansas University Affiliated Facility at Lawrence. She has served in the UAF in various capacities for the last 10 years, and for the last 4 years has served at vice-chair of the Kansas Planning Council on Developmental Disabilities. Her research interests include families with disabled children and analysis of developmental disabilities policy.

Craig Thornton, Ph.D., Mathematica Policy Research, Inc., P.O. Box 2393, Princeton, New Jersey 08540

Craig Thornton is a researcher and economist with Mathematica Policy Research of Princeton, New Jersey. During the past several years, he has developed, with many of his associates at Mathematica, strategies for assessing the benefits and costs of social programs. He is currently working on a national benefit-cost study of vocational training programs for mentally retarded people.

Ann P. Turnbull, Ed.D., Bureau of Child Research, University of Kansas, 223 Haworth Hall, Lawrence, Kansas 66045

Ann P. Turnbull is an associate professor of special education at the University of Kansas. She has published extensively on a wide range of issues related to the education and development of severely handicapped children, with particular reference to the needs of families. She has authored several publications on the issues of cooperative planning between families and schools, the needs of families, and strategies for increasing the coping capacity of family members with developmentally disabled children and youth. As a parent of a developmentally disabled youth who has been deinstitutionalized, she has experienced the impact of deinstitutionalization directly and upon members of her family.

Preface

Living and Learning in the Least Restrictive Environment examines a range of topics relating to the origins, implications, and substance of important social changes in the past decade that have granted handicapped citizens a fuller share of legal equality and social participation in society. It is the spirit of these changes that has been most important and has led to the growing realization that differentness and disfranchisement from opportunities should not go hand in hand. As a result of important changes in ideology and in public policies, social advances have occurred throughout Western society in the treatment of handicapped persons. These changes are most evident today in the provision of residential, educational, and related services in community settings with nonhandicapped citizens.

This volume focuses primarily on services for persons whose handicaps are so substantial that they are likely to require some degree of lifelong support. In the past, individuals in this group who received extrafamilial residential services would have been placed in one of the various institutional settings created for their care. Those who were fortunate enough to receive any education at all would have been provided school experiences devoid of much contact with anyone but those sharing the status of deficiency. In the past two decades this two-option services system, providing either disability-centered care in segregated settings or nothing, has evolved into a system with numerous and widely ranging alternatives. Although much has yet to be accomplished to make contemporary services effective and efficient in responding to the individual needs of handicapped persons, recent progress has been remarkable. Visages of archaic models still linger, but no longer does a serious disability preordain young people to a segregated childhood and near-certain institutionalization at whatever age those upon whom they are dependent cannot or will not provide for their basic needs.

Although this volume discusses services to persons whose needs are numerous and substantial, it contains no suggestion that degrees or types of dependence can ever justify depriving people of the opportunity to develop and demonstrate their maximum personal levels of independence. Our society has come a long way in its development from early in this century when dependence was perceived largely as a sign of irreversible deficiency, for which the only option of a civilized society was to construct asylums that, at minimal costs to society, would at least keep "them" off the streets and from starving.

Today our society is more sensitive to the fact that all human beings spend a substantial portion of their lives in some form of dependent relationship and that, indeed, one of the most important distinguishing characteristics of humans is the amount of their lives spent in dependent relationships before being prepared for independent living. Society has developed hundreds of programs that recognize the need to treat periods of dependence as developmental opportunities to enhance growth and social assimilation, through its schools, training programs for unemployed persons, and even self-care training programs in medical or nursing facilities. It is also generally assumed by society and its institutions, however, that dependency is transitory (e.g., in the case of children) or periodic (e.g., in the case of the millions of unemployed persons). In larger measure, such assumptions have served the important social function of giving structure to interventions to "get people on their own feet," to ready and to rehabilitate them, or to assist them to function more independently. Effective social programs in recent decades have been structured to serve such purposes—not to accept dependent conditions, but to combat them through education, training, and opportunity.

This volume is organized around major philosophical, social, organizational, and research issues affecting the delivery of residential living and habilitative services to handicapped children and youth under conditions that emphasize social integration. In today's terminology, such services are provided in the least restrictive environment with opportunity for experiences with nonhandicapped peers and adults in circumstances that are as normal as possible. The opening section of this volume discusses current trends in philosophy and practice within service programs, as well as important conceptual and practical issues in the general integration movement. In Chapter 1, K. Charlie Lakin and Robert H. Bruininks present a background on current trends, problems, and issues related to the full implementation of deinstitutionalization and the provision of appropriate educational services to handicapped children and youth. Chapter 2, by Leona L. Bachrach, carefully examines the substance of the semantics related to *deinstitutionalization* and the *least restrictive alternative* movement. Rather than being a replay of platitudes, the chapter challenges readers to focus on semantics or ideology to replace substance in their evaluation of programs for severely handicapped children and youth. Robert L. Schalock, in Chapter 3, the closing chapter of this section, outlines the elements of a comprehensive services system and discusses a number of important problems involved in providing integrated and effectively coordinated services.

Part II examines the constitutional and judicial bases of the services discussed in this volume. In Chapter 4, Frank J. Laski discusses the history, trends, and current status of judicial litigation to achieve adequate services. Following Laski's chapter, Valerie J. Bradley evaluates the past effects of litigation on reforming services for handicapped persons and looks at the future potential and probable use of litigation in this area.

Part III of this book is devoted to important implications derived from research on community attitudes and considerations in working with parents of handicapped persons. Marsha Mailick Seltzer, in Chapter 6, discusses what is known about the attitudes of community members toward establishing community residences and how program developers can approach the problem of implementing community residential programs. Chapter 7, by Ann P. Turnbull, Mary Jane Brotherson, and Jean Ann Summers, describes a family systems approach for working with parents of severely handicapped persons in community-based programs. The final chapter in this section, by James W. Conroy, reviews recent research and theory on parents' initial and long-term reactions to the deinstitutionalization of their children.

Important issues in evaluating environments and a synthesis of available research on residential environments are contained in Part IV. Lisa L. Rotegard, Robert H. Bruininks, Julie Gorder Holman, and K. Charlie Lakin, in Chapter 9, explore the findings of past research on the relationships among characteristics of environments, client treatment practices, and changes in adaptive behavior. In Chapter 10, Sharon Landesman-Dwyer examines the current status of research on the effects of environments on severely handicapped persons. While mainly focused upon residential living settings, both chapters address important issues involved in assessing environmental influences, in designing integrated settings, and in researching the impact of environments upon behavior and adjustment.

Part V, the last major section of the volume, looks at program and policy evaluation strategies. Laird W. Heal, in Chapter 11, presents a thorough discussion of outcome-oriented evaluation methodologies for community services and discusses the strengths and weaknesses of each. In Chapter 12, Craig Thornton describes how cost-benefit analyses can be used to improve evaluation and research efforts in community-based programs for handicapped persons. And in Chapter 13, Janis G. Chadsey-Rusch provides a perspective on program development and evaluation that includes an ecological psychology focus on the environmental effects on behavior, the technology of applied behavioral psychology, and the careful use of observable behavior to measure program effects that is shared by both perspectives.

Finally, in Part VI, volume editors Robert H. Bruininks and K. Charlie Lakin use the book's discussions of social and organization aspects of community-based services and related program and policy perspectives as a base to examine future directions for community-based residential, educational, and related service programs for severely handicapped children and youth in Chapter 14.

This book recounts the many achievements of the past decade, while delineating the multitude of tasks left to be accomplished. By thoroughly examining contemporary standards, practices, and problems in programs and policies affecting severely handicapped children and youth, it is hoped that the volume will assist in making the state-of-the-practice equal to the state-of-the-art and, in the process, contribute to the future improvement of both.

Acknowledgments

The initial content of some of the chapters in this volume was first presented in a working conference on deinstitutionalization and education, supported in part through a grant from the U.S. Department of Education (Grant No. G008100277). Significant work on this conference was done by Colleen Wieck in preparing the initial grant application and by JoAnne Putnam who assumed major responsibilities in coordinating the working conference activities.

Assistance in copyediting and checking references was provided by Elizabeth Balow Laraway and Cheri Gilman. Preparation of the final manuscript was done by Renee Wegwerth, with timely assistance from Steven McGuire and Sharon Olson. The patience for missed deadlines and diligent editing of our editor, Melissa Behm, were especially appreciated in the final preparation of the volume. Their assistance and support helped produce, with our knowledgeable and talented authorial colleagues, what we feel are important statements about the many accomplishments and challenges in providing full opportunity to severely handicapped children and youth. Any errors and omissions that remain are the unfortunate responsibility of the editors.

Part I

TRENDS IN PHILOSOPHY AND PRACTICE IN SERVICE PROGRAMS

Chapter 1

Contemporary Services for Handicapped Children and Youth

K. Charlie Lakin and Robert H. Bruininks

The life experiences of most handicapped persons and of those who share in their lives have improved dramatically in recent years. These improvements demonstrate society's increased concern for furthering integration, individual opportunity, and equitable treatment for all citizens. For handicapped citizens and their families, social advances have been reflected in an evolving, more progressive philosophy toward integrating handicapped individuals into society, toward recognizing and extending their legal rights, and toward substantially increasing public support for educational, residential, income maintenance, training, and other essential services. The results of these changes have provided numerous alternatives to the segregated institutional service models that were virtually the only options available not long ago.

Few events in our society have so radically transformed the lives of handicapped citizens as the public policies of deinstitutionalization of residential services and of mainstreaming in educational programs (Reynolds & Birch, 1977). These policies, sharing common philosophical and legal principles, not only signify recent progress but, at the same time, have come to signify many of the complex problems involved in assuring full opportunity for severely handicapped persons in our society.

This book explores many of the philosoph-ical, conceptual, and family and community research and development issues that remain in guaranteeing full opportunity for the development and social integration of severely handicapped persons. The focus of this exploration is primarily upon the provision of residential and educational services for severely handicapped persons, services and programs that form the core of public and private support for the severely handicapped population. Moreover, these services provide some of the most significant means by which society provides opportunities for development and social integration of handicapped children and youth. They also comprise the necessary context for examining more fully the entire range of issues and services needed by citizens who depend upon society for assistance.

This first chapter describes the severely handicapped target population on whom this book concentrates, it outlines significant trends in social and public responses to these individuals, and it identifies the significant programmatic and policy issues in providing effective service programs that are addressed in the remainder of the volume.

THE TARGET POPULATION

Before discussing contemporary perspectives and practices in providing services for severely handicapped children and young adults, an attempt should be made to identify the target population. Individuals with severe handicaps present extremely heterogeneous characteristics, typically with limitations in learning, mobility, language, and sensory functioning. Such disabilities and handicaps limit the individual's ability to function in culturally normative ways without special assistance or environmental adaptations. Within the joint perspectives of deinstitutionalization and education, the focus of this book is upon individuals with substantial handicaps who require some assistance throughout their lives. Most of these individuals will exhibit varying degrees of comparative deficiency in maturation, learning, and social adjustment.

Most handicapped persons in the United States and other Western societies who require supervised residential care outside of the natural or adopted family are defined as mentally retarded persons. Published definitions of mental retardation vary somewhat in emphasis, but most stress the criteria advocated by the American Association on Mental Deficiency (AAMD). This definition states: "Mental retardation refers to significantly subaverage general intellectual functioning resulting in or associated with concurrent impairments in adaptive behavior and manifested during the developmental period" (Grossman, 1973, p. 11). This definition stresses difficulties in the ability to learn, in combination with inadequacies in development of maturational skills (e.g., walking, toileting, language), school achievement, and social and vocational adjustment. While not all persons with substantial handicaps are classified as retarded, the vast majority of those who receive extrafamilial, supervised residential and extensive special education services meet the criteria of the AAMD definition.

Another term used to describe the target population addressed in this volume is *developmentally disabled*. The term was adopted by the U.S. Congress in 1970 with the passage of the Developmental Disabilities Services and Facilities Construction Act to describe a number of substantial disabilities that require some form of lifelong assistance to an individual in order for him or her to live and function in society. The early definition emphasized a number of categorical disabilities such as mental retardation, cerebral palsy, epilepsy, autism, and other disabilities that were presumed to originate during the developmental period of life. In the early 1970s, the exclusive focus of this definition upon often imprecisely characterized and usually overlapping categorical disabilities began to be questioned and led to a study by a national definitional task force.

As a result of the task force's recommendations (Gollay, Freedman, Wyngaarden, & Kurtz, 1978), the federal definition of developmental disability was modified from a diagnostic categorical approach to a more functional orientation. Public Law 95-602 as amended, the Developmental Disabilities Assistance and Bill of Rights Act, defines a developmental disability as a severe, chronic disability of a person that a) is attributable to a mental or physical impairment or combination of mental and physical impairments; b) is manifested before the person attains age 22; c) is likely to continue indefinitely; d) results in substantial functional limitations in three or more of the following areas of major life activity: self care, receptive and expressive language, learning, mobility, self-direction, capacity for independent living, and economic self-sufficiency; and e) reflects the person's need for a combination and sequence of special interdisciplinary or generic care, treatment, or other services that are of lifelong or extended duration and are individually planned and coordinated (Section 102[7]).

Throughout this volume, the term *developmental disabilities* is often used interchangeably with other terms such as *severely handicapped* or *substantially handicapped*. Despite normal confusion and ambiguity in this definition, people meeting these criteria often require residential services and invariably need specialized educational and other training programs.

Projecting the number of developmentally disabled persons needing services is difficult today, owing to the lack of comprehensive and accurate survey research studies. Bruininks (1983) and Bruininks, Lakin, and Rotegard (1984) have reviewed available research studies on the incidence and prevalence of mental retardation and developmental disabilities. The most extensive research in this area has been reported on persons defined as mentally retarded. Using the current AAMD definition, a rate of 2.3% to 3% of the general population could be projected as mentally retarded in the course of their lifetimes (Grossman, 1973). Some authorities, however, point out that the actual prevalence of mental retardation, that is the number of people formally identified as mentally retarded at any one time, is closer to 1% (Birch, Richardson, Baird, Horobin, & Illsley, 1970; Dingman & Tarjan, 1960; Farber, 1968; MacMillan, 1977; Mercer, 1973; Tarjan, Wright, Eyman, & Keeran, 1973). This lower estimate takes account of the higher mortality rates throughout life among moderately, severely, and profoundly retarded persons and the highly variable nature of the diagnosis, particularly for mildly retarded individuals, during the preschool, school, and adult stages of life.

A number of studies and analyses have been conducted to estimate the prevalence of developmentally disabled persons. Most studies rely extensively upon diagnostic categories to estimate prevalence rates, generally including mental retardation, cerebral palsy, epilepsy, autism, and associated disabilities. From an analysis of many published studies, Bruininks (1983) estimates the prevalence of developmentally disabled persons at 1.6% of the general population. This estimate seems defensible, based upon available empirical studies and reports on persons in specialized service programs. But although it is quite useful as a general index, as an indicator of prevalence for particular subgroups or under local circumstances, it is likely subject to some error.

Prevalence rates for all handicaps and disabilities vary as a function of age, gender, patterns of migration, nature and severity of disabilities, socioeconomic status, and regional location. This point is illustrated by the analysis of Patrick and Reschly (1982) of prevalence rates of mental retardation for the school-age population (5–17 years old), using the number of students in special education reported by states to the U.S. Department of Education. A national average of 1.63% of the school population was defined as mentally retarded on the basis of being provided special education services by public school programs. Percentage rates by states or school districts, however, varied widely, from 0.37% to 3.93%. These statistics, plus those cited earlier, attest to the importance of the many social-cultural, environmental, demographic, biomedical, and technical/administrative factors in the definition and diagnosis of disabilities.

Despite the limitations of prevalence estimates, these estimates are nonetheless useful in assessing service needs and in describing the context of service programs. The general estimate for developmental disabilities would conservatively project a total of approximately 3.6 million or more substantially handicapped persons in the United States. This estimate, however, represents a statistical average that should be increased when applied to children of school age or to periods or places of serious economic decline and high poverty (see chapter by Conley in Lakin & Bruininks, in press). Given current statistics on children and youth in special education programs, it is plausible to project that approximately 1 million children and youth would probably meet the definition of developmentally disabled.

SOCIAL AND PUBLIC RESPONSES TO SEVERELY HANDICAPPED PERSONS

Historically, the underlying structure of society's response to providing for a dependent member has been founded on the assumption that there are two essentially dichotomous forms of dependency, one being organic, the other cultural. Persons viewed as organically dependent generally included those persons with biologically impaired mental or physical processes that precluded independent functioning, whatever the environmental or social modifications that might be made in their behalf (e.g., aged/disabled and severely retarded individuals). On the other hand, culturally dependent persons generally included persons who were fortuitously dependent because the specific physical and social demands for independence in their culture were ones they were not presently meeting, although, under other physical or social (including economic) circumstances, independence might be attainable. These distinctions, although never completely dichotomous and never formally labeled, have served for decades as the primary basis for planning the types of care and treatment alternatives to be provided by social service agencies.

In part because principles of effective treatment of organically dependent persons were historically so poorly understood and articulated, it was largely assumed that services to these people would not substantially alter conditions of dependency and, therefore, that social responses were in nature largely ethical. On the other hand, social responses to culturally dependent poeple were seen as technological, with an orientation toward training or treatment. Programs for culturally dependent people required considerations of cost-effective utilization of resources allocated for habilitation to achieve and increase eventual productivity. Programs for organically dependent persons, on the other hand, were largely based on the moral costs to the culture of not making sufficient allocation of resources to an otherwise helpless group. Social responses to such individuals, therefore, were characterized more by concern for life-sustaining care than by an orientation to active treatment.

The decade of the 1970s saw a remarkable change in both the social perspective on the care and habilitation of severely (organically) handicapped persons and in the amount of funding made available to implement programs based on these changing perspectives. Several highly related factors promoted changes in the societal response to severely handicapped persons. The most important of these are discussed briefly below.

Parent-Consumer Movement

The effect of parents as consumer-advocates for handicapped persons has been felt since the end of World War II. One of most influential parent-consumer groups has been the Association for Retarded Citizens (ARC). Begun in 1950 with about 40 parents and advocates for mentally retarded persons, the ARC has been particularly influential in the establishment of improved educational, residential, and support services for retarded persons. The evolving advocacy of this organization has played a major role in defining each decade's standards for programs serving handicapped persons. For example, in the 1950s the ARC called for restrictions on the size of institutions; in the 1960s it assisted with establishing minimum standards for residential care facilities; in the 1970s it passed a resolution to recommend "residential facilities consist[ing] of small living units, each replicating a normal home environment to the closest extent possible" and "that such residential facilities take absolute precedence over further capital investments in existing or new scale institutions" (National Association for Retarded Citizens, 1976, p. 3); and in the 1980s it is supporting legislation to phase out Medicaid funding for institutional settings. The ARC has also been an active plaintiff in federal and state court cases regarding the rights of retarded citizens to adequate treatment in residential and community services (e.g., *Michigan Association for Retarded Citizens v. Smith,* 1979; *New York Association for Retarded Citizens v. Carey,* 1975).

Parents have been equally active in promoting education and related services for handicapped children and youth. In addition to the ARC, parent groups like the National Society for Crippled Children, United Cerebral Palsy Associations; and, more recently, the Association for Children with Learning Disabilities have actively and politically pursued special education and related services for handicapped children and youth. In many instances, this has been done with the concerted cooperation of professional groups like the Council for Exceptional Children, the American Association on

Mental Deficiency, and the National Education Association. In recent years, when serious proposals were made at state and federal levels to alter the fundamental guarantees contained in Public Law 94-142 (the Education for All Handicapped Children Act of 1975), and other statutes, the potency of this parent-professional coalition caused rapid retractions of the proposals.

There has also been growing activism among severely handicapped persons to function as their own advocates. One such self-advocacy organization is People First, originally a Canadian organization. One of the primary foci of this organization is advocating for the rights and means to permit handicapped persons to live as independently as their ability allows. Tacitly promoted by this and other self-advocacy groups is that personal rights and human dignity are too precious to be taken from the individual and entrusted solely to professional discretion.

Civil Rights Movement

The great social movement in the 1960s to grant full civil rights to this nation's ethnic and racial minorities spread in the 1970s to other minorities, including groups of handicapped persons. In part this movement was related to the parent-consumer movement but, in large measure, it went beyond mere advocacy for improved services, to publicizing the plight of severely handicapped persons, contending that the conditions of their treatment, in many specific instances, represented a deprivation of constitutional rights. The landmark decision in this movement was *Wyatt v. Stickney*, a 1972 Alabama case in which the court ruled that mentally retarded persons have a right to treatment in the "least restrictive" alternative:

> Residents shall have a right to the least restrictive conditions necessary to achieve the purposes of habilitation. To this end, the institution shall make every attempt to move residents from: (a) more- to less-structured living; (b) larger to smaller facilities; (c) larger to smaller living units; (d) group to individual residence; (e) segregated from community to integrated into the community living; (f) dependent to independent living (1972, p. 396).

In the decade following *Wyatt*, a host of other court cases have approached issues related to the constitutional rights of severely handicapped individuals in residential care. These cases and their impact on both the residential care system and the clients of that system are discussed in depth in Chapters 4 and 5 in this volume (by Laski and Bradley). In addition to court cases affecting residential placements, there has been significant judicial impact on the provision of education for handicapped children and youth.

Perhaps the most significant case in granting handicapped children and youth equal access to a free and appropriate education was *Pennsylvania Association for Retarded Citizens (PARC) v. Commonwealth of Pennsylvania* (1971). The consent agreement in that case stated that

> It is the Commonwealth's obligation to place each mentally retarded child in a free, public program of education and training appropriate to the child's capacity, within the context of the general educational policy that among the alternative program of education and training required by statute to be available, placement in a regular public school class is preferable to placement in a special school class and and placement in a special school class is preferable to placement in any other program of education and training (p. 1260).

While constitutional issues regarding residential placement of handicapped persons have been raised frequently in recent years, with regard to educational programs, the most important actions have been legislative. The most significant pieces of national legislation have been Public Law 94-142 (passed in 1975) and Public Law 93-112, Section 504 of the Rehabilitation Act of 1973. The states also have been extremely active in assuring the educational rights of their handicapped children and youth.

Federal and State Legislative Activity

Following the Civil Rights Act of 1964 and in the wake not only of the constitutional interpretation of a number of federal and state court cases but of mounting pressure from parents and advocates and a growing realization of the underdeveloped potential and discriminatory treatment of handicapped persons, the federal government passed two major pieces of legislation in the mid-1970s. The first of these was Section 504 of the Rehabilitation Act of 1973, which dealt largely with the issue of discrimination. The legislation stated that no handicapped person "shall solely by reason of his handicap, be excluded from participation in, be denied the benefits of, or be subjected to discrimination under any program or activity receiving federal financial assistance" (Sec. 84.4[a]). The provisions of the Section 504 regulations required states to make efforts to remedy practices, to avoid unnecessary segregation of services, and to modify programs so that they serve handicapped persons with equal effectiveness.

The second principal piece of legislation affecting handicapped children and youth was PL 94-142, the Education for All Handicapped Children Act of 1975. As noted in the legislation, the act promises:

a free, appropriate education which emphasizes special education and related services [to handicapped children] designed to meet their unique needs, to assure that the rights of handicapped children and their parents or guardians are protected, to assist states and localities to provide for the education of all handicapped children and to assess and assure the effectiveness of efforts to educate handicapped children (Sec. 601[c]).

This enabling legislation and its subsequent regulations specify that there can be *no exclusion* of handicapped children from a *free, appropriate education,* as outlined in an *individualized education plan* (IEP) based on a *nondiscriminatory evaluation* and *parental* and *professional participation* that provides for placement in the *least restrictive setting* appropriate. Despite the fact that this federal legislation promises far more than it was willing to pay for, a 1981 report of the U.S. General Accounting Office concluded that these guarantees for severely handicapped children and youth have in large measure been realized (General Accounting Office, 1981).

One of the major reasons for the high level of compliance with PL 94-142 has been owing to

parallel and, in most cases, prior legislation to provide for the education of handicapped children at the state level. In fact, much of the advocacy for PL 94-142 began with judicial and political pressures on states to increase special education services. These were soon reflected in state legislation providing financial assistance, which led, in turn, to appeals from local and state school systems, often in concert with advocates, for the federal government to share in the costs of these programs. While legislation at the federal level has been essential to the growth of integrated services for handicapped children and youth, it is important to emphasize that most of the financial support (probably 80% to 90%) for special educational services is derived from local and state, rather than federal, sources of revenue.

Government Advocacy

In addition to the substantial government-initiated advocacy across local, state, and federal levels, important advocacy and program development agencies are also nested within federal and state (and sometimes local) levels of government. These agencies are most visible at the federal level where they exercise considerable influence on the policies and programs of the U.S. Departments of Health and Human Services, Education, Housing and Urban Development, Transportation, and others.

The first internal advocacy organization for severely handicapped persons to be established within the federal government was the President's Committee on Mental Retardation (PCMR), founded by an executive order in 1966. Among the functions given to PCMR were: a) advising the president regarding efforts to combat mental retardation, coordinating services among federal agencies, establishing liaisons among federal, state, local, and private agencies, and developing and disseminating information to the general public regarding mental retardation and its effects; b) mobilizing support for mental retardation programs and related activities; and c) making policy recommendations to the president. Although limited in budgetary power, the direct line of the PCMR to the Executive Branch has had a considerable influence on public policies affecting handicapped citizens.

A second organization of considerable influence within the federal government is the Administration on Developmental Disabilities (ADD). This agency was created by Public Law 91-5176, the Developmental Disabilities Services and Facilities Construction Act of 1970, amended by Public Law 95-602 in 1975. The agency is located within the U.S. Department of Health and Human Services. To accomplish the legislative intent of PL 95-602, the ADD manages programs in four broad areas: 1) a *Basic State Grant Program,* which provides grants to states for planning, coordination, and systems advocacy; 2) a *Protection and Advocacy System,* which provides grants to states to protect and advocate for the rights of developmentally disabled individuals; 3) a *University Affiliated Facilities Program,* which provides grants for administrative and operational costs related to the training and research programs conducted by the facilities; and 4) a *Special Projects Program,* which provides grants to public and nonprofit organizations to develop improved methods of service delivery and protection and advocacy services.

The major expenditure of resources under Public Law 95-602 has been for the Basic State Grant Program and the Protection and Advocacy System. A central focus of the act is the requirement that each state assess the service needs of all developmentally disabled citizens, with special emphasis upon four service areas. The act further requires each State Developmental Disabilities Program to commit at least 65% of the federal allotment to ''service activities'' in one out of four or, at the state's option, two out of four targeted service areas. These targeted areas, referred to as the State's Priority Service Areas, are defined as follows:

1. *Case Management:* Services which will assist persons with developmental disabilities in gaining access to needed social, medical, educational and other services; includes follow along services which ensure a continuing relationship, lifelong if necessary, between a provider and a person with developmental disabilities and the person's immediate relatives or guardians; includes

coordination services which provide support, access to and coordination of other services, information on programs and services and monitoring of progress (Section 102[8][C]).

2. *Child Development Services:* Services which will assist in the prevention, identification, and alleviation of developmental disabilities in children, and includes early intervention, counseling and training of parents, early identification and diagnosis and evaluation (Section 102[8][D]).

3. *Alternative Community Living Arrangement Services:* Services which will assist persons with developmental disabilities in maintaining suitable residential arrangements in the community, including in-house services (such as personal aides and attendants and other domestic assistance and supportive services), family support services, foster care services, group living services, respite care, and staff training, placement and maintenance services (Section 102[8][E]).

4. *Non-Vocational Social Developmental Services:* Services which will assist persons with developmental disabilities in performing daily living and work activities (Section 102[8][F]).

State Developmental Disabilities Planning Councils work with state agencies that have primary responsibility for programs for developmentally disabled persons, generally to identify gaps and needs in service availability, to plan and evaluate programs, and to act as advocates for developmentally disabled individuals through independent protection and advocacy agencies in each state.

A third agency of broad influence in intragovernmental advocacy is the Office of Special Education and Rehabilitation Services (OSERS) within the U.S. Department of Education. Established in 1964, this agency served as the primary federal funding agent for special education demonstration projects and personnel training prior to the passage of Public Law 94-142. It also served as the chief internal advocate of increased federal commitment to educational programs for handicapped children and youth. Since the passage of Public Law 94-142, OSERS has remained a strong advocate for full compliance with the regulations implementing PL 94-142. Its efforts have gone beyond issues of strict implementation to building support and advocacy for the tenets of the legislation.

A multiplicity of other state and federal advisory groups advocate on behalf of handicapped citizens. For example, the National Committee on Employment of the Handicapped and the National Committee on the Handicapped work with other agencies to promote programs affecting the welfare of handicapped and disabled persons. Many other groups operate largely through volunteer efforts at the state and local level (e.g., special educational advisory councils). Such organizations at all levels of government have increased public awareness and support for services and have argued strongly for the full social integration of handicapped individuals.

Public Exposés

Another important influence in promoting socially integrated approaches to serving the needs of handicapped persons has been that of numerous and potent exposés on life in institutional settings. One of the first, and perhaps most important, derived from Robert F. Kennedy's unannounced tour of two New York state institutions two decades ago (''Where toys . . . ,'' 1965). Kennedy's outrage at the conditions he found was well publicized in the media. His visits were followed by Blatt and Kaplan's (1966) powerful photographic essay of a Christmas visit to another New York state facility. This work, plus a *Look* magazine article containing many of the same photographs, focused national attention on the condition of state institutions (Blatt & Mangel, 1967). Another exposé of enormous impact was Geraldo Rivera's videotaping of life in yet another New York state institution in the early 1970s. That video-essay (*Willowbrook: The Last Disgrace*), which was shown on local and national television, had a powerful effect on attitudes about state institutions. Since that time, the media has documented on numerous occasions instances of institutional neglect and client abuse, not just in New York but throughout the country. These reports have kept deinstitutionalization on the agenda of citizens and legislators who would otherwise have little contact with the status of services for handicapped persons.

Research Findings

Another major source of influence on contemporary services for handicapped children and youth has been the findings of research. Although it has been well established for over a half a century that handicapped persons are able generally to function, if adequately supported, in community settings (Lakin, Bruininks, & Sigford, 1981), it was more recent research on the nature and effects of total institutions that provided the greatest research support to the deinstitutionalization movement. By the beginning of the 1970s, a number of sociological and anthropological studies had pointed to dehumanizing and debilitating effects of institutional placement (Blatt, 1970; Braginsky & Braginsky, 1975; Goffman, 1961; King, Raynes, & Tizard, 1971; Vail, 1967). The power of these presentations was supported by concurrent research suggesting that community-based placements presented clients with a substantially different reality (e.g., Edgerton, 1967; Jackson & Butler, 1963; Kraus, 1972; Krishef, 1959; Wolfson, 1956). Research on the characteristics and adjustment of community-based services clients continues today to support the view that community services can be adjusted to accommodate for handicapped persons at all levels of need.

Research findings related to school placement have been much less conclusive than those of residential placement. Much of the support for the integration of handicapped young persons into their neighborhood schools has been based on their right to participate in their own community. Furthermore, since the integration of mildly handicapped students into regular classrooms with appropriate supports and interactions has been generally accompanied by greater student academic and social outcomes than those exhibited by students in more restrictive settings (Carlberg & Kavale, 1980; Maddin & Slavin, 1983), mainstreaming (i.e., the education of handicapped students to the maximum extent feasible with their nonhandicapped peers) has been widely accepted as the treatment of choice for mildly handicapped children and youth. However, support for integration of severely handicapped students has come more slowly, not unlike support for deinstitutionalization, with people withholding judgment pending outcomes on the effectiveness of integration with mildly handicapped persons. It is important to note that recent research is beginning to provide evidence suggesting substantial benefits to severely handicapped students and their classmates in integrated programs (Brown, Branston, Hamre-Nietupski, Johnson, Wilcox, & Gruenewald, 1979; Voeltz, 1980; see also chapters by Liberty and by Meyer & Kishi in Lakin & Bruininks, in press).

The results stimulated by these social forces have been remarkable, both in terms of the opportunities they have provided to handicapped persons and, in turn, by what the results of those opportunities have taught other members of society about severely handicapped persons' potential. In developing programs referenced to the conditions and necessities of community life, it has been demonstrated repeatedly, although it is perhaps still not fully appreciated, that promoting a person's relative competence and independence stimulates that person to greater levels of reciprocity with other members, elements, and practices of the culture. Through such interaction, the person learns more of the ways of the society and enjoys fuller membership in it. In so doing, a person's basic organic condition is not substantially altered, but the individual's needs are addressed in ways that increase his or her ability to participate in society and that reduce his or her own general levels of dependency. It is in helping to make persons less dependent than they would have otherwise been that social programs have found justification and merit greater than that of charity.

GUIDING PRINCIPLES OF CONTEMPORARY SERVICES

Of all the terms used in this volume and elsewhere to describe the nature of recent changes in the philosophy and substance of contemporary services for handicapped persons, none has been more appropriate or influential than *normalization*. Normalization at its most fundamental level does not focus on services or imply an attempt, or even a desire, to make disabled persons normal; it merely sets a standard by which the treatment of individuals, both professional and human, can be appraised. This standard dictates that the residential, educational, employment, and social and recreational conditions of the individual must be as close to the cultural norm for a person of that age as the extent of the individual's disability reasonably allows (Nirje, 1969; Wolfensberger, 1972). Normalization means always contending with the disabled person's membership in the community, with all due legal and human rights, while considering his or her unique qualities and any special treatment that might be seen as deriving from them. It further recognizes that learning to take one's place in society demands active participation in that society. Any type of living that restricts a person from participating in the normal settings, patterns, and activities of community life must be justified on the basis that the individual's disability precludes participation in a more normal setting. As is noted again and again in this volume, such justifications are harder and harder to find as research and practice, legislation and judicial decisions, and the achievements of handicapped persons themselves continue to confirm a place in the natural community for persons with severe disabilities. As Sarason and Doris (1978) stated:

> Handicapped and nonhandicapped students are human beings, not different species, and their basic make-up in no way justifies educational practices that assume that the needs they have for social intercourse, personal growth and expression, and a sense of mastery are so different that one must apply different theories of human behavior to the two groups (p. 391).

Normalization should not be seen as a dogmatic assertion intended to serve as a rallying point of any particular group of persons that care for or care about seriously impaired persons. It is, instead, a counterpoint to attitudes that once provided segregated and professionalized programs for handicapped individuals with virtually no recognition of their rights and potential to participate in their own culture (Wolfensberger, 1972). Normalization as a concept has endured primarily because it is elegant in its simplicity, yet it provides both a utilitarian and an equalitarian guide against which to measure the coherence of programs and services for handicapped citizens. Experiences in normalized settings are not enough in themselves to develop the potential of handicapped youth (just as they are not for nonhandicapped persons); socially and developmentally oriented training is also needed. But, the normalization principle and the specific policies that have evolved from it make clear that the absence of habilitation programs in normalized settings is no justification for removing people from community life in the name of supplying such programs in institutionalized settings. Contemporary views of normalization include both living in culturally normal settings and having opportunities to exploit those settings in ways that enhance one's culturally normative personal development and social integration (Flynn & Nitsch, 1980; Wolfensberger, 1980).

Two social policies derive from the assumptions and values of normalization. One relates to the place of residence of handicapped persons and is termed *deinstitutionalization*. This policy has been founded on the recognition that large public and private institutions, once virtually the only model of extrafamilial care for handicapped persons, are both aberrant social settings and have debilitating effects that increase the future probability of segregated living (Balla, Butterfield, & Zigler, 1974; Bernstein, 1927; Braginsky & Braginsky, 1975; Doll, 1934; Goffman, 1961; Zigler, Butterfield, & Capobianco, 1970). Clearly, the provision of residential care needs constant scrutiny, both in terms of whether residents' present living arrangements are appropriate for persons who have done no harm to society and whether the commitment of a person to a setting temporarily restricting personal liberty will, in fact, increase his or her probability for improved living in the future. Such standards have been difficult for large institutions to meet. For example, in one recent case involving an institution in Pennsylvania State, a district court found: "Pennhurst provides confinement and isolation, the antithesis of habilitation. We found that Pennhurst has produced regression and, in many instances, has destroyed life skills possessed by its retarded residents at the time of their admission" (*Halderman v. Pennhurst State School and Hospital,* 1978, p. 1318).

The policy of deinstitutionalization is concerned with reducing and preventing the need for residential living in large institutional environments. It is concerned with preventing admissions to institutional environments and promoting the placement, with appropriate habilitation and support services, of people in more normal living environments within the community. Deinstitutionalization became a dominant social policy over a decade ago and shows no signs of losing momentum. The conviction that this policy is sound and that the use of institutional settings to provide residential care for handicapped persons should be substantially reduced or altered, if not eventually totally eliminated, continues to grow. A recent statement from the U.S. Department of Health and Human Services reflects this view:

It is widely accepted that the great majority of persons with developmental disabilities are more likely to achieve their maximum potential residing in small facilities which allow them to participate more fully in the normal life of the community rather than in institutions (*Federal Register,* 1983, p. 48383).

A second policy that derives directly from the concept of normalization relates not only to residential care but also to the educational, habilitative, work, and support programs in which handicapped persons participate. This concept is generally referred to as placement in the "least restrictive environment," although its underlying promise and relationship to normalization might also be conveyed as "maximum feasible integration." The choice of least restrictive environment as the hallmark of this policy comes primarily from the institutional and ethical perspective that social agencies should assume the burden of proving necessity or probable benefit to a client before depriving a person of normal social conditions and experiences. In general, the policy of placing handicapped persons in the least restrictive environment means that developmentally appropriate care, training, and support based on an individual's needs should be, to the maximum extent possible, provided in the types of community settings that are used by nonhandicapped persons. For example, the regulations implementing Public Law 94-142, the Education for All Handicapped Children Act of 1975, require that, "To the maximum extent appropriate, handicapped children, including children in public or private institutions or other care facilities, [shall be] educated with children who are not handicapped" (Education of All Handicapped Children Act, 1975).

Inherent in the concept of the least restrictive, appropriate placement is that: a) needed services will be available, that is, persons needing educational, habilitative, residential, or other services will be provided them; and b) there will be recourse (e.g., due process hearings) should there be disagreement about the appropriateness and/or restrictiveness of placements. One of the most thoroughly developed explications of the concept of the least restrictive alternative is the statement of the American Association on Mental Deficiency's Task Force on Least Restriction (Turnbull, 1981). In the pages following, the impact of these twin policies is examined.

DEINSTITUTIONALIZATION

It is easy to overlook the complexity of a social policy like deinstitutionalization. In its simplest sense, deinstitutionalization involves reforming the residential services system so that handicapped persons in it are less likely to live within the formalized and routinized conditions that have characterized state and private institutions (King et al., 1971). To bring about significant improvements in the living conditions of persons who do, did, or would have

lived in such settings, states (often under court order, consent decrees, or the threat of legal action as noted by both Laski and Bradley, in this volume) have reduced or halted admissions to state institutions, have placed former residents in other, less institutional, residences, and have attempted, with varying degrees of success, to make the state facilities less institutional in nature (*National Association for Superintendents,* 1974). These changes have brought about easily documented effects on the locus of residential provisions for handicapped persons.

The movement of handicapped persons in extrafamilial placements to community-based residences is a relatively recent phenomenon. For example, from the funding of the first institution in the U.S. for mentally retarded persons in 1848, state institutions in this country grew steadily in resident population through 1967. Fiscal year (FY) 1968 saw the first drop in almost 120 years in the annual average daily population of public institutions for mentally retarded persons, from 194,650 to 194,000 (Lakin, 1979). A decade later, there were 148,752 mentally retarded persons in public institutions, a decrease of 23% in 10 years (Krantz, Bruininks, & Clumpner, 1979). Steady annual decrements in average populations have also occurred every year since, reaching a daily average in FY 1982 of 117,160 (Lakin, 1979; Lakin, Krantz, Bruininks, Clumpner, & Hill, 1982; Rotegard & Bruininks, 1983; Scheerenberger, 1982).

Deinstitutionalization began in state and county hospitals for mentally ill persons earlier than it did in state institutions for mentally retarded individuals. It also took place at a much more accelerated pace. The population of state and county hospitals for mentally ill persons peaked in 1955 at 559,000 residents. Ten years later it was 475,000 and 20 years later 193,436, decreasing by about 65% in only two decades (Bassuck & Gerson, 1978; National Institute of Mental Health, 1979). The number of mentally retarded persons in state and county mental hospitals peaked at about 40,000 in 1959, 8 years before the peak in state institutions for mentally retarded persons. By 1978, that number had decreased to about 13,000. An estimated 10,600 mentally retarded individuals were residing in state and county mental hospitals in 1980 (Lakin, Bruininks, Doth, Hill, & Hauber, 1982).

Nursing and personal care homes have been used extensively in some states as major sources of placement for mentally retarded persons. The National Center for Health Statistics' 1977 survey of nursing homes indicated that about 65% (48,500) of 79,800 mentally retarded residents in nursing homes were placed there primarily because of mental retardation rather than because of specific physical or health needs (National Center for Health Statistics, 1979). While data on national trends on the population of mentally retarded persons in nursing homes are difficult to derive, national studies of resident movement by the Center for Residential and Community Services at the University of Minnesota from 1977 and 1980 suggest a net decline of about 10,000 nursing home placements for mentally retarded persons between those years (Lakin, Bruininks, Doth, Hill, & Hauber, 1982). In addition, approximately 17,000 persons in the nursing placements (nursing homes and personal care homes) were in facilities that were specially licensed or contracted for mentally retarded persons. Therefore, the number of mentally retarded persons in nursing facilities without mental retardation program licenses is probably in the range of 50,000 to 55,000, although there is a serious lack of information about the number and characteristics of these persons and the nature of their lives within nursing facilities. Special concern about the adequacy of these services and placements for retarded citizens has been expressed by a number of state and national advocacy organizations (National Association for Retarded Citizens, 1976; Wisconsin Coalition for Advocacy, 1980).

Matching the decline in institutional placements has been the rapid growth of community-based, private proprietary and nonprofit residential facilities. From 1969 to 1982, the number of residents of privately managed, generally smaller community-based facilities quadrupled from 24,000 to approximately 98,000 (Center for Residential and Community Services, 1983). While the total population of private, community-based facilities has increased substantially, the average number of residents per private placement has decreased correspondingly from 47 (34 of whom were mentally retarded persons) in 1969 to 15 (12 of whom were mentally retarded persons) in 1982.

Another expanding model of residential care is the specially licensed foster home. In addition to regular foster care licenses, providers of these homes are specially licensed or contracted by state or regions to provide residential and habilitative services to developmentally disabled persons. Indicative of the rapid growth of this model of care is the fact that a national survey of specially licensed foster homes for retarded persons open on June 30, 1977, found that about one-quarter (26%) had been providing foster care for fewer than 18 months and nearly one-half (44%) for 30 or fewer months (Bruininks, Hill, & Thorsheim, 1982). Based on national studies of movement of mentally retarded persons between 1977 and 1980, an approximate 80% increase in residents served in this model was projected over that 3-year period (Lakin, Bruininks, Doth, Hill, & Hauber, 1982). However, statistics on foster care placements are difficult to gather and to assess. One problem is that states do not generally maintain data on mentally retarded individuals in the generic foster care placements that are usually a part of county social services programs. About 30,000 mentally retarded children were estimated to be in such placements in 1977 (Shyne & Schroeder, 1978). Another problem is determining what constitutes a foster care placement. In a number of states, providers offer residential care within their family's primary domicile but without the level of integration normally associated with foster care. Nationally, state-licensed programs providing care in "a home or apartment owned or rented by a family, with one or more retarded people living as family members" had a total of about 17,150 residents in 1982 (Center for Residential and Community Services, 1983).

An important factor in evaluating statistics

on residential services is change in the placement rate per 100,000 of the general population. Based on facility population data and resident movement data, it can be estimated that from 1970 to 1980, the number of mentally retarded persons in the residential service system per 100,000 of the general population decreased from 152.8 (105.9 in public institutions for mentally ill and mentally retarded persons and 46.9 in other licensed residential facilities) to an estimated 136.8 (62.3 in institutions and 74.5 in other licensed facilities). These numbers reflect an approximate 10% increase in the total U.S. population and a concurrent general stability in the total number of mentally retarded persons in full-time, supervised residential settings (Lakin, Bruininks, Doth, Hill, & Hauber, 1982).

In analyzing the trend toward lower rates of extrafamilial placements (outside of natural, adoptive, or normal foster care) over the past decade, it is important to look at data on persons entering the residential services system. Data on age at first admission to residential care explain many of the changes that have been noted in the ratio of system residents to the general population. Data gathered from a number of National Institute of Mental Health facility surveys and a national probability sample of residents in public and private residential facilities show that the average age at first admission and the median age at first admission to residential placements rose significantly in the 1970s (Lakin, Hill, Hauber, & Bruininks, 1982). In 1967, the average age of people entering the residential care system was approximately 13 years; the median was about 11 years. By the years 1976–1978, the average age of first admission to residential care had risen to 18 years old and the median had climbed to 16 years old.

The trend toward increased age at admission to residential placements can also be evidenced by the percentage of persons entering the residential service system prior to their 20th birthday. Throughout the decades of the 1950s and 1960s, the percentage of 0–19 year olds at first admission to residential care remained stable, ranging from 83% to 89% of all first admissions. By the 3-year period between 1976 and 1978, less than two-thirds (65%) of the first admissions to residential care were less than 20 years old. Concordant data on the same general trend show that the percentage of children and youth (0–21 years old) in the total public and private residential care system dropped from 30% in 1977 to 25% in 1982 (Bruininks, Hauber, & Kudla, 1979; Center for Residential and Community Services, 1983; Scheerenberger, 1978). While there is no way to directly prove causative relationships in these changes, the only plausible explanation can be found in the growth of community-based education and training and family-oriented support programs that have allowed and encouraged families to keep their children at home. The fact that the growth of special education programs is directly proportional to the average age of first admission to extrafamilial residential care should not be surprising, but is significant in that it shows one potent effect of the social commitment toward enhancing opportunities for handicapped children in the least restrictive environment.

Deinstitutionalization is certainly more than a set of policies that affect where handicapped persons will live. Of greater importance is that it is a descriptive label of a changing social perception and of related social action concerning how society will respond to the needs of its handicapped members. It is, indeed, an evolving concept that has taken its present form after decades of active consumerism and lobbying by parents and other advocates, as well as numerous judicial and legislative battles. While the progress of deinstitutionalization in recent years may have seemed slow, in terms of time demanded for most social change, its speed seems dramatic. Until the second half of this century, state institutions were the primary locus of services to handicapped persons. Although it seems remarkable today, it was not until the mid-1950s that the number of mentally retarded persons in public schools equaled the number in state institutions (Lakin, 1979; Mackie & Robbins, 1960). Therefore, deinstitutionalization has not only involved the depopulation of state institutions but also has been a process of transferring the central locus and orientation of services from institutional to natural communities. In fact, foundations for deinstitutionalization actually were laid before depopulation became evident. For example, Public Law 88-164 was passed in 1963 to stimulate states' expansion of community mental retardation services and to create research and leadership training centers related to the care and habilitation of mentally retarded persons. Special education placements more than doubled to over 2 million between 1958 and 1966 (Mackie, 1969). Similarly, fledgling sheltered work and day activity programs (often, out of necessity, operated and staffed by parents) began to appear during this same period (Cortazzo, 1972; Office of Mental Retardation Coordination, 1972). Much of this dramatic growth in community services is traceable to the efforts of parents and professionals who supported expansion and changing approaches to service programs.

By the time the many pressures to drastically alter the residential provisions for severely handicapped persons were fully felt, there were already model programs and community-oriented bureaucracies able to provide direction as well as needed services. Without these foundations, it is inconceivable that deinstitutionalization as a policy and process could ever have progressed as rapidly and as effectively as it did. Further, it became evident that the ability to carry out deinstitutionalization programs was inextricably linked to the capacity to provide the necessary residential, habilitative, and support services in community settings (Davies, 1959; General Accounting Office, 1977; Joint Commission on Mental Illness and Mental Health, 1961). Toward the end of the 1970s, the deinstitutionalization movement had indeed reached the point where such options were available. Mildly and moderately handicapped individuals who were capable of self-care, although perhaps not consistently of economic self-sufficiency, were recognized as having the right to live and learn with a reasonable measure of independence in more normal environments. And more and more commonly, severely-impaired persons were being placed in community residences with appropriate habilitative, social, and recreational activities to aid their development and constructively occupy their time. While the deinstitutionalization movement will not have achieved its goals until there is a community-based system of adequate residential, habilitation, and support services for all handicapped citizens, so much has been accomplished in the past 15 years that, to many, such an aspiration no longer seems unrealistic.

THE LEAST RESTRICTIVE ENVIRONMENT

The meaning of the term *least restrictive environment* could be expressed in a number of ways (e.g., "as normal a placement as possible," "maximum reasonable level of integration"), but its essence is captured in a 1976 statement of the Council for Exceptional Children:

> [a] child should be educated in the least restrictive environment in which his educational and related needs can be satisfactorily provided. This concept recognizes that exceptional children have a wide range of special educational needs, varying greatly in intensity and duration; that there is a recognized continuum of educational settings which may, at a given time, be appropriate for an individual child's needs; that to the maximum extent appropriate, exceptional children should be educated with nonexceptional children; and that special classes, separate schooling, or the removal of an exceptional child from education with nonexceptional children should occur when the intensity of the child's special education and related needs is such that they cannot be satisfied in an environment including nonexceptional children, even with the provision of supplementary aids and services (Council for Exceptional Children, 1976, p. 43).

The primary social principle underlying the concept of least restrictive environment is the commitment to finding a place for handicapped individuals in settings that enhance their participation in the society. The importance of this principle is not tied merely to basic social values, although in large measure it originated from them, but stems also from the fact that it is a powerful habilitation concept. Throughout this book, two habilitative points are reiterated in discussions of the many facets of life that severely handicapped persons share with non-handicapped persons. First, the best classroom for developing any single repertoire of skills is the environment in which the individual is ultimately expected to demonstrate these behaviors, a fact known by employers for centuries but which has only recently become evident to human service professionals (Brown, Wilcox, Sontag, Vincent, Dodd, & Gruenewald, 1977; chapter by Liberty in Lakin & Bruininks, in press). Institutional settings are best for teaching people how to live in institutional settings; normal family settings are most effective for teaching people to live like normal members of a family; and classes with predominantly normal children are best for teaching persons to act normally. The second habilitative point relates to a factor that is true of all human beings but is more visibly so to those working with handicapped persons: the uniqueness of the human species is reflected as much by the amount its members must learn in order to take their place in society as by its impressive capacities to learn. Because learning is so critical, our society invests much in inculcating its developing members with the lessons seen as fundamental to independent participation as an adult member. The same goal is essential to social programs for severely handicapped persons, not because the result can usually be expected to be complete independence, but because the extent to which independence is achieved is more greatly affected by the quality of opportunities to learn independent living skills than on any other manipulatable factor (Brown, Branston, Hamre-Nietupski, Pumpian, Certo, & Gruenewald, 1979). Virtually all severely handicapped persons can master something of what makes up the normal patterns of family, educational, social, and leisure patterns in a society, but more than their nonhandicapped peers, they need direct, systematic instruction to master the specific skills required in daily living (Brown, Nietupski, & Hamre-Nietupski, 1976; chapter by Liberty in Lakin & Bruininks, in press). Perhaps one of the greater ironies in social services is that while handi-

capped persons have been known to have relatively less ability to generalize across settings than their nonhandicapped peers, it is the non-handicapped persons who have generally been raised in normal social settings. Handicapped individuals, on the other hand, have been more often socialized in abnormal settings, thus greatly limiting their potential to develop the skills necessary for living in normal, integrated social settings. From a strictly educational perspective, severely handicapped persons must be immersed in normal social environments as much as possible if they are to be given the maximum opportunity to learn to participate in society. A number of chapters in this volume deal with the need for bringing about this fuller participation.

The potent habilitative effects of the least restrictive environment doctrine notwithstanding, it is important to reemphasize that this concept is a derivative of philosophical principles, reflected in judicial and legislative activity, that focus on the rights of handicapped persons to have conditions of their lives determined by their citizenship rather than by their handicap. In large measure, the multitude of legal actions of the past decade related to America's residential and educational treatment of handicapped persons have been largely about (re)enfranchising them, with the same protections of a community and its laws as are afforded nonhandicapped persons. In case after case, American courts have expressed their abhorrence that rights to education, to movement, to social participation, to integrated housing, and to due process have been limited to handicapped individuals solely on the presumption that the contemporary cadre of professionals bestowed with their care must be doing a decent job (see New Jersey Supreme Court, 1981). Without question, the removal of handicapped persons primarily from the "protective custody" of professional judgment was a major intent and outcome of litigation on behalf of handicapped persons in the early 1970s.

With remarkable consistency, courts affirmed the right of handicapped persons of school age to access appropriate habilitative programming, whether in institutional (e.g., *Welsch v. Likins,* 1974) or school (e.g., *Mills v. Board of Education of the District of Columbia,* 1972) settings. In explaining the necessity of actively pursuing this goal in the most normative placement possible within the educational services system, *Pennsylvania Association for Retarded Children v. Commonwealth of Pennsylvania* (1971) is exemplary:

> It is the Commonwealth's obligation to place each mentally retarded child in a free, public program of education and training appropriate to the child's capacity, within the context of the general education policy that, among the alternative programs of education and training required by statute to be available, placement in a regular public school class is preferable to placement in any other type of program of education and training (p. 1260).

In addition to ruling that handicapped persons have the right to appropriate habilitative programs in the least restrictive alternative, courts have affirmed the necessity of due process procedures to ensure that decisions regarding a person's residential and school placement can be openly scrutinized and challenged and that professionals are held accountable for their judgments. They have also recognized the right of handicapped persons to periodic and appropriate assessments that relate to program and placement, as well as their right to a formal written program that outlines publicly a plan of education and habilitation.

In the area of providing education to handicapped children and youth, national legislation (Public Law 94-142) has institutionalized each of these obligations. The guarantee of access to appropriate education opportunities for handicapped children and youth has brought about large-scale changes in both the quantity and locus of special education services. In fiscal year 1981–82, about 4.23 million children were provided special education, with 3.99 million of these served under Public Law 94-142 and the rest under Public Law 89-313, the latter of which provides grants for special education to children in state-operated or state-supported institutions (U.S. Department of Education, 1982).

There are few data on the prevalence of children with severe handicaps within the educational system, making it impossible to estimate statistically the need for or the numerical growth in special education placements of severely handicapped young persons. Data reported annually on special populations in schools are presented according to categorical classifications rather than severity of disability (U.S. Department of Education, 1982). Such classification schemes are highly susceptible to the vacillating popularity of one or more diagnostic categories. For example, in the 4 years between the 1976–1977 and 1980–1981 school years, the number of children diagnosed as mentally retarded in U.S. school programs decreased from 969,547 to 844,180, while the number of children diagnosed as learning disabled increased from 797,213 to 1,468,014. Most of the decrease in the former category was simply a shift to the latter.

One study has assessed severity of disabilities of students receiving special education (Pyecha, 1980). This study, which suffers from unknown reliability, indicated that students with severe levels of single or multiple disability (severely/profoundly retarded, multiply handicapped, severely disturbed children, etc.) comprised 13% of the public school special education population and 58% of the state school/institution population. Therefore, the best estimate of the number of severely handicapped children and youth receiving school services would be approximately 650,000. Of these, about 605,000 would be in the 6-to-17-year-old range. It was noted earlier that the incidence of developmental disabilities is probably about 1.6% of the general population. This estimate is based on U.S. Bureau of the Census data for 1980 (U.S. Bureau of the Census, 1981) on the number of 6–17 year olds in the United States, which would indicate a total of 668,000 developmentally disabled children of school age. Since an average prevalence estimate across all ages likely underestimates the extent of service needed for severely handicapped children in schools, the number of such children and youth likely reaches nearly 1 million students.

Unfortunately, there are not data to evaluate how adequately severely handicapped students are being served. It may be instructive to compare observations prior to Public Law 94-142, such as that by Kirp, Buss, and Kuriloff (1974) that "the severely handicapped generally go without an education [while the] enrollment in programs for the mildly handicapped continually climbs" (p. 45), with the report of the General Accounting Office (GAO) just 7 years later that "the priorities to first serve the unserved and second the most severely handicapped children within each category may have been realized" (GAO, 1981). However, the only published survey of the educational status of children and youth in a national sample of extrafamilial and residential placements suggests that, at least for that particular group, the GAO's observations were overly optimistic for the period studied in 1978–1979 (Lakin, Hill, Hauber, & Bruininks, 1983). The authors further note that, unfortunately, there is no way to evaluate compliance with Public Law 94-142 on a national level, given the lack of meaningful prevalence data on the handicaps of children and youth. They also caution that the process of ensuring children and youth their legislated educational rights can only take place on the local level.

Data from U.S. Department of Education reports to the U.S. Congress (U.S. Department of Education, 1982) and a sample survey conducted by the Research Triangle Institute (Pyecha, 1980) show that well over 90% of identified handicapped students are served in regular schools. In recent years placement rates in regular classrooms have increased compared to placements in segregated classroom and school settings. Within public schools, experiences in normal classrooms are now provided to over two-thirds of handicapped students. These placements are typically supported by a variety of supplementary special education programs. As experience and success with integrated programs increase, so does the ability to create classrooms and schools that can respond to even greater ranges of student ability, among them increasing numbers of classrooms for severely handicapped students (see also

chapter by Meyer & Kishi in Lakin & Bruininks, in press).

DELIVERY OF SERVICES

The fundamental principles under which residential and educational services are governed have required, and will continue to require, far more than a simple fine-tuning of previously existing school and residential programs for handicapped persons. These changes have necessitated substantially increased resources, in addition to revising the relationships among professionals, clients, and other caregivers (whether family or surrogate family), and more generally with citizens in thousands of communities. Operationalizing the principle of normalization involves significantly changing the beliefs and expectations of many professionals and citizens about the value of integration and the capacity of handicapped persons to benefit from it.

Systems providing residential, habilitative, and social/recreational services to handicapped individuals are generally survivors from a period when normalization was an inconceivable notion upon which to plan services for individuals. The fact that many of the same administrative and programmatic structures that were originally organized to provide segregated residential care in state institutions and segregated training in special education settings are expected to suffice to operate substantially different programs today portends problems that indeed can be found in contemporary efforts to implement the principles of normalization and least restrictive placements.

On the basis of what we now know about the benefits of deinstitutionalized treatment settings, one might expect that long-term care and special education professionals would have long since deserted state institutions and segregated schools in favor of these other settings. Despite positive changes, however, this has not happened, and examples of outmoded, discredited practices are still too prevalent. Whether, in the future, social principles and principles of learning will be more powerful than political clout is hard to predict. Clearly, in the future human service professionals will need to better use what has been learned about the values of their society and about how best to teach socially meaningful skills to seriously handicapped children and youth. Certainly knowledge, expertise, and conducive attitudes are presently available for continuing to improve the quality of contemporary programs for handicapped children and youth.

This book seeks to bring together the ideas of authorities who share a commitment that severely handicapped persons should be inte-

grated into their community. Within their respective areas of expertise, the volume's contributors discuss contemporary trends and the social context of providing integrated learning and living opportunities for severely handicapped persons. Many of the foundational concepts and issues that affect the full integration of handicapped citizens are discussed. It is hoped that these discussions will contribute to improving the state-of-the-practice of providing community living and learning opportunities for severely handicapped children and youth.

REFERENCES

Balla, D.A., Butterfield, E.C., & Zigler, E. Effects of institutionalization on retarded children: A longitudinal cross-institutional investigation. *American Journal of Mental Deficiency,* 1974, *78,* 530–549.

Bassuk, E., & Gerson, S. Deinstitutionalization and mental health services. *Scientific American,* 1978, *238,* 46–53.

Bernstein, C. Advantages of colony care for mental defectives. *Psychiatric Quarterly,* 1927, *1,* 419–425.

Birch, H., Richardson, S., Baird, D., Horobin, G., & Illsley, R. *Mental subnormality in the community: A clinical and epidemiological study.* Baltimore: Williams & Wilkins Co., 1970.

Blatt, B. *Exodus from pandemonium: Human abuse and a reformation of public policy.* Boston: Allyn & Bacon, 1970.

Blatt, B., & Kaplan, F. *Christmas in purgatory.* Boston: Allyn & Bacon, 1966.

Blatt, B., & Mangel, C. Tragedy and hope of retarded children. *Look,* 1967, *31.*

Braginsky, D., & Braginsky, D. *Hansels and Gretels.* New York: Holt, Reinhart & Winston, 1975.

Brown, L., Branston, M.B., Hamre-Nietupski, S., Johnson, F., Wilcox, B., & Gruenewald, L.A. A rationale for comprehensive longitudinal interactions between severely handicapped students and non-handicapped students and other citizens. *AAESPH Review,* 1979, *4,* 3–14.

Brown, L., Branston, H., Hamre-Nietupski, S., Pumpian, I., Certo, N., & Gruenewald, L. A strategy for developing chronological age appropriate and functional curricular content for severely handicapped adolescents and young adults. *Journal of Special Education,* 1979, *13,* 81–90.

Brown, L., Nietupski, J., & Hamre-Nietupski, S. The criterion of ultimate functioning and public school services for severely handicapped children. In: M.A. Thomas (ed.), *Hey, don't forget about me: New directions for serving handicapped children.* Reston, VA: Council for Exceptional Children, 1976.

Brown, L., Wilcox, B., Sontag, E., Vincent, B., Dodd, N., & Gruenewald, L. Toward the realization of the least restrictive educational environment for severely

handicapped students, *AAESPH Review,* 1977, *2*(4), 195–201.

Bruininks, R.H. Client oriented service indicators in developmental disabilities. Unpublished manuscript, University of Minnesota, Minneapolis, 1983.

Bruininks, R.H., Hauber, F.A., & Kudla, M.J. *National survey of community residential facilities: A profile of facilities and residents in 1977.* Minneapolis: University of Minnesota, Department of Educational Psychology, 1979.

Bruininks, R.H., Hill, B.K., & Thorsheim, M.J. Deinstitutionalization and foster care for mentally retarded people. *Health and Social Work,* 1982, *7,* 198–205.

Bruininks, R.H., Lakin, K.C., & Rotegard, L.L. Epidemiology of mental retardation and trends in residential services in the United States. In: S. Landesman-Dwyer & P. Vietze (eds.), *The social ecology of handicapped people.* Baltimore: University Park Press, 1984.

Carlberg, C., & Kavale, K. The efficacy of special versus regular class placement for exceptional children: A meta-analysis. *Journal of Special Education,* 1980, *14*(3), 295–309.

Center for Residential and Community Services. *1982 national census of residential facilities: Summary report.* Minneapolis: University of Minnesota, Department of Educational Psychology, 1983.

Cortazzo, A. *Activity centers for retarded adults.* Washington, D C : President's Committee on Mental Retardation, 1972.

Council for Exceptional Children. *Official actions of the Delegate Assembly.* Reston, VA: Council for Exceptional Children, 1976.

Davies, S. P. *The mentally retarded in society.* New York: Columbia University Press, 1959.

Dingman, H.F., & Tarjan, G. Mental retardation and the normal distribution curve. *American Journal of Mental Deficiency,* 1960, *64,* 991–994.

Doll, E.A. Social adjustment of the mental subnormal. *Journal of Educational Research,* 1934, *28,* 36–43.

Edgerton, R.B. *The cloak of competence.* Berkeley: University of California Press, 1967.

Education for All Handicapped Children Act, Public Law 94-142, 20 U.S.C. 1412 (1975).

Farber, B. *Mental retardation: Its social context and social consequences.* Boston: Houghton-Mifflin Co., 1968.

Federal Register, 1983 (October 18), *48*(202), 48381.

Flynn, R.J., & Nitsch, K.E. Normalization: Accomplishments to date and future priorities. In: R.J. Flynn & K.E. Nitsch (eds.), *Normalization, social integration and community services.* Baltimore: University Park Press, 1980.

General Accounting Office (GAO). *Returning the mentally disabled to the community: Government needs to do more.* Washington, D C : U.S. Government Printing Office, 1977.

General Accounting Office (GAO). *Disparities still exist in who gets special education.* Washington, D C : U.S. Government Printing Office, 1981.

Goffman, E. *Asylums: Essays on the social situation of mental patients and other inmates.* Garden City, NY: Doubleday & Co., 1961.

Gollay, E., Freedman, R., Wyngaarden, M., & Kurtz, N. *Coming back: The community experiences of deinstitutionalized mentally retarded people.* Cambridge, MA: Abt Books, 1978.

Grossman, H.J. (ed.). Manual on terminology and classification in mental retardation. Washington, D C : American Association on Mental Deficiency, 1973.

Halderman v. Pennhurst State School and Hospital, 446 F. Supp. 1295 (E.D. Pa. 1978).

Jackson, S.K., & Butler, A.J. Prediction of successful community placement of institutionalized retardates. *American Journal of Mental Deficiency,* 1963, *68,* 211–217.

Joint Commission on Mental Illness and Mental Health. *Action for mental health.* New York: Basic Books, 1961.

King, R.D., Raynes, N.V., & Tizard, J. *Patterns of residential care: sociological studies in institutions for handicapped children.* London: Routledge & Kegan Paul, 1971.

Kirp, D., Buss, W., & Kuriloff, P. Legal reform of special education: Empirical studies and procedural proposals. *California Law Review,* 1974, *62,* 40–155.

Krantz, G.C., Bruininks, R.H., & Clumpner, J.C. *Mentally retarded people in state operated residential facilities: Year ending June 30, 1978.* Minneapolis: University of Minnesota, Department of Educational Psychology, 1979.

Kraus, J. Supervised living in the community and residence and employment of retarded male juveniles. *American Journal of Mental Deficiency,* 1972, *77,* 283–290.

Krishef, C.H. The influence of urban-rural environments upon the adjustment of discharges from the Owatonna State school. *American Journal of Mental Deficiency,* 1959, *63,* 860–865.

Lakin, K.C. *Demographic studies of residential facilities for mentally retarded people: A historical review of methodologies and findings.* Minneapolis: University of Minnesota, Department of Educational Psychology, 1979.

Lakin, K.C., & Bruininks, R.H. (eds.). *Strategies for achieving community integration of developmentally disabled citizens.* Baltimore: Paul H. Brookes Publishing Co., in press.

Lakin, K.C., Bruininks, R.H., Doth, D., Hill, B.K., & Hauber, F.A. *Sourcebook on long-term care for devel-opmentally disabled people.* Minneapolis: University of Minnesota, Department of Educational Psychology, 1982.

Lakin, K.C., Bruininks, R.H., & Sigford, B.B. Early perspectives on the community adjustment of mentally retarded people. In: R.H. Bruininks, C.E. Meyers, B.B. Sigford, & K.C. Lakin (eds.), *Deinstitutionalization and community adjustment of mentally retarded people.* Washington, D C : American Association on Mental Deficiency, 1981.

Lakin, K.C., Hill, B.K., Hauber, F.A., & Bruininks, R.H. Changes in age at first admission to residential care of mentally retarded people. *Mental Retardation,* 1982, *20,* 216–219.

Lakin, K.C., Hill, B.K., Hauber, F.A., & Bruininks, R.H. A response to the GAO report, "Disparities still exist in who gets special education." *Exceptional Children,* 1983, *50*(1), 30–34.

Lakin, K.C., Krantz, G.C., Bruininks, R.H., Clumpner, J.L., & Hill, B.K. One hundred years of data on public residential facilities for mentally retarded people. *American Journal on Mental Deficiency,* 1982, *87*(1), 1–8.

Mackie, R.P. *Special education in the United States: Statistics, 1948–1966.* New York: Teachers College Press, 1969.

Mackie, R.P., & Robbins, P.P. Exceptional children in the local public schools. *School Life,* 1960, *13,* 15.

MacMillan, D.L. *Mental retardation in school and society.* Boston: Little, Brown & Co., 1977.

Maddin, N.A., & Slavin, R.E. Mainstreaming students with mild handicaps: Academic and social outcomes. *Review of Educational Research,* 1983, *53,* 519–569.

Mercer, J.R. The myth of the 3% prevalence. In: R.K. Eyman, C.E. Meyers, & G. Tarjan (eds.), *Socio-behavioral studies in mental retardation.* Washington, D C : American Association on Mental Deficiency, 1973.

Michigan Association for Retarded Citizens v. Smith, 475 F. Supp. 990 (E.D. Mich. 1979).

Mills v. Board of Education of the District of Columbia, 348 F. Supp. 866 (D.D.C., 1972).

National Association for Retarded Citizens (NARC). A position statement of the NARC. In: NARC, *Nursing homes in the system of residential services.* Arlington, TX: NARC, 1976.

National Association for Superintendents of Public Residential Facilities for the Mentally Retarded (NASPRFMR). *Contemporary issues in residential programming.* Washington, D C : President's Committee on Mental Retardation, 1974.

National Center for Health Statistics. *The National Nursing Home Survey: 1977 summary for the United States.* Washington, D C : U.S. Department of Health, Education and Welfare, 1979.

National Institute of Mental Health. *Patients in state and county mental hospitals, 1977.* Washington, D C : National Institute of Mental Health, Division of Biometry and Epidemiology, 1979 (microfiche).

New Jersey Supreme Court. In re Grady, 85 N.J. 235, 426 A. 2d 427 (1981).

New York Association for Retarded Citizens v. Carey, 393 F. Supp. 715 (E.D. N.Y. 1975).

Nirje, B. The normalization principle and its human management implications. In: R. Kugel & W. Wolfensberger (eds.), *Changing patterns in residential ser-*

vices for the mentally retarded. Washington, D C : President's Committee on Mental Retardation, 1969.

Office of Mental Retardation Coordination. Mental retardation source book. Washington, D C : U.S. Department of Health, Education and Welfare, 1972.

Patrick, J.L., & Reschly, D.J. Relationships of state educational criteria and demographic variables to school system prevalence of mental retardation. American Journal of Mental Deficiency, 1982, 86(4), 351–360.

Pennsylvania Association for Retarded Children (PARC) v. Commonwealth of Pennsylvania, 334 F. Supp. 1257 (E.D. Pa. 1971).

Pyecha, J.N. A national survey of individualized education programs for handicapped children. Research Triangle Park, Raleigh, NC: Research Triangle Institute, Center for Educational Research and Evaluation, 1980.

Reynolds, M.C., & Birch, J.W. Teaching exceptional children in all America's schools. Reston, VA: Council for Exceptional Children, 1977.

Rotegard, L.L., & Bruininks, R.H. Mentally retarded people in stage-operated residential facilities: Years ending June 30, 1981 and 1982. Minneapolis: University of Minnesota, Department of Educational Psychology, 1983.

Sarason, S., & Doris, J. Mainstreaming: Dilemmas, opposition, opportunities. In: M.C. Reynolds (ed.), Futures of education for exceptional children. Reston, VA: Council for Exceptional Children, 1978.

Scheerenberger, R.C. Public residential services for the mentally retarded, 1977. Minneapolis: University of Minnesota, Department of Educational Psychology, 1978.

Scheerenberger, R.C. Public residential services for the mentally retarded, 1981. Minneapolis: University of Minnesota, Department of Educational Psychology, 1982.

Section 504 of the Rehabilitation Act of 1973, 29 U.S.C. 794.

Shyne, A.W., & Schroeder, A.G. National study of social services to children and their families (Publication # OHDS-78-30150). Washington, D C : U.S. Department of Health and Human Services, 1978.

Tarjan, G., Wright, S.W., Eyman, R.K., Keeran, C.V. Natural history of mental retardation: Some aspects of epidemiology. American Journal of Mental Deficiency, 1973, 77, 369–379.

Turnbull, H.R. (ed.). The least restrictive alternative:

Principles and practices. Washington, D C : American Association on Mental Deficiency, 1981.

United Nations General Assembly. The declaration on the rights of disabled persons (adopted on December 9, 1975). Reprinted in The White House Conference on Handicapped Individuals, Vol. 1: Awareness papers. Washington, D C : U.S. Government Printing Office, 1977.

U.S. Bureau of the Census. Age, sex, race and Spanish origin of the population by regions, divisions and states: 1980. Washington, D C : U.S. Government Printing Office, 1981.

U.S. Department of Education. Fourth annual report to Congress on the implementation of Public Law 94-142: The Education of All Handicapped Children Act. Washington, D C : U.S. Department of Education, 1982.

Vail, D. Dehumanization and the institutional career. Springfield, IL: Charles C Thomas, 1967.

Voeltz, L.M. Children's attitudes toward handicapped peers. American Journal of Mental Deficiency, 1980, 84, 455–464.

Welsch v. Likins, 373 F. Supp. 487 (D. Minn. 1974).

Where toys are locked away. Senator R. F. Kennedy's indictment of New York State's institutions for mentally retarded children. Christian Century, 1965 (September 19), 1179–1180.

Wisconsin Coalition for Advocacy. Life in limbo: A report on people with disabilities in nursing homes. Madison: Wisconsin Coalition for Advocacy, 1980.

Wolfson, I.N. Follow-up studies of 92 male and 131 female patients who were discharged from the Newark State School in 1946. American Journal of Mental Deficiency, 1956, 61(1), 224–238.

Wyatt v. Stickney, 344 F. Supp. 387 (M.D. Ala. 1972).

Wolfensberger, W. The principle of normalization in human services. Toronto: Canadian National Institute on Mental Retardation, 1972.

Wolfensberger, W. The origin and nature of our institutional models. Syracuse, NY: Human Policy Press, 1975.

Wolfensberger, W. A brief overview of the principle of normalization. In: R.J. Flynn & K.E. Nitsch (eds.), Normalization, social integration and community services. Baltimore: University Park Press, 1980.

Zigler, E., Butterfield, E.C., & Capobianco, F. Institutionalization and the effectiveness of social reinforcement: A five- and eight-year follow-up study. Developmental Psychology, 1970, 3, 255–263.

Chapter 2

Deinstitutionalization

The Meaning of the Least Restrictive Environment

Leona L. Bachrach

The notion of the least restrictive environment (LRE), which is central to both the philosophy and social policy of deinstitutionalization, permeates program planning for mentally disabled persons in the last quarter of the 20th century. This chapter presents an analysis of emerging trends in service delivery for chronically mentally ill persons (Bachrach, 1983a) and is intended to provide a theoretical foundation for planning of services for mentally retarded persons. Although the history of deinstitutionalization for these two populations varies in a number of critical ways (Boggs, 1981; Braddock, 1981), there are points at which the interests of these groups converge, so that an exchange of the concepts and methods of treatment holds the potential for benefiting both.

This cross-fertilization of concepts and research findings is in no way intended to minimize the uniqueness of the two populations. Certainly there are major distinctions between mentally retarded and chronically mentally ill persons, and for many purposes it is inappropriate and perhaps even counterproductive to treat them as a generic, mentally handicapped population. Indeed, viewing the two together has at times had the unfortunate effect of diluting bases of support for one or the other.

For example, several years ago an article in the *New York Times* reported that the success of a program for hiring mentally retarded persons in noncompetitive municipal jobs in New York City had been slowed because agency supervisors confused mentally ill and mentally retarded persons (Gupte, 1977). In the strong language of the Liaison Task Panel on Mental Retardation (1978) of the President's Commission on Mental Health, the confusion between mental illness and mental retardation has had unfortunate consequences for retarded persons and their families. It has, moreover, led to public misunderstandings and has fostered inappropriate professional services and administrative models.

Nonetheless, there are occasions when combining the two populations appears to make sense. It is both possible and productive to view simultaneously the social processes that affect program development for mentally retarded and chronically mentally ill people without doing violence to the uniqueness of either group. Since deinstitutionalization is very much a series of sociological events (Bachrach, 1976, 1981c), with certain attributes pertaining to the process irrespective of the particular persons who experience it (Lerman, 1981; Rutman, 1981; Scull, 1977), some of its con ceptual elements may be distilled for the purpose of developing a theoretical base regarding program planning.

The common interests of the two mentally disabled populations are, of course, readily apparent in the case of those persons diagnosed as both mentally retarded and chronically mentally ill (Bachrach, 1981a; Dietz, 1982; Levie, Roberts, & Menolascino, 1979; Russell & Tanguay 1981; Smull, 1980; West & Richardson, 1981). Although such individuals represent a relatively small portion of either target group, their problems in receiving adequate care are intensified by the presence of multiple handicaps, and they experience disproportionate barriers to the receipt of services (North Carolina Division of Mental Health, 1981). The earlier-mentioned Liaison Task Panel (1978), in its concern for the special problems of this group of disabled individuals, devoted the bulk of its report to their service requirements.

The shared problems of mentally retarded and chronically mentally ill persons, however, extend beyond the interests of this multiply disabled group of individuals. For example, literature in the mental retardation field is rich in techniques for assessing client needs, skills, and satisfaction (Bruininks, Meyers, Sigford, & Lakin, 1981), while planners of services for chronically mentally ill persons are only now beginning to focus in depth on these practical and basic concerns (Anthony, 1977, 1980). Considerable trial and error in developing assessment techniques for the mentally ill population can potentially be avoided through careful study of programmatic procedures developed in the mental retardation area for these and other concerns.

On the other hand, the massive depopulation of institutions for mentally ill persons, which both predates and outnumbers that for mentally retarded people (Bachrach, 1981a) may now be regarded with something approaching historical detachment (Bachrach, 1983b). The psychiatric literature is replete with analyses of the sociopolitical dimensions of deinstitutionalization, and many of the planning and implementation difficulties currently surfacing in the literature on mental retardation (Bradley, 1978) have a déjà vu quality for practitioners who have encountered similar problems in planning for chronically mentally ill persons.

The following discussion explores two primary concepts that have permeated service systems for both mentally ill and mentally retarded persons: deinstitutionalization and least restrictive environment. This discussion is based more heavily in the author's area of greater expertise, treatment of mentally ill persons, but it is assumed that what has been learned about this system also has relevance to systems of care for mentally retarded persons.

DEFINITION OF BASIC TERMS

Deinstitutionalization has been used to refer to recent efforts to reverse the trend of providing treatment or care for certain dependent populations in custodial environments that are physically separated from home settings (Bachrach, 1976, 1978). Closely related to notions such as normalization (Wolfensberger, 1970) and mainstreaming (Omang, 1979; Silverman, 1979), deinstitutionalization has been pursued for a variety of target populations, including mentally retarded and chronically mentally ill persons (Rutman, 1981). Since traditional services for mentally disabled populations have generally been provided away from the mainstream of society, the clients enrolled in them have had different social exposures and environments from those of the majority of the population. Deinstitutionalization has sought to eliminate the physical isolation and the exclusionary practices inherent in institutional care.

Planners of services for the chronically mentally ill segment of the mentally disabled population have generally oversimplified the meaning of deinstitutionalization by limiting its definition to the depopulation of public institutions. Thus, in the mental health field a deinstitutionalized individual is commonly regarded as one who has been discharged from an institution and placed for care in a community-based setting (Bachrach, 1983b). This essentially geographic understanding of the concept is, however, limited and lends a distorted picture of the numerous dimensions of deinstitutionalization.

Willer, Scheerenberger, and Intagliata (1978) note that among mental retardation programs there has been a broader conceptualization of deinstitutionalization that has included, in addition to institutional depopulation, the parallel goal of reducing institutional admissions. The most widely acknowledged concept of deinstitutionalization of mentally retarded persons (one first put forth by the National Association of Superintendents of Public Residential Facilities for the Mentally Retarded, 1974) actually goes beyond discussions of altered geographic settings and also includes new concepts of care *within* institutions, such as institutional reform and enhancement of institutional facilities for those clients who continue to utilize them.

This broader view of deinstitutionalization is critically important because it demonstrates that deinstitutionalization is more than a physical event, an exchange of treatment settings for client care. Deinstitutionalization is also a sociological event that has altered the entire service delivery system by requiring basic accommodations in all elements of that system. Moreover, these system-wide changes have been accompanied by dramatic shifts in the service utilization history of mentally disabled clients. Thus, mentally disabled persons today, precisely because of deinstitutionalization, fall into at least five primary subgroups:

1. Individuals who have been institutionalized and have been released to the community
2. Individuals who, as the direct result of deinstitutionalization policies and practices, have never been institutionalized (although they probably would have been in the predeinstitutionalization era)
3. Individuals who have remained in institutions despite deinstitutionalization efforts—that is, veteran residents of public facilities who are unlikely to be released
4. Individuals who are now entering institu-

tions and are unlikely to be released in the future
5. Individuals who are now entering institutions and will probably be released to the community within a short period of time

The boundaries of these subgroups are permeable, and the passage of clients from one to another is responsible for the phenomenon known popularly as the "revolving door."

Obviously, individuals with such disparate institutional histories require different kinds of programmatic interventions, so that even for clients who might appear comparatively homogeneous in level of functioning, the deinstitutionalization movement has created a need to plan highly diversified programs. In short, although deinstitutionalization is a motivating force in program philosophy today, it is also, by itself, a powerful variable intervening between the assessment of client needs and the development of appropriate services.

For many caregivers and program planners the notion of the least restrictive environment is the essence of deinstitutionalization. Least restrictive environment refers basically to the "objective of maintaining the greatest degree of freedom, self-determination, dignity, and integrity of body, mind, and spirit for the individual while he or she participates in treatment or receives services" (President's Commission, 1978, p. 44). Clearly a close relationship exists between this idea and the humanitarian assumptions that justify the philosophy of deinstitutionalization (Bachrach, 1978).

The idea of the least restrictive environment has several dimensions. It is, of course, a legal concept, one that has stood at the center of a number of court decisions closely identified with the deinstitutionalization movement (Appelbaum, 1980; Klein, 1981; Rachlin, 1983). But intertwined with the concept's legal implications are basic clinical considerations, so that the question of providing treatment in the least restrictive environment fundamentally involves efforts to grant to mentally disabled persons a full complement of personal and civil liberties, while ensuring them the most effective interventions for their disabilities. Chambers (1978) refers to the least restrictive environment as "an idea about justice that rests on the apple-pie premise that people should in general be free to live as they please" (p. 24), and he draws an analogy regarding its legal overtones: "when you swat a mosquito on a friend's back, you should not use a baseball bat" (p. 25). In addition, the concept of the least restrictive environment has extensive sociological and semantic implications (Bachrach, 1980a), which are discussed next.

The idea of the least restrictive environment plainly purports to deal with a question that is basic to the care of mentally disabled persons in an era of deinstitutionalization: How can we ensure that services and treatments provided in community-based settings are humane, relevant, and responsive to the varied needs of mentally disabled persons? A corollary to this question is: How can we ensure that the services and treatments we provide, in addition to being clinically and educationally sound, are also consistent with the best interests of mentally disabled persons as American citizens—that is, with their civil rights?

Thus, the LRE concept is meant to serve as an aid in deinstitutionalization program planning. However, as currently employed, the notion of the least restrictive environment is both inexact and unrefined, and this limits its usefulness (Klein, 1981). In order for a concept to have value as a planning device, it must be precisely defined and its empirical referents clearly designated; neither requirement has been met with the concept of the least restrictive environment.

In fact, it is extremely difficult to find an operational definition for LRE that translates readily into tangible, empirical referents. Friedman and Yohalem (1978) suggest that the concept is "relatively simple in theory, [but] it becomes complex to apply on a practical level" (p. 8), and they raise these critical questions:

> How should the determination be made that one treatment setting or treatment modality is less restrictive than another? Is living in a halfway house or in the community on long-term psychoactive medication injected intramuscularly a less re-

strictive alternative to institutionalization? If the patient is incompetent and unable to decide which mode of treatment is less restrictive, how should this decision be made? (p. 8).

EMERGING ISSUES IN DEINSTITUTIONALIZATION

A central aspect in the popularization of the deinstitutionalization movement was its ideology. Although the roots of deinstitutionalization in this country may be traced to the 19th century (Grob, 1983), for all practical purposes, the current movement began in post–World War II America, when a variety of civil rights protests gained widespread support. These protests, which reached their peak in the 1960s, shared an ideological commitment to the goal of improving the lot of individuals who were perceived as helpless in gaining access to life's entitlements (Bachrach, 1978; Willer et al., 1978). Like other civil rights protests of that era, the deinstitutionalization movement emphasized the inalienable rights of disfranchised citizens—in this case, the mentally disabled population—and their legitimate claims on society. Pioneers in deinstitutionalization planning objected to both the content and the quality of care in large, usually secluded, public facilities and sought to exchange these treatment settings for services provided in clients' home communities, on the assumption that community-based care is both more humane and, ultimately, more therapeutic (Bachrach, 1983a; Hersch, 1972).

In addition to the deinstitutionalization movement's ideological impetus, other powerful factors have contributed to its history. For example, community-based care was widely perceived as more cost-effective than institutional care (Cramer, 1978; Elshtain, 1981), and the ability of social reformers to ally themselves with fiscal conservatives resulted in a rare coalition of ideologies. Thus, deinstitutionalization owes much of its popularity to its historical appeal to conservative forces. Acceptance of the progressive philosophy of deinstitutionalization was, in reality, facilitated by its attractiveness to people who were more interested in fiscal reform than social reform.

Moreover, there was a desire on the part of some state legislatures to reduce their budgets by shifting to a different level of government the cost and responsibility of caring for formerly institutionalized persons (Cramer, 1978). With the depopulation of large public institutions, many disabled individuals relied on federal public-assistance funds for support.

Also important in the history of deinstitutionalization was the rapidly expanding ability to contain the most obvious symptoms of mental illness through psychopharmacological advances. Seriously disabled persons were beginning to *seem* less impaired than they had in the past, and this reinforced the commitment of deinstitutionalization advocates to the basic desirability of emptying, and eventually closing, institutions.

All of these factors contributed to the emergence of service initiatives that were unique in scope and consequence. Never before had the nation's mentally disabled population exhibited such an array of treatment histories (Bachrach, 1978). Some service recipients were released from institutions after as many as five or six decades in residence, while other equally disabled persons were denied admission to institutions in the first place. Of those released from institutions, some were shunted to places that could be described as ''mini-institutions,'' facilities where, by most measures, clients' quality of life deteriorated. Other deinstitutionalized individuals showed a persistent dependency on institutional care and developed patterns of repeated admission and discharge. At the same time, substantial numbers of persons remained institutionalized—individuals who, even in an era that idealized the benefits of community-based care, were deemed ''poor risks'' for discharge.

To make matters more complicated, many service providers, perhaps to ease their own situations, recognized only one kind of mentally disabled individual—the kind their programs dealt with. There was a great deal of ego investment in specific approaches to client care, and this tended to result in deeply rooted territorial feelings that exacerbated service delivery difficulties.

It was inevitable that in such a climate chaos would result, and it did. And, of course, the ensuing tensions did little to ease the transition to a new style of service delivery. Mentally disabled persons, who were to have been the beneficiaries of John F. Kennedy's (1963) ''bold new approach'' continued to suffer as they had before, from inadequate attention to their most basic needs.

Certainly, there were notable exceptions to this picture. In fact, the implementation of successful programs that improved the lives of *some* mentally disabled individuals (Bachrach, 1980b, 1982; Wehbring & Ogren, 1976) reinforced the notion that it is, in fact, possible to attend humanely to the needs of mentally disabled persons in noninstitutional settings. These extraordinary programs offered, and still continue to provide, great hope for the future. Yet there is mounting evidence that the most severely mentally disabled persons have not, in general, been adequately and humanely served by the new service initiatives and have often been overlooked altogether by the service delivery system in this era of deinstitutionalization (Bachrach, 1983b). Indeed, in most parts of the country, serious problems associated with deinstitutionalization today appear to outweigh positive developments. In short, the historical developments noted here have culminated in the 1980s, in a series of interrelated problems.

In the first place, the very process of service planning today is far more complex than it was prior to deinstitutionalization. The one-time institution-based population of mentally disabled individuals has been splintered into so many subgroups that there is now a need to plan highly diversified programs—a task for which our imagination and creativity, and also our pocketbooks, have generally proven inadequate. When differences in institutional history are superimposed on disparities in level of functioning, the result is a complicated multidimensional array of program and service requirements.

Second, it is now apparent that the service needs of mentally disabled persons tend to endure, despite the fact that in the early years of deinstitutionalization many predicted that, without the negative effects of institutional residence, chronic disability would disappear, at least for many clients. In sharp contrast to the persistence of service needs, however, are community-based programs, which tend to ignore the long-term aspects of chronic disability. Hansell (1978) has written that community mental health services tend to be patterned after programs for the "single-episode user of services" and so exhibit "a deficiency of interest in people with lifelong disorders" (p. 105). Thus, emergent service structures in deinstitutionalization have tended to underemphasize the need for *continuity* in clients' care (Bachrach, 1981b).

Third, there have been problems in providing *comprehensive* care to the mentally disabled population. These individuals require a combination of psychiatric, medical, social, rehabilitative, vocational, and quasi-vocational services. In the past, providing comprehensive care was relatively simple, because virtually all required services could be delivered within a single physical setting. But today services are divided along many health, human service, and educational agencies in the public and private sectors; and successful programming depends upon the fine-tuning of initiatives originating with separate—and sometimes competing—authorities. The task of coordinating service delivery today is often hopelessly complex.

Fourth, many efforts ostensibly designed as deinstitutionalization programs actually resist treating the most severely impaired individuals. As a consequence, there is a deepening concern among service providers throughout the nation who deplore the deflection of community resources away from those who are most disabled and least equipped to compete successfully for scarce resources (Bachrach, 1980b; Langsley, 1980). Furthermore, when resources are expended on least disabled persons, often there is little left over for those with the most severe disabilities (Hockstader, 1981; Kleiman, 1981).

Fifth, the delivery of services to mentally disabled persons continues to take place against a backdrop of stigma that is exceedingly difficult to penetrate (Clendinen, 1981; President's Commission, 1978). Neither the successes of model programs in delivering community-based care nor the active and growing concern of client advocacy groups has succeeded in bringing about the revolution in the public's thinking that ideally was to accompany deinstitutionalization.

SPECIAL PROBLEMS IN SEMANTICS

As service planners and providers have attempted to come to terms with these serious issues, a new language has come into fashion to describe the deinstitutionalization movement and its by-products. Semantic confusion has become a hallmark of deinstitutionalization, as new concepts have been sought to explain and deal with arising problems. As pointed out earlier, even today, the term *deinstitutionalization* is rarely defined with precision, but this does not stop it from being used either as a planning concept or a rallying cry.

Other vague words and phrases also appear to have taken on lives of their own in deinstitutionalization planning efforts. Thus, the literature discusses "revolving door" clients—individuals whose service utilization patterns demonstrate that a gulf invariably separates an ideology from its practical implementation. Some clients who have great difficulty adapting to life outside of institutions are said to be "falling through the cracks" of a "fragmented service system," as agencies fail to engage them in services. There is growing recognition that some of the functions routinely provided by institutions—like asylum, respite, and social support—are enormously difficult to duplicate in noninstitutional settings (Bachrach, 1976), and the search for "support networks" to help implement some of these functions has emerged as a major planning emphasis. Similarly, "case management" has become a popular planning initiative toward the end of "coordinating" services (Bachrach, 1983a; Willer et al., 1978). Innovative residential sites have been developed to ease the transition from one service orientation to another, and now there are "quarterway," "halfway," and, in some places, even "fullway" houses. And a search for "model programs" with proven effectiveness has been undertaken so that they may be easily and quickly duplicated in a variety of settings (Bachrach, 1980b).

From a sociological perspective, the prevalence and popularity of these vague terms is no accident. The study of semantics demonstrates that language has social uses that extend beyond denotation and description (Hayakawa, 1972). Words reflect ideology, beliefs, and social status; they determine the questions we ask and, coincidentally, those that we fail to ask. Imprecision in language, in short, itself has certain functions, although these are not always conscious or intended. For example, imprecision may enable an individual to read into any word or concept whatever definition fits his or her own experience or purposes. It may in this way eliminate the need to search for alternative perspectives or points of view. Frank (1979) suggests that "members of a changing society seek to maintain a sense of control over events by clinging to a belief system that promises to provide this control" (p. 401), and imprecise language is one way of clinging.

In addition to the function of protecting vested interests, the inexact use of language may also serve to cover up inaction. Things that *sound* busy may help persuade individuals that they *are* busy—that they are basically sound and aggressive. Hayakawa (1972) points out that "fine-sounding speeches, long words, and the general *air* of saying something important are affective in result, regardless of what is said" (p. 103). Slogans and other bandwagon terms, irrespective of how well they reflect reality, are capable of deflecting critical thought.

Finally, imprecision in language may act to preserve the status quo. It is difficult for society to accept changes that occur too precipitously, and imprecision helps keep the rate of change within the limits of cultural tolerance.

The Least Restrictive Environment: A Special Example of Semantic Confusion

The concept of the least restrictive environment, which, as stated earlier, is thought by many to represent the heart of the deinstitutionalization movement, appears to work in all these ways. It is vague enough to mean many things to many people, and often what it means has something to do with turf that is being defended. Yet, it is an idea that, because of its concerned and idealistic sound, can persuade individuals that they are really doing something and that what they are doing is basically good. Moreover, lack of consensus about the empirical referents of the least restrictive environment slows the pace of change and reinforces polarized viewpoints concerning the entire deinstitutionalization movement.

Thus, by employing a concept whose empirical referents are fuzzy, we have stalled action and given de facto support to the conservative forces that delay social intervention. Of course, this may have some positive value. Although most service planners and providers, and many legislators, are committed to the goal of providing effective community-based care for most mentally disabled clients, they are not exactly certain how to proceed, so that their attempts to progress are often tentative. Unclear goals couched in imprecise language thus become braking devices, as the service system adopts trial-and-error efforts. Without these brakes, more precipitate deinstitutionalization programs would probably exist than do already, and the problems described earlier would be multiplied proportionately.

Whatever purposes have been served by vagueness, it is obvious that the least restrictive environment now has something of an Alice in Wonderland aura, where words sound like deeds and have the power to elicit emotions although they have little shared meaning. One is reminded of Humpty Dumpty's assertion in *Through the Looking Glass:* "When *I* use a word, it means just what I choose it to mean— neither more nor less" (Carroll, 1969, p. 74).

Assumptions Underlying the Least Restrictive Environment

What contributes specifically to the extreme lack of clarity associated with the idea of the least restrictive environment? Webster tells us that to restrict may mean either to limit, to confine, or to restrain. These several meanings, although related, may, in terms of the LRE, be considered to deal respectively with clients' personal autonomy, social isolation, and civil rights. Thus, when different individuals seek to limit the restrictiveness of environments for mentally disabled persons, they may be referring to any one or more of these qualities. As a result, their ends may be at variance, and this is a first source of confusion in using the concept of the least restrictive environment as a planning device.

The second source of confusion comes from a failure to clarify the assumptions that are made as planners and service providers attempt to translate their individual understandings of the least restrictive environment into specific actions. It appears that this concept generally rests upon the uncritical acceptance of at least three assumptions that are logically weak and largely unwarranted: first, it is assumed, for all practical purposes, that the quality of restrictiveness resides outside the client and in the environment; second, that the quality of restrictiveness is primarily a function of class of residential facility; and, third, that there is a relationship between restrictiveness and residence that may be expressed in terms of a continuum. These assumptions are discussed further in the paragraphs following.

Assumption 1—The quality of restrictiveness resides outside the client and in the environment. Implicit in the words *least restrictive environment* is the notion that certain settings have intrinsic qualities that make them good or bad for mentally disabled persons. The concept of restrictiveness, when thus expressed environmentally, minimizes the fact that individuals who have mental disabilities vary extensively in their needs and that what may unduly restrict one client may not restrict another. In short, this environmental approach to restrictiveness lacks the flexibility needed to make it client-specific. With it, one is more likely to say, "This is a good place for people with mental disabilities," than "This particular client, with his or her special needs and clinical history, would fare well in this particular place at this particular time."

It is conceivable that for some individuals the least restrictive environment is an institution, *if the only available community facilities fail to provide conditions that enhance their well-being.* The argument that being inside an institution is necessarily worse than anything on the outside does not hold; there are cases where clients would indeed show improved functioning outside institutions *under certain conditions,* but would be better off inside if those conditions could not be met (Fitzgerald, 1982). However, because of the essentially environmental emphasis in service planning, those conditions too often go unspecified.

At times, deinstitutionalization has literally been a matter of life and death, as illustrated by a tragic event several years ago in Washington, D.C., when 10 patients released from St. Elizabeths Hospital died in a foster care home fire. Although these patients had been evaluated prior to community placement, the particular facility to which they were sent did not provide the supervision or the environmental safeguards necessary to ensure their safety (Bowman & Valentine, 1979; Sherwood, 1979). Placement had, in short, confused locus of care with kind, or quality, of care. Having these patients outside the institution had become a goal in itself, or at least a goal of such critical importance that the means for effecting it were not subjected to the scrutiny that humanitarian concerns demand.

This illustration is not, of course, intended as an indictment of St. Elizabeths Hospital, which has many exemplary programs and is the recipient of an award from the American Psychiatric Association's Institute on Hospital and Community Psychiatry for its innovative programming (The 1979 APA Achievement Award Winners, 1979). The incident, which is hardly unique, is singled out here only because the deaths of 10 individuals in a fire in an uninspected residence provide dramatic illustration of the misfortune that often ensues when client concerns are subordinated to environmental considerations in deinstitutionalization planning.

Assumption 2—The quality of restrictiveness is primarily a function of type of residential facility. Closely related to the idea that restrictiveness resides in the environment is the notion that specific types of residence are either more or less heavily endowed with restrictiveness. The error here comes from overlooking the fact that restrictiveness is multivariate in nature. In other words, restrictiveness is associated with a variety of circumstances that are not necessarily related to whether the client resides independently in his or her own home, in a halfway house, in an institution, or in some other class of residential facility (Barbash, 1982; Hill & Bruininks, 1981; Rotegard, Bruininks, & Hill, 1981). Table 1 lists 13 variables that may be judged to be related in some way to restrictiveness. The last 12 of these transcend the first (type of residence), and relate highly to the degree to which a given client might be said to experience restrictiveness. And, although these variables are by no means exhaustive, it is clear that any measure of restrictiveness based upon a single criterion, like class of residence, is a gross oversimplification. If type of residence were in

Table 1. Selected environmental (nonclient) factors affecting restrictiveness of environments for the care of mentally disabled persons

1. Type of residence—class of facility
2. Location—urban versus rural; low-profile versus highly visible, etc.
3. Staffing—types and distribution of personnel
4. Specific programs and treatment modalities provided
5. Selection of clients—mix according to level of functioning, diagnosis, demographic and socioeconomic characteristics, institutional history, etc.
6. Presence of "normal catalysts"—mix of client and nonclient residents
7. Rehabilitation efforts—degree and kind emphasized
8. Expectations of clients—anticipation of clients' capabilities and behavior
9. Degree of autonomy accorded clients
10. Extraresidential programs for clients
11. Limitations on length of stay
12. History of facility—record of "success" in providing care
13. Agenda (stated and unstated program goals)—degree of precision or ambiguity in program goals and subgoals

Source: Based on a discussion in Carpenter, M.D., Residential placement for the chronic psychiatric patient: A review and evaluation of the literature. *Schizophrenia Bulletin,* 1978, *4,* 384–398.

fact a valid indicator of the quality of restrictiveness, it would have a predictable relationship to all of the other variables listed. One would be able to say, for example, that living in a place called a halfway house ensures maximum training in daily living skills; or that residence in an institution affords less autonomy in daily activities than does residence in a foster care home; or that medical care is of the best quality when a client is in an independent residence. But, of course, these generalizations cannot be logically or empirically supported.

Assumption 3—There is a relationship between restrictiveness and residence that is best expressed in terms of a continuum.   This assumption is, in effect, a corollary of the first two assumptions. If restrictiveness resides in the environment, where it is primarily a function of type of residence, it follows that some classes of residence are superior to others according to this characteristic. Implied in this assumption is a straight line, or continuum, of restrictiveness along which different kinds of facilities may be plotted, as if one class were inherently better or worse than another.

A simple example is provided in Figure 1, which plots residential environments for mentally disabled persons along a hypothetical continuum of restrictiveness. Independent living represents the least restrictive setting and institutional residence the most restrictive setting for the care of these clients. The problem with this illustration, of course, is the unwarranted assumption that there is enough uniformity within classes of residence to allow us to speak of them as if each contained a dependable core of characteristics. In fact, however, there is tremendous variation within residential facility categories. Two different nursing homes are not necessarily similar and, in many instances, one nursing home may be more like a halfway house than another nursing home. There is a great range of styles within any residential category, so that, depending on the criteria employed, a given community-based facility may be difficult to distinguish from the back wards of some institutions. The converse may also be true: depending on the criteria used, an institution-based program for mentally disabled per-

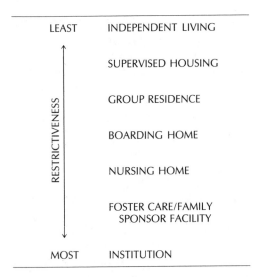

Figure 1.   Sample typology of residential settings for mentally disabled persons along a continuum of restrictiveness.

sons may be difficult to distinguish from some community-based model programs (Dickey, Gudeman, Hellman, Donatelle, & Grinspoon, 1981; Shadish & Bootzin, 1981; Steel, 1980).

REDEFINING RESTRICTIVENESS

Failure to be exact in defining the concept of the least restrictive environment has, unfortunately, often resulted in program initiatives that do little to benefit mentally disabled persons. Clearly, any program planned solely on the basis of residence—or on any other single variable—will overlook important considerations in the delivery of services. Growing awareness of this fact has been evidenced in some recently documented programmatic efforts that, by providing a more realistic approach to defining restrictiveness, point up the inadequacy of a single-criterion concept.

Polak and Mushkatel (1981) suggest a schema of treatment settings cross-classified by degree of supervision and by ability of individual clients to perform in selected functional areas. Similarly, Lund (1976) cross-classifies treatment settings by clients' level of functioning and uses indexes like degree of infirmity, ambulation, and required supervision to determine restrictiveness. Butler and Bjaanes

(1977, 1978) argue that placement should be based on the client's personal and family characteristics, as well as on intrafacility, extrafacility, and type-of-care variables. They also discuss the need for programs to be responsive to either therapeutic, maintenance, or custodial needs of clients.

Each of these approaches combines residential setting with other variables to yield a more sophisticated determination of restrictiveness than is found in a single-criterion, class-of-residence approach. Indeed, the sophistication of these approaches results from two important factors that serve as antidotes to oversimplification. First, all make an effort to reflect the multivariate reality of restrictiveness by covarying several conditions in assigning clients to treatment settings. Second, all proceed from conceptual frameworks that acknowledge the individual client as a vital force in determining restrictiveness. By including level of functioning or other indices of client status, these programs make it possible to address the question of whether a given environment is restrictive *for a particular client*.

Discussion

The concept of the least restrictive environment is, as Klein (1981) eloquently points out, "fundamentally flawed." He summarizes some of the serious logical limitations of the concept: "Treatment and liberty cannot be viewed as independent variables, thereby suggesting that one—treatment—can be kept constant, while the other—liberty—is titrated along a continuum of restrictiveness. The provision of treatment is ultimately a clinical matter" (p. 13).

From the semanticist's perspective the concept of the least restrictive environment suffers from the tendency to confuse levels of abstraction and to draw faulty inferences. Hayakawa's (1972) well-known semantic paradigm, "Cow$_1$ is not cow$_2$," may be paraphrased in the case of the least restrictive environment for the mentally disabled: Institution$_1$ is not institution$_2$; and community residence$_1$ is not community residence$_2$. Also, client$_1$ is most assuredly not client$_2$. These simple and fundamental statements remind us of the dangers inherent in placing clients in least restrictive environments without further elaborating upon the conditions that affect restrictiveness.

Planning services for mentally disabled persons requires a conceptual framework in which vagueness is minimized and principles of effective care are stressed. Instead of a unidimensional continuum of restrictiveness based on residential setting, a matrix with multiple cells should be employed, so that the numerous environmental variables that affect restrictiveness may be taken into account. In addition to these environmental variables, client variables must also be considered—a process that provides the matrix with additional dimensions and gives it increased depth. Admittedly, such a multidimensional approach is exceedingly difficult to summarize verbally or even to illustrate graphically, and its complexities may at first glance appear forbidding. But this kind of thinking is, in fact, used whenever truly appropriate placements are made, even though the entire logical process may not be conscious. This type of approach is the essence of planning for people, not places.

As suggested earlier, the concept of the least restrictive environment may be viewed as symptomatic of widespread conceptual deficits in program planning for mentally disabled persons in an era of deinstitutionalization. Indeed, efforts to reduce imprecision must be extended beyond the concept of the least restrictive environment and applied more generally. One of the first steps in that direction must be the conscientious delineation of who—what particular clients—are to be treated in the community in deinstitutionalization programs. An accompanying consideration must be: Are there some clients who cannot be regarded as appropriate candidates for community-based care, because such placement would ultimately increase the level of their restrictiveness? Such careful identification of the target population is part of a more global need for competent goal setting in deinstitutionalization (Bachrach, 1974; Bradley, 1978).

These points lead logically to a basic program-planning principle for mentally disabled persons. Effective and humane programs for these individuals must always begin with the fundamental question of whether all persons in the planning universe are covered in a proposed program plan. If the plan discriminates against some kinds of clients (Bradley, 1978), the plan must be revised, for no group of individuals in need—most particularly mentally disabled persons, who are generally unable to be their own advocates,—should be placed in the position of having to compete for services.

CONCLUSIONS

Attention to basic planning principles—principles of effective care—instead of to slogans, should form the basis for programmatic initiatives for mentally disabled persons. By focusing on such principles, instead of on a single dimension of planning such as class of residence, planners can begin to develop programs that acknowledge that the mentally disabled client's individuality is more important for effective treatment than is the nature of a predetermined residential designation. Several recent additions to the literature attest to the importance of redefining the meaning of the least restrictive environment so that it is a more realistic, more precise, and more operational planning concept (Allen, Weinman, Lorimor, & Claghorn, 1980; Killebrew, Harris, & Kruckeberg, 1982; Kloss, 1980; Ransohoff, 1980; Ransohoff, Zachary, Gaynor, & Hargreaves, 1982; Schwarz, 1981; Segal & Baumohl, 1981).

Another way of stating this conclusion is to suggest that the concept of the least restrictive environment be viewed in a new way in order that it may have relevance to program planning for mentally disabled persons. To some extent this can be accomplished by consideration of the concept's polar opposite, the idea of the most therapeutic environment. These paired concepts, although complementary, differ in what semanticists call intensional meaning: each one elicits different mental images. While *least restrictive* has come to suggest environmental conditions, *most therapeutic* urges examination of the status and needs of individual clients. And while the notion of *least restrictive* encourages us to look at places, *most therapeutic,* a more dynamic concept, puts the emphasis on the client's changing level of functioning.

A quotation from Thiele, Paul, and Neufeld (1977) epitomizes the major points in this chapter's discussion:

The institutionalizing process . . . is deeply entrenched in the culture of caregiving systems. The purpose of programming for deinstitutionalization is not to stop institutionalization. It is, rather, to minimize the negative impact of institutions and institutional practices. Stated positively, deinstitutionalization is an attempt to revitalize the potential of service-delivery systems for responding appropriately and efficiently to the needs of persons that those systems are established to serve (p. 28).

REFERENCES

Allen, R.H., Weinman, M., Lorimor, R., & Claghorn, J.L. A multi-tiered screening system for the least restrictive setting. *American Journal of Psychiatry,* 1980, *137,* 968–971.

Anthony, W.A. Psychological rehabilitation: A concept in need of a method. *American Psychologist,* 1977, *32,* 658–662.

Anthony, W.A. *Principles of psychiatric rehabilitation.* Baltimore: University Park Press, 1980.

Appelbaum, P.S. Least restrictive environment: Some comments, amplification. *Hospital and Community Psychiatry,* 1980, *31,* 420.

Bachrach, L.L. Developing objectives in community mental health planning. *American Journal of Public Health,* 1974, *64,* 1162–1163.

Bachrach, L.L. *Deinstitutionalization: An analytical review and sociological perspective.* Rockville, MD: National Institute of Mental Health, 1976.

Bachrach, L.L. A conceptual approach to deinstitutionalization. *Hospital and Community Psychiatry,* 1978, *29,* 573–578.

Bachrach, L.L. Is the least restrictive environment always the best? Sociological and semantic implications. *Hospital and Community Psychiatry,* 1980a, *31,* 97–103.

Bachrach, L.L. Overview: Model programs for chronic mental patients. *American Journal of Psychiatry,* 1980b, *137,* 1023–1031.

Bachrach, L.L. A conceptual approach to deinstitutionalization of the mentally retarded: A perspective from the experience of the mentally ill. In: R.H. Bruininks, C.E. Meyers, B.B. Sigford, & K.C. Lakin (eds.), *Deinstitutionalization and community adjustment of mentally retarded people.* Monograph No. 4, 51–67. Washington, D C : American Association on Mental Deficiency, 1981a.

Bachrach, L.L. Continuity of care for chronic mental patients: A conceptual analysis. *American Journal of Psychiatry,* 1981b, *138,* 1449–1456.

Bachrach, L.L. Deinstitutionalization: Development and theoretical perspective. In: I.D. Rutman (ed.), *Planning for deinstitutionalization: A review of principles, methods, and applications.* Human Services Monograph Series No. 28, 5–22. Rockville, MD: Project Share, 1981c.

Bachrach, L.L. Assessment of outcomes in community support systems: Results, problems, and limitations. *Schizophrenia Bulletin,* 1982, *8*(1), 39–61.

Bachrach, L.L. (ed.). *Deinstitutionalization.* New Directions for Mental Health Services Series No. 17. San Francisco: Jossey-Bass, 1983a.

Bachrach, L.L. An overview of deinstitutionalization. In: L.L. Bachrach (ed.), *Deinstitutionalization.* New Directions for Mental Health Services Series No. 17, 5–14. San Francisco: Jossey-Bass, 1983b.

Barbash, F. High court establishes rights for retarded in institutions. *Washington Post,* June 19, 1982, pp. A1, A5.

Boggs, E.M. Contrasts in deinstitutionalization. *Hospital and Community Psychiatry,* 1981, *32,* 591.

Bowman, L., & Valentine, P.S. Officials cite violations in fire fatal to nine. *Washington Post,* April 12, 1979, pp. A1, A14.

Braddock, D. Deinstitutionalization of the retarded: Trends in public policy. *Hospital and Community Psychiatry,* 1981, *32,* 607–615.

Bradley, V.J. Deinstitutionalization of developmentally disabled persons: *A conceptual analysis and guide.* Baltimore: University Park Press, 1978.

Bruininks, R.H., Meyers, C.E., Sigford, B.B., & Lakin, K.C. (eds.). *Deinstitutionalization and community adjustment of mentally retarded people.* Monograph No. 4. Washington, D C : American Association on Mental Deficiency, 1981.

Butler, E.W., & Bjaanes, A.T. A typology of community care facilities and differential normalization outcomes. In: P. Mittler (ed.), *Research to practice in mental retardation: I. Care and intervention,* 337–347. Baltimore: University Park Press, 1977.

Butler, E.W., & Bjaanes, A.T. Activities and the use of time by retarded persons in community care facilities. In: G.P. Sackett (ed.), *Observing behavior: Theory and applications in mental retardation,* 379–399. Baltimore: University Park Press, 1978.

Carroll, L. *Through the looking glass.* London: Mayflower, 1969.

Chambers, D.L. Community-based treatment and the constitution: The principle of the least restrictive alternative. In: L.I. Stein & M.A. Test (eds.), *Alternatives to mental hospital treatment,* 23–39. New York: Plenum Publishing Corp., 1978.

Clendinen, D. Willowbrook's goals still unmet 6 years after order for reforms. *New York Times,* May 25, 1981, pp. A1, B5.

Cramer, P.K. *Report on the current state of deinstitutionalization: Period of retrenchment.* Philadelphia: Health and Welfare Council, May, 1978.

Dickey, B., Gudeman, J.E., Hellman, S., Donatelle, A., & Grinspoon, L. A follow-up of deinstitutionalized chronic patients four years after discharge. *Hospital and Community Psychiatry,* 1981, *32,* 326–330.

Dietz, J. Persons mentally ill and retarded need better care. *Psychiatric News,* July 2, 1982, pp. 8–9.

Elshtain, J.B. A key to unlock the asylum? *The Nation,* March 16, 1981, pp. 585, 602–604.

Fitzgerald, S.J. Letter to the editor. *Washington Post,* April 13, 1982, p. A18.

Frank, J.D. Mental health in a fragmented society: The shattered crystal ball. *American Journal of Orthopsychiatry,* 1979, *49,* 397–408.

Friedman, P.R., & Yohalem, J.B. The rights of the chronic mental patient. In: J.A. Talbott (ed.), *The chronic mental patient,* 51–64. Washington, D C : American Psychiatric Association, 1978.

Grob, G.N. Historical origins of deinstitutionalization. In: L.L. Bachrach (ed.), *Deinstitutionalization.* New Directions for Mental Health Services Series No. 17. San Francisco: Jossey-Bass, 1983.

Gupte, P. Program provides city jobs for mentally retarded. *New York Times,* January 31, 1977.

Hansell, N. Services for schizophrenics: A lifelong approach to treatment. *Hospital and Community Psychiatry,* 1978, *29,* 105–109.

Hayakawa, S.I. *Language in thought and action* (3rd ed.). New York: Harcourt Brace Jovanovich, 1972.

Hersch, C. Social history, mental health, and community control. *American Psychologist,* 1972, *27,* 749–754.

Hill, B.K., & Bruininks, R.H. *Family, leisure, and social activities of mentally retarded people in residential facilities.* Developmental Disabilities Project Report No. 13. Minneapolis: University of Minnesota, Department of Psychoeducational Studies, 1981.

Hockstader, L. Retarded Fairfax girl is caught in a legal tug-of-war. *Washington Post,* July 20, 1981, pp. B1, B3.

Kennedy, J.F. Message from the President of the United States to the 88th Congress. 88th Cong., February 6, 1963. H.Doc. 58.

Killebrew, J.A., Harris, C., & Kruckeberg, K. A conceptual model for determining the least restrictive treatment-training modality. *Hospital and Community Psychiatry,* 1982, *33,* 367–370.

Kleiman, D. Many disabled still not placed by city schools. *New York Times,* August 31, 1981, pp. A1, D10.

Klein, J. *The least restrictive alternative: More about less.* Paper presented at the Conference on Housing the Elderly Deinstitutionalization Patient in the Community, sponsored by the International Center for Social Gerontology, Inc., Arlington, VA, May, 1981.

Kloss, J.D. Restrictiveness: Defining its multiple dimensions. *Hospital and Community Psychiatry,* 1980, *31,* 422.

Langsley, D.G. The community mental health center: Does it treat patients? *Hospital and Community Psychiatry,* 1980, *31,* 815–819.

Lerman, P. *Deinstitutionalization: A cross-problem analysis.* Rockville, MD: National Institute of Mental Health, 1981.

Levie, C.A., Roberts, B.D., & Menolascino, F.J. Providing psychiatric services for clients of community-based mental retardation programs. *Hospital and Community Psychiatry,* 1979, *30,* 383–384.

Liaison Task Panel on Mental Retardation. *Report of the President's Commission on Mental Health,* Vol. 4. Washington, D C : President's Commission on Mental Health, 1978.

Lund, D.A. *Appropriateness of level of care: The pilgrim project.* Working paper no. 1, revised. Albany, NY: New York Department of Mental Hygiene, Office of Evaluation and Inspection, May 6, 1976.

National Association of Superintendents of Public Residential Facilities for the Mentally Retarded (NASPRFMR). *Contemporary issues in residential programming.* Washington, D C : President's Committee on Mental Retardation, 1974.

The 1979 APA achievement award winners. *Hospital and Community Psychiatry,* 1979, *30,* 488.

North Carolina Division of Mental Health, Mental Retardation and Substance Abuse Services. *Mentally retarded clients in regional psychiatric hospitals, report of a task force.* Raleigh, NC: North Carolina Division of Mental Health, December 1981.

Omang, J. Entry of handicapped children into schools brings problems. *Washington Post,* January 14, 1979, pp. G1, G4.

Polak, P.R., & Mushkatel, L.G. A community mental health center model. In: J.A. Talbott (ed.), *The chronic mentally ill: Treatment, programs, systems,* 198–211. New York: Human Sciences Press, 1981.

President's Commission on Mental Health. *Report.* Washington, D C : President's Commission on Mental Health, 1978.

Rachlin, S. The influence of law on deinstitutionalization. In: L.L. Bachrach (ed.), *Deinstitutionalization.* New Directions for Mental Health Services Series No. 17. San Francisco: Jossey-Bass, 1983.

Ransohoff, P. A comment on the dimensions and context of restrictiveness. *Hospital and Community Psychiatry,* 1980, *31,* 639.

Ransohoff, P., Zachary, R.A., Gaynor, J., & Hargreaves, W.A. Measuring restrictiveness of psychiatric care. *Hospital and Community Psychiatry,* 1982, *33,* 361–366.

Rotegard, L.L., Bruininks, R.H., & Hill, B.K. *Environmental characteristics of residential facilities for mentally retarded people.* Developmental Disabilities Report No. 15. Minneapolis: University of Minnesota, Department of Psychoeducational Studies, May, 1981.

Russell, A.T., & Tanguay, P.E. Mental illness and mental retardation: Cause or coincidence? *American Journal of Mental Deficiency,* 1981, *85,* 570–574.

Rutman, I.D. (ed.). *Planning for deinstitutionalization: A review of principles, methods, and applications.* Human Services Monograph Series No. 28. Rockville, MD: Project Share, September 1981.

Schwarz, F. Least restrictive alternative and utilization review: Meeting requirements in a single system. *Hospital and Community Psychiatry,* 1981, *22,* 204–206.

Scull, A. *Decarceration: Community treatment and the deviant—A radical view.* Englewood Cliffs, NJ: Prentice-Hall, 1977.

Segal, S.P., & Baumohl, J. Toward harmonious community care placement. In: R. Budson (ed.), *Issues in community residential care.* New Directions for Mental Health Services Series No. 11, 49–61. San Francisco, Jossey-Bass, 1981.

Shadish, W.R., & Bootzin, R.R. Nursing homes and chronic mental patients. *Schizophrenia Bulletin,* 1981, *7*(3), 488–498.

Sherwood, T. 10th victim of Lamont St. blaze dies. *Washington Post,* April 30, 1979, p. C3.

Silverman, M. Beyond the mainstream: The special needs

of the chronic child patient. *American Journal of Orthopsychiatry,* 1979, *49,* 62–68.

Smull, M.W. A community support system using multi-source funding. *National Association of Private Psychiatric Hospitals Journal,* 1980, *11,* 36–41.

Steel, E. Long-term care: The hospital as least restrictive setting. *CME Newsletter* (St. Elizabeths Hospital Department of Psychiatry), 1980, *2,* 1–3.

Thiele, R.L., Paul, J.L., & Neufeld, G.R. Institutionalization: A perspective for deinstitutionalization program development. In: J.L. Paul, D.J. Stedman, & G.R. Neufeld (eds.)., *Deinstitutionalization: Program and policy development.* Syracuse, NY: Syracuse University Press, 1977.

Wehbring, K., & Ogren, C. *Community residences for mentally retarded persons: A summary of a study of seven community residences.* Arlington, TX: National Association for Retarded Citizens, 1976.

West, M.A., & Richardson, M. A statewide survey of CMHC programs for mentally retarded individuals. *Hospital and Community Psychiatry,* 1981, *32,* 413–416.

Willer, B., Scheerenberger, R.C., & Intagliata, J. Deinstitutionalization and mentally retarded persons. *Community Mental Health Review,* 1978, *3,* 1–12.

Wolfensberger, W. The principle of normalization and its implications to psychiatric services. *American Journal of Psychiatry,* 1970, *127,* 291–297.

Chapter 3

Comprehensive Community Services

A Plea for Interagency Collaboration

Robert L. Schalock

This chapter seeks to define and outline comprehensive community services for handicapped persons, particularly those for public school-age children and young adults. The chapter's focus in on the current community service delivery system and what might be done to improve community-based services in the 1980s. The development of the topic was guided by three premises. First, deinstitutionalization and placement in the least restrictive alternative (mainstreaming) do not end with community placement or with the authorization of any particular set of services. The hallmarks of handicapism and of the institutional structures that have often fostered it have been inappropriately low levels of independence, productivity, and community integration. Therefore, the primary goal of comprehensive community services is to increase a person's independence, productivity, and community integration, or to paraphrase Seneca (A.D. 63), "The blessing is not in living [in the community], but in living well [in the community]." Second, there is frequently a less than optimal match, if not an outright mismatch, between the characteristics of handi-

capped individuals and the environments in which they live, are educated, or work. This mismatch generally increases the effects of a person's disability. An effective service delivery system maximizes the congruence between what the individual can accomplish and what the environment demands. How well that is done constitutes an essential criterion against which community services are judged. And third, service determination by means of categorical diagnoses and single-agency service delivery is no longer viable. The result of past shortcomings of such approaches has been and will continue to be a significant shift toward functional definitions of disability, with a corresponding trend toward interagency collaboration in meeting individual service needs.

This chapter responds to three basic questions about services for handicapped persons, each of which is addressed in a major section of the chapter. The questions are: 1) What does the knowledge gained about deinstitutionalization and mainstreaming tell us about the present and future needs for comprehensive community services? 2) What are the critical problems involved in implementing needed

services? and 3) What are the policy and research issues that need resolution if community
services are indeed to be determined by client
needs rather than agency provisions?

Over the last 10–15 years, it has been apparent that human rights, related judicial and legislative activity, agressive advocacy, and significant amounts of financial and human
resources have made a major difference in the
care and treatment of handicapped persons.
However, the enthusiasm generated by these
accomplishments should be somewhat re-
strained by three observations. The first is that
deinstitutionalization and mainstreaming are
social experiments whose efficacy and effectiveness have not yet been fully established.
The second is that a number of problems must
be overcome in order to provide appropriate
and desired services to handicapped persons in
community settings. Such problems relate to
inadequate services for specific client groups,
continued dependence on institutions, mixed
results of changes brought about by litigation
or its threat, and problems in personnel preparation and utilization. Finally, there is a continued lack of clearly defined long-term goals
by which to define the parameters of needed
services and criteria against which to judge
their quality. Without these goals, policy and
program effort has been focused on placement
issues, rather than on the content and the most
appropriate method of service delivery. This
third problem area is the primary focus of the
last part of this chapter.

NEED FOR COMPREHENSIVE
COMMUNITY SERVICES

Services for handicapped persons are currently
offered by a number of separate systems including health, education, welfare, rehabilitation, recreation, employment, and housing.
None of these systems separately can solve the
multiple problems of handicapped persons
(Pollard, Hall, & Kiernan, 1979). Therefore
the need for collaboration among human service agencies and their components is being
increasingly stressed.

Community services include providing the
resources, technology, and staff necessary to
prevent, intervene, or (re)habilitate handicapping conditions. Planning for these services
must be based on an awareness of the needs of
handicapped persons, as well as on an understanding of the status of the current service
delivery system. Finally, the criteria for designing and evaluating comprehensive community services must be related to the principles underlying the services system and its
component parts. Such principles should be
implicitly and explicitly evident in the qualities
and goals of individual programs and in the
purposes of society regarding the care and
treatment of handicapped individuals as reflected by legislation and judicial interpretation. These criteria provide the parameters of a
comprehensive community service that are discussed later in the chapter.

Handicapped persons affected by the deinstitutionalization movement share a need for
community living alternatives, habilitation
programs, and support services. These needed
services are listed and diagrammed in Figure 1
and are referenced to current literature in
Table 1.

The following points are considered particularly important in structuring the array of community living and habilitation alternatives as
shown in Figure 1:

Natural environments are the preferred service
settings.
Generic services should be utilized to the greatest extent possible.
Assistance to the person should be provided
only at the level actually needed to promote
independence and self-sufficiency.
Training provided should focus on increasing
the person's independence, productivity,
and community integration.
Everyone has potential for growth regardless of
his or her current functioning level.
There are definable aspects of programs that
can be placed within discrete steps of a continuum so that alternatives/programs can be
rank-ordered along the dimensions outlined
in Figure 1.

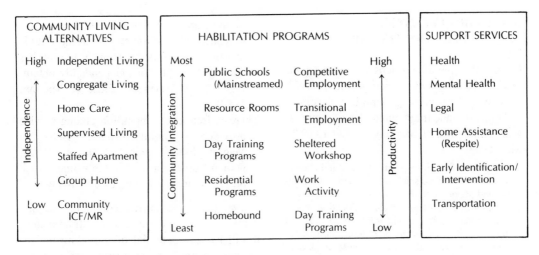

Figure 1.   Interrelationships of needed comprehensive community services.

Table 1.   Literature referenced to needed community services

				Component				
					Support services			
References	Community living alternatives	Habili-tation	Health	Mental health	Legal	Home assis-tance (respite)	Early identifi-cation/ intervention	Trans-portation
Brewer & Kakalik (1979)		X	X	X			X	X
Bruininks et al. (1980)	X	X	X	X	X		X	X
Bruininks et al. (1981)	X	X	X		X	X		X
Copeland & Iverson (1981)	X					X		
Elder & Magrab (1980)		X	X		X	X		X
Gibson (1978)	X		X					X
Gollay et al. (1978)	X	X	X	X	X	X		X
Haywood & New-brough (1981)	X			X				
Kenowitz, Gallaher & Edgar (1977)			X			X		X
Koch & Dobson (1976)		X	X	X		X		X
Larsen (1977)	X	X		X	X	X	X	X
Ramirez (1978)	X	X						
Schalock (1982)	X	X		X		X		X
Scheerenberger (1981)	X	X	X	X	X		X	X

STATUS OF CURRENT
SERVICE DELIVERY SYSTEMS

Despite the overall consensus regarding the service needs of handicapped persons, service delivery systems are in general best described as duplicative and fragmented. This situation is well summarized by Magrab and Elder (1979) who state,

> The service delivery system for the handicapped in the United States is really a series of fragmented service delivery systems in the areas of community and social services, education, vocational rehabilitation, and health delivery. Each of these systems was developed independently in response to needs within each of these areas over the past decades (p. x).

A number of observers have proposed explanations for this situation. The explanations include:

Needed services may overlap traditional boundaries of generic, community services such as health care and education (Gettings, 1981; Magrab & Elder, 1979).

Problems exist in defining target populations and in establishing whether services should be delivered to a categorically versus functionally defined clientele (Magrab & Elder, 1979).

Overlapping legislation and lack of a clear national policy (Brewer & Kakalik, 1979; Gettings, 1981; Magrab & Elder, 1979; Whitehead, 1981).

Multiple funding sources often exist without any means of financial coordination (Bellamy, Sheehan, Horner, & Boles, 1980; Copeland & Iverson, 1981; Gettings, 1981).

Multiple planning bodies frequently exist without any one group having adequate control or responsibility (Brewer & Kakalik, 1979; Magrab & Elder, 1979).

There is a clear lack of reliable data on program benefits and effectiveness (Brewer & Kakalik, 1979; Gottlieb, 1981).

Adequate resources including facilities, technology, and experienced and trained staff are in short supply (Brewer & Kakalik, 1979; Bruininks, Kudla, Hauber, Hill, & Wieck, 1981; Harper, 1979; Scheerenberger, 1981).

Despite notable changes in recent years, a significant portion of society retains the attitude that the handicapped person (or family) has the responsibility for independently obtaining effective services (Elder & Magrab, 1980).

There is frequent competition among service providers for limited resources (Elder and Magrab, 1980; Schalock & Harper, 1983), without any means of establishing which programs use the resources effectively.

Even though the current community service delivery system is duplicative and fragmented, it still has the potential of providing the resources, technology, and personnel adequate to fulfill the needs of handicapped persons. It will be necessary, however, to restructure, redefine, and redirect some of the service components.

CRITERIA FOR COMPREHENSIVE
COMMUNITY SERVICES

Specific criteria and guidelines for transforming the present array of services for handicapped persons in community settings are outlined in this section. In approaching the problem of developing comprehensive community services, it is necessary to conceptualize the goal as the *conversion of a service system,* rather than simply as deinstitutionalization or mainstreaming of individuals. Principles guiding such a system should include, to the maximum extent possible, that

Services are provided as a right, rather than a privilege (Biklen, 1973, 1976).

Services are provided on a noncategorical basis (Blatt, Bogdan, Biklen, & Taylor, 1977).

Services constitute a continuum to ensure that a person's needs are met in the most appropriate manner possible (Blatt et al., 1977).

Services are provided under the least restrictive, most normalized circumstances possible (Wolfensberger, 1972).

Agencies providing services are accountable to the consumers (Ashbaugh, 1981; Bellamy & Wilcox, 1982; Blatt et al., 1977; Laski & Spitalnik, 1980; Schalock, 1983).

Services use the most up-to-date techniques

available and meet at least minimum performance standards regarding their provision and results (Baum, Flanigan, Hoke, Parker, Rydman, & Schalock, 1982).

Program Qualities

A number of program qualities should guide the design and implementation of community services. Some of the more significant of these are mentioned briefly below. However, this volume contains numerous detailed elaborations of each. Perhaps the central quality that should be incorporated into programs relates to the *integration* of the handicapped person into the life of the community (Aloia, 1978; Bellamy & Wilcox, 1982). By *life of the community* is meant the normal routines and activities of daily living, the normal use of community facilities and resources, and normal (to the extent possible) social contact with other members (handicapped and nonhandicapped persons) of the community. *Age appropriate* training and development of adaptive behavior is also important. To the maximum extent possible, developmental activities of handicapped individuals should reflect those of nonhandicapped persons (Grossman, 1977). These activities should include:

During infancy and early childhood, skill development related to sensorimotor, communication, self-help, and socialization

During childhood and early adolescence, application of basic academic skills in daily life activities; application of appropriate reasoning and judgment in mastery of the environment; and participation in group activities and interpersonal relationships

During late adolescence and adulthood, vocational and social activities

Programs should be *community referenced* in regard to the demands and expectations both of the program and program participants. The implications of community referencing of programs include:

Emphasizing functional skills related to the basic demands of work, leisure, community participation, and residential living (Bellamy & Wilcox, 1982).

Using an ecological approach to assessing vocational and community living skills (Karan & Schalock, 1982).

Designing community-based training on an environmental inventory consisting of performance demands, naturally occurring cues and consequences, and environmental characteristics (Brown, Branston, Hamre-Nietupski, Pumpian, Certo, & Gruenewald, 1979).

Programs should also be *future oriented,* focusing on increasing use of community living alternatives commensurate with a person's level of functioning, increasing opportunities for nontrivial work, and decreasing tolerance for "eternal preschool" programs (Bellamy & Wilcox, 1982; Brown, Branston, Baumgart, Vincent, Falvey, & Schroeder, 1979). In that sense, programs should be *comprehensive* in their service delivery components (such as those outlined in Figure 1), including community living alternatives, habilitation programs, and necessary support services.

Finally, programs should enhance *family involvement* in a handicapped person's individual education/treatment program(s). The importance of the family's involvement in the deinstitutionalization process, their acceptance of community-based programs, and the relationship between these two variables and successful community placement has been well documented (see, for example, Heal, Sigelman, & Switzky, 1978; Schalock, Harper, & Garver, 1981; Schalock, Harper, & Genung, 1981).

Legislative Intent

The U.S. Congress and state legislatures have enacted several pieces of legislation to protect handicapped persons against discrimination and other forms of unjust treatment. Comprehensive community services should fulfill the intent of existing legislation through nondiscriminatory availability of services, physical accessibility to facilities and programs, and financial accessibility through free, appropriate education and habilitation.

In summary, comprehensive community services for handicapped persons must involve community living alternatives, a progression of habilitation-training programs, and necessary support services that will help maintain handicapped persons' successful community placement. Currently, the service delivery system attempting to provide these services is most accurately characterized as duplicative and fragmented. A number of criteria—including service delivery principles, program qualities, and legislative intent—that should guide the development and implementation of the needed comprehensive community services have been noted.

IMPLEMENTING COMPREHENSIVE COMMUNITY SERVICES

Truly comprehensive service systems for handicapped persons are based on an ecological or person-environment perspective. The theoretical basis of this approach is discussed in Chapter 13 by Chadsey-Rusch in this volume. A service system that operates from this perspective incorporates the following premises: 1) individuals cannot be separated from their living-working environments (Scott, 1980; Stucky & Newbrough, 1981); 2) both persons and their environments can be assessed (Dokecki, 1977; Karan & Schalock, 1984; Moos, 1974a, 1974b); 3) the mismatch between persons and their environment can be reduced in a number of ways, including the development of behavioral skills on the part of the client, the use of prosthetics, and modifying the environment (Schalock, 1983; Weisgerber, Dahl, & Appleby, 1980); 4) intervention should focus on caregivers and settings as much as on the handicapped person (Berkson & Romer, 1981; Karan, 1982; Willer & Intagliata, 1981); 5) assessment and training activities should have ecological validity, in that they should have value in the context of clients' daily lives (Brooks & Baumeister, 1977); and 6) handicapped persons should have access to both generic and specialized services (Gettings, 1981; Gollay, 1981). The ecological service delivery model outlined in this section incorporates these premises and suggests that:

Training activities should focus on functional skills taught in the natural environment.

Prosthetic devices should be used to assist in meeting the environment's demands or requirements.

Environments can be modified to facilitate access for and accommodation of persons with special needs.

Persons and environments can be matched to provide optimal opportunity for growth and development.

A number of critical questions are involved in implementing comprehensive community services and, in this author's view, good approaches exist for responding to them. The question of "What services will be provided and where" is best determined by an ecological service delivery model; "Who will provide them" involves a competency based staff utilization model; and "How will they be provided" requires consideration of interagency collaboration. Each of these questions is examined more fully in the following discussion.

Ecological Service Delivery Model

Recent studies suggest that environmental variables have significant influence on the behavior of persons with substantial mental impairments (Crawford, Aiello, & Thompson, 1979; Hull & Thompson, 1980; Landesman-Dwyer, 1981; Sutter, 1980; Sutter, Mayeda, Call, Yanagi, & Yee, 1980; Thiel, 1981; Wicker, 1979; Willems, 1977). Therefore, efforts to match persons to appropriate environments are clearly important. A model that reflects this process is outlined in Figure 2. Linking clients with environments requires conceptualization of two profiles: one profile summarizes a person's behavioral skills and needed prosthetics; the second profile summarizes the environment's available living-training services and service options, behavioral skill requirements, and environmental characteristics. These two profiles are then integrated through a process that might be referred to as "person-environment match." The steps in such a process are described below:

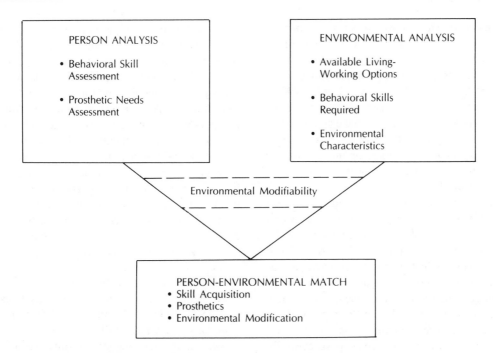

Figure 2.   An ecological assessment-placement model.

Person Analysis   Client characteristics account for between 21% to 36% of the variance of successful community placement (Gollay, Freedman, Wyngaarden, & Kurtz, 1978; Hull & Thompson, 1980; Schalock, Harper, & Genung, 1981). Recent summaries of characteristics associated with successful community living and vocational placement can be found in Karan and Schalock (1984), Landesman-Dwyer (1981), and Martin, Rusch, and Heal (1982). Social behavioral assessment instruments are available that can be used to determine a person's *behavioral skill profile* related to behaviors required by the person's living-habilitation environments and/or to the goals established on the person's program plan. A description and critique of available instruments can be found in Mayeda, Pelzer, and Magni (1979) and Chadsey-Rusch (this volume).

Behavioral skill assessment represents one aspect of person analysis. The second component includes assessing the need for *prosthetic devices* that would smooth the interface between the person and environment (Weisgerber

et al., 1980). Prosthetic devices include special aids or modification of the environment that compensate for or eliminate the effects of disabilities. Examples of such devices might be wheelchairs, ramps, and elevators for individuals of limited mobility. A *prosthetic need profile* would include an outline of needed sensory, motor, communication, cognitive, and staff support (facilitator-enabler) prosthetics. Specific examples are found in Schalock (1983) and Weisgerber et al. (1980).

Environmental Analysis   Evaluating the characteristics and behavioral requirements of different environments is a core component to ecological service delivery (Karan, 1982; Price, 1979; Chadsey-Rusch, this volume). Comprehensive environmental analysis techniques have not been adequately developed. However, a number of components are clearly important; these include assessment of the living-habilitation options within the environment, behaviors required to adapt successfully to those environments, and the characteristics of the environments.

In an environmental analysis the first step is

to list *available options*. An array of program-related services, such as that outlined in Figure 1, has been associated with community placement and programmatic success (Gollay et al., 1978; Schalock, Harper, & Genung, 1981). Delineating that array is the first step in the environmental analysis, since the options identified will establish the parameters and stages of habilitation programming (Brown, Branston, Baumgart, Vincent, Falvey, & Schroeder, 1979).

Once the list of services is prepared, the environmental analysis proceeds to the second step, that of identifying the behavioral skills required for each option in the array. Those skills required by the person's current and subsequent environments are determined through a process analogous to that done in manufacturing industries. A ''job'' or ''living'' analysis requires delineation of the personal, social, and supportive skills required to adapt successfully to the environment in question. For example, Table 2 summarizes the relationship, based on the author's research, between specific types of living-habilitation facilities and the behavioral skills generally required within several behavioral domains. As is reflected in the table, different environments are associated with increased demand on clients for independence and vocational productivity.

A third aspect of environmental analysis is listing environmental characteristics. A number of environmental characteristics—many of which have been associated with successful community living and integration—can be assessed. They include:

Normalizing qualities as typically assessed by Program Analysis of Service Systems (PASS-3) (Hull & Thompson, 1980; Wolfensberger & Glenn, 1975a, 1975b)
Social climate including relationships, person-

Table 2. Behavioral skill training areas associated with living-training facility progressions

	Community living-facility progression		
	ICF/MR $\longrightarrow$	**Group home/transitional living** $\longrightarrow$	**Staffed apartment/independent housing**
	Grooming	Health care	Handles medication
	Dressing	Laundry skills	Clothing repair/replacement
	Independent eating	Meal preparation	Meal planning and shopping
CLS Training Areas[a]	Self-referenced behaviors	Social integration	Interpersonal relations
	Expresses needs	Uses an expressive language system	Language generalization
	Cleaning	Home safety	Coping skills
	Utility of money	Money concepts	Independent money usage
	Prompted daily routine	Unprompted daily routine	Independent scheduling
	Perceptual-motor	Recreation and leisure activities	Uses community recreation facilities
	Community awareness	Community access	Independent community use
	Vocational training-placement progression		
	Extended employment $\longrightarrow$	**Sheltered workshop** $\longrightarrow$	**Center industry/competitive employment**
	Self-help skills	Job-related skills	On-the-job evaluation
Vocational Training Areas[a]	Personal/interpersonal behaviors	Work performance	On-the-job training
	Information processing	Work behavior	Industrial practica
	Learning/coping strategies	Job-seeking skills	Job enabler-facilitator (assistance)
	Prevocational skills		

[a]Referenced to behavioral domains contained in Schalock, R. L. *Community living and vocational training screening tests and remediation manuals*. Hastings: Mid-Nebraska Mental Retardation Services, 1982.

al growth orientation, and systems maintenance and change (Moos, 1974a, 1974b; Moos & Insel, 1974; Wandersman & Moos, 1981)

Staff attitudes including job satisfaction, standard setting, equality with residents, shared values, goals and beliefs, and overprotectiveness (Sutter et al., 1980; Willer & Intagliata, 1981)

Administrative organization such as shared management (Raynes, Pratt, & Roses, 1977), monitoring (Schalock, 1983), and perceived management problems

Family/benefactor involvement with persons residing within community-based facilities (Edgerton, 1975; Gollay et al., 1978; Reagan, Murphy, Hill, & Thomas, 1980; Schalock, Harper, & Genung, 1981)

Peer support including peer relationships, affiliation patterns, and agency-related friendships (Berkson & Romer, 1981)

Environment's Modifiability At least four steps are involved in facilitating and monitoring environmental change (Curtis, 1976; Wandersman & Moos, 1981), including:

1. Systematic assessment of the environment, including its environmental characteristics (see preceding discussion) and the degree to which it can be modified
2. Providing feedback to participating groups/individuals with particular stress on feasibility, advantages, and differences between the real and ideal characteristics of the setting
3. Planning and instituting specific changes
4. Monitoring and evaluation

Each of these steps is outlined later in the discussion of interagency collaboration.

Person-Environmental Match Like all persons, handicapped individuals have unique strengths and weaknesses that enable them to perform better in certain environments than in others; therefore, one should look for the best fit between persons and environments (Chadsey-Rusch, this volume; Stucky & Newbrough, 1981). A number of techniques can be used to facilitate a ''good fit'' or, as discussed earlier, reduce the mismatch between the person and the environment. These techniques include training functional skills, utilizing prosthetics, and modifying the environment.

The most common approach to increasing person-environmental match is *training functional skills*. The recent emphasis on adaptive behavior, personal competence, and functional skills has led to a complimentary emphasis on training these skills within environments that require and will help maintain them. Community living skills, including travel training, money management, meal preparation, clothing and personal care, telephone usage, housekeeping skills, self-medication, leisure, and social skills are increasingly being taught *in the community* and within the client's living-working-leisure environment (Bauman & Iwata, 1977; Brickey, 1978; Close, Irvin, Taylor, & Agosta, 1981; Dennis & Mueller, 1981; Johnson & Cuvo, 1981; Martin et al., 1982; Matson, 1980, 1981; Matson & Marchetti, 1980; Schalock, Gadwood, & Perry, 1984). Similarly, job training and work performance are being taught within a more normal employment environment, using one or more of the following models:

Cooperative classroom and vocational training areas (Forness, 1981)

Labor market survey and job analysis/training (Alper, 1981; Mithaug, 1981)

Utilization of training strategies that foster generalization of acquired skills (Bellamy, Wilson, Adler, Clarke, 1980)

Work experience and cooperative placement (Kingsbury, 1980; Lynch, Kiernan, & Stark, 1982)

Career exploration (Kiernan & Petzy, 1982; Phelps & Lutz, 1977)

On-the-job support services (Merwick, 1980)

Training for placement (Schutz & Rusch, 1982)

Transitional employment and on-the-job training (Kiernan, 1978)

Person-environmental match can also be influenced by *utilizing prosthetics*. Prosthetics can be conceptualized as devices that help meet the demands of a task and thereby facilitate community integration. They include mechanical devices, behavioral-chemical intervention strategies, and enabler-facilitator assistance. Mechanical prosthetics facilitate sensory, motor, communicative, and cognitive processing. Examples can be found in Brewer and Kakalik (1979), Brehner, Hallworth, and Brown (1981), Hallworth and Brehner (1978), Schalock (1983), Smeets (1981), Thomas (1981), and Weisgerber et al. (1980).

Behavioral-chemical intervention strategies have been used commonly to treat handicapped persons. In fact, to the extent that drug abuse means the overuse of prescription drugs, drug abuse is common among handicapped persons. Psychotropic medication is often used as a substitute for habilitative training, a particularly disturbing fact when one considers that high dosages of either psychotropic or anticonvulsant medication are related to impaired learning, cognitive performance, and adaptive behavior (Gardner & Cole, 1981; Menolascino, 1982). In addition, current drug treatment evaluation and monitoring practices are generally inadequate, with low levels of interaction between the person who prescribes, the agency staff person or parent who transmits the information on the client's behalf to the prescribing physician, and the person(s) in a position to monitor the drug's effects. A number of strategies to improve the interaction between drug givers, consumers, and monitors are beginning to be recognized in the literature. These include:

Behavioral-chemical intervention and monitoring (Schalock, 1983)
Inservice training for physicians serving handicapped persons (Powers & Healy, 1982; Wolraich, 1982)
Clinical pharmacology services (Inone, 1982; Van Krevelen & Harvey, 1982)

Facilitator assistance is a third type of prosthetic support. The need to assist an individual in his or her daily living environment has recently received considerable attention. For example, a teacher-broker approach has been proposed by Sabatino (1982) as the proper role for a special educator at the secondary level. In this role, the teacher-broker becomes the instructional advisor and advocate for youth in both regular and vocational programs. Similarly, the community-based mental retardation program with which this author works has implemented a new staff position, referred to as a facilitator assistant. The role of this staff person is to provide direct assistance to clients as they are placed into more independent and productive living-work environments. Examples of assistance provided include supervision of medication, shopping, legal-financial help, transportation, job supervision, and apartment monitoring.

A third general method of enhancing person-environmental match is through *modifying the environment*. Accessibility and environmental accommodation can be facilitated through architectural and task modifications. Examples include ramps; lowered appliances; wider doorways; grab bars; handibuses; and modified work equipment, work space, and assembly sequences. There is, furthermore, an increasing awareness of the role that the physical environment plays in both client and staff behaviors (Knight, Zimring, Weitzer, & Wheeler, 1977).

To conclude the discussion of matching persons and environments, it should be stressed that the primary purpose of this effort should be to ensure the environmental consistency, security, challenge, success, and opportunities for growth that result in increasing the client's independence, productivity, and community integration. This author, as well as others (Landesman-Dwyer, 1981; Moos, 1974a, 1974b; Sundberg, Snowden, & Reynolds, 1978), are actively pursuing a technology to improve environmental assessments and client-environment matching.

Competency-Based Staff-Utilization Model

The previous discussion stressed that community services should encompass an ecological or person-environment interaction perspective. Staff-utilization models should also be developed from this perspective. How to approach such a goal is the focus of the pages following. First, however, it is important to review recent personnel-utilization issues. These include both the needs of deinstitutionalized or mainstreamed persons and political-economic demands for increased effectiveness, efficiency, and accountability.

Current Personnel-Utilization Issues Deinstitutionalization and mainstreaming have caused strains in the utilization of habilitation personnel and have thereby resulted in considerable rethinking about how to increase efficiency in the use of staff across the environments and agencies involved in comprehensive community services. The following discussion briefly examines a number of personnel-utilization issues. However, no review of labor-market trends among professionals and paraprofessionals dealing with the handicapped population is included. Excellent recent reviews can be found in Beauregard and Indek (1979), Comptroller General (1976), Hanley (1981), National Commission (1976), and Schafer and McGough (1976).

The most important personnel issue involves delineating necessary skills for training personnel. The acceptance of mainstreaming has probably been hindered, owing to the confusion about skills needed by the personnel involved in mainstreaming (Crisci, 1981). Increasingly, however, researchers are beginning to delineate the competencies required of professionals if handicapped students are to be provided services in mainstream settings (Haring, 1978; Horner, 1977; Lilly, 1974). Stamm (1980), for example, suggests several generic teaching competencies for special educators, including that educators should:

Individually assess and diagnose specific skill strengths and weaknesses in order to develop appropriate instructional programming

Discriminate between assessment for classification purposes and that for instructional purposes

Design effective instructional programs (specify learning requirements and instructional objectives)

Systematically analyze instructional objectives (task analysis) and specify alternative program strategies to achieve them

Evaluate learner outcomes

Work effectively with other professionals and parents (communication and consulting skills)

Similarly, Byford (1979) has designed a training model for regular classroom teachers that includes the following skill areas:

Diagnostic skills—the ability to use case histories, clinical-observation techniques, the assessment of learning modalities, and formal and informal testing skills

Remediation skills—individualizing instruction, appropriate selection of teaching materials, varied instructional methods, and effective use of supportive services

Behavior management—understanding social and emotional problems, knowledge of affective skills development, understanding the relationship of self-concept and learning, and possessing knowledge of personal adjustment mechanisms

In comparing these and other lists, it is reasonable to conclude that the knowledge and skills perceived as needed by both regular and special education personnel are very similar. These competencies relate to assessment, task analysis, behavior management, motivation, communication, evaluation, and human relations (Crisci, 1981; Reynolds, 1978). Proposed approaches to training these competencies include specialized training (Horner, 1977, Wilcox, 1977), noncategorical teacher training programs (Blackhurst, 1981; Heward, 1981; Idol-Maestas, Lloyd, & Lilley, 1981; NARC-Education Committee, 1981), and inservice programs (Barrett & Buscher, 1981; Hardin, 1982; Phelps, 1975; Ziarnik & Bernstein, 1982).

A second personnel issue involves increased use of paraprofessionals. The use of paraprofessionals has expanded in both public schools (Bennett, 1981; Frith, 1981; May & Marozas, 1981; Pickett, 1979) and community-based mental health and retardation programs (Bruininks, Kudla, Wieck, & Hauber, 1980; Bruininks, Thurlow, Thurman, & Fiorelli, 1980). In reference to the latter, it is estimated that 80% of the personnel who come in contact with handicapped persons in community-based programs are paraprofessionals who are typically the least trained, lowest paid, and frequently least qualified (Schalock, 1983). In terms of the public schools' use of paraprofessionals, 20 states in 1979 were employing more than 1,000 special education paraprofessionals. From 1972 to 1979, there was a 42% increase in such usage. The most common activities conducted by special education paraprofessionals include (in descending order) work with individuals, behavior management, feeding, toileting, assisting the therapist, preparing materials, craftmaking, and instruction planning (May & Marozas, 1981).

A major personnel issue involves increased interdisciplinary collaboration. Public laws, entitlement programs, and accreditation agencies require an interdisciplinary approach to service delivery that includes individualized habilitation program plan development, implementation, and review. Although there is no standard composition of the team, the intent is reflected in the following accreditation standard:

> Each individual's interdisciplinary team is constituted of persons drawn from, or representing, the professions, disciplines or service areas that are relevant to identify the individual's needs and designing programs to meet them . . . (and) who work most directly with the individual in each of the professions, disciplines or service areas that provide services to the individual (Accreditation Council for Services for Mentally Retarded and Other Developmentally Disabled Persons, 1980).

Interdisciplinary *service* has increasingly been implemented; however, interdisciplinary *collaboration* has developed less rapidly. Barriers to this collaboration relate in part to concern about professional "territorial domains," confusion about practitioners' role(s) as participating professionals, and the lack of an agency-based person to interpret, integrate, assign priorities to, and implement the interdisciplinary team's evaluations and recommendations (Magrab & Schmidt, 1980). The author has found that two positions, that of diagnostic programmer and systems-level case manager, in the staff-utilization model presented on the following pages have helped significantly to overcome these barriers to effective interdisciplinary collaboration.

Features of the Staff-Utilization Model
Staff training and utilization should focus on developing the knowledge and skills necessary to assess environmental characteristics and requirements, to assess the client's functional level in reference to those environmental requirements, to implement individualized training programs to overcome significant behavioral skill deficits, and to provide assistance to the client in the critical steps or skills necessary to adapt successfully to less-restrictive and more-productive environments. A proposed personnel-utilization model is diagrammed in Figure 3. The model's essential features involve separating the process of assessment and training from that of case management and assistance, identifying within each process three levels of staff functioning, and linking the two intraorganizational processes (assessment/training and case management/assistance) with generic components of the service delivery system. Figure 3 also depicts the relationship between levels of service needs, specialization of personnel, and percentage of the client population.

The three staff levels involved in the *assessment/training component* derive from the data summarized in the preceding discussion of current personnel utilization issues. The general skills required at each level are listed in Table 3. Paraprofessional competencies (Level I) relate to knowledge about client groups, behavior management, behavioral analysis skills, and attitudes toward clients. Instructor competencies (Level II) relate to classroom organization, classroom management, curriculum, instructional methods/materials, and prescriptive program writing. Diagnostic programmer competencies (Level III) relate to client assessment, individual program planning, and evaluation.

The three staff levels have been identified within the *case management/assistance* component, based on the following research findings: 1) a significant proportion of case management (social service) staff time is spent

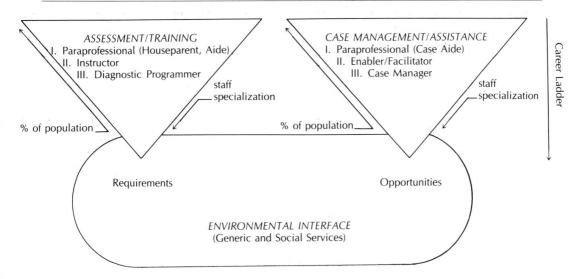

Figure 3.   Personnel-utilization model.

either on paperwork or on accompanying clients to various appointments and waiting for them; 2) the preceding activity does not require many skills short of patience and a driver's license; 3) lower-functioning clients can be placed into less-restrictive living and more-productive vocational environments if some staff support and training (not just advice) is provided; and 4) successful deinstitutionalization and mainstreaming require the integration of agency-based training programs, agency-sponsored assistance in maintaining a client's placement, and community-based generic services focused on living and working environments.

Basic duties for each of the three staff levels are listed in Table 4 and include:

Level I (aide): Persons at this staff level are involved with case-finding and paper-oriented procedures involving evaluation, diagnosis, and certification. In addition, the staff person monitors client progress and maintains records and information system requirements. The Level-I person also handles client-maintenance functions such as appointments, errands, correspondence, and recertification.

Level II (enabler/facilitator): Persons at this staff level provide assistance to clients

placed from the training program and function to facilitate their successful adaptation to the increased environmental requirements. Although the assistance provided is client specific, the general areas relate to community living, vocational placement, and community integration.

Level III (case manager): Case managers work to assure appropriate services and maximum client development through three major activities: 1) working with the diagnostic programmer in identifying the available placement options and specific behavioral skills required in those environments; 2) working with other components of the service delivery system, including generic community services to maintain client movement toward less restrictive placements; and 3) procuring the agency and community-based services that the client requires (such as additional assessment, specialized intervention, housing, transportation, and so forth).

The three activities performed by the case manager require two levels of case management and two types of individualized programs. *Client-level* case management utilizes the *individualized education program* (IEP) to structure activities and services promoting clients' growth and development toward the goal

Table 3.   Competencies for Levels I, II, and III assessment training staff

Level I (paraprofessional)	Level II (instructor)	Level III (diagnostic programmer)
Knowledge	**Classroom organization**	**Client assessment**
1. Characteristics of client population	1. Uses learning centers	1. Analyzes client's occupational and independent living interests and aptitudes
2. Interdisciplinary process	2. Adapts materials to student's needs	
3. Rights of client population	3. Manages time and resources	2. Collaborates with other educators, specialists, parents, and clients in developing an individualized education plan
Skills	**Classroom management**	
1. Behavioral management	1. Utilizes behavior-management techniques	3. Uses diagnostic and prescriptive assessment for planning intervention programs
a. Arranges environment to maximize learning	2. Employs reinforcement techniques	
b. Applies behavioral analysis and change principles	3. Integrates all clients into training activities	4. Develops individual performance goals and behavioral objectives
(a) Antecedent conditions	4. Utilizes paraprofessionals productively	**Program planning and evaluation**
(b) Behaviors	5. Recognizes variables affecting client behaviors	1. Analyzes local or regional job market and employment trends
(c) Consequences (deceleration techniques)	**Curriculum**	
2. Skill development	1. Utilizes and adapts local curriculum	2. Analyzes available community living alternatives
a. Uses task analysis	2. Utilizes prevocational, vocational, and independent living curriculum	3. Identifies and uses community resources in planning program and services
b. Incorporates principles of imitation training, generalization, discrimination, and maintenance into prescriptive programs	**Instructional methods/materials**	4. Establishes program advisory committees
c. Measures client performance	1. Utilizes individualized instructional methods	5. Identifies occupations and living environments to determine instructional content
d. Uses appropriate acceleration and deceleration consequences (rewards, negative consequences)	2. Documents instruction on an ongoing basis	6. Designs and implements a system for monitoring client progress
	3. Uses multiple resources and materials	7. Obtains information following placement
	4. Modifies materials to client's functional level	**Implementing individual programs**
Attitudes	**Prescriptive program writing**	1. Coordinates vocational and independent living with academic areas
1. Respect of person's individuality	1. Understands developmental and behavior sequences and the characteristics of different developmentally disabled groups	2. Uses diagnostic and prescriptive assessment techniques for planning intervention programs
2. Commitment to client's growth and development	2. States specific target behaviors or behavioral objectives based on either a task analysis or an "ABC" analysis	3. Uses instructional techniques that individualize instruction
	3. Completes all parts of prescriptive program sheet, including graphing of results	4. Selects or modifies instructional materials appropriate for different special-needs learners
		5. Plans and coordinates off-campus work and living instructions

Adapted from Batsche (1980), Phelps (1975), and Schalock (1983).

Table 4. Competency areas for Levels I, II, and III case management/assistance staff

Level I (paraprofessional)	Level II (enabler/facilitator)	Level III (case manager)
Enrollment	**Assists community living**	**Client-level case management**
1. Case finding	1. Medication	1. Individualized education plan (IEP) development
2. Certification	2. Clothing repair/replacement	2. IEP implementation
Monitoring	3. Meal planning/grocery shopping	3. IEP monitoring
1. Maintains records	4. Crisis intervention/emergency services	**Systems-level case management**
2. Information system input (computer)	5. Money usage	1. Determines placement alternatives
3. Client progress/movement documentation	6. Time awareness and utilization	2. Coordinates services (individualized transition plan)
Maintenance	**Assists vocational placement**	3. Interfaces with generic services
1. Appointments	1. Career counseling and guidance	
2. Errands	2. Work-adjustment counseling	
3. Correspondence	3. Develops and uses simulated job application and interview procedures	
4. Recertification	4. Provides and/or coordinates job placement services	
	5. Trains employers and supervisors to work effectively with special-needs learners on the job	
	Assists community integration	
	1. Recreation/leisure	
	2. Transportation	
	3. Community utilization	
	4. Interpersonal relations	

Adapted from Rosen, Clark, and Kivitz (1977); Schalock (1983); and Smith and Cooney (1979).

of eventually moving into, through, and out of the agency's training program. This is the traditional orientation of case management; but increasingly, *systems-level* case management is becoming necessary. This level, utilizing an *individualized transition plan* (ITP), structures interagency collaboration in developing and implementing a plan of sequential moves as clients progress along continua of independence and productivity. The ITP process requires that representatives from the clients' current and future living-training environments work together to identify potentially appropriate environments, required skills, and related training activities (Brown, Branston, Baumgart, Vincent, Falvey & Schroeder, 1979; Brown, Branston, Hamre-Nietupski, Pumpian, Certo & Gruenewald, 1979; Maher, 1981; Schalock, 1983).

Interagency Collaboration

The last major issue related to implementing comprehensive community services involves determining how those services can best be delivered. Earlier it was suggested that comprehensive community services must fulfill handicapped persons' needs for community living alternatives, for a progression of living-training programs, and for generic support services that facilitate successful community placement. It has been suggested that the ''what and where'' of these services involves training functional skills in natural environments and reducing the possible mismatch between the individual and the environment through systematic client and environmental assessments, prosthetic usage, and environmental modification. The most efficacious response to ''Who will provide those services'' involves a multi-level staff demonstrating knowledge and skills related to assessment, training, and case management and providing assistance in the client's living-work environments. In the following pages, major steps toward developing interagency collaboration are outlined. Such collaboration, in the author's opinion, is the best vehicle and in many, if not most, areas the *only* way to effectively implement comprehensive community services.

The current human service delivery system was previously described as duplicative and fragmented. The deficiencies of this uncoordinated system have been highlighted in a Rand Corporation study (cited in Brewer and Kakalik, 1979), which found that the service delivery system dealing with children and youth was so complex and disorganized as to defy efficient and effective operation. The two basic premises of this chapter's discussion are first, that collaboration should occur among agencies providing community living alternatives and habilitation-training programs (see Figure 1); and second, that interagency collaboration is the best potential solution for improving the efficiency and effectiveness of human service programs. The initiative for interagency collaboration has already been established at the federal level through written joint policy statements between the offices of special education programs and community health services, and between vocational education, vocational rehabilitation, and special education programs. These initiatives, plus parallel developments at both state and national levels in legislative, judicial, fiscal, and policy arenas, have increasingly mandated interagency collaboration (Elder & Magrab, 1980). Additional impetus for interagency collaboration comes from current environmental conditions such as limited dollars, rising consumer expectations, and a political-economic philosophy that demands increased effectiveness, efficiency, and accountability.

Needless to say, interagency collaboration is easier proposed than accomplished. In fact, the difficulties inherent in this area have led to the development of general guidelines and relevant observations for those pursuing cross-agency collaborative efforts (Barth, 1963; Baum et al., 1982; Dunham, 1970; Elder & Magrab, 1980; Evans, 1966; Zeitz, 1975). Some general considerations and observations in this regard include:

Changes tend to originate from the actions of individuals at the grass roots level.

Political issues should be avoided as much as possible in seeking to secure community agency coordination and cooperation.

Organizing efforts and decision making should be decentralized and are most effective when they rely on persuasion and mutual agreement rather than on authoritarianism.

Agencies tend to avoid creating interdependencies except in relatively safe areas that are auxiliary to the main organizational objective.

Conflict occurs among agencies owing to overlapping domains, different philosophies and goals, and competition for either financial or public support.

Cooperation occurs when the benefits and advantages outweigh the costs and disadvantages.

Communities and their organizations have a relatively high degree of autonomy.

Clearly there is no best model to follow in developing interagency collaboration within a community (Elder and Magrab, 1980). Indeed, collaboration can take place in different ways and at different levels. For example, levels of coordination may include (Baumheimer, 1979):

Policy level coordination involving collaboration in needs identification, in selection of options, and in making allocative choices on a jurisdictionwide or cross-agency level

Administrative linkages that include goal-oriented interactions between two or more agencies that are designed to facilitate the organizational, administrative, or management dimensions of agency relationships

Case management linkages that include interactions between agencies to improve client services

Similarly, there are different types of multi-institutional arrangements (Magrab & Elder, 1979; Mason, 1979; Zuckerman, 1979) including:

Formal affiliations involving a close association under formal agreement, most commonly used for conducting joint educational activities

Shared or cooperative services involving formal or informal agreements to share or provide one or more administrative or clinical service by one of a group of agencies in a geographic area, or through a separate, newly formed special purpose agency

Consortia involving a voluntary alliance of existing agencies within the same geographic area that are organized for a specific purpose

In many instances, consortium arrangements seem to represent the best vehicle for implementing interagency collaboration and thereby for improving the comprehensiveness of a community's service delivery system. At a time when the level of resources allocated for human services programs requires a special concern for efficiency as well as effectiveness, the consortium concept provides a means for

agencies to blend their programs productively. Although the concept of consortia is relatively new in human services, both hospitals and educational agencies have been involved for years in such cooperative efforts (Cochrane, 1979; Grupe, 1974; Martinson, 1982; Nelson, 1972; Schwenkmeyer & Goodman, 1972).

Figure 4 diagrams how a consortium would facilitate interagency collaboration and thereby better integrate community living alternatives and habilitation programs. The steps in implementing such efforts are described next, followed by discussion of three catalysts that will facilitate the collaborative process required in consortium arrangements.

Considerable work has recently been done to formulate the steps involved in consortium formation. The author has been involved in one such effort (Baum et al., 1982) outlining a rationale, steps, and procedures required to develop, implement, and evaluate consortia for community living alternatives. The six critical phases in this process include: 1) determining feasibility and expected outcomes of collaboration; 2) choosing a collaborative model and membership; 3) developing an operational plan; 4) operating and monitoring to provide

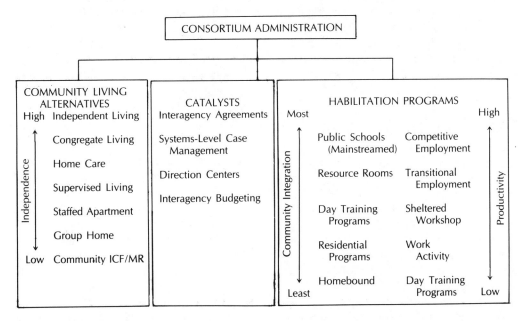

Figure 4. Interagency collaboration.

feedback; 5) monitoring for improvement and evaluation; and 6) evaluating outcomes and implementing change strategies. These six phases, along with process steps and suggested outcomes, are outlined in Table 5.

Interagency collaboration cannot occur unless two things happen: First, agencies involved must anticipate improved outcomes from the collaboration; and second, one or more catalysts must exist to initiate and guide the process. The major expected advantages of such cooperation include (Zuckerman, 1979):

Economic Benefits

Operating advantages (increased productivity, improved utilization of resource capacity, lower staffing requirements, and reduced unit costs from joint activities)

Financial advantages (access to capital markets, improved credit standing, reduced borrowing costs)

Staffing Benefits

Improved recruitment and retention of clinical and management staff

Strong clinical and management capability

Organizational Benefits

Organizational growth (extended referral networks, penetration of new geographical areas, expansion of existing services)

Organizational survival (financial improvements, accreditation standards, greater political power)

Service Delivery Benefits

Improved resource allocation

Improved distribution of health personnel

Increased availability of services

Broader, more comprehensive scope of services

Catalysts that facilitate interagency collaboration include interagency agreements, systems-level case management, direction centers, and interagency budgeting. Each is briefly discussed in the paragraphs following; the reader is referred to cited references for more in-depth treatments.

Interagency Agreements Written agreements are an integral part of the interagency process regardless of the multi-institutional arrangement chosen. Interagency agreements can vary from a broad statement of commitment to work together to a detailed description of the objectives, roles, and responsibilities of each party to the agreement. A review of the information elements contained in a number of interagency agreements suggests that the following elements are the most important (Aram & Stratton, 1974; Baumheimer, 1979; Elder, 1979; Gross & Skopin, 1977; Johnson, McLaughlin, & Christensen, 1982):

Clear statement of the purpose of the agreement between parties, with delineation of goals and measurable objectives for the central components of the agreement

Definitions of any terms that could be ambiguous between the parties

Clear definitions of specific programs, services, or special targeting within the agreement so that there is clear communication of the need for and intent of the agreed-upon effort

Specific actions, roles, and responsibilities of each party to the agreement

Designation of specific staff within each agency to implement and monitor the agreement

General administrative procedures including time lines, revision/termination procedures, meetings, confidentiality safeguards, referral mechanisms, and information sharing;

Evaluation procedures and guidelines for the utilization of evaluation data;

Assurances that each agency will maintain its autonomy.

Systems-Level Case Management This level of case management involves a primary role of linking clients with appropriate and needed components of the larger service system. A similar role position, referred to as a human development liaison specialist, examines what ecological systems an individual is currently involved with and then establishes links with needed community resources to maximize the person's independence, productivity, and community integration (Dokecki, 1977; Newbrough, 1977; Williams, 1977). Family support-units and broken systems rep-

Table 5. Consortium development, implementation and evaluation phases

Phase and outcome	Critical process steps/variables
I. Determine feasibility and expected outcome of collaboration	1. *Assess:* a. Preexisting conditions b. Success indicators/criteria c. Expected benefits (economic, staffing, organizational) d. Agreement/commitment to specific service performance indicators (availability, awareness, accessibility, extensiveness, appropriateness, efficiency, effectiveness, acceptability) 2. *Evaluate:* a. Possibility of collaboration b. Expectations of potential members c. Baseline of service performance indicators d. Major purpose(s) of the collaboration e. Potential initial leaders
II. Choose collaborative model and membership	1. *Assess among existing collaborative models:* a. Shared services—agencies share services b. Contractual services/referral agency—each agency provides own services and contracts service(s) from other agencies c. Centralized planning and administration—centralized entity services all member agencies d. Decentralized, geographically dispersed—centralized entity monitors member agencies in dispersed geographical areas 2. *Assessment variables:* a. Agency domain factors—purpose, population serve, geographical jurisdiction, services offered b. Agency resources—money, facilities, staffing, technology c. Existing interagency relations—communication, trust, shared expectations, information exchange 3. *Choose model/membership that best:* a. Meets needs of service delivery system b. Consistent with social-political environment c. Has highest probability of success
III. Develop an operational plan	1. *Assess and categorize client needs* 2. *Inventory current program resources* 3. *Compare available resources with client/service needs* 4. *Assess heterogeneous constituency* 5. *Determine range of service options* 6. *Develop a strategic (or "ideal") plan that:* a. Organizes service needs in order of priority b. Utilizes service delivery standards to plan needed service components c. Identifies funding/interagency sources 7. *Evaluate strategic plan and develop an operational plan that specifies:* a. Needed service components considered most feasible and utilitarian b. Necessary interagency agreements c. Critical performance indicators used to monitor progress and evaluate results
IV. Operate and monitor to provide feedback	1. *Implement operational plan:* a. Establish loci of responsibility b. Implement administrative and policies manual (with specific reference to role(s) of fiscal and lead agencies) c. Implement interagency agreements d. Maintain awareness of critical realities during implementation—political issues, consumer/provider relations, time lines and responsibilities, accountability

(continued)

Table 5. (*Continued*)

Phase and outcome	Critical process steps/variables
	2. *Monitor organizational variables reflecting the "health" of the consortium and its success at:* a. Problem solving b. Conflict resolution c. Communication d. Future planning e. Optimism f. Delineating clear roles g. Maximizing client welfare h. Developing policies/procedures for client access, quality assurance, client movement
V. Monitor for improvement and evaluation	1. *Develop consortium information system variables such as:* a. Access/client characteristics b. Screening data c. Referral-placement d. Optimal client-provider match e. Client tracking f. Record keeping g. Fiscal recording h. Reporting functions 2. *Implement monitoring/review procedure:* a. Choose variables to be monitored—critical performance indicators such as goals, consortium health indicators, service performance indicators, client progress, status of consortium collaboration b. Link monitored variables to consortium information system (CV-1) c. Define when and how data will be gathered and the party or entity from which it will be obtained d. Establish judgmental criteria for acceptance/rejection of evidence in relation to each variable e. Conduct the monitoring activities f. Interpret the data and specify action/correction procedures
VI. Evaluate outcomes and implement change	1. *Use monitoring data (Phase V) to evaluate outcomes such as:* a. Changed service performance indicators b. Status of anticipated benefits c. Degree of consortium collaboration 2. *Verify status of required accountability relationships:* a. Goal accountability—consortium board responsible to client and to public b. Program accountability—agency/consortium management responsible to agency/consortium board c. Outcome accountability—program staff and management responsible to (consortium) management 3. *Implement planned change (based upon information from VI-1 and VI-2)* a. Change areas include resources (money and facilities), staffing, and technology (methods and machines). b. Change strategies include top-down, bottom-up and shared responsibility.

Note: Specific methodology and tools are available in Baum et al. (1982).

resent extensions of this catalyst (Karnes & Zehrback, 1975). The complex issues involved in effective case management services are discussed extensively by Wray and Wieck in Lakin and Bruininks (in press).

Direction Centers The concept of a direction center was proposed by Brewer and Ka-

kalik (1979) as a result of the Rand study's conclusion regarding the disarray among human service programs. It was the position of Brewer and Kakalik that the center should "be separate from other major direct service programs in the bureaucracy, so that it is not captured by those programs, and so that too much emphasis is not placed on direction to certain services'' (p. 222).

The U.S. Bureau of Education for the Handicapped has funded a number of direction-center demonstration projects as an outgrowth of the Rand study's recommendations. Basic tasks conducted to date by the direction centers include:

Assisting in the location of and access to the most appropriate combination of services and resources to meet the needs of handicapped children

Systematically collecting and maintaining information on services and resources available to meet the needs of handicapped children

Assisting in the development and support of relationships among agencies that promote coordinated services to children

Interagency Budgeting Copeland and Iverson (1981) suggest that it is possible to link program optimization to fiscal optimization by "organizing programs along a continuum of care, adopting an interagency budgeting approach to financing them, and establishing a continuum management function to ensure continuing program and fiscal optimality" (p. 315). Interagency budgeting involves tying program design to fiscal incentives through:

Treating all human service budgets as a single budget

Maximizing client entitlements through integrated eligibility and referral

Intertitle transfers, to the extent permitted by clients' eligibility for more than one entitlement program, to help finance continuum management

One or more of these catalysts should effectively bring about better interagency collaboration, including possible consortium formation. When such arrangements can be structured, improvement in the comprehensive community services provided to handicapped persons should be seen.

POLICY AND RESEARCH ISSUES

This chapter has so far focused on three observations related to providing comprehensive community services for handicapped persons.

The first observation is that despite some apparent successes of the deinstitutionalization and mainstreaming movements, both are social experiments whose efficiency, effectiveness, and comprehensiveness have not yet been well established. The second observation is that handicapped persons' varied needs can best be met by a progression of living-training programs and the support services required for success and further development in those programs. The third observation involves the author's experience that certain specific conditions enhance comprehensive community services and that these include the use of models for ecological service delivery, staff utilization, and interagency collaboration. The last part of this chapter addresses unresolved research and policy issues that, among other factors, will be codeterminants in the future success, or lack thereof, in developing and evaluating comprehensive community services.

Several policy research issues need to be addressed in the immediate future; these are listed here. But first, a note of caution: research and policy priorities will need to be established that reflect the reality of diminishing financial resources. Furthermore, it must be recognized that under such conditions distinctions between policy issues and research questions will be fewer and narrower. While the distinction between policy and research issues is maintained in this chapter, it is important to emphasize that the two are intertwined.

Policy Issues

The development of valid outcome measures for mainstreaming and deinstitutionalization programs is critically important, providing the criteria against which the efficacy of these two movements and programs generated by them can be evaluated. Areas in which outcome-sensitive measures must be developed and utilized include increased client competence, skills, and productivity; increased morale, well-being, and satisfaction; improved ability to cope with new situations; and increased involvement with regular community-based activities, particularly those measures that reflect greater personal independence. A related issue involves the need to develop the means to fund programs on the basis of demonstrated client outcomes, as well as to create funding incentives for improved program efficiency.

Another funding issue that remains particularly important is the establishment of a medical assistance/income maintenance system that provides incentives for moving clients into environments that are more independent and productive and ultimately less expensive. As the present reimbursement system is structured, social and fiscal policies are not harmonious. Finally, efforts should be made to structure personnel preparation and continuing education around the particular skills needed to perform in an integrated, community-based service system as outlined in the earlier-proposed personnel-utilization model.

Research Issues

Although deinstitutionalization and least restrictive placement programs have been ongoing for many years, there remains a very limited amount of longitudinal research on their outcomes. It should be remembered that the implementation of deinstitutionalization and of least restrictive placements has been predicated more on perceptions of client rights than on claims of significantly improved outcomes. Therefore, the longitudinal assessment of outcome is critically important to answering both *general* questions about program effects and *specific* questions about the relative merits of system refinements such as the ecological service delivery model discussed earlier. Further research is also needed in developing and implementing competency-based staff utilization models that increase demonstrated staff competencies, that clarify roles, and that enhance abilities to implement interdisciplinary recommendations, analyze environments, and make and carry out interagency agreements.

Finally, there is an urgent need for policy research related to interagency collaboration. Such research should focus on both the process of establishing collaborative arrangements and the outcomes of various collaboration/consortium models. Important outcome variables in this research include the following: 1) client movement within living-work progressions; 2) units of service and costs; 3) number of clients served; and 4) staff turnover and other job attitude measures.

Any discussion of future research and policy issues must take three realities into consideration. One is reflected in Winston Churchill's observation that, "First we shape our programs, and then they shape us." We have developed, somewhat haphazardly to be sure, programs for providing residential, educational, and habilitative programming in the least restrictive setting. We must be willing to distinguish the good from the bad and to discard those that do not work. The second reality deals with the recognition that the 1980s is much more likely to be a political-economic era than a philosophical one. Economics is the overriding issue of today, and the major issue of the 1980s will be how the economy affects policies, rather than how constituencies affect politics. The third reality deals with social movements, examples of which are deinstitutionalization and mainstreaming. Social movements are born, grow fast, age prematurely, and either die or are absorbed into new movements. In this sense, they are like scientific revolutions in which specific scientific paradigms or movements are supplanted by other theories or movements that can solve problems better. Ultimately, this issue will become the issue of the 1980s. The notion of interagency collaboration presented in this chapter represents to the author both that upcoming movement and the best hope we have of providing comprehensive community services for handicapped citizens in the 1980s.

REFERENCES

Accreditation Council for Services for Mentally Retarded and Other Developmentally Disabled Persons. (5101 Wisconsin Avenue, NW, Suite 405, Washington, DC 20016). 1980.

Aloia, G. Assessment of the complexity of the least re-

strictive environment doctrine of Public Law 94-142. In: *LRE: Developing criteria for the evaluation of the least restrictive environment provision.* Philadelphia: Research for Better Schools, 1978.

Alper, S. Utilizing community jobs in developing vocational curriculum for severely handicapped youth. *Education and Training of the Mentally Retarded*, 1981,*16*(3), 217–221.

Aram, J.D., & Stratton, W.E. The development of interagency cooperation. *Social Service Review*, 1974, *48*, 412–421.

Ashbaugh, J.W. Accountability of community providers for services to the mentally retarded and other developmentally disabled persons. In: T.C. Muzzio, J.J. Koshel, & V. Bradley (eds.), *Alternative community living arrangements and non-vocational social services for developmentally disabled people*. Washington, D C : Urban Institute, 1981.

Barrett, J.C., & Buscher, J.B. The circular paradigm: An answer to inservice needs. *Journal of Learning Disabilities*, 1981, *14*(8), 455–458.

Barth, E. The cause and consequences of interagency conflict. *Social Inquiry*, 1963, *33*, 31–33.

Batsche, C. Personnel preparation for serving special vocational needs populations. In: G.D. Meers (ed.), *Handbook of special vocational needs education*. Rockville, MD: Aspen Systems Corp., 1980.

Baum, B., Flanigan, R., Hoke, G., Parker, R., Rydman, R., & Schalock, R. (eds.), *Consortia for community living alternatives*. Springfield, IL: Illinois Governor's Planning Council on Developmental Disabilities, 1982.

Bauman, K.E., & Iwata, B. Maintenance of independent housekeeping skills using scheduling plus self-recording procedures. *Behavior Therapy*, 1977, *8*, 554–560.

Baumheimer, E. Interagency linkages in the field of developmental disabilities. In: J. Adams (ed.), *Readings in interagency evaluation*. Columbus, OH: University of Ohio Press, 1979.

Beauregard, R.A., & Indek, B.P. *Human service labor market: Developmental disabilities*. New Brunswick: New Jersey Press, 1979.

Bellamy, G.T., Sheehan, M.R., Horner, R.H., & Boles, S.M. Community programs for severely handicapped adults: An analysis of vocational opportunities. *TASH Review*, 1980, *5*(4), 307–324.

Bellamy, G.T., & Wilcox, B. Secondary education for severely handicapped students: Guidelines for quality services. In: K.P. Lynch, W.E. Kiernan, & J.A. Stark (eds.), *Prevocational and vocational education for special needs youth: A blueprint for the 1980s*. Baltimore: Paul H. Brookes Publishing Co., 1982.

Bellamy, G.T., Wilson, D.J., Adler, E., & Clarke, J.Y. A strategy for programming vocational skills for severely handicapped youth. *Exceptional Education Quarterly*, 1980, *1*(2), 85–97.

Bennett, R.E. Professional competence and the assessment of exceptional children. *Journal of Special Education*, 1981, *15*(4), 437–446.

Berkson, G., & Romer, D. A letter to a service provider. In: H.C. Haywood & J.D. Newbrough (eds.), *Living environments for developmentally retarded persons*. Baltimore: University Park Press, 1981.

Biklen, D. Human report: I. In: B. Blatt (ed.), *Souls in extremis: An anthology on victims and victimizers*. Boston: Allyn & Bacon, 1973.

Biklen, D. Advocacy comes of age. *Exceptional Children*, 1976, *42*, 308–313.

Blackhurst, A.E. Noncategorical teacher preparation: Problems and promises. *Exceptional Children*, 1981, *48*(3), 197–205.

Blatt, B., Bogdan, R., Biklen, D., & Taylor, S. From institution to community: A conversion model. In: E. Sontag, J. Smith, & N. Certo (eds.), *Educational programming for the severely and profoundly handicapped*. Reston, VA: Council for Exceptional Children, 1977.

Brehner, A., Hallworth, H.J., & Brown, R.I. Computer-assisted learning with the handicapped. In: P. Mittler (ed.), *Frontiers of knowledge in mental retardation*, Vol. 1. Baltimore: University Park Press, 1981.

Brewer, G.D., & Kakalik, J.S. *Handicapped children: Strategies for improving services*. New York: McGraw Hill Book Co., 1979.

Brickey, M. A behavioral procedure for teaching self medication. *Mental Retardation*, 1978, *16*, 29–32.

Brooks, R., & Baumeister, A. A plea for consideration of ecological validity in the experimental psychology of mental retardation. *American Journal of Mental Deficiency*, 1977, *81*, 407–416.

Brown, L., Branston, M.B., Baumgart, D., Vincent, L., Falvey, M., & Schroeder, J. Utilizing the characteristics of a variety of current and subsequent least restrictive environments as factors in the development of curricular content for severely handicapped students. *AAESPH Review*, 1979, *4*, 407–424.

Brown, L., Branston, M.B., Hamre-Nietupski, A., Pumpian, I., Certo, N., & Gruenewald, L. A strategy for developing chronological age-appropriate and functional curricular content for severely handicapped adolescents and young adults. *Journal of Special Education*, 1979, *13*, 81–90.

Bruininks, R.H., Kudla, M.J., Hauber, F.A., Hill, B.K., & Wieck, C.A. Recent growth and status of community-based residential alternatives. In: R.H. Bruininks, C.E. Meyers, B.B. Sigford, & K.C. Lakin (eds.), *Deinstitutionalization and community adjustment of mentally retarded persons*. (Monograph #4). Washington, D C : American Association on Mental Deficiency, 1981.

Bruininks, R.H., Kudla, M.J., Wieck, C.A., & Hauber, F.A. Management problems in community residential facilities. *Mental Retardation*, 1980, *18*(3), 125–130.

Bruininks, R.H., Thurlow, M.L., Thurman, S.K., & Fiorelli, J.S. Deinstitutionalization and community services. In: J. Wortis (ed.), *Mental retardation and developmental disabilities*, Vol. 9. New York: Brunner/Mazel, 1980.

Byford, E.M. Mainstreaming: The effects on regular teacher training programs. *Journal of Teacher Education*, 1979, *30*(6), 23–24.

Close, D.W., Irwin, L.K., Taylor, V.E., & Agosta, J. Community living skills instruction for mildly retarded persons. *Exceptional Education Quarterly*, 1981, *2*(1), 75–85.

Cochrane, J.D. Hospital consortia: State of the art. In: J.D. Cochrane (ed.), *Hospital consortia*. Sacramento: California Hospital Association, 1979.

Comptroller General of the United States. *Training educators for the handicapped: A need to redirect federal programs*. Washington, D C : U.S. General Accounting Office, Manpower & Welfare Division, 1976.

Copeland, W., & Iverson, I. An optimization approach to reforming and refinancing state programs for mentally retarded and developmentally disabled persons. In: T.C. Muzzio, J.J. Koshel, & V. Bradley (eds.), *Alternative community living arrangements and non-vocational social services for developmentally disabled people*. Washington, D C : Urban Institute, 1981.

Crawford, J.L., Aiello, J.R., & Thompson, D.E. Deinstitutionalization and community placement: Clinical and environmental factors. *Mental Retardation*, 1979, *17*(2), 59–65.

Crisci, P.E. Competencies for mainstreaming: Problems and issues. *Education and Training of the Mentally Retarded*, 1981, *16*(3), 175–182.

Curtis, S. The compatability of humanistic and behavioristic approaches in a state mental hospital. In: A. Wandersman, P. Poppen, & D. Ricks (eds.), *Humanism and behaviorism: Dialogue and growth*. New York: Pergamon Press, 1976.

Dennis, S.S., & Mueller, H.H. Self-management training with the mentally handicapped: A review. *Mental Retardation Bulletin*, 1981, *9*(1), 3–31.

Dokecki, P. The liaison perspective on the enhancement for human development: Theoretical, historical, and experimental background. *Journal of Community Psychology*, 1977, *5*, 13–17.

Dunham, A. *The new community organization*. New York: Thomas Y. Crowell Co., 1970.

Edgerton, R.B. Issues relating to the quality of life among mentally retarded persons. In: M.J. Begrab & S.A. Richardson, (eds.), *The mentally retarded and society: A social science perspective*. (Proceedings of conference supported by the National Institute of Child Health and Human Development, Niles, MI., April 18–20, 1974). Baltimore: University Park Press, 1975.

Elder, J.O. Coordination of service delivery systems. In: P.R. Magrab & J.O. Elder, (eds.), *Planning for services to handicapped persons: Community, education, health*. Baltimore: Paul H. Brookes Publishing Co., 1979.

Elder, J.O., & Magrab, P.R. *Coordinating services to handicapped children*. Baltimore: Paul H. Brookes Publishing Co., 1980.

Evans, W.M. The organization-set: Toward a theory of interorganizational relations. In: J.D. Thompson (ed.), *Approaches to organizational design*. Pittsburgh: University of Pittsburgh Press, 1966.

Forness, S.R. Prevocational academic assessment of children and youth with learning and behavior problems: The bridge between the school classroom and vocational training. In: K.P. Lynch, W.E. Kiernan, & J.A. Stark (eds.), *Prevocational and vocational education for special needs youth: A blueprint for the 1980s*. Baltimore: Paul H. Brookes Publishing Co., 1981.

Frith, G.H. Paraprofessionals: A focus on interpersonal skills. *Education and Training of tbe Mentally Retarded*, 1981, *16*(4), 306–309.

Gardner, W.I., & Cole, C.L. Meeting the mental health needs of the mentally retarded. *Community Services Bulletin*, 1981, *1*(3), 1–3.

Gettings, R.M. Generic vs. specialized services: The yin and yang of programming for developmentally disabled clients. In: T.C. Muzzio, J.J. Koshel, & V. Bradley (eds.), *Alternative community living arrangements and non-vocational social services for developmentally disabled people*. Washington, D C : Urban Institute, 1981.

Gibson, W.M. Health care services for the developmentally disabled. In: R.L. Schalock (ed.), *A model comprehensive service delivery system for persons with developmental disabilities*. Springfield, IL: Illinois Developmental Disability Council, 1978.

Gollay, E. Some conceptual and methodological issues in studying the community adjustment of deinstitu-

tionalized mentally retarded people. In: R.H. Bruininks, C.E. Meyers, B.B. Sigford, & K.C. Lakin (eds.), *Deinstitutionalization and community adjustment of mentally retarded persons* (Monograph # 4). Washington, D C : American Association on Mental Deficiency, 1981.

Gollay, E. Freedman, R., Wyngaarden, M., & Kurtz, N.R. *Coming back: The community experience of deinstitutionalized mentally retarded people*. Cambridge, MA: Abt Associates, 1978.

Gottlieb, J. Mainstreaming: Fulfilling the promise? *American Journal of Mental Deficiency*, 1981, *86*(2), 115–126.

Gross, J., & Skopin, J. *Deinstitutionalization consortium final report*. Columbus, OH: Ohio State University, Nisonger Center, 1977.

Grossman, H.J. (ed.). *Manual on terminology and classification in mental retardation*. Washington, D C : American Association on Mental Deficiency (Special Publication No. 2), 1977.

Grupe, F.H. Consortia and academic change. In: C. Dwyer & L.D. Patterson (eds.), *Interinstitutional interface: Making the right connection*. Washington, D C : American Association for Higher Education, 1974.

Hallworth, H.J., & Brehner, A. Computer assisted instruction and the mentally handicapped: Some recent developments. In: *Proceedings of the 16th Annual Convention—Association for Educational Data Systems*. Washington, D C : Association for Educational Data Systems, 1978.

Hanley, E. Labor market trends. In: T.C. Muzzio, J.J. Koshel, & V. Bradley (eds.), *Alternative community living arrangements and nonvocational social services for developmentally disabled people*. Washington, D C : Urban Institute, 1981.

Hardin, V.B. Designing continuing education programs for special educators. *Exceptional Education Quarterly*, 1982, *2*(4), 69–76.

Haring, N.G. Conclusion: Classroom two. In: N.G. Haring (ed.), *Behavior of exceptional children* (2nd ed.). Columbus, OH: Charles E. Merrill Publishing Co., 1978.

Harper, R.S. Resources for MR/DD programs in rural settings. In: R.L. Schalock (ed.), *MR/DD services in rural America . . . It is time*. Washington, D C : Institute for Comprehensive Planning, 1979.

Haywood, H.C., & Newbrough, J.R. *Living environments for developmentally retarded persons*. Baltimore: University Park Press, 1981.

Heal, L.W., Sigelman, C.K., & Switzky, H.N. Research on community residential alternatives for the mentally retarded. In: N.R. Ellis (ed.), *International review of research in mental retardation*, Vol. 9. New York: Academic Press, 1978.

Heward, W.L. Noncategorical teacher training in a state with cateogrical certification requirements. *Exceptional Children*, 1981, *48*(3), 206–212.

Horner, R.D. A competency-based approach to preparing teachers of the severely and profoundly handicapped: Perspective II. In: E. Sontag, J. Smith, & N. Certo (eds.), *Educational programming for the severely and profoundly handicapped*. Reston, VA: Council for Exceptional Children, Division on Mental Retardation, 1977.

Hull, J.T., & Thompson, J.C. Predicting adaptive functioning of mentally retarded persons in community settings. *American Journal of Mental Deficiency,* 1980, *85,* 253–261.

Idol-Maestas, L., Lloyd, S., & Lilly, M.S. A noncategorical approach to direct service and teacher education. *Exceptional Children,* 1981, *48*(3), 213–220.

Inone, F. A clinical pharmacy service to reduce psychotropic medication use in an institution for mentally handicapped persons. *Mental Retardation,* 1982, *20*(2), 70–74.

Johnson, B., & Cuvo, A.J. Teaching cooking skills to mentally retarded persons. *Behavior Modification,* 1981, *5,* 187–202.

Johnson, H.W., McLaughlin, J.A., & Christensen, M. Interagency collaboration: Driving and restraining forces. *Exceptional Children,* 1982, *48*(5), 395–398.

Karan, O.C. From the classroom into the community. In: K.P. Lynch, W.E. Kiernan, & J.A. Stark (eds.), *Prevocational and vocational education for special needs youth.* Baltimore: Paul H. Brookes Publishing Co., 1982.

Karan, O.C., & Schalock, R.L. An ecological approach to assessing vocational and community living skills. In: C. O'Connell-Mason (ed.), *Assessing moderate and severe handicaps.* Columbus, OH: Charles E. Merrill Publishing Co., 1984.

Karnes, M., & Zehrbach, R. Matching families to services. *Exceptional Children,* 1975, *42*(8), 545–549.

Kenowitz, L.A., Gallaher, J., & Edgar, E. Generic services for the severely handicapped and their families: What's available? In: E. Sontag, J. Smith, & N. Certo (eds.), *Educational programming for the severely and profoundly handicapped.* Reston, VA: Council for Exceptional Children, 1977.

Kiernan, W. Rehabilitation planning. In P.R. Magrab & J.O. Elder (eds.), *Planning for services to handicapped persons: Community, education, health.* Baltimore: Paul H. Brookes Publishing Co., 1978.

Kiernan, W.E., & Petzy, V. A systems approach to career and vocational enducation programs of special needs students: Grades 7–12. In: K.P. Lynch, W.E. Kiernan, & J.A. Stark (eds.), *Prevocational and vocational education for special needs youth.* Baltimore: Paul H. Brookes Publishing Co., 1982.

Kingsbury, D. Work experience and cooperative placement programs. In G. D. Meers (ed.), *Handbook of special vocational needs education.* Rockville, MD: Aspen Systems Corporation, 1980.

Knight, R.C., Zimring, C.M., Weitzer, W.H., & Wheeler, H. C. (eds.). *Social development and normalized institutional settings: A preliminary research report.* Amherst: Institute for Man and Environment. University of Massachusetts Press, 1977.

Koch, R., & Dobson, J.C. *The mentally retarded child and his family: A multi-disciplinary handbook.* New York: Brunner/Mazel, 1976.

Lakin, K.C., & Bruininks, R.H. (eds.). *Strategies for achieving community integration of developmentally disabled citizens.* Baltimore: Paul H. Brookes Publishing Co., in press.

Landesman-Dwyer, S. Living in the community. *American Journal of Mental Deficiency,* 1981, *86*(3), 223–234.

Larsen, L.A. Community services necessary to program effectively for the severely/profoundly handicapped. In

E. Sontag, J. Smith, & N. Certo (eds.), *Educational programming for the severely and profoundly handicapped.* Reston, VA: Council for Exceptional Children, 1977.

Laski, F. J., & Spitalnik, D. M. A review of Pennhurst implementation. *Community Services Forum,* 1980, *1*(1), 1–8.

Lilly, M.S. *Classroom teacher competencies for mainstreaming.* Duluth: University of Minnesota, 1974.

Lynch, K.P., Kiernan, W.E., & Stark, J.A. Sociological, educational, and behavioral/biomedical advances and their future implications for special needs youth. In: K.P. Lynch, W.E. Kiernan, & J.A. Stark (eds.), *Prevocational and vocational education for special needs youth.* Baltimore: Paul H. Brookes Publishing Co., 1982.

Magrab, P.R., & Elder, J.O. *Planning for services to handicapped persons: Community, education, health.* Baltimore: Paul H. Brookes Publishing Co., 1979.

Magrab, P.R., & Schmidt, L.M. Interdisciplinary collaboration: A prelude to coordinated service delivery. In: J.O. Elder & P.R. Magrab (eds.), *Coordinating services to handicapped children: A handbook for interagency collaboration.* Baltimore: Paul H. Brookes Publishing Co., 1980.

Maher, C.A. Decision analysis: An approach for multidisciplinary teams in planning special service programs. *Journal of School Psychology,* 1981, *19*(4), 340–349.

Martin, J.E., Rusch, F.R., & Heal, L.W. Teaching community survival skills to mentally retarded adults: A review and analysis. *Journal of Special Education,* 1982, *16,* 243–268.

Martinson, M.C. Interagency services: A new era for an old idea. *Exceptional Children,* 1982, *48*(5), 389–394.

Mason, S.E. *Multihospital arrangements: Public policy implications.* Chicago: American Hospital Association, 1979.

Matson, J.L. A controlled group study of pedestrian skill training for the mentally retarded. *Behavior Research and Therapy,* 1980, *18,* 99–106.

Matson, J.L. Use of independence training to teach shopping skills to mildly mentally retarded adults. *American Journal of Mental Deficiency,* 1981, *86,* 178–183.

Matson, J.L., & Marchetti, A. A comparison of leisure skills training procedures for the mentally retarded. *Applied Research in Mental Retardation,* 1980, *1,* 113–122.

May, D.C., & Marozas, D.S. The role of the paraprofessional in educational programs for the severely handicapped. *Education and Training of the Mentally Retarded,* 1981, *16*(3), 228–231.

Mayeda, T., Pelzer, L., & Magni, T. *Performance measures of skill and adaptive competencies of mentally retarded and developmentally disabled persons.* Los Angeles: University of California, 1979.

Menolascino, F.J. *Mental retardation and mental health: Bridging the gap.* New York: McGraw-Hill Book Co., 1982.

Merwick, S. Identification and utilization of support services in serving special vocational needs students. In: G.D. Meers (ed.), *Handbook of special vocational needs education.* Rockville, MD: Aspen Systems Corp., 1980.

Mithaug, D.E. *Prevocational training for retarded students.* Springfield, IL: Charles C Thomas, 1981.

Moos, R. H. *Community oriented program environment scale manual*. Palo Alto, CA: Consulting Psychologists Press, 1974a.

Moos, R.H. *The social climate scales: An overview*. Palo Alto, CA: Consulting Psychologists Press, 1974b.

Moos, R.H., & Insel, P.M. The work environment scale. In: R.H. Moos, P.M. Insel & B. Humprey (eds.), *Combined preliminary manual—family work and group environment scales*. Palo Alto, CA: Consulting Psychologists Press, 1974.

NARC-Education Committee. Competency-based teacher education in mental retardation: A model of self-analysis for teacher training programs. *Education and Training of the Mentally Retarded*, 1981, *16*(3), 21–29.

National Commission for Manpower Policy. *Second annual report to the president and the Congress of the National Commission for Manpower Policy: An employment policy for the United States: Next Steps*. Washington, D C : National Commission for Manpower Policy, 1976.

Nelson, W.C. Entrepreneurship and innovation in consortia. *Journal of Higher Education*, 1972, *43*, 544–551.

Newbrough, J.R. Liaison services in the community context. *Journal of Community Psychology*, 1977, *5*, 24–27.

Phelps, L.A. *Instructional development for special needs learners: An inservice resource guide*. Urbana, IL: University of Illinois Press, 1975.

Phelps, L.A., & Lutz, R.J. *Career exploration and preparation for the special needs learners*. Boston: Allyn & Bacon Co., 1977.

Pickett, A.L. *Paraprofessionals in special education: The state of the art—1979*. New York: National Resource Center for Paraprofessionals in Special Education, Center for Advanced Study in Education, City University of New York, 1979.

Pollard, A., Hall, H., & Kiernan, C. Community services planning. In: P.R. Magrab & J.O. Elder (eds.), *Planning for services to handicapped persons: Community, education, health*. Baltimore: Paul H. Brookes Publishing Co., 1979.

Powers, J.T., & Healy, A. Inservice training for physicians serving handicapped children. *Exceptional Children*, 1982, *48*(4), 332–336.

Price, R.H. The social ecology of treatment gains. In: A. Goldstein & F. Kanfer (eds.), *Maximizing treatment gains*. New York: Academic Press, 1979.

Ramirez, R. Community living alternatives for persons with developmental disabilities. In: R. L. Schalock (ed.), *A model comprehensive service delivery system for persons with developmental disabilities*. Springfield, IL: Illinois Developmental Disability Council, 1978.

Raynes, N., Pratt, M., & Roses, S. Aides' involvement in decision-making and the quality of care in institutional settings. *American Journal of Mental Deficiency*, 1977, *81*(6), 570–577.

Reagan, M.W., Murphy, R.J., Hill, Y.F., & Thomas, D.R. Community placement stability of behavior problems among educable mentally retarded students. *Mental Retardation*, 1980, *18*(3), 139–142.

Reynolds, M.C. Basic issues in restructuring teacher education. *Journal of Teacher Education*, 1978, *29*(6), 25–29.

Rosen, M., Clark, G.R., & Kivitz, M.S. *Habilitation of the handicapped*. Baltimore: University Park Press, 1977.

Sabatino, D.A. Rx for better secondary programming: A teacher-broker. *Academic Therapy*, 1982, *17*(3), 289–296.

Schafer, R.C., & McGough, R.L. *Statewide cooperative manpower planning in special education: A status study*. Columbia: University of Missouri, 1976.

Schalock, R.L. *Services for the adult developmentally disabled: Development, implementation, and evaluation*. Baltimore: University Park Press, 1983.

Schalock, R.L., Gadwood, L.S., & Perry, P.B. Effects of different training environments on the acquisition of community living skills. *Journal of Applied Research in Mental Retardation*, 1984.

Schalock, R.L., & Harper, R.S. A systems approach to community living skills training. In: R.H. Bruininks, C.E. Meyers, B.B. Sigford, & K.S. Lakin (eds.), *Deinstitutionalization and community adjustment of mentally retarded people* (Monograph # 4). Washington, D C : American Association on Mental Deficiency, 1981.

Schalock, R.L., & Harper, R.S. Untying some Gordian knots in program evaluation. *Journal of Rehabilitation Administration*, 1983, *7*(1), 12–20.

Schalock, R.L., Harper, R.S., & Garver, G. Independent living placement: Five years later. *American Journal of Mental Deficiency*, 1981, *86*(2), 170–171.

Schalock, R.L., Harper, R.S., & Genung, T. Community integration of the developmentally disabled: Variables affecting community placement and program success. *American Journal of Mental Deficiency*, 1981, *85*(5), 478–488.

Scheerenberger, R.C. Deinstitutionalization: Trends and difficulties. In: R.H. Bruininks, C.E. Meyers, B.B. Sigford, & K.C. Lakin (eds.), *Deinsititutionalization and community adjustment of mentally retarded persons* (Monograph # 4). Washington, D C : American Association on Mental Deficiency, 1981.

Schutz, R.P., & Rusch, F.R. Competitive employment: Toward employment integration for mentally retarded persons. In: K.P. Lynch, W.E. Kiernan, & J.A. Stark (eds.), *Prevocational and vocational education for special needs youth: A blueprint for the 1980s*. Baltimore: Paul H. Brookes Publishing Co., 1982.

Schwenkmeyer, B., & Goodman, M.E. *Putting cooperation to work*. New York: Academy for Educational Development, Management Division, 1972.

Scott, M. Ecological theory and methods for research in special education. *Journal of Special Education*, 1980, *14*, 279–294.

Smeets, P.M. Developing a calculator to enable retarded adults to make financial transactions. In: P. Mittler (ed.), *Frontiers of knowledge in mental retardation*, Vol. 1. Baltimore: University Park Press, 1981.

Smith, C.B., & Cooney, L.L. *Illinois case management study*, Vols 1–3. Springfield, IL: Illinois Governor's Planning Council for Developmental Disabilities, 1979.

Stamm, J.M. Teacher competencies: Recommendations for personnel preparation. *Teacher Education and Special Education*, 1980, *3*(1), 52–57.

Stucky, P.E., & Newbrough, J.R. Mental health of mentally retarded persons. In: H.C. Haywood & J.R. Newbrough (eds.), *Living environments for developmentally retarded persons*. Baltimore: University Park Press, 1981.

Sundberg, N.D., Snowden, L.R., & Reynolds, W.M. Toward assessment of personal competence and incompetence in life situations. *Annual Review of Psychology,* 1978, *29,* 179–221.

Sutter, P. Environmental variables related to community placement failure in mentally retarded adults. *Mental Retardation,* 1980, *18*(4), 189–191.

Sutter, P., Mayeda, T., Call, T., Yanagi, G., & Yee, S. Comparison of successful and unsuccessful community-placed mentally retarded persons. *American Journal of Mental Deficiency,* 1980, *85,* 262–267.

Thiel, G.W. Relationship of IQ, adaptive behavior, age, and environment demand to community-placement success of mentally retarded adults. *American Journal of Mental Deficiency,* 1981, *86*(2), 208–211.

Thomas, M.A. Educating handicapped students via micro-computer/videodisc technology: A conversation with Ron Thorkildsen. *Education and Training of the Mentally Retarded,* 1981, *16*(4), 262–269.

Van Krevelen, N.D., & Harvey, E.R. Integrating clinical pharmacy services into the interdisciplinary team structure. *Mental Retardation,* 1982, *20*(2), 64–68.

Wandersman, A., & Moos, R.H. Evaluating sheltered living environments for mentally retarded people. In: H.C. Haywood & J.R. Newbrough (eds.), *Living environments for developmentally retarded persons.* Baltimore: University Park Press, 1981.

Weisgerber, R.A., Dahl, P.R., & Appleby, J.A. *Training the handicapped for productive employment.* Rockville, MD: Aspen Systems Corp., 1980.

Whitehead, C.W. *Final report: Training and employment services for handicapped individuals in sheltered workshops.* Washington, D C : U.S. Department of Health and Human Services, Office of the Assistant Secretary for Planning and Evaluation, 1981.

Wicker, A.W. Ecological psychology: Some recent and prospective developments. *American Psychologist,* 1979, *34*(9), 755–765.

Wilcox, B. A competency-based approach to preparing teachers of the severely and profoundly handicapped: Perspective I. In: E. Sontag, J. Smith, & N. Certo (eds.), *Educational programming for the severely and profoundly handicapped.* Reston, VA: Council for Exceptional Children, 1977.

Willems, E.P. The interface of the hospital environment and patient behavior. In: A. Rogers-Warren & S. Warren (eds.), *Ecological perspectives in behavior analysis.* Baltimore: University Park Press, 1977.

Willer, B., & Intagliata, J. Social-environmental factors as predictors of adjustment of deinstitutionalized mentally retarded adults. *American Journal of Mental Deficiency,* 1981, *86*(3), 252–259.

Williams, J. Liaison functions as reflected in a case study. *Journal of Community Psychology,* 1977, *5,* 18–23.

Wolfensberger, W. *The principle of normalization in human services.* Toronto: National Institute on Mental Retardation, 1972.

Wolfensberger, W., & Glenn, L. *PASS 3. Program Analysis of Services Systems field manual.* Toronto: National Institute on Mental Retardation, 1975. (a)

Wolfensberger, W., & Glenn, L. *PASS 3. Program Analysis of Services Systems field manual.* Toronto: National Institute on Mental Retardation, 1975. (b)

Wolraich, M.L. Communication between physicians and parents of handicapped children. *Exceptional Children,* 1982, *48*(4), 324–329.

Zeitz, G. Interorganizational relationships and social structure: A critique of some aspects of the literature. In: A. Nagandhi (ed.), *Interorganizational theory.* Kent, OH: Kent State University Press, 1975.

Ziarnik, J.P., & Bernstein, G.S. A critical examination of the effect of inservice training on staff performance. *Mental Retardation,* 1982, *20*(3), 109–114.

Zuckerman, H.S. *Multi-institutional hospital systems.* Chicago: Hospital Research and Educational Trust, 1979.

Part II

CONSTITUTIONAL AND LEGAL
ISSUES IN SOCIAL
INTEGRATION AND HABILITATION

This book was largely developed around the premise that the central focus of the struggle to improve opportunities for severely handicapped persons in the mid-to-late-1980s will shift from courts and the U.S. Congress to policies, programs, and professional practices. Therefore, the bulk of this volume is devoted to describing the best contemporary practices in community-based service delivery, organization, administration, and policy. In the future, it seems likely that judicial and legislative activity will be less sweeping but more precisely targeted. There will be fewer major new programs, but careful consideration will be given to how existing programs can be refined and regulated to promote the best of contemporary programs for their target populations. Recent U.S. Supreme Court decisions strongly suggest that future judicial action can be expected to be more often focused on specific instances of denial of recognized rights to habilitation, to freedom from undue restraint, to safety, and to nondiscrimination, and less often directed toward reforming the traditional provision of service to handicapped persons.

Given this assessment of the future, a number of major questions are raised. Among these are: 1) What rights have been established in past judicial and legislative decisions regarding handicapped children and youth? 2) What are the major issues that courts have tended to see as programmatic or professional rather than legal? 3) What kinds of judicial and legislative interventions can be expected to be successfully negotiated in the remainder of the decade? 4) What strategies can be recommended as alternatives to the utilization of courts and to totally new federal programs in continuing the improvement of services for severely handicapped children and youth?

The chapters in this section have been developed by persons who, by direct involvement with these and related issues, are particularly well qualified to examine the role of the courts and of Congress in shaping the contemporary legal standards governing educational, habilitation, residential, and other support services for handicapped children and youth. In Chapter 4, Frank J. Laski examines the legal foundation of the rights to habilitation and to education that have been the cornerstone of the greatly expanded and improved system of services for handicapped children and youth. Laski notes the commonalities and differences in the development of the current legal status of right to education and right to habilitation (the general concept most influencing the nature and quality of residential services). The present status of court and congressional activity is summarized and critically analyzed. The chapter concludes by emphasizing the need for improved federal policy regarding the regulation of existing programs as the most direct and effective way of continuing the reform of programs for persons with handicaps in the United States.

Chapter 5, by Valerie J. Bradley, critically evaluates the past effects of using litigation in bringing about major changes in long-term care for severely handicapped persons. Bradley examines the factors underlying the efforts in the 1970s (which lasted into the early 1980s) to use the courts as principal agents of reform, as well as the likely effects of recent Supreme Court decisions on the future of judicial activity. The actual benefits, in addition to the economic and programmatic costs, of past court interventions are also explored. The chapter concludes with suggestions for the use of judicial remedies in promoting continued reform of programs for handicapped persons.

Chapter 4

Right to Habilitation and Right to Education

The Legal Foundation

Frank J. Laski

Constitutional values, legal principles, and law-based notions of equality and personal liberty provide the foundation for the movement to integrate handicapped persons into society. The legal developments of the 1970s fueled the efforts of handicapped persons and their families to secure effective access to education, community services, vocational training, employment, and transportation. In the courts and in the U.S. Congress, much of the advocacy on behalf of handicapped persons has had as its overriding objective the active participation and access of disabled persons to effective services in the community. Of central importance in the achievement of the integration objective for handicapped persons has been the development of legally enforceable rights to education for handicapped children and the right to habilitation, including services in the community, for developmentally disabled children and adults.

This chapter, in addition to addressing the constitutional and federal statutory basis for the right to education and right to habilitation, also explores the commonalities and interre-

lationships between the legal concerns in the two areas. Although the course of legal developments in each of the two areas has encompassed specific procedural issues bearing on the general issue of integration (for example, in education, testing, and student classification in *Diana v. State Board of Education,* 1970, and *Larry P. v. Riles,* 1972; in habilitation, admission, and commitment procedures and parental rights in *Parham v. J.R.,* 1979), it is important to note the origins, legal principles, stages of development, and judicial and congressional interrelationships that are common to both areas.

Despite the significant role played by the lower courts in developing legal rights and remedies for handicapped persons, it was nearly a decade after the seminal court actions in education (*Pennsylvania Association for Retarded Citizens v. Commonwealth of Pennsylvania,* 1971; henceforth, *PARC*) and habilitation (*Wyatt v. Stickney,* 1971) that the U.S. Supreme Court directly addressed constitutional rights to habilitation and federal statutory rights to education.[1] In 1981 *Halderman v.*

---

[1]In 1975, the Court did affirm the right to liberty of nondangerous persons civilly committed to mental institutions, avoiding, for the time being, the question of right to treatment or to habilitation.

Pennhurst (State School and Hospital) and 1982 (*Youngberg v. Romeo*), the Court dealt with the right to habilitation under federal statute and the U.S. Constitution and, in 1982, the Court addressed the right to education, interpreting for the first time the Education for All Handicapped Children Act of 1975 (Public Law [PL] 94-142) in *Board of Education of Hendrick Hudson School District et al. v. Amy Rowley* (1982). Together with its option in *Southeastern Community College v. Davis* (1979), which interpreted Section 504 (the antidiscrimination clause of the Rehabilitation Act of 1973), these decisions provide a baseline for understanding and making judgments about the future of court decisions regarding the right to habilitation of persons with handicaps.

Using these Supreme Court decisions as a foundation, five observations emerge:

1. Each handicapped child has a statutory right to appropriate education that includes "education sufficient to confer educational benefit upon the handicapped child" (*Board of Education of Hendrick Hudson School District et al. v. Amy Rowley,* 1982).
2. Each developmentally disabled person in an institution or other restrictive facility has a constitutionally protected liberty interest in safety, freedom of movement, and training, and constitutionally protected rights to "safe conditions," and to "freedom from bodily restraint and minimally adequate or reasonable training to ensure safety and freedom from undue restraint" (*Youngberg v. Romeo,* 1982).
3. The training opportunities provided in institutional and other settings must be based upon the judgment of qualified professionals (*Youngberg v. Romeo,* 1982).
4. Each handicapped person has a right to nondiscriminatory treatment and access to services. Affirmative obligations to provide effective services are limited to the extent that those services are perceived as costly special services (*Southeastern Community College v. Davis,* 1979).

5. There is no federal statutory right to habilitation or to services in less-restrictive community settings. Congressional imposition of substantive standards upon states for the habilitation of developmentally disabled persons must be explicit, both in terms of what is required and in terms of the constitutional basis for the federal requirement (*Halderman v. Pennhurst [State School and Hospital],* 1981).

While these statements provide a simple preview of current law, of greater significance is that they pose issues that must be addressed in both professional and public policy forums, including: a) whether professionals, parents, and advocates will be able to effectively use existing statutes (PL 94-142) to secure state-of-the-art programs; b) whether the constitutional right to habilitation can eventually be applied to securing community living; c) whether the integrity of professional judgments concerning appropriate education and adequate habilitation can be bolstered and freed from administrative pressures and constraints; and d) whether federal legislation can be structured to establish legally enforceable rights and funding patterns that support integrated settings.

As an aid to understanding current law and to provide a framework for dealing with the legal issues that the Supreme Court decisions raise, it is important to trace the legal development in rights to education and habilitation through the following stages: a) early judicial protection under the Constitution; b) congressional codification of constitutional principles; and c) Supreme Court interpretation.

EARLY CONSTITUTIONAL PROTECTIONS

In the early 1970s, faced with the reality of subcustodial state institutions for retarded persons and the claims that persons in those institutions suffered abuse, injury, and regression, lower courts referred to the Constitution in attacking two aspects of the states' treatment of mentally retarded persons: level of treatment within institutions and exclusion from public education in the community. The initial questions surrounding the issue of constitutional violations were deceivingly simple: a) Should severely handicapped children be excluded from school (based upon the judgment of school officials that certain handicapped children could not benefit from schooling)? and b) Should severely handicapped children and adults be protected from abuse, neglect, and inhumane conditions of confinement?

While the litigation tactics and constitutional theories used to confront these questions were different, the underlying problems they addressed—the segregation of severely handicapped persons and their exclusion from services in the community—were two sides of the same coin.

Historically, state institutions were developed as surrogates for the public schools. Davies (1925) in describing the early development of these institutions, wrote:

> These early institutions were, in a sense, a branch of the public school system. . . . When these early education methods proved less fruitful than had been anticipated in the intellectual rehabilitation of the mentally defective, the institutions . . . . entered upon that second and familiar stage in which custodial care and segregation were the most prominent (p. 220).

Throughout the country, state laws excluding retarded children from public schools codified and legitimized the practice of institutionalization of young children and continued to encourage institutional admissions of school-age children even during the late 1960s when the institutional census began to decrease. In 1970, when parents of retarded children were actively preparing to litigate for rights to education and treatment, 87% of the first admissions to institutions were below age 20 (Butterfield, 1976).

Given this background, it was no accident that early litigation efforts were the result of parents who began to organize out of concern for inhumane conditions in institutions and their frustration with traditional political solutions to chronic neglect, abuse, and maltreatment. The first right to education case (*PARC v. Commonwealth*, 1971) was triggered by

continuing evidence of significant physical abuse and dangerous institutional practices at the Pennhurst State Institution in Pennsylvania (Wilson, 1980). The parents association at Pennhurst resolved to retain counsel to take legal action against the state "to either have it close Pennhurst or show just cause for its continuance" (Lippman & Goldberg, 1973, p. 18). Instead of a direct attack on the institution via a right to treatment suit, PARC chose to pursue its objective by attacking school exclusion based in part on the association's view that education in the community was a necessary condition of dismantling the institutions (Lippman & Goldberg, 1973).

The 1972 federal court decisions in the *PARC* case marked the beginning of the end of school exclusion for severely handicapped children and, if not the beginning of the closing of state institutions, at least the stemming of the tide of admissions to institutions by securing needed alternative services and by establishing the importance of habilitation in programs for severely handicapped persons. The facts in the case that gained access to the classroom for retarded children also demonstrated that the institution was unnecessary for the students' "education and training."

Approving the decree in the *PARC* case, the three-judge federal court found:

> all mentally retarded persons are capable of benefitting from a program of education and training; that the greatest number of retarded persons, given such education and training, are capable of achieving self-sufficiency and the remaining few, with such education and training are capable of achieving some degree of self-care (1972, p. 279).

The *PARC* consent decree legally established the principle that a state could not deny any mentally retarded child access to a free public education. Moreover, it established a legal foundation that extended beyond the principle of nonexclusion. As Supreme Court Justice William Rehnquist recently acknowledged, the decree incorporated the standard that each child receive "access to a free public program of education and training appropriate to his learning capacities," and that the state be required to take action in the event that "the needs of the mentally retarded child are not being served" (*Board of Education of Hendrick Hudson School District et al. v. Amy Rowley*, 1982, 102 S. Ct. 3034, 3044, at note 15, quoting *PARC I*, 334 F. Supp. 1258 and 1266). The *PARC* decree furthermore set forth the integration principle, stating that

> Among the alternative programs of education and training required . . . to be available, placement in a regular public school class is preferable to placement in a special public school class, and placement in a special public school class is preferable to placement in any other type of program of education and training (334 F. Supp. at 1257).

The chief programs of the "other type" were in state institutions. In Pennsylvania at the time of the *PARC* decree, 4,154 school-age retarded children were in institutions; over 3,000 received no program of education or training.

A few months after the *PARC* decree was approved, a federal court extended the right to education to all handicapped children in the District of Columbia (*Mills v. D.C. Board of Education*, 1972), basing its decision on the due process and equal protection clauses of the U.S. Constitution. The thrust of the constitutional doctrine invoked by the three-judge *PARC* court and applied by the *Mills* court can be summarized as follows:

> First, the unjustified exclusion of any child from all public schooling denies to that child the equal protection of the laws when the state makes the opportunity freely available to other children. Second, the operation of our unfair procedure in the stigmatization by public authority of any person or the denial to him of any public good denies the process due each person under the 14th Amendment. Such a stigmatization and denial is involved in labeling children as exceptional, retarded, or handicapped and placing them in a special class, or excluding them from schooling entirely. These two rights, equal protection and due process, merge to form the emerging constitutional right to an education which guarantees to every child a minimally adequate publicly supported education opportunity (Dimond, 1973, p. 1087).

This constitutional doctrine provided the foundation supporting the four major principles of right to education:

Zero reject education. Access to free public education must be provided for all children and youth regardless of degree of exceptionality or fiscal impact on the school system.

Integrated education. Education should be provided in the most integrated, normal setting possible that is consistent with the learning needs of the invididual. A presumption is made against segregation and in favor of the most integrated, least restrictive environment possible.

Appropriate education. Education must be based on an individualized program that is appropriate to the needs of the child.

Due process. Opportunity must be made available for a notice or a hearing appeal with respect to placement or other changes in educational programs.

When bolstered by principles of normalization and integration, the constitutional doctrine advanced in the *PARC* and *Mills* cases, especially the equal protection aspect, was applied in litigation in almost every state. By 1975, there were 46 pending or completed court cases raising constitutional claims of right to education for handicapped children (121 *Cong. Rec.* 19487–19491). At the same time many states, following the example of Massachusetts in 1972, scrapped categorical exclusionary school codes and enacted comprehensive special education laws incorporating the zero reject and due process principles of the federal court cases.

During the time that the right to education cases were being developed and presented, an emerging constitutional theory of right to treatment for persons involuntarily confined in state institutions came to be applied to mentally retarded persons. First, in Alabama as part of a wholesale attack on the state mental health system (*Wyatt v. Stickney,* 1971) and then in New York (*New York Association for Retarded Citizens* [henceforth, *NYARC*] *v. Rockefeller,* 1973), lower courts proclaimed that persons in institutions had a constitutional right to habilitation or at least a right to protection from harm.

Although the major focus and immediate impact of the right to habilitation cases was an attempt to improve institutional conditions (for example, staffing, physical environment, and habilitation within existing facilities) and to stimulate substantial investment in institutional programs, the court orders themselves also contained the germ of the community services and integration remedies that were directly addressed in *PARC* and the right to education cases. The original Willowbrook decree required reduction of population from 3,000 to 250 (*NYARC v. Rockefeller*, 1975). In the *Wyatt* case, Judge Frank Johnson invoked normalization principles and adopted a standard of least restrictive setting for habilitation (in other words, educational training of retarded persons, which required the institution "to make every effort to move residents from facilities segregated from the community to those integrated into the community" [*Wyatt v. Stickney*, 1971, p. 396]).

Despite the intentions of the parties, the emphasis on institutional standards and protections in the early right to habilitation cases overwhelmed the imprecise least-restrictive-setting standard. The formulation of the right to habilitation in due process terms allowed the courts to order that institutions be improved without addressing the justification for continuing the institutional mode of services. Burt (1976), in an analysis of the early right to treatment cases, noted the serious limitation in the *Wyatt* approach to habilitation for institutionalized persons—a limitation not inherent in the *PARC* doctrine. Burt saw the rights at stake in *Wyatt* and *PARC* as the same rights to "equal state services for all citizens." Examining the right to habilitation in *Wyatt* in the terms of the equality principles of *PARC*, Burt concluded:

As in *PARC*, the court is not requiring the state to provide educational facilities for children in general. But if the state chooses to provide services for some, it must provide some such services to all. . . . The state was obligated to provide "habilitation"—that is, opportunities for cognitive and social growth—for mentally retarded children wherever they resided, because the state provided these opportunities—denoted "education"—for other children who cannot be treated

so much differently from the mentally retarded (p. 425).

While the right to education cases (*PARC*) and the right to habilitation cases (*Wyatt*) both aimed for elimination of the same evil—segregation—both left a place for the segregated setting. But as Burt (1976) points out, the *PARC* doctrine and its equal protection underpinnings could be applied to replace institutions with community services. Presaging the *Halderman v. Pennhurst* (1977) case, he wrote:

There is . . . ample evidence that *all* mentally retarded persons can benefit from individualized educational programs. But existing large-scale geographically remote institutions cannot, by their nature, provide adequate programs to remedy the intellectual and emotional shortcomings and the galling social stigma that led the retarded residents to these institutions. If this evidence is fully marshalled in litigation, courts can be led to rule that present patterns of state segregation of retarded persons for "habilitation" or "educational" purposes are impermissible. Courts can be led, that is, to force states to close the Partlows and Willowbrooks and, even more important, to require alternative programs for mentally retarded persons, which treat them as indistinguishably as possible from other persons (p. 425).

The evidence Burt refers to was "fully marshalled" in the *Halderman v. Pennhurst* (1977) case. There, grounding its decision in *PARC* equal protection terms and *Wyatt* due-process terms, as well as federal and state law, the district court concluded:

On the basis of the evidence presented . . . we find that the retarded residents of Pennhurst have not received, and are not receiving, minimally adequate habilitation. Furthermore, on the basis of the record, we find that minimally adequate habilitation cannot be provided in an institution such as Pennhurst. . . . Pennhurst does not provide an atmosphere conducive to normalization, which is so vital to the retarded if they are to be given the opportunity to acquire, maintain and improve their life skills. Pennhurst provides confinement and isolation, the antithesis of habilitation (*Halderman v. Pennhurst*, 446 F Supp. at 1295).

The *Pennhurst* remedy of replacing segregated institutional services with integrated community services has been substantially affirmed twice (see 612 F.2d 84 [3rd Cir. 1979]; 673 F.2d. 645 [3rd Cir. 1982]) and acknowledged by state officials to be the proper remedy. However, the full dimensions of its constitutional holdings were precluded from full judicial review and development by the intervening congressional codification of the integration and normalization principles.

CONGRESSIONAL CODIFICATION OF RIGHTS TO EDUCATION AND TO INTEGRATED COMMUNITY SERVICES

The institutional conditions and practices of exclusion of severely handicapped persons from community services that spurred court action also caught the attention of Congress, which enacted a series of laws substantially expanding the scope of federal statutes and dramatically changing the focus of federal legislation from merely encouraging program development to directing that exclusion of severely handicapped persons be ended and that programs established be nondiscriminatory, integrated, and community-based.

More specifically, during the legislative years 1972–1975, Congress held extensive hearings to review the operation of federal disability programs and the various litigative and court approaches intended to improve the situation of persons with severe handicaps. These deliberations resulted in the passage of a number of related statutes all directed to the equal and full participation of severely handicapped persons in society. The most significant of these statutes were the Education for All Handicapped Children Acts of 1974 and 1975, Section 504 of the Rehabilitation Act of 1973, and the Developmentally Disabled Assistance and Bill of Rights Act (DD Act) of 1975. Each of the three statutes has been interpreted separately by the Supreme Court within the context of particular aspects of educating and habilitating severely handicapped persons (Section 504, higher education; PL 94-142, appropriate education; and DD Act, as a basis for mandatory deinstitutionalization). The impact of these court interpretations is discussed later in the chapter. First, however, it is important to consider the common origins and history of each enactment.

The three statutes originated in the wake of congressional concern about the exclusion and segregation of handicapped persons in our society, as exemplified most dramatically by the institutionalization of severely developmentally disabled children and adults. Section 504, which was passed first, dealt with exclusion, unequal treatment, and segregation most directly and comprehensively. Introduced originally by Senators Hubert Humphrey and Charles Percy and Congressman Claude Vanik as an amendment to the Civil Rights Act of 1964, the legislation was ultimately incorporated as Section 504 of the Rehabilitation Act of 1973. Using the form and language of the Civil Rights Act of 1964, the act contained three prohibitions, which were that

> No otherwise qualified handicapped individual, solely by reason of his handicap, *be excluded* from participation in, *be denied the benefits* of, or *be subjected to discrimination* under any program or activity receiving federal financial assistance (Rehabilitation Act of 1973, Sec. 84.4[a].[2]

The use of the Title VI Civil Rights language in Section 504 suggests that Congress was concerned with eliminating segregation. The legislative history of Section 504 shows the concern to be directed centrally at conditions in institutions and at the exclusion of handicapped persons from public school programs. On introducing the bill that was to become Section 504, Senator Humphrey tied the two discriminatory practices together. He stated:

> The time has come when we can no longer tolerate the invisibility of the handicapped in America . . . I am calling for public attention to three-fourths of the nation's *institutionalized mentally retarded* [emphasis supplied], who live in public and private residential facilities which are more than 50 years old, functionally inadequate, and designed simply to isolate these persons from society. . . .

---

[2]Interestingly, two years before, Congress had authorized substantial open-ended Medicaid financial assistance for institutions as Intermediate Care Facilities for the Mentally Retarded (42 U.S.C. 1936[d], 117 *Cong. Rec.* 44720).

These people have the right to live, to work to the best of ability—to know the dignity to which every human being is entitled. But too often we keep children, whom we regard as "different" or a "disturbing influence" out of our schools and community activities altogether. . . . More than one million children are denied entry into public schools, even to participate in special classes (118 *Cong. Rec.* 525, January 20, 1972).

Referring to the rights established in the *PARC* and *Wyatt* cases, Senator Humphrey concluded, "These *are* people who *can* and must be helped to help themselves. That this is their constitutional right is clearly affirmed in a number of recent decisions in various judicial jurisdictions" (emphasis supplied; 118 *Cong. Rec.* 525, January 20, 1972).

Contemporaneous with nondiscrimination provisions of the Rehabilitation Act, Congress moved to enact federal law to mandate the rights established in the right to education cases. The report of the U.S. Senate Committee on Labor and Public Welfare accompanying Bill S. 6, which was to become Public Law 94-142, stated:

This legislation was originally introduced as S. 3614 on May 16, 1972. It followed a series of landmark court cases establishing in law the right to education for all handicapped children. Since those initial decisions in 1971 and 1972, and with similar decisions in 27 states, it is clear today that this "right to education" is no longer in question (U.S. Senate Report 94-168, 1975, p. 6).

It is plain in the legislative history of the Education for All Handicapped Children Acts that Congress was legislating to render unnecessary the institutionalization of severely handicapped persons. The Senate committee saw the connection between provision of educational services and freedom from institutionalization:

Providing educational services will ensure against persons needlessly being forced into institutional settings. One need only to look at public residential institutions to find thousands of persons whose families are no longer able to care for them and who themselves have received no educational services. Billions of dollars are spent each year to maintain persons in these subhuman

conditions (U.S. Senate Report 94-168, 1975, p. 9).

The Education for All Handicapped Children Acts of 1974 and 1975 (20 U.S.C. Section 1401 *et seq.*) were, like Section 504, premised upon congressional findings about the need for individualized attention and about the competence of severely disabled persons. Both acts incorporate the principles of normalization, recognize individualization as a necessary condition of learning (e.g., 20 U.S.C. Sec. 1412[4]), and emphasize services to children with the most severe handicaps (e.g., 20 U.S.C. Section 1413[3]). Both state their own integration requirements, on the basis of the same findings and purposes similar to Section 504's integration imperative: that, "to the maximum extent appropriate, handicapped children, including children who are in public or private institutions or other care facilities, [shall be] educated with children who are not handicapped . . ." (20 U.S.C. Sec. 1412[5]).

The problem of institutionalization was addressed most directly by the Congress in the evolution of developmental disabilities legislation. In 1970, Congress passed the Developmental Disabilities Services and Facilities Construction Amendments, PL 94-517. This legislation, which established a new federal grant-in-aid program to encourage states to meet the needs of mentally retarded persons and other developmentally disabled individuals, expressly adopted the developmental view that all persons with retardation, including those most severely handicapped, have potential for learning and growth. Congress's acknowledgment of the developmental potential of severely handicapped persons led to its rejection of custodial care facilities and its recognition of integrated settings as essential to the growth in disabled persons.

In 1975, following extensive hearings and testimony concerning Willowbrook, Partlow, Rosewood, and other institutions, Congress passed the Developmentally Disabled Assistance and Bill of Rights Act, PL 94-103. In addition to extending and revising the programs, the 1975 Act established a bill of rights for mentally retarded and other developmentally disabled persons. The DD Bill of Rights (42 U.S.C. Sec. 6010) originated in Senator Jacob Javits's personal experiences of what he called "the tragedy of Willowbrook." In the bill's summation of the rights of disabled persons, Congress asserted that "state residential programs" should be designed to maximize the developmental potential" of every severely retarded person and that this design could be best accomplished "in the setting that is least restrictive of . . . personal liberty."

Although, as noted later is this chapter, the Supreme Court in *Halderman v. Pennhurst* (1981) held that Congress did not create substantive rights in enacting the DD Bill of Rights, the findings of Congress and its rejection of the custodial care model were not disputed. As stated in the Senate Report accompanying the DD Bill of Rights:

From [the] developmental model, it follows that custodial care—which is predicated on *the assumption that certain individuals are essentially incapable of development—must be rejected.* The newer developmental model emphasizes concrete program goals for individuals and, therefore, encourages evaluation based on specific outcomes. *A final, but critically important dimension of [the developmental] model is that developmentally disabled persons should live like nondevelopmentally disabled persons to the greatest degree possible.* Every effort should be made to assist developmentally disabled persons to maximize their ability for self-care and to live normal lives. From this, it also follows that each developmentally disabled person should be allowed to live in the least restrictive environment conducive to his or her maximum development (U.S. Senate Report 94-160, 1975, pp. 27–28).

The early congressional resolve to secure for retarded persons a right to habilitation was reemphasized when, after the *Pennhurst* decision in August 1981, Congress reauthorized funding for the DD Act. In so doing, the Conference Committee explicitly reaffirmed the findings contained in the DD Bill of Rights, stating:

[t]he Conferees reemphasize that they believe that developmentally disabled persons have a right to habilitative services in a setting which is least restrictive of their personal liberty in accordance

with Section 111 of the Developmental Disabilities Assistance and Bill of Rights Act (42 U.S.C. Section 6010).

The 1975 DD Bill of Rights, Section 504, and the Education for All Handicapped Children Act, together with other enactments directed to equal opportunity for handicapped persons (e.g., employment, 29 U.S.C. 792; and access to buildings and transportation, 29 U.S.C. 790, 42 U.S.C. 1612[a]) all had a common purpose and congressional objective. That purpose was set forth in a 1974 Act of Congress that reads:

The Congress finds that . . . it is essential to assure that all individuals with handicaps are able to live their lives independently and with dignity, and that the complete integration of all individuals with handicaps into normal community living, working, and service patterns be held as the final objectives (29 U.S.C. Section 701[n], December 7, 1974).

The 1972–1975 Congressional legislation provided the basis for lower-court decisions mandating integrated education (e.g., *Hairston v. Drosick,* 1976), prohibiting unnecessarily separate services (e.g., *Lloyd v. Regional Transit Authority,* 1977), and mandating movement from large-scale segregated settings to integrated community living arrangements (e.g., *Halderman v. Pennhurst,* 1977; *NYARC v. Carey,* 1978).

In terms of educational programs, the legislative basis for integration and for affirmative programming to secure educational benefits remains strong (*Roncker v. Walters,* 1983). In other areas, including deinstitutionalization, the impact of congressional findings is somewhat impaired by two factors. First, as detailed below, is the refusal of a majority of the Supreme Court to make the standards declared in Section 504 and the DD Act enforceable (against state officials) as substantive rights. Second, and perhaps more important, is the continued federal funding of large-scale, admittedly custodial institutions under Title XIX (Medicaid), in direct contradiction of the congressional findings mentioned earlier in this chapter.

SUPREME COURT INTERPRETATIONS

The Supreme Court has recently interpreted Public Law 94-142, Section 504, and the DD Act. It has also, for the first time, in *Youngberg v. Romeo* (1982) acknowledged the existence of a constitutionally based right to habilitation. While the Court's decisions provide valuable guidance in defining the rights of handicapped persons under federal law and the Constitution, it is important here to clarify the extent of the initial round of Supreme Court opinions. Neither the *Board of Education of Hendrick Hudson School District et al. v. Rowley* case (1982), which interpreted PL 94-142, nor *Southeastern Community College v. Amy Davis* (1979), which interpreted Section 504, dealt directly with the integration requirements of those federal statutes. The Court in *Halderman v. Pennhurst* (1981) acknowledged that the Rehabilitation Act, the Education for All Handicapped Children Acts, as well as the DD Act were among the "laws designed to improve the way in which the nation treats the mentally retarded" (101 S. Ct. 1547), but held only that Section 6010 of the DD Act did not create enforceable rights to habilitation in the least restrictive setting. The recent rulings of the Court deserve careful analysis.

Board of Education v. Rowley

The Court in *Board of Education v. Rowley* (1982), although reversing the lower court's decision that under Public Law 94-142 Amy Rowley, a deaf elementary school student, was entitled to a sign-language interpreter to maximize her educational potential, does provide a helpful standard to determine the appropriateness of educational offerings to students who are apt to be excluded from anything but preschool in integrated settings, and are likely to be kept in segregated settings. In *Rowley*, the Court held that federal law requires that the education provided must "be individually designed to provide educational benefit to the handicapped child" and "be sufficient to confer some educational benefit upon the handicapped child." In support of this conclusion,

the Court further reasoned, "It would do little good for Congress to spend millions of dollars in providing access to a public education only to have the handicapped child receive no benefit from that education" (102 S. Ct. 3048). Referring to the statistics before the Congress on school exclusion, the Court specifically noted the taxpayer cost of school exclusion of "billions of dollars over the lifetime of these individuals to maintain such persons as dependents in a minimally acceptable lifestyle" (102. S. Ct. 3048, n. 23).

The Court emphasized that the standard of "educational benefit" to be applied by the courts would differ from case to case, but the Court made clear that the standard applied to all children no matter how severely handicapped. Criticizing a lower court proposal that "self-sufficiency" should be the primary standard by which educational benefit is determined, the Court noted that the self-sufficiency standard was "an inadequate protection and overly demanding requirement." Therefore, a majority of the justices concluded that it was Congress's intention "that the services provided handicapped children be educationally beneficial whatever the nature or severity of their handicap" (102 S. Ct. 3048, n. 23).

Since the student in the *Rowley* case was receiving instruction in a regular class with nonhandicapped children, the Supreme Court did not address the issue of separate schooling. Justice William Rehnquist, writing for the majority, treated the integration provision of PL 94-142 as a principle requirement and, in the context of the case, suggested that the grading and advancement system used for nonhandicapped children could be used as an important factor in determining educational benefit to a "mainstreamed" handicapped child.

Court decisions since *Rowley* indicate that the integration requirement will be strictly enforced. In *Roncker v. Walters* (1983), the U.S. Court of Appeals for the Sixth Circuit, applying the Supreme Court's educational benefits to the case of a severely handicapped child assigned to a segregated facility, found that interaction with nonhandicapped children was required by the law. The court of appeals stated:

> The proper inquiry is whether a proposed placement is proper under the Act. . . . The perception that a segregated insitution is academically superior for a handicapped child may reflect no more than a basic disagreement with the mainstreaming concept. Such a disagreement is not, of course, any basis for not following the Act's mandate (700 F.2d 1063).

As to the standard to be applied in a case where segregated placement is recommended, the *Roncker* (1983) court held as follows:

> In a case where the segregated facility is considered superior, the court should determine whether the services which made that placement superior could be feasibly provided in a nonsegregated setting. If they can, the placement in the segregated setting would be inappropriate under the Act (700 F.2d 1063).

In response to the contention made in the wake of *Rowley* that courts should not resolve questions of education methodology, in *Roncker* the court stated that the integration question:

> is not one of methodology but rather involves a determination of whether the school district has satisfied the Act's requirement that handicapped children be educated alongside nonhandicapped children to the maximum extent appropriate. . . . Since Congress has decided that [interaction with handicapped] children is appropriate, the states must accept that decision, if they desire federal funds (700 F.2d 1062).

The holding by the court of appeals that integration is a substantive rather than a procedural requirement seems to comport with Justice Rehnquist's reading of the statute (102 S. Ct. 3049). The Supreme Court has declined to review the *Roncker* case, allowing the decision to stand.

Hadlerman v. Pennhurst and Southeastern Community College v. Davis

Unlike the Supreme Court's interpretation of Public Law 94-142, the Court's decisions regarding the congressional intention in the DD Act and Section 504 greatly limit the reach of existing federal legislation in enforcing rights to habilitation in normalized, integrated en-

vironments. As to Section 504, the Court's opinion in *Southeastern Community College v. Davis* (1979) provided good reason to suggest that Section 504 will be largely limited to prohibiting discriminatory practices and unequal treatment without imposing further substantial affirmative obligation upon recipients of federal funds. According to the Court in *Davis,* "neither the language, purpose, nor history of Section 504 reveals an intent to impose an affirmative action obligation on recipients of federal funds" (p. 410). "Substantial modifications" are not required, nor are accommodations required if they cause "undue financial and administrative burdens." Despite these limitations, Section 504 is still a useful instrument to secure equivalent and equally effective services for institutionalized populations. After the Supreme Court's decisions in *Pennhurst* and *Davis,* a federal district court in the Laconia (New Hampshire) deinstitutionalization case (*Garrity v. Gallen,* 1981), applied Section 504 to secure evenhanded treatment in community placement for severely handicapped residents of the state institution. Judge Devine found:

> Defendants have . . . made placements and disbursed services not on an individual assessment of the abilities and potentials of each resident but on the generalized assumption that certain *groups* of people (e.g., profoundly retarded or nonambulatory people) are unable to benefit from certain activities and services. This kind of blanket discrimination against the handicapped, and especially against the most severely handicapped, is unfortunately firmly rooted in the history of our country (522 F. Supp. at 214).

Since severely and profoundly retarded persons are capable of benefiting from community placement, the court held, a failure to consider them for placement in small-scale community programs violates Section 504 (522 F. Supp. at 215).

The Supreme Court itself in *Southeastern Community College v. Davis* (1979) did not foreclose the possibility of affirmative relief under Section 504. "It is possible," the Court suggested:

> to envision situations where an insistence on continuing past requirements and practices might ar-

bitrarily deprive genuinely qualified handicapped persons of the opportunity to participate in a covered program. . . . Thus, situations may arise where a refusal to modify an existing program might become unreasonable and discriminatory (p. 410).

The chief lesson in *Pennhurst* and *Davis* is that in situations where Congress intends to impose affirmative obligations upon the states or other grant recipients to protect rights or provide particular community services, it must do so directly, invoking its powers to enforce the equal protection clause of the Constitution and with particularity as to the conditions it seeks to impose. Or, in the words of Justice Rehnquist in *Pennhurst,* "if the Congress intends to impose a condition on the grant of federal monies, it must do so unambiguously" (101 S. Ct. at 1540). Given the Supreme Court's distinction between encouraging community programs and mandating such programs (101 S. Ct. at 1545), as well as its differentiation between national policy and enforceable legal duties (101 S. Ct. at 1542), future congressional action to secure what was promised in the several enactments of the 1970s must take the form of the Education for All Handicapped Children Acts rather than the DD Act.

Youngberg v. Romeo

Given the hurdles the Supreme Court has set for Congress in legislating enforceable federal law for habilitation for mentally retarded persons, the Court's opinion in *Youngberg v. Romeo* (1982), which acknowledged the existence of constitutional rights of retarded persons to adequate training and habilitation, provides a basis for additional developments in judicially enforceable rights to treatment and community services. In *Romeo,* the Court unanimously held that a retarded person in state custody has, under the 14th Amendment to the U.S. Constitution, protected liberty interest to have: a) reasonable care and safe conditions, b) freedom from bodily restraint, c) adequate food, shelter, clothing, and medical care,

d) adequate training or habilitation to ensure the enjoyment of liberty interest.

In light of the facts of the *Romeo* case and the nonfactual stipulation that Nicholas Romeo would not be capable of leaving the Pennhurst institution,[3] the Supreme Court's ruling on treatment was stated in terms of training and habilitation necessary "to ensure safety and freedom from undue restraint." However, three members of the Court acknowledged the necessity of skills training in order to prevent regression as a result of institutionalization. The extent to which the right to habilitation as expressed in the *Romeo* case can be applied to secure habilitation in community settings remains to be tested. Cook (1983) has suggested the following possibilities:

An important factual question will be presented in each particular case as to whether required training opportunities can be provided appropriately at a particular facility or for particular residents. Where such training cannot be provided at an institution, for example, mentally retarded people have a right to placement in a setting where training *can* be provided. Moreover, where such training, in the judgment of the state's professionals, is necessary for particular residents to provide them reasonable care, prevent harm as regression, or permit greater freedom of movement, and where the residents can appropriately be placed in training programs in alternative settings, those residents have a right to such placement (p. 346).

The Court in *Romeo* signaled a new emphasis on deference to professional judgment as to the adequacy of treatment and habilitation options. However, the obligations of courts to determine whether professional judgments are made will remain and will put in issue decisions made not on a professionally prepared record but on the basis of political convenience. The role of the court post-*Romeo* was put into perspective by Chief Judge Weinstein in *Society for Good Will to Retarded Children v. Carey* (1979):

The substantive rule of deference to on-the-scene professionals may present substantial difficulty in application at the trial level. . . . Experts charged with administration of the institution may not feel free to exercise untrammeled professional judg-

---

[3]Some 6 months after the Court's decision, Nicholas Romeo left Pennhurst and now lives in a community-living arrangement.

ment since they are part of a team and statewide structure. The desire to comply with budgetary pressures and statewide standards may cause a yielding of professional judgment to personal career perspectives. Should these pressures cause the professional in charge to neglect his professional duty to his clients, the court will step in and provide guidance (p. 2546).

CONCLUSION

The legal advocacy of the early 1970s and federal legislation incorporating the principles of right to education and right to habilitation have provided a strong foundation for the steady development of public education programs and community-based habilitation programs. Even considering recent Supreme Court interpretations, the legal structure supporting the claims of handicapped persons to integrated services in the community is sound. Its further development, however, depends not so much on a refined articulation by the Congress and the Court of the rights at stake as upon the careful formulation of federal legislation to provide funding in concert with the previously articulated federal mandates of right to education and right to habilitation. Current federal-funding patterns conflict with federal-state objectives. In 1980, total federal funds across the statutory fabric of federal-state programs for retardation services were at least $3.168 billion dollars.[4] By far the largest amount of federal dollars to state programs are in the form of Title XIX funds (for intermediate care facilities for the mentally retarded— ICF/MRS). Although, under statute, regulations, and the recent 1981 waiver amendments, Title XIX can be used to support community-based residential facilities, it has been used almost exclusively for open-ended funding of segregated institutional programs. For example, in Massachusetts, where state institutions are under federal court orders to secure and maintain minimal levels of habilitation, and where the state has undertaken substantial efforts to develop community residential programs, Braddock (1981) reports that from 1977–1983 federal funds for substandard institutional programs were 10 times greater than federal support for community programs.

The contradiction of continued congressional funding of segregated programs through Title XIX, while at the same time Congress espouses the rights of habilitation in the least restrictive setting, was noted by the Supreme Court in *Pennhurst*. Characterizing the funds available to Pennsylvania under the DD Act as "woefully inadequate" to provide habilitation in the least restrictive setting, the Court opined, "[w]hen Congress does impose affirmative obligations on the states, it usually makes a far more substantial contribution to defray costs" (101 S. Ct. 1543).

After *Pennhurst,* the Congress initiated action to redistribute Title XIX funds to conform to the principles of the DD Act, Section 504, and the Education for all Handicapped Children Acts. Enactment of the Home and Community-Based Services Waiver in 1981 was the first step. Under the waiver legislation, states are able, under certain conditions, to secure federal funds for community-based programs to serve persons who otherwise would be institutionalized. A second step was initiated in November 1983 with the introduction of the Community and Family Living Amendments (S. 2053). If enacted, this bill would, after a transition period, permit states to use Title XIX funds for community settings only and not for institutional settings. Senator Chaffee (1983), sponsor of the bill, describes its purpose as follows:

> The Community and Family Living Amendments Act will gradually shift the federal bill of Medicaid funds from institutional to community-based integrated settings. . . . It is designed to encourage states to reduce the number of persons living in institutions by providing community living arrangements. Services funded through the federal Medicaid program to severely disabled individuals gradually would have to be provided in a community environment (S. 2053, p. 515485).

---

[4]Hearings before the Subcommittee on Departments of Labor, Health, and Human Services, and related agencies for the Committee on Appropriations, 96th Congress, 2d. Session, pp. 641–644.

Whether via S. 2053 or another legislative vehicle, it is essential for the Congress to structure funding to support national policy as embodied in the legislative acts of Congress a decade ago and first set into motion more than 20 years ago with President John F. Kennedy's 1963 directive that "Services to the retarded *must* be community-based. . . . We *must* move from the outmoded use of distant custodial institutions to the concept of community-centered agencies" (Kennedy, 1963).

The movement from segregated custodial institutions to the community over the last decade has been aided by litigation and by legislative responses to court actions in the direction of community services. In order for the trend to continue and yield the intended results, the judicial-legislative dynamic must be maintained. The next step is legislative reform of federal financial assistance to programs for persons with severe handicaps.

REFERENCES

Board of Education of Hendrick Hudson School District et al. v. Amy Rowley, 102 S. Ct. 3034 (1982).

Braddock, D. Deinstitutionalization of the retarded: Trends in public policy. *Hospital and Community Psychiatry*, 1981, *32*(9), 607–615.

Burt, R. Beyond the right to habilitation. In M. Kindred, J. Cohen, D. Penrod, & T. Shaffer (eds.), *Mentally retarded citizens and the law*. Washington, D C : President's Committee on Mental Retardation, 1976.

Butterfield, E. Some basic changes in residential facilities. In: President's Committee on Mental Retardation, *Changing patterns in residential services for the mentally retarded* (2nd ed.). Washington, D C : U.S. Government Printing Office, 1976.

Chaffee, J.H. Community and Family Living Amendments Act. *Congressional Record*, 1983, (Nov. 4), 98–150, S15480–S15485.

Cook, T. The substantive due process rights of mentally disabled clients. *Mental Disability Law Reporter*, 1983, *7*(4), 346.

Davies, S.P. The institution in relation to the school system. *Journal of Psycho-Asthenics*, 1925, *30*, 210–226.

Developmentally Disabled Assistance and Bill of Rights Act of 1975, 42 U.S.C. Sec. 6010.

Diana v. State Board of Education, C.A. No. 70-37 RFP (N.D. Cal. Jan. 7, 1970 and June 18, 1973).

Dimond, P. The constitutional right to education: The quiet revolution, *Hastings Law Journal*, 1973, *24*, 1087.

The Education for All Handicapped Children Act of 1975, 20 U.S.C. 1401.

Garrity v. Gallen, 522 F. Supp. 171 (D.NH. 1981).

Hairston v. Drosick, 423 F. Supp. 180 (S.D.W. Va. 1976).

Halderman v. Pennhurst (State School and Hospital), 446 F. Supp. 1295 (E.D. Pa. 1977); aff'd. 612 F.2d 84 (3rd Cir. 1979); rev'd in part 451 U.S. 1 (1981); aff'd 673 F.2d 645 (3rd Cir. 1982), *cert granted* 100 S. Ct. 3046.

Kennedy, J.F. Message from the President of the United States to the 88th Congress. 88th Cong., February 6, 1963. H. Doc. 58.

Larry P. v. Riles, 343 F. Supp. 1306 (N.D. Cal. 1972), aff'd 502 F.2d 963 (9th Cir. 1974).

Lippman, L., & Goldberg, I. *Right to education: Anatomy of the Pennsylvania case and its implications for exceptional children*. New York: Teachers College Press, 1973.

Lloyd v. Regional Transit Authority, 548 F.2d 1277 (7th Cir. 1977).

Mills v. D.C. Board of Education, 348 F. Supp. 866 (D.D.C. 1972).

New York Association for Retarded Citizens v. Carey, 446 F. Supp. 479 (E.D. NY. 1978), aff'd 612 F.2d 644 (2nd Cir. 1979).

New York Association for Retarded Citizens v. Rockefeller, 357 F. Supp. 752 (E.D. NY. 1973).

New York Association for Retarded Citizens v. Rockefeller, 393 F. Supp. 715 (E.D. NY. 1975).

Parham v. J.R., 442 U.S. 584 (1979).

Pennsylvania Association for Retarded Citizens v. Commonwealth of Pennsylvania, 334 F. Supp. 1257 (E.D. Pa. 1971), 343 F. Supp. 279 (E.D. Pa. 1972).

Roncker v. Walters, 700 F.2d 1058 (6th Cir. 1983).

Section 504 of the Rehabilitation Act of 1973, 29 U.S.C. 794.

Society for Good Will to Retarded Children v. Carey, 47 U.S.L.W. 2546 (E.D. NY. 1979).

Southeastern Community College v. Davis, 442 U.S. 397, 99 S. Ct. 2361 (1979).

Wilson, J. Reaching for the last straw. In: P. Roos, R. McCann, & M. Addison (eds.), *Shaping the future: Community-based residential services and facilities for mentally retarded people*. Baltimore: University Park Press, 1980.

Wyatt v. Stickney, 344 F. Supp. 373 and 387 (M.D. Ala. 1971), aff'd sub nom. *Wyatt v. Aderholt*, 503 F.2d 1305 (5th Cir. 1974).

Youngberg v. Romeo, 102 S. Ct. 2452 (1982).

Chapter 5

Implementation of Court and Consent Decrees

Some Current Lessons

Valerie J. Bradley

O ver a decade has passed since the advent of litigation as a serious tool for reforming facilities and programs for mentally disabled children and adults. Although the drama of judicial intervention into the previously walled-off area of human services has generated spirited debate in the field, little has been written—except in the legal literature—about the influence of judicial remedies on the shape and content of services for mentally handicapped individuals (Note, 1977, p. 428). The current effort to synthesize information and research on deinstitutionalization and its impact on the education of children and youth presents a much-needed opportunity to explore the positive and negative consequences of resorting to the courts to restructure mental disabilities systems.

The paucity of serious analyses of the ramifications of judicial oversight of the care and habilitation of mentally disabled persons is striking, given the ways in which litigation has changed both the general service landscape and individual expectations of what mentally disabled persons have a right to demand from society. Without the ruling in *Pennsylvania Association for Retarded Children v. Commonwealth of Pennsylvania* (1972; henceforth, *PARC*) and related suits, it is questionable whether the Education for All Handicapped Children Act of 1975 would have passed—at least in its current form. Litigators in these cases gave substance to the right of all children to a free public education and to enjoy equal protection under the law. The assertion of these rights laid the groundwork for further litigation, and their implementation made it possible to show, concretely, that mentally disabled citizens could be served outside institutional settings. This premise has been made manifest in the declines in institutional admissions and populations over the past 10 to 15 years.

Much of the material that forms the basis for this chapter was collected as part of the Longitudinal Study of Court-Ordered Deinstitutionalization of Pennhurst. The study, funded by the Office of the Assistant Secretary for Planning and Evaluation of the U.S. Department of Health and Human Services, is a multifaceted 5-year analysis of the implementation of the court decree in *Halderman v. Pennhurst State School and Hospital* (1977). The study is jointly being conducted by the Human Services Research Institute (HSRI) and Temple University. The author is the project director for the HSRI portion of the study.

Clearly, litigation has led to progressive changes in many instances. From the vantage point of the early 1980s, however, it is possible to examine litigation more critically and to draw conclusions regarding both the benefits and costs of asking judges to superintend state mental disabilities systems. In addition to shedding light on the efficacy of legal-reform strategies, such an exploration provides a unique perspective on deinstitutionalization. Because litigation has reached into almost every corner of the human services system, it has brought many policy issues into strong relief, illuminating the nooks and crannies in the system and pointing out major stresses and strains. An assessment of the efficacy of litigation furthermore helps to isolate those instances where litigation may be the only way to achieve desired results, as well as those situations in which other strategies would suffice or are preferable.

The purpose of this chapter is to begin the dialogue regarding the role of litigation in reforming services for mentally disabled children and adults. Specifically, the following topics are discussed: a) the antecedents of litigation and the governing legal theories; b) the influence of recent U.S. Supreme Court rulings; c) the benefits of litigation, including exposure of the problems of severely disabled persons, the development of standards and accountability mechanisms, increased leverage for systemic reform, and an expansion of programmatic frontiers; d) the costs of litigation, including diversion of resources, creation of bureaucratic intransigence, polarization of interest groups, and legislative backlash; and e) the future of litigation in the mental disabilities field.

OVERVIEW OF LITIGATION

Motivating Factors

The use of the legal process to affirm and secure the rights of mentally disabled children and adults—both through class and individual action—has been motivated by a desire to increase the "bargaining power" of consumers

of services and to hold state and local officials accountable for the delivery of appropriate services (Fremouw, 1974). The increasing use of litigation and kindred forms of advocacy to redress individual and collective grievances has resulted from a variety of forces that coalesced in the late 1960s and early 1970s, among them:

1. There was a growing recognition that the objectives pursued by minority groups during the civil rights movement of the sixties were common to a variety of groups that had been figuratively or literally disenfranchised (e.g., the elderly, handicapped persons, women, prisoners, children, and mentally ill persons held against their will).

2. Reformers began to realize that mentally disabled persons—because of their inability to vote and/or owing to the stigma associated with their condition—had no direct access to the political process, and that those who represented their case before administrative and political bodies had a self-interest, albeit well-intentioned, in the structure of the existing delivery system (Wright, 1973).

3. There was a forcible recognition of the widening gulf between the moral purposes and responsibilities of public institutions and the grim reality of institutional conditions.

4. Skepticism developed regarding the ability of education and mental disabilities officials to provide appropriate care and habilitation, constrained as they were by tight budgets and staffing shortages.

5. Anger increased regarding the exclusion of some mentally disabled children from educational services, especially in the face of a growing body of research that suggested that such children could develop and learn in mainstreamed settings.

These factors, taken together, explain the sense of impotence, frustration, and impatience that led many concerned reformers to seek legal means to rectify what they considered to be inequities and arbitrariness in the way mentally disabled persons were treated.

By resorting to a less-conventional arena for social change, reformers hoped also to circumvent the inevitable balancing of interests that is part of the political process and that, historically, had placed mentally disabled persons at a distinct disadvantage in terms of resource allocation, owing to their lack of political "clout" or leverage. Courts, on the other hand, are more or less insulated from political pressures and judges are free to pursue singular aims without the political constraints of compromise and negotiation.

Departure from Traditional Litigation

Attempts to use the courts to rectify the "wrongs" done to mentally disabled children and adults became part of a larger legal movement to redress major social ills (e.g., racism, employment discrimination, intolerable prison conditions, etc.). The resulting litigation departed significantly from the traditional dispute resolution type of adjudication. A number of suits took the form of a broad-based class-action suit aimed at reforming large social institutions, a type of lawsuit that has been variously referred to as "structural litigation" (Fiss, 1979), "complex enforcement" (Sargentich, 1978), and "public law litigation" (Chayes, 1976). The public nature of the lawsuit stems from the public character of the values or norms (either statutory or constitutional) used by the judge to assess the particular social reality under scrutiny. In many such suits, the object of reform is also a public agency such as a state department of mental health or a local housing authority. Fiss (1979) provides the following rationale for the emergence of this form of litigation:

Structural reform is premised on the notion that the quality of our social life is affected in important ways by the operation of large-scale organizations, not just by individuals acting either beyond or within these organizations. It is also premised on the belief that our constitutional values cannot be fully secured without effectuating basic changes in the structures of these organizations (p. 2).

The overarching characteristic of this form of litigation is that it attempts to reorganize a sizable social institution rather than merely to recompense victims for discrete wrongs. As Fiss (1979) states, the structural suit "undertakes to restructure the organization to eliminate a threat to those values posed by the present institutional arrangements" (p. 2).

Evolution of Legal Theories

More than 10 years have passed since Judge Frank Johnson decided *Wyatt v. Stickney* (1972)—the first significant attempt to use the courts to upgrade the quality of life for large groups of mentally disabled persons. *Wyatt* and other similar cases in the early 1970s (e.g., *Horacek v. Exon,* 1973; *New York State Association for Retarded Citizens and Parisi v. Rockefeller,* 1973, henceforth, Willowbrook; *Welsch v. Likins,* 1974) concentrated primarily on the conditions of mentally disabled persons living in institutions. Such cases were premised on constitutional theories of right to treatment and habilitation and right to protection from harm. As litigation of this type expanded, it became clear that complying with broad-based right to treatment injunctions required an enormous investment of resources in the institutional system in order to bring such facilities up to mandated standards.

These cases, because of their emphasis on conditions in institutions, tended to further legitimize insitutions and to ignore comparisons between the treatment of mentally retarded and non–mentally retarded individuals. In commenting on the institutional improvement approach and its limitations, Burt (1976) made the following observation:

The approach permitted the court and parties to address institutional habilitation resources in isolation without forcing them to justify the very existence of the institutional habilitation modality. Neither the court nor the parties were ignorant of the inherent shortcomings of residential institutional care. Rather, they either failed to perceive or were unwilling to use a legal principle that would have brought this problem into the high visibility and relevance it properly deserved (p. 424).

In fact, some of the cases in this general category of litigation did depart from Judge Johnson's historic decision by decreeing major institutional population decreases and expansion of community-based resources. The consent decrees in the Willowbrook (New York) and *Horacek v. Exon* (1973) (Nebraska) cases are important examples of mixed institutional improvement and mandated deinstitutionalization premised on care in the least restrictive alternative. Though both decrees allowed for a residual population, they formed, to some extent, a legal bridge between *Wyatt* and the more recent *Halderman v. Pennhurst State School and Hospital* (1977; henceforth, *Pennhurst*) case.

During this same time period, another strand of cases directed at the rights of mentally retarded persons began to develop. This line of litigation, best exemplified in the 1972 *PARC* case, focused on the unconstitutionality of exclusion or segregation of mentally retarded and other disadvantaged individuals. In *PARC,* the plaintiffs argued that excluding mentally retarded children from public education is an unconstitutionally invidious discrimination. Unlike the right to treatment and habilitation cases, *PARC* stressed the rights of mentally retarded persons to receive the same services granted their nonhandicapped peers. The case also was premised on the delivery of services in nonsegregated settings rather than on the improvement of care in a special-purpose and segregated institution.

These two strands of legal reasoning ultimately converged in the *Pennhurst* case. When the suit was first brought in 1974 on behalf of Terri Lee Halderman and other residents of Pennhurst, the relief sought was institutional improvement and determination of the "minimum constitutional statutory common law standards for care." Ferleger and Boyd (1979), the lawyers for the original plaintiffs in *Pennhurst,* provided the following explanation for the nature of the relief sought in the early stages of the case:

> It was May 1974, and, no matter what one's personal views toward institutions, there was no reason to believe that any court in the United States would embrace an "anti-institutionalization" position. A lawsuit could certainly be filed to

clean up and fix up the institution and thus to alleviate, at least minimally, the worst of Pennhurst and to illuminate the broader social and political questions regarding the utility and wisdom of institutions (p. 724).

As the case progressed, however, a broader legal theory emerged. The ultimate arguments presented to the federal district court on behalf of Pennhurst residents included the right to habilitation but also attacked the inability of the institution to provide such care given conditions at the facility *and* the segregated nature of the facility. By superimposing the *PARC* theory on the traditional line of right to treatment and right to habilitation cases, the plaintiffs preserved the fundamental gains that had been made but moved beyond institutional improvement to a community imperative based on constitutional and federal statutory bases.

RECENT DEVELOPMENTS

The *Pennhurst* case, owing to its ambition and the scope of restructuring intended by the remedy, represented the full flowering of public law litigation in the field of mental disabilities. Some would suggest that the *Pennhurst* decision is in fact the high-water mark, as evidenced by subsequent retrenchment brought about by recent Supreme Court decisions. That the pendulum may be swinging back toward a more conservative judicial attitude regarding social change should not be surprising. As Scheingold (1981) has observed, "Judicial support for policy change responds to its own internal logic as well as to cyclical patterns of activism and self-restraint" (p. 219).

Judicial "self-restraint" is clearly present in three key decisions—two of which involve the Pennhurst litigation—recently handed down by the Supreme Court. The first is the initial ruling in *Pennhurst v. Halderman* (1981). On April 20, 1981, the Supreme Court ruled, in a six-to-three decision, that Section 6010 of the Developmental Disabilities Assistance and Bill of Rights Act does not create any substantive rights to "appropriate treatment" in the "least restrictive" environment. The Court, therefore, rejected Section 6010 as a legitimate basis for the comprehensive district court remedy that had been affirmed in the main by the court of appeals. In its opinion, the Court did not address any of the legal underpinnings relied on by the district court, including Section 504 of the Rehabilitation Act of 1973, the Fourteenth Amendment to the U.S. Constitution, and the state's Mental Health and Mental Retardation Act of 1966. These grounds were left to the circuit court to consider further, along with alternative provisions of the Developmental Disabilities Act not addressed by the Supreme Court.

The initial *Pennhurst v. Halderman* decision provided only partial guidance to lower courts regarding the future course of similar litigation. It did not have the effect of automatically vacating the 1977 *Pennhurst* ruling nor did it require an immediate dismantling of the compliance mechanisms established by the district court. Strictly speaking, the decision knocked out the Developmental Disabilities Act as a legal basis for *Pennhurst*-type suits and left the viability of the remaining legal justification (i.e., Section 504, state law, and the Fourteenth Amendment) in doubt.

The rhetoric of the majority and dissenting opinions in the first Supreme Court decision in the *Pennhurst* case, however, conveyed a somewhat negative attitude regarding the extent of the remedy and the elaborate monitoring and compliance entities set up to ensure implementation of the decree. Although the Court decided on very narrow grounds, the language of the opinions suggested that further arguments before the Court on alternative grounds would be equally unsuccessful. The Court was not unsympathetic with the plight of mentally retarded persons but was also not enthusiastic about the use of federal courts to do anything more than support improvements in the immediate circumstances of institutionalized persons.

The second ruling in *Romeo v. Youngberg* (1982), represents the first time that the Supreme Court considered the substantive constitutional rights of involuntarily committed mentally retarded persons. In reviewing the lower court opinion in *Romeo,* a majority of the Supreme Court found that involuntarily detained mentally retarded persons have the following constitutionally protected rights: reasonably safe conditions of confinement; freedom from unreasonable bodily restraints; and minimally adequate training as reasonably may be required by these interests.

With respect to "right to treatment," the Court defined the term narrowly to mean habilitation that would diminish the dangerous behavior of Romeo, the mentally retarded plaintiff, and therefore avoid unconstitutional infringement of Romeo's safety and freedom of movement rights. This interpretation was far different from the court of appeals finding that such persons have a right to treatment in the least restrictive fashion and according to accepted medical practice. The Supreme Court also noted that in determining whether an individual's constitutional rights had been violated, his or her liberty interests must be balanced against relevant state interests. The Court also stated that in ascertaining liability, the U.S. Constitution requires only that courts make certain that professional judgment is exercised; and, furthermore, that judges should not take sides regarding which of several professionally acceptable choices should have been made.

In its second opinion in the *Pennhurst* case (*Pennhurst State School and Hospital,* 1984), issued on January 23, 1984, the Supreme Court—in a five-to-four decision—held that the sovereign immunity principle of the Eleventh Amendment to the Constitution prohibits a federal district court from ordering Pennsylvania state officials to comply with state law. The ruling reversed the Third Circuit's earlier ruling (which followed the Court's 1981 decision noted above) that affirmed the district court's decree in *Pennhurst* based on state law grounds alone. The Supreme Court decision significantly altered the traditional jurisdiction of federal courts in state law matters and may force litigators with state as well as federal claims to file in state and federal court respectively. This second Supreme Court ruling in *Pennhurst* is in keeping with the decisions described earlier in regard to its emphasis on judicial restraint and its deference to state law and state mental retardation professionals.

As in the first decision, the Court left open the constitutional as well as Section 504 claims as possible bases for affirming the district court's broad-based order The reception that these issues might receive in the Supreme Court was foreshadowed by the less-than-hospitable attitude toward comprehensive system restructuring by the judiciary evinced in the majority opinion. The constitutional and Section 504 questions will not, however, come to the Court—at least in the *Pennhurst* context, given the decree recently signed by the defendants (with the exception of the Parent/Staff Association) and the plaintiffs.

These narrow and extremely cautious decisions, coupled with the Court's recent rulings on the scope of Section 504 of the Rehabilitation Act of 1973 and of PL 94-142, suggest a period of retrenchment in the federal judiciary and a "cooling off" of structural reform litigation. This trend is consistent with the increasing reluctance of state officials to enter into consent agreements, which may also contribute to at least a temporary hiatus in the spate of litigation that characterized the decade of the 1970s.

Although there may be a pause in the use of public law litigation to effect change in the mental disabilities field, much of the litigation of the 1970s is ongoing. In only a few of the major cases (e.g., *Wuori v. Zitnay*, 1978) has a judge terminated oversight over some or all of the decree. This fact, together with the real probability that the pendulum of judicial involvement will swing back to the more activist end of the continuum, makes an assessment of the benefits and costs of litigation central to understanding litigation's ultimate impact on public policy.

LITIGATION: THE BENEFITS

As mentioned earlier in the chapter, the use of litigation to secure the rights of devalued groups within society has one major benefit—it removes the debate from the political arena and places it into the more insulated forum of the courts. Some would argue that this shift also makes it possible to reinforce the moral, as opposed to practical and expedient, aims of the mental disabilities delivery system. This more general and ideological vision of the gains of litigation is compelling theoretically, but what concrete gains have been made as the direct result of litigation? The section following describes some of these benefits and speculates upon whether such outcomes could have been achieved by other means.

Shedding Light on the Subject

One of the major accomplishments of litigation to date is the illumination of the problems and needs of more seriously handicapped persons. Because of the severity of the disabilities of many of the plaintiffs in large-scale suits and their virtual invisibility, it is probably safe to say that without the pressure created by litigation, their plight might have been only partially ameliorated.

Over the past decade, suits have been brought on behalf of institutionalized mentally ill and mentally retarded persons, involuntarily detained mentally ill persons, disabled children denied access to education, involuntarily detained mentally disabled children, institutional residents forced to work without pay, mentally disabled offenders, and mentally ill persons "dumped" into inappropriate community facilities. Because of the disabilities of such persons and their physical distance from the public view, most of the traditional avenues for the redress of grievances had been closed to them.

The victories achieved by these plaintiffs resulted in a reallocation of resources to seriously disabled children and adults. Because of *PARC,* for instance, resources were made available to children previously excluded from school. The *Wyatt* and Willowbrook cases resulted in a significant increase in the level of resources devoted to the care of institutionalized mentally disabled persons. Peonage cases have required state officials to pay institutional residents for their work, and suits like *Pennhurst* have required states to develop community-living arrangements for severely handicapped institutional residents.

Even when suits have not been totally successful, many would argue that litigation has served as a catalyst for change (Gambitta, 1981; Lee & Weisbrod, 1978). This may be in part because class-action suits aimed at systemic problems garner considerable attention. As Scheingold (1981) has said, ''. . . there is evidence that among the important side effects of litigation are changes in the political arena. Most obviously, litigation is a way of gaining a good deal of publicity, thus creating general awareness of a problem'' (p. 207).

The fact that most of the major suits in the field have not been fully litigated but rather have been settled by consent agreement, underscores the power of litigation to frame issues and to influence political decision making. Though consent in some states was the result of shared aims between the plaintiffs and the defendants, suits like the one against Plymouth Center in Michigan (*Michigan Association for Retarded Citizens et al. v. Donald Smith*, 1978; henceforth, *MARC*) were settled because of public reaction to the abuses alleged by the plaintiffs (Bradley, Allard, & Epstein, 1982).

Monitoring and Accountability

A second area in which litigation has resulted in at least temporary gains is in quality assurance. As a means of protecting the rights of individual plaintiffs, many remedies have included provisions for individualized habilitation programs, individualized program plans, or individualized education programs. Variously referred to as IHPs, IPPs, and IEPs, these plans have been a key ingredient in institutional improvement, deinstitutionalization, and right to education cases. The requirement for individualized planning has subsequently been included in federal statutes and regulations— specifically in the provisions of PL 94-142 and the Title XIX regulations for intermediate care facilities for the mentally retarded (ICF/MRs).

Right to treatment suits in particular have reinforced the legitimacy of externally developed staffing standards for institutional settings. Several remedies, including the decree in the landmark *Wyatt* case, have required states to bring staffing levels in state facilities in conformance with the standards of the Accreditation Council for Services for Mentally Retarded and Other Developmentally Disabled Persons and also of the American Association on Mental Deficiency. The inclusion of such standards has not only made compliance easier to measure, but it has also lent credence to the assumption that state institutions should be judged by the same professional standards to which community-based and private facilities must adhere.

In order to assess the appropriateness of community placement plans, remedies that envision significant deinstitutionalization in many instances include review by the court-appointed compliance officer. In the 1978 *MARC* case, the court master reviews all community IHPs. In the *Pennhurst* case, the court special master reviews and approves all transitional IHPs and final IHPs. To carry out these duties, court masters have developed guidelines for the preparation of IHPs and internal criteria for plan approval.

In addition to reviewing individualized plans, some masters and monitors are responsible for monitoring the quality of community-living arrangements. In the *Pennhurst* case, for example, staff of the office of the special master were required by the court to monitor the quality of all community-living arrangements in which class members resided. This function and the IHP approval responsibility have since been transferred to the state. Some of the monitoring has already been extended to facilities beyond those serving class members, and the individual client monitoring is likewise rapidly expanding beyond the more narrow target group. Monitoring and quality assurance are key ingredients in the settlement reached between the state and the plaintiffs.

Finally, litigation has given the families of mentally disabled persons a formal role in decision making regarding placement plans for their family members. In *Pennhurst*, the court has required that families be involved at all stages of the placement process. Families also have a right to appeal placement decisions to the hearing master and ultimately to the judge himself. In the *Wuori* consent decree, a consumer panel was established to assist the court in monitoring compliance. In other suits, parent-appeal rights and participation in planning have become routine.

Despite the fact that quality-assurance procedures surrounding the provision of services to class members in suits around the country have improved, it is uncertain whether these benefits will be extended to non–class members or whether they will survive if and when courts relinquish jurisdiction. What is clear is that litigation has hastened improvements in the technology of quality assurance and has stimulated the development of planning and monitoring requirements in federal regulations and statutes.

Leverage for Systemic Reform

In many states litigation has provided the external impetus required to give system reformers the tools to bring about change in the service system. Some state mental retardation officials have suggested that their willingness to enter into consent agreements was motivated by their desire to further their own programmatic aims (Bradley et al., 1982). These admissions support Diver's (1979) observation:

> A judicial finding of violation gives the sympathetic operating official a powerful lever with which to pry loose cooperation from intransigent policymakers. He approaches them no longer as a supplicant but as one armed with the enhanced legitimacy conferred by a sense of legal duty (p. 81).

A specific example of the concurrence of aims between plaintiffs and defendants is seen in the *Wuori* case in Maine. In that state, the consent agreement was viewed by many in the system as a vehicle to accomplish desired change and as a means to obtain necessary financial resources from other state agencies and from the legislature (Bradley et al., 1982, p. 45). Although the enthusiasm of reform-oriented state program officials for litigation as a way of facilitating change in the system may

be contingent on the availability of resources, some would still have to admit that without public law litigation, their ability to move the system in more progressive directions would have been hampered.

In addition to providing political leverage to those within the bureaucracy, litigation may also mobilize previously disparate and unorganized constituencies into cohesive, politically active groups (Scheingold, 1981, pp. 204–205). This may be particularly true in cases where consumers and/or families are the plaintiffs. In Massachusetts, for example, all of the five class-action suits in the state were brought by parents—three by institutional parents groups (*Ricci v. Greenblatt*, 1972 [Belcherton]; *McEvoy v. Mitchell*, 1974 [Fernald]; *Gauthier v. Benson*, 1975 [Monson]) and two by the state Association for Retarded Citizens (*Massachusetts Association for Retarded Citizens v. Dukakis*, 1975 [Wrentham]; and *Massachusetts Association for Retarded Citizens v. Dukakis*, 1975 [Dever]).

Expansion of Programmatic Frontiers

Litigation, especially those suits aimed at more severely disabled persons, has stimulated the development of innovative program approaches and hastened the utilization of state-of-the-art techniques. In other words, by forcing service systems to respond to the needs of new populations (e.g., in right to education suits), or to create alternative services (e.g., in deinstitutionalization suits), court decrees have indirectly caused the generation of new programmatic resources and strategies.

For instance, in Pennsylvania, those persons who have been moved out of Pennhurst State Center have been primarily severely and profoundly retarded, many with multiple handicaps. At first, there was concern among providers that the service system—which until then had served more moderately and mildly retarded persons—would be unable to cope with the special needs of this client group. Most of those involved with the implementation of the decree in the southeast region of Pennsylvania would now agree, however, that, with time, providers were able to build the capacity to provide appropriate services to *Pennhurst* class members.

Research on the progress of former Pennhurst residents now living in the community tends to support the view that community-based programs have found successful ways to address the multiple needs of these individuals (Conroy, Efthimiou, & Lemanowicz, 1982). An analysis of the characteristics of matched comparison groups (one group stayed at Pennhurst and another group moved to the community) showed that over a 2-year period, those living in community facilities showed significant growth in adaptive behaviors compared to minimal growth among their opposite numbers in the institution.

The *Pennhurst* decree is particularly interesting since it prohibited the movement of class members to other institutions and diverted deinstitutionalized residents to small, three-person community living arrangements. It also virtually eliminated the possibility of class members returning to the institution. Thus, communities were put on notice that they had to develop backup services to cope with the inevitable crises that would arise in placements. Although this process has not gone altogether smoothly, there is now more sophistication in the affected counties regarding behavior management and the medical requirements of severely retarded persons. Given the types of persons who had been placed outside institutions in the state prior to *Pennhurst,* it is fairly safe to say that any exploration of programmatic approaches for the habilitation of more disabled individuals would have remained a low priority.

By moving disabled children and adults into the mainstream of the public school classroom and into residential neighborhoods, litigation may also have helped to improve attitudes regarding persons with disabilities. In a survey of the neighbors of community-living arrangements housing former Pennhurst residents, researchers at the Institute for Survey Research at Temple University found that, after an increase in negative feeling immediately after the residence opened, community members came to accept the retarded residents (Walbridge, 1982).

Finally, by mandating individualized plans, litigation directed at disabled persons both in institutions and in the community has pressed program staff to design service regimens much closer to what might be considered the ideal array of supports. Though clearly not all of these plans have been fully funded and/or implemented, the litigation did stimulate case managers to explore a wider range of options and to bring techniques into play that might not otherwise have been considered or applied.

LITIGATION: THE COSTS

As the previous section reaffirms, the use of litigation to bring about system reform has resulted in some positive gains in the delivery of services to mentally disabled persons. However, the interjection of the courts into programmatic and bureaucratic arenas has not been an unalloyed success. For one thing, judges are limited in terms of staff and experience and can therefore only paint the broad outlines of system reform and must rely on the bureaucracy to fully implement judicial intent. Further, litigation is of necessity focused on a delimited group of individuals rather than on all persons whose rights have been violated in similar circumstances. And, finally, implementation of a complex decree—in the face of finite resources—must to some extent draw resources away from other target populations whose needs may be equally acute. The next section describes some of the specific "costs" of litigation and attempts to distinguish these negative effects from the deinstitutionalization movement generally.

Diversion of Resources

As discussed early in the chapter, some of the large class-action suits around the country have resulted in a major investment of resources into institutional programs. The classic example is the Willowbrook litigation, which to date has resulted in an expenditure of close to $100 million. Some would argue that even though this staggering infusion of resources has resulted in improvements in the facility, serious deficits still remain (Rivera, 1982).

In Massachusetts, each of the state's five institutions for mentally retarded people is under a consent decree. In the past four years, the requirements of these decrees have doubled if not tripled the staff-to-patient ratios in those facilities. Again, whereas distinct improvements have been made, there are no comparable requirements for the development of alternative community services.

Even in the *Pennhurst* case, which originally sought to close the Pennhurst State Center, the institution derived substantial benefits from the presence of the suit. Unlike other state centers in Pennsylvania, Pennhurst was, until recently, more or less insulated from budget and staff reductions, and the facility has the only private physicians' services contract in the state. The contract, which includes the bulk of medical services at the facility, at one point cost approximately $1 million per year. Finally, because of the requirement in the decree that medications for Pennhurst residents be reviewed, the facility has been able to contract with a highly regarded expert in pharmacology and mental retardation to perform monthly reviews and staff training sessions.

More recently, however, the picture has changed. Pennsylvania mental retardation officials have announced that they plan to close Pennhurst State Center and their intention has been memorialized in the recent consent agreement in the case. With the announcement of the closure, there has been funding and staff cutbacks at Pennhurst State Center as the population continues to decline. Money saved as a result of the decline in the Pennhurst budget is being channeled into the community to support those who have left the facility. Many of those interviewed in the state have argued that the concentration of resources necessary to bring about the closure of Pennhurst and to expand the community system for those who were moved out would have been politically problematic without the presence of the litigation.

The *MARC* suit in Michigan (*Michigan ARC et al. v. Smith, 1978*) originally included standards for the provision of institutional care at Plymouth Center. Over time, however, the richness of the staffing ratios became a source of resentment among other facilities and programs in the state. The situation was exacerbated by the state's declining financial condition and budget cutbacks in mental retardation services. As the population at the institution declined, the costs of maintaining the facility skyrocketed, while the level of care did not change appreciably. As a result, in 1981, the plaintiffs and the defendants entered into a stipulation to close the facility on a phased placement schedule.

These examples point to one of the major negative side effects of litigation—the creation of a special class of individuals who, by virtue of the resources devoted to their needs, are "worthier" than other similarly handicapped individuals in the state. For example, several parents in New York who had children who had never been institutionalized, attempted to sue in state court to secure the same community-placement resources allotted to Willowbrook class members. Similarly, parents of children in two other state institutions in New York have brought suit in federal court under an equal protection theory to gain the same institutional improvements granted Willowbrook residents.

Clearly, the allocation of resources, as performed by state legislatures and state agencies, is not always equitable. However, such policies do not usually result in eligibility determinations that are as arbitrary as the isolation of a "class" for purposes of a remedy.

Bureaucratic Resistance

Complex litigation in the field of mental disabilities, regardless of whether it aims merely at institutional improvement or at total deinstitutionalization, requires significant restructuring of bureaucratic practice. The ways in which the bureaucracy views such reforms is a key factor in the ultimate success or failure of the court's intervention. As Diver (1979) has stated:

The sweeping reform sought by plaintiffs in these cases necessarily impacts upon a wide range of organizational relationships. The prospects for success, therefore, depend critically on the *amenability of these relationships to change* (p. 53).

As state officials become increasingly angry about the "interference" of the courts in policy making, there is a danger that they will also become more resistant to the directions dictated by decrees—even if such directions are consistent with their goals for the mental disabilities system. This seeming perverseness can be explained in part by the fact that organizations, like organisms, resist change at some level in order to preserve their integrity and the regularity of their operations. Because organizations are vested with the responsibility of performing a discrete set of tasks in a reliable fashion, they erect strong defenses against innovation in order to protect their ability to maintain these prescribed operations (Shepherd, 1969, pp. 519–520).

As a result, organizations must develop means of coping with externally imposed change that will serve to maximize the integrity of the entity and permit the continuation of its core functions. Depending on the nature of the external pressure, the organization has three basic choices: to "ingest" or co-opt the group pressuring for change, to adapt to change (Katz & Kahn, 1966), or to resist change. Resistance is certainly the course chosen by the defendants in *Pennhurst*—the only suit in this field that will have been heard by the Supreme Court not once, but three times.

Although difficult to prove, it is possible that some state officials may respond to court orders by doing exactly the opposite. In litigation pending in Kentucky, for example, the state was ordered to significantly improve the conditions in a state institution for mentally retarded persons. Instead, the state has set upon a course of deinstitutionalization in the facility. As another example, in the early stages of the *Horacek* (1973) case, the state was directed to minimize improvements at Beatrice State School and to concentrate on a plan for deinstitutionalization. Instead, for the first several months, most of the state's efforts were devoted to institutional improvement. And in Pennsylvania, as placement outside of Pennhurst slowed to a trickle, the state Office of Mental Retardation implemented plans to close a 250-bed state facility and to phase out a large mental retardation unit at a state hospital.

If increasing numbers of state bureaucrats show their disdain for the court's presence by resisting compliance, the difficulties that the judiciary has in enforcing compliance will become more apparent. The only real sanction available to judges is the contempt power which, in cases like *Pennhurst,* is generally regarded as a last resort—in part because it must be directed at an individual or individuals within the broader bureaucracy implicated in the litigation. By focusing the punishment for noncompliance on one actor, the greater and more complex wrongdoing is ignored.

Bureaucratic resistance, therefore, may have two negative consequences—obstruction of reform goals, and a diminution of the moral suasion that courts have been able to exercise in complex suits.

Polarization of Interests

As discussed earlier, litigation has the power to mobilize previously disparate individuals into political coalitions. In some instances, this mobilization is positive and results in a unification of like interests. In other instances, however, the mobilization effect acts to drive wedges in existing coalitions and to create antagonism and animosity. This phenomenon is partially explained by the increasing complexity of some decrees and the entry of the courts into the less discrete and more complicated realms of community-based care. As the second and third generations of the *Wyatt* case have evolved, the interests of more and more groups have been drawn into the debate, including institutional employees, parents of institutionalized children, parents of children in the community, community care-givers, and other human service providers and administrators.

The *Pennhurst* litigation in particular appears to have exacerbated, if not created, tensions among parents of mentally retarded persons in Pennsylvania. Because of the frank deinstitutionalization character of the remedy, proinstitution parents felt compelled to take sides, ultimately forming a separate organization and becoming intervenors on the state's side of the litigation. This means that, formally, there are parents of mentally retarded persons on both sides of the case. Given the community orientation of the Office of Mental Retardation in Pennsylvania, this polarization might have occurred in any event, but certainly not as quickly or as intensely.

This schism among parents groups has not been as dramatic in other states. In Michigan, the MARC suit was originally brought by parents of Plymouth Center residents who were concerned about institutional conditions. The state Association for Retarded Citizens (ARC) eventually joined the suit and, more recently, the defendants have signed a stipulation to close the facility. Despite the fact that Plymouth parents felt somewhat left out of the negotiation process and were initially hesitant about the impact of closure, they now agree with the ARC that the viability of the institution is in serious doubt.

Litigation has also activated employee unions in those states where consent decrees have mandated significant deinstitutionalization. In Pennsylvania, the American Federation of State, County and Municipal Employees (AFSCME) is a significant factor in the policy arena surrounding the mental retardation system in the state. The intensity of AFSCME's activities definitely increased once the community-oriented character of the *Pennhurst* decree became clear; union actions have included the use of litigation to attempt to block institutional closures; payment of the legal fees of the Parent/Staff Association (the institutional parent group that intervened on the defendants' side of the litigation); and legislative lobbying, including successful opposition to zoning legislation that would have opened up residential neighborhoods to small group-living arrangements.

In contrast to the divisive effect of mobilization on institutional parents, the *Pennhurst* de-

cree gave AFSCME a distinct rallying point. Unions in Pennsylvania were clearly predisposed to a negative view of deinstitutionalization and had worked against institutional phasedowns in Pennsylvania since the early 1970s.

Legislative Backlash

One of the major constraints faced by judges in the enforcement of complex decrees is their lack of power to command the state legislature, which is ultimately responsible for providing funds for reform. Though some judges, such as Johnson in *Wyatt,* have threatened to circumvent the legislature by attaching public lands or taking other action that would inhibit the legislature's ability to control specific public funds, by and large courts have been unwilling to confront the legislature directly.

The legislature, then, is pivotal to the successful implementation of consent decrees and court orders. During the 1970s, most legislators were willingly guided by the advice of state program officials—many of whom were sympathetic to the aims of litigation in their states. However, as judicial intervention continued, some legislatures began to assert their independence from the executive and judicial branches of government. In the Willowbrook case, for example, the legislature refused to appropriate funding for the review panel. The defendants' argument that they were therefore unable to support the panel was upheld by the federal court of appeals. In Pennsylvania, the state legislature cut the budget of the *Pennhurst* special master from $900,000 to $35,000 and barred the executive branch from exceeding the limit it had set. And in Massachusetts, the chairman of the House Ways and Means Committee formed a special subcommittee on Federal and Court Consent Decrees, the purpose of which was to assess the impact of the court's intervention and to explore the state department's management of the funds provided by the legislature to meet the decree requirements.

In most states legislative hostility toward the courts' intrusion into policy making has not necessarily colored the legislature's commitment to system improvement for mentally retarded persons; in Pennsylvania, however, the two issues have coalesced. In part because of its concern about the *Pennhurst* litigation and in part because of complaints from parents of institutionalized persons, the legislature conducted its own investigation of the management of the state system. One of the recommendations resulting from the investigation includes amending the state's mental health and mental retardation statute in order to remove the intent language regarding least restrictive environments (Bradley & Allard, 1982). If the committee is successful in carrying out its recommendations, some in the state suggest it will be because of the *Pennhurst* litigation. The political context in Pennsylvania, however, is much too complex to be swayed by one factor only. It is probably more accurate to say that the litigation has forced an airing of the issue of deinstitutionalization and has required the legislators to reexamine their views on community services.

Whether this pattern will be repeated in other states is not clear—especially since the decrees vary from state to state. What is clear is that legislators are increasingly concerned about an erosion of their prerogatives as a result of court intervention and are increasingly more willing to do something about it.

LITIGATION: THE FUTURE

The previous discussion of the pluses and minuses of litigation may be somewhat academic given the current political, legal, and economic realities. The legal realities are exemplified by the recent Supreme Court rulings in *Pennhurst* and *Romeo*. Political shifts have made it more difficult for state program officials to use litigation to hasten reform. And financial realities have severely dampened the optimism and enthusiasm that accompanied the spread of litigation in the 1970s.

Diminished Willingness to Consent

Of cases brought in the last few years, more are going to trial, and consent agreements are being more aggressively negotiated by the de-

fendants. In the *Iasimone v. Garrahy* (1977) litigation in Rhode Island, for instance, defendants and plaintiffs worked for almost four years to forge an agreement. Further, attorney generals around the country are in relatively close communication regarding litigation strategies in these types of cases. In 1981, several state attorney generals submitted an amicus brief for the defendants in the *Romeo v. Youngberg* case. Some of the state officials who signed the brief were from states where cases had been settled.

In the *Connecticut Association for Retarded Citizens v. Mansfield State Training Center* (1978) case, the plaintiffs and defendants finally reached a settlement 6 years after the litigation was filed. The *Garrity v. Gallen* (1981) case in New Hampshire, like *Pennhurst*, has been fully litigated. In August 1981, the federal district court judge denied the plaintiffs' claims that there are constitutional or statutory bases for a right to least restrictive care in the community. The judge did, however, mandate substantial reforms in the institutional and community system and approved one of the state's alternative plans for eventual phasedown of Laconia State School and Training Center. The point of the latter example is the fully litigated character of the case and the lack of consent before trial.

Further, although the rulings in the Supreme Court on *Pennhurst* were limited to one aspect of the Developmental Disabilities Act and to the state law claim, there is reason to suspect that federal courts may be less willing now to grant the sweeping relief seen in many earlier cases. The Court's conservative ruling in *Romeo*—though it did support some form of constitutional protection for institutionalized mentally retarded persons—will almost certainly send a signal to federal district courts that judicial intervention to restructure mental disabilities systems will not be upheld.

Even without a shift in the case law, many state officials are increasingly reluctant to submit control over aspects of the service system to federal court oversight. This reluctance stems in part from officials' direct experience with other decrees and in part from a growing consensus among such individuals that the price paid for consent may not be worth the benefits that may be conferred on the system. One state official was recently asked whether he would support consent if he had it to do all over again and his answer was a reluctant no (Bradley, Allard, & Epstein, 1982, p. 80).

Increasing Financial Pressures

The growing resistance to federal court interventions is also strongly influenced by the gloomy financial picture emerging at the federal level and in several states. So long as resources were relatively flexible, there was enough "play" in the system to accommodate comprehensive consent agreements. As resources become diminished, however, meeting court requirements may be accomplished at the expense of expansion or improvement in other parts of the system. The uncertainty surrounding future cutbacks in federal funds also may mean that many state officials will be loathe to contemplate significant system reform projects.

Another related fiscal issue has to do with the Medicaid program. Those states that have certified a significant number of institutional beds for Title XIX reimbursement may resist court-mandated deinstitutionalization unless they can be assured that the Title XIX funds will follow the clients into the community. In states where there is an aggressive ICF/MR program in the community, this shift may be accomplished with no substantial loss to the state treasury. However, in states where community programs are funded primarily with state dollars, deinstitutionalization will result in a direct loss of federal funding and a concomitant drain on scarce state funds. The rumored cap on Medicaid may even lessen the ability of those states with community intermediate care facilities for the mentally retarded (ICF/MRs) facilities to expand the program, given the reluctance of providers to invest funds in the face of an uncertain potential for reimbursement.

All of these factors lead to the conclusion that the increasing shortage of resources will influence the response of state officials to continued litigation. To what extent such concerns will alter the trends of the last 10 years is still to be explored. The irony is that if resources begin to decline for mentally retarded individuals and service systems are in fact compromised as a result, state officials may once again find that their interests are synonymous with plaintiffs seeking system reform.

Reform Strategies in the 1980s

For the time being, it is highly unlikely that there will be any dramatic breakthroughs in securing additional constitutional rights for mentally disabled persons. This fact, coupled with the hard realities described above, means that litigators and others concerned with protecting the rights of mentally disabled persons will have to develop alternative litigation and political strategies. The following points represent some speculations regarding the course that future rights protection and system reform will take:

1. Reformers may begin to target suits on specific and discrete system problems in order to garner publicity for an issue, while simultaneously implementing extrajudicial strategies such as lobbying, demonstrations, and so forth.

2. Litigators, given the uncertain state of the case law, may be more likely to pursue rights based on highly definite legal rules rather than on more open-ended provisions. This preference may lead to statutory litigation in which the plaintiffs' priority is "remedy over principle" (Olson, 1981, p. 253).

3. The necessity to litigate textual or statutory entitlements, as opposed to the more debatable claims based upon constitutional interpretation, may lead to more suits brought in state courts. Since many of the major federal statutory programs have now disappeared in the wake of budgetary block grants, state laws will become a primary source of direction for the mental disabilities system. Litigators may

also begin to use state courts to pursue more open-ended entitlements based on state constitutions.

4. The time and resources involved in bringing a case to trial and, if necessary, carrying it through the appeals process are significant. Further, even if the case is successful, the principle that is ultimately extracted may take years to become fully operational. Lawyers' training orients them to the orderly development of legal doctrine and "can create an inclination toward broad principles over tangible solutions" (Olson, 1981, p. 242). On the other hand, clients or plaintiffs may become more concerned about the risks of continued litigation and impatient for solutions. The result may be growing pressure from plaintiffs for settlement.

5. Given a reduction in legal-services funding and intensified competition for other funding to support litigation, the numbers of public interest law professionals are likely to decrease. Thus, recruitment of paraprofessionals in public law practice may increase and a diversion of resources to more repetitive, client-centered tasks, such as representation at administrative hearings, may result.

CONCLUSION

Litigation is clearly responsible for major improvements in the lives of mentally disabled persons. However, in the absence of authoritative reaffirmation of the legal theories that underpin public law cases in this area, the pace of broad-based suits brought in this country may slow considerably. In those instances where litigation continues to be pressed, warning signals such as reluctance to consent and growing legislative resistance should be heeded. Given these realities, now is the time to consolidate and enforce the direct and indirect gains of public law litigation. The appeal to broad principles made in the 1970s should be followed by concrete and concentrated efforts at implementation. The armamentarium of those who continue to seek change, therefore, cannot be limited to one tactic, but must include multiple judicial and extrajudicial strategies.

REFERENCES

Bradley, V., & Allard, M.A. *Longitudinal study of court-ordered deinstitutionalization of Pennhurst: Historical overview, IV, April, 1982–September 30, 1982.* Boston: Human Services Research Institute, 1982.

Bradley, V., Allard, M.A., & Epstein, S. *Longitudinal study of court-ordered deinstitutionalization of Pennhurst: Implementation analysis.* Department of Public Welfare. Boston: Human Services Research Institute, 1982.

Burt, R.A. Beyond the right to habilitation. In: President's Committee on Mental Retardation, *The mentally retarded citizen and the law.* New York: Free Press, 1976.

Chayes, A. The role of the judge in public law litigation. *Harvard Law Review,* 1976, *89*(7), 1281–1316.

Connecticut Association for Retarded Citizens v. Mansfield State Training Center, C.A. No. H78-653 (D. Conn. 1978).

Conroy, J., Efthimiou, J., & Lemanowicz, J.A. Matched comparison of the developmental growth of institutionalized and deinstitutionalized mentally retarded clients. *American Journal of Mental Deficiency,* 1982, *86*(6), 581–587.

Diver, C.S. The judge as political powerbroker: Superintending structural change in public institutions. *Virginia Law Review,* 1979, *65*, 43–106.

Ferleger, D., & Boyd, P. Anti-institutionalization: The promise of the *Pennhurst* case. *Stanford Law Review,* 1979, *31*(4), 717–752.

Fiss, O.M. The forms of justice. *Harvard Law Review,* 1979, *93*(1), 1–58.

Fremouw, W.J. A new right to treatment. *Journal of Psychiatry and Law,* 1974, *2*(1), 7–31.

Gambitta, R.A.L. Litigation, judicial deference, and policy change. In: R.A.L. Gambitta, J.L. May, & J.C. Foster (eds.), *Governing through the courts.* Beverly Hills, CA: Sage Publications, 1981.

Garrity v. Gallen, 522 F. Supp. 171 (D. NH. 1981).

Gauthier v. Benson (Monson State Hospital), C.A. No. 75-3910-T (D. Mass. 1975).

Halderman v. Pennhurst State School and Hospital, 446 F. Supp. 1295 (E.D. Pa. 1977).

Horacek v. Exon, 357 F. Supp. 71 (D. Neb. 1973).

Iasimone v. Garrahy, C.A. No. 77-0727 (D. RI. 1977).

Katz, D., & Kahn, R.L. *The social psychology of organizations.* New York: John Wiley & Sons, 1966.

Lee, A.J., & Weisbrod, B.A. Public interest law activities in education. In: B.A. Weisbrod (eds.), *Public interest law: An economic and institutional analysis.* Berkeley: University of California Press, 1978.

McEvoy v. Mitchell (Fernald State Hospital), C.A. No. 74-02768-T (D. Mass. 1974).

Massachusetts Association for Retarded Citizens v. Dukakis (Wrentham State Hospital), C.A. No. 75-5023-T (D. Mass. 1975).

Massachusetts Association for Retarded Citizens v. Dukakis (Dever State Hospital), C.A. No. 75-52/0-T (D. Mass. 1975).

Michigan Association for Retarded Citizens et al. v. Donald Smith, (C.A. No. 78-70384 (D. Mich. 1978).

New York State Association for Retarded Children and Parisi v. Rockefeller, 357 F. Supp. (E.D. N.Y. 1973), order entered as *NYSARC and Parisi v. Carey,* 393 F. Supp. 715 (E.D. NY. 1975).

Note. Implementation problems in institutional reform litigation. *Harvard Law Review,* 1977, *91*(2), 428–463.

Olson, S.M. The political evolution of interest group litigation. In: R.A.L. Gambitta, M.L. May, & J.C. Foster (eds.), *Governing through the courts.* Beverly Hills, CA: Sage Publications, 1981.

Pennhurst v. Halderman, 101 S. Ct. 1531 (1981).

Pennhurst State School and Hospital v. Halderman, 104 S. Ct. 900 (1984).

Pennsylvania Association for Retarded Children v. Commonwealth of Pennsylvania, 343 F. Supp. 279 (E.D. Pa. 1972).

Ricci v. Greenblatt (Belcherton State Hospital), C.A. No. 72-0469-T (D. Mass. 1972).

Rivera, G., correspondent. *Willowbrook: Ten years after* (television documentary). New York: ABC News, January 7, 1982.

Sargentich, L.D. *Complex enforcement.* Unpublished manuscript, 1978.

Scheingold, S.A. The politics of rights revisited. In: R.A.L. Gambitta, M.L. May, & J.C. Foster (eds.), *Governing through the courts.* Beverly Hills, CA: Sage Publications, 1981.

Shepherd, H. Innovation resisting and innovation producing organizations. In: W.G. Bennis, K.D. Benne, & R. Chin (eds.), *The planning for change.* New York: Holt, Rinehart & Winston, 1969.

Walbridge, H. Community attitudes. In: V.J. Bradley & J.W. Conroy (eds.), *Third year comprehensive report of the Pennhurst Longitudinal Study.* Philadelphia: Temple University Developmental Disabilities Center, 1982.

Welsch v. Likins, 373 F. Supp. 487 (D. Minn. 1974).

Wright, B.A. Changes in attitudes toward people with handicaps. *Rehabilitation Literature,* 1973, *34*(12), 354–368.

Wuori v. Zitnay, No. 75-80-SD (D. Maine, July 14, 1978).

Wyatt v. Stickney, 344 F. Supp. 373 and 387 (M.D. Ala. 1972), aff'd sub. nom., *Wyatt v. Aderholt,* 503 F.2d 1305 (5th Cir. 1974).

Youngberg v. Romeo, 102 S. Ct. 2452 (1982).

Part III

COMMUNITY AND FAMILY
PERSPECTIVES ON INTEGRATION

The past decade has witnessed a remarkable change in social perspectives on the care and habilitation of severely handicapped persons. For over a century, services to severely handicapped persons in the United States had operated largely from a "placed away" policy. But, by the early 1960s, there was growing awareness that such practices were isolating people in settings that both violated their rights to normal social protections and exposed them to "treatments" that actually reduced rather than increased the probability of their growth and development. This realization led to the evolution of such new philosophies and practices as normalization and deinstitutionalization and to the implementation of community integration strategies.

The results stimulated by these social forces have been remarkable, not only in terms of the opportunities they have provided to handicapped persons but also in terms of what the results of those opportunities have taught other members of society about handicapped persons' potential. Obviously, however, moving toward community integration after decades of segregating handicapped children, youth, and adults is a difficult process. Such extensive changes in philosophy and practice depend largely upon effective intervention strategies and upon the level of commitment to people and organizations.

This section focuses on the changes in attitudes and perspectives, both among community members and among the families of handicapped persons, that have been experienced as deinstitutionalization has progressed. Any movement to enhance social integration of handicapped children, youth, or adults must involve all affected parties, including the general public and particularly the parents, whose unique perspective on the changing situation for their children must be appreciated.

For community members, stereotypic impressions of handicapped individuals and fears of neighborhood deterioration or other adverse consequences from social integration must be confronted and dispelled. Chapter 6, the first chapter in this part, examines the problem of neighborhood opposition to community-based residential facilities. Author Marsha Mailick Seltzer addresses the reasons for community opposition and the results of attempts to deal with it. She notes that it is erroneous to believe that "community education" alone will assuage fears and that often such efforts merely activate resistance. Suggestions are made for social policy and for further research in promoting residential integration of severely handicapped persons.

Chapters 7 and 8, the other two chapters in this section, focus on the roles and attitudes of families with handicapped members. Nearly everyone in society is a part of a family unit. Despite the central importance of the family in development and support of its members, few meaningful generalizations can be made about the condition of families that have severely handicapped members. Certain features in the lives of these families can be identified, however, even if only in terms of their counterpoint to the lives of families whose members are not handicapped. One feature of families with handicapped members is their inability to establish congruence with a contemporary model of the American family. The families receive the same messages about family rhythms and accomplishments, and about personal self-actualization and development, but must deal personally with the ambivalence created by the possibility that their "normal" expectations about raising a family will not be fulfilled.

Members of families with severely handicapped members experience considerable pain, isolation, and disruption of typical patterns of family life. They are aware of normal expectations for children to develop toward eventual independence but are deprived the satisfaction and personal freedom associated with seeing their children attain it. A family with severely handicapped members is torn between two conflicting views of reality: the "normal," with emphasis on accomplishment, personal freedom, and self-realization, and the family's own deviation from "normal," which is largely affected by the nature of its members' handicap(s) and the qualities and expectations of the nonhandicapped members. These deviations from normal permeate the lives of families with severely handicapped members but are manifested and interpreted differently by each member.

The second chapter in this section focuses primarily on parents who are still caring for their own children. In it Ann P. Turnbull, Mary Jane Brotherson, and Jean Ann Summers discuss a family systems approach to supporting the vast majority of families who care for severely handicapped members in their own homes. The family systems model and related research is organized around three central factors in family life—structure, function, and life cycle. Vignettes of families with handicapped members are used to underscore both the importance of the central factors but also the great differences among families in regard to these factors. The chapter describes how variations in family dynamics create different needs that require individualized rather than normative, global approaches to family support. The authors provide specific suggestions for persons providing services directly to families and outline future directions in research related to working with families.

The third chapter in this section, by James W. Conroy, looks at parents involved in another phase of the community integrating movement, i.e., those parents whose children were once institutionalized but are now returning to community settings. The chapter reviews past research and reports recent work involving Pennhurst—a large state facility involved in court-ordered reduction of residents—concerning the feelings of families of institutionalized persons about deinstitutionalization. It is noted that past research has largely failed to yield accurate measures of the extent of opposition to deinstitutionalization among families, and none has explored differences between families of children and adults. A few studies have interviewed families after relocation of their relative, but none has used the pretest/posttest design to assess *actual* changes in opinions, support, and/or contact before and after placement from an institution to a community placement. This chapter concentrates on research on the families of persons who were moved from a large state institution to community-based group homes. Initial resistance to the notion of deinstitutionalization was greater among families of adults than among families of children. After the relocation, however, both groups were about equally supportive of the move. The author casts these differences into a cognitive dissonance framework, suggesting that initial family resistance to deinstitutionalization is a function of the client's time at the institution, but that defense mechanisms built up over years can be dissipated through appropriate planning and work with families.

Chapter 6

Public Attitudes Toward Community Residential Facilities for Mentally Retarded Persons

Marsha Mailick Seltzer

The clients who live in community-based residential facilities are diverse in age, level of retardation, special problems, and the services that they need and receive. Similarly, community residences are characterized by considerable variability in size, program philosophy, staffing pattern, and location. The purpose of community residential facilities is to provide housing for mentally retarded persons who, for a variety of reasons, do not live with family, with friends, or independently. In addition, most community residential facilities attempt to maximize residents' personal development and participation in society. The ideological thrust of the community residence movement during the past 15 years has been to develop the least restrictive environment in order to deinstitutionalize and mainstream mentally retarded children and adults. According to Hill, Lakin, Sigford, Hauber, & Bruininks (1982):

> the essence of the normalization concept is that mentally retarded people will share in the activities of their community, not because it is the most effective site for habitation, but because it is

"their" community as much as it is "our" community (pp. 76–77).

During the same period of time that community residences have been established to help mentally retarded persons become integrated into the larger community, many neighborhoods have become increasingly well organized and have gained a greater degree of control over their resources. It is often precisely in those communities in which neighborhood revitalization and social reorganization have occurred most intensively that community residences have been placed. In such circumstances, and in middle class neighborhoods as well, there have been reports of active opposition by community groups to the establishment of community residences. Reportedly, neighbors fear that nontraditional family living arrangements will have a negative impact on the integrity of their community and on property values.

To date, only limited research has been conducted on the phenomenon of community opposition. Community residences have been established largely without an adequate under-

Partial support for this chapter was provided by the National Science Foundation through a subcontract with the Boston Neighborhood Network.

standing of how best to foster favorable community relationships. In addition, many state agencies have developed rather inflexible policies to guide the manner in which community residences deal with community opposition when it occurs (Seltzer & Litchfield, 1983). In general, these state policies require advance notification of the community and/or formal public education about community residences. However, little is known about the actual effects of public education on community attitudes, and thus such policies, although well-intentioned, may not in fact maximize community acceptance.

This chapter reviews the research literature about community attitudes toward community residences for mentally retarded persons. An understanding of the causes of community opposition, its consequences, and the best ways to minimize the problem is important for organizations that sponsor community residences, for groups that hope to establish new facilities in the future, and for state governmental agencies that have control over the development, location, and funding of community residences. The chapter examines research on attitudes toward mental retardation in general and toward community residences in particular. In addition, data about the scope of the problem of community opposition, factors associated with its occurrence, and strategies that have been used to minimize the problem are presented. The chapter concludes with a discussion of policy implications and an agenda for future research. It should be noted that most of the literature on this topic is either specifically about community residences for adults or does not make distinctions among residences according to the age of the client group. Thus, there is a need to extrapolate the findings of the available studies to community residences specifically for children and youth.

ATTITUDES TOWARD MENTALLY RETARDED PERSONS AND COMMUNITY RESIDENCES

Attitudes toward Mental Retardation

It has been argued that "nothing is more essential to the eventual success of the community

mental retardation services movement than the goodwill, acceptance, and support of the general public" (Kastner, Reppucci, & Pezzoli, 1979, p. 137). In general, there is much truth to this perspective. However, little is known about the specific effects of community members' attitudes on specific types of services or on the mentally retarded persons who receive these services. In addition, the available research does not reveal which types of community members are likely to hold more positive or more negative attitudes toward mentally retarded children and adults.

The research on attitudes toward mentally retarded individuals and toward the integration of such persons into the community suffers from several methodological and conceptual problems. For example, there is the tendency for people when interviewed to give the response they believe is desired by the researcher. This type of response bias reduces the validity of the data considerably. Second, the relationship between expressed attitudes and actual behavior tends to be weak, and therefore even if attitudes could be accurately assessed, it would be difficult to use them reliably to predict the behavior of community members. Third, no minimum level of acceptance has been identified, either conceptually or empirically, as necessary for a minimum degree of integration. Despite these limitations, a number of interesting findings about community attitudes have been reported.

The literature suggests that public attitudes toward mental retardation are both positive and negative, depending on the degree of the public's interaction with handicapped persons. At one extreme, a Gallup Organization poll conducted for the President's Committee on Mental Retardation (Gallup, 1976) found that 85% of those polled would not object to having a home on their block for six mildly or moderately retarded persons who were prepared for community living. At the other extreme, Gottlieb (1975, 1981), in his reviews of literature on the effect of increased contact between retarded and nonretarded children, concluded that "the majority of evidence indicates that proximity is associated with increased *rejection of* mentally retarded individuals" (p. 121, emphasis supplied). Assuming that both the Gallup poll's and Gottlieb's conclusions are valid, the picture that emerges is that the public's attitudes toward mental retardation are positive so long as mental retardation remains an abstract phenomenon. However, this general positive attitude may become more negative following actual interaction with retarded persons, at least among school-age children.

Ashmore (1975) proposed a model that may provide an understanding of these seemingly conflicting findings. He explained that although American public schools attempt to socialize feelings of sympathy toward handicapped children, the school setting does not afford children the opportunity to become truly comfortable in situations involving retarded or otherwise handicapped persons. Although in the abstract children may hold positive attitudes, feelings of discomfort are common when there is direct contact with mentally retarded children. Although most professionals in the mental retardation field expected that mainstreaming would provide nonhandicapped children with precisely the sorts of experiences that would foster positive attitudes, Gottlieb's recent review (1981) suggests otherwise, concluding that increasing contact with mentally retarded children does little to reduce the extent to which they are stigmatized by their agemates. Gottlieb suggested that unless the *behavior* of retarded children is normalized, the level of acceptance of others toward them will remain low.

Attitudes toward Community Residences

Somewhat similar conclusions can be drawn about attitudes held by the general public about community residences for mentally retarded individuals. Sigelman (1976) posed the following hypothetical question to over 600 community members: "Should homes for retarded adults be allowed in residential districts?" Approximately half (45%) responded favorably.[1] However, when such a question becomes less hypothetical, attitudes become less positive.

Kastner et al. (1979) compared two groups of neighborhood residents with respect to their attitudes toward community residences for mentally retarded persons. One group was led to believe that a residence might be opening up on their block, and the other group was told that the questions were purely hypothetical. The authors found significant differences between the two groups in terms of their attitudes about "immediate personal neighborhood issues," including whether they would like to have a group home in their neighborhood. As predicted, those who were told that such a home might in fact become a reality responded less favorably than those who knew they were responding to hypothetical questions.

Conroy and his colleagues (Conroy, 1980; Walbridge & Conroy, 1981; Walbridge, Whaley, & Conroy, 1981) interviewed community members before and after a community residence opened in their neighborhood. The first set of interviews did not inform neighbors about the community residence that would open nearby but rather posed questions about a hypothetical community residence. Nearly 70% of the neighborhood residents said that they would not be bothered at all if a community residence for between two and five mildly retarded persons opened close by, and about 50% felt this way about a community residence for severely retarded persons. These community members were reinterviewed after community residences actually opened in their neighborhoods. Two unexpected findings emerged when the pairs of interviews were compared. First, there was a small but significant ($p < .0001$) *negative* shift in attitudes toward community residences. Second, there was a small *decrease* in the amount of contact with retarded persons reported by the community members who were interviewed. It is possible that this reported decrease was in part responsible for the negative shift in attitudes; however, many other explanations for the attitude change can be posited as well. These findings are provocative because they raise doubts about

---

[1]The discrepancy of 40 percentage points between Sigelman's (1976) findings and those of the Gallup Organization (1976) poll may be due to the differences in the way the questions were worded. The Gallup poll question made specific reference to level of retardation and degree of preparation for the community, possibly reducing fears to some extent. Geographic differences in the samples may also have contributed to the difference in the findings.

the belief that placing a community residence in a neighborhood results in increased contact between neighborhood residents and mentally retarded persons and consequently produces more favorable community attitudes.

Additional analysis of the data (Walbridge & Conroy, 1981), which examined the responses of only those community members who were actually aware of the existence of the community residence when they were interviewed for the second time, indicated that there was a positive shift (p < .001) among these neighbors in their attitudes toward the community residence over time. Thus, it is possible that familiarity with the facility is associated with increased positive attitudes.

A third analysis of these data (Walbridge et al., 1981) attempted to identify the characteristics of community members who hold more positive attitudes toward the idea of having a community residence established in their neighborhood. They found that nearly 20% of the variance in this dependent variable was accounted for by knowledge about mental retardation. The authors concluded that these findings support the desirability of public education about mental retardation, presumably because public education is expected to increase knowledge, which in turn is expected to be associated with more favorable attitudes. However, the section following on community opposition to community residences indicates public education efforts are not always associated with these desired positive outcomes. Moreover, even when public education activities produce favorable community attitudes, these attitudes are not necessarily expressed as actual support for a community residence once it opens. Heal, Sigelman, and Switzky (1978) noted that opposition from the community can occur even after neighbors have expressed initial support for the establishment of the facility. This is because attitudes may change and because the leadership of community groups may shift over time. The translation of attitudes into behavior is complex and not easily predicted.

In sum, attitudes about hypothetical community residences in a given neighborhood are generally more favorable than attitudes about potential or established community residences. A complex and as yet poorly understood relationship exists among knowledge about mental retardation, contact with retarded persons, and support for community residences. Moreau, Novak, and Sigelman (1980) concluded that the available research indicates that "community receptivity regarding residential alternatives is more enthusiastic from a distance than from 'next door' " (p. 98). Increasing our knowledge about how to influence the attitudes and behavior of those who live "next door" is of critical importance in future research.

THE SCOPE OF COMMUNITY OPPOSITION TO COMMUNITY RESIDENCES

Surveys of Community Residences

Surveys of community residences conducted over the past decade have found that between one-quarter and one-half of existing facilities reported that they had encountered opposition from members of the community at some time since they were established.[2] The lowest rate of opposition was reported by Berdiansky and Parker (1977), who found that 26% of the community residences in North Carolina encountered *major* difficulties with the community. The highest rate was reported by Seltzer and Seltzer (1982), who found that 49% of the community residences they sampled in the Boston area met some opposition from the community. Between these extremes several researchers (Baker, Seltzer, & Seltzer, 1977; Lubin, Schwartz, Zigman, & Janicki, 1982; O'Connor, 1976; Piasecki; 1975) found that

---

[2]The validity of the findings of all of the surveys reported here may be questioned because the data about community opposition were provided by staff members of community residences rather than by community members directly. The authors of a number of the studies noted that they feared that direct assessment of community members could spark additional opposition, and for this reason community residence staff were used as the source of data. However, confidence in the validity of the findings is enhanced by the substantial degree of agreement in findings across the studies.

approximately one-third of the sampled community residences encountered opposition. Possible explanations for the variability in reported rates of opposition across studies include differences among communities, differences in the community's level of tolerance at various times, and differences in the phrasing or content of the questions used in the various studies. The rates of opposition reported by all studies are underestimates of the true extent of opposition, because some community residences never succeed in opening as a result of the community opposition they encounter. However, even when the highest estimate is used, it is clear that opposition is not routinely encountered by all community residences that are in existence. Thus, it may be valuable to examine the factors that differentiate between situations in which communities have opposed community residences and situations in which there has not been opposition.

The primary source of community opposition in a number of studies was reported to be neighbors of the community residence (Lubin et al., 1982; O'Connor, 1976; Piasecki, 1975). Among the frequently reported *causes* of opposition were neighbors' fears regarding: 1) a decrease in property value, 2) a change in neighborhood character, 3) an increase in crime and danger to the community, 4) lack of supervision of the residents, 5) an increase in noise or traffic or other disturbances. Interestingly, Berdiansky and Parker (1977) found that the concerns of community members were almost as likely as not to have been resolved prior to the time that the residence opened. Since as many community residences opened when neighbors' concerns were resolved as not, it is possible that the resolution of neighbors' concerns, although desirable, may not be so critical to the establishment of a community residence as is commonly assumed.

Several studies have reported marked shifts in community attitudes over time. Lubin et al. (1982) found that even though 30% of the community residences initially encountered opposition, only 2% of the community residences reported opposition at the time the research was

conducted. Seltzer and Seltzer (1982) documented a similar shift, with 36% of the community residences reporting opposition at the time of opening and 2% reporting opposition at the time of the research (an average of $2\frac{1}{2}$ years later). O'Connor (1976) also found that nearly all (89%) of the community residences that initially faced opposition reported a decrease in the level of opposition over time. However, the absence of opposition once the facilities are established and operating for some time does not necessarily indicate that positive relationships have developed to replace opposition.

In summary, community opposition has been experienced by approximately one-third of the established facilities. The primary source of opposition tends to be neighbors who express a variety of concerns. Substantial improvement in community relationships appears to occur over time. Thus, the problem seems to be most acute when community residences are first established and less so after the community has had direct contact over a period of time with residents and staff.

Impact of Community Residences on Property Values

A commonly reported cause of concern among community members is that community residences will have a negative impact on the neighborhood, particularly on the property values of homes for sale. Even those who have positive attitudes toward mentally retarded persons may oppose the establishment of a community residence if they believe that their home will decrease in value if a community residence were opened nearby. This problem may become especially acute when the economy is in a downswing.

A number of studies have examined community members' concerns about property values and/or conducted analyses of changes in property values in neighborhoods that contain one or more community residences. Conroy (1980) asked 350 community members to estimate the effect on property value of a hypothetical community residence for between two and five mentally retarded persons. When the hypothetical clients were described as mildly retarded, 21% of the community members believed that the community residence would have some or a marked impact on the property value of the neighborhood; when the residents were described as severely retarded, the percentage of neighbors who gave this estimate rose to 31%.

Similar conclusions are suggested by studies examining neighbors' beliefs about the impact of property values of real (as opposed to hypothetical) community residences. Lubin et al. (1982) reported that 32% of the community residences in their sample encountered community opposition, owing to fears about lowered property values. A study in Ohio (Community Acceptance of Group Homes in Ohio, n.d.) reported that 34% of those interviewed believed that group homes have caused property values to decline. Similarly, this was the most frequently cited cause for opposition to a group home in North Carolina, as reported by Berdiansky and Parker (1977).

In fact, analysis of the real estate market in neighborhoods in which community residences for mentally retarded persons have been located reveals that these facilities have had no impact on property value. Wolpert (1978), for example, compared 42 neighborhoods in New York State in which a community residence was located with 42 matched control neighborhoods, and found that there was no significant difference between the two groups of neighborhoods in the rate of increase of property values. Moreover, no relationship was found between the distance of a property from a community residence and its value. In another study, Wagner and Mitchell (1979) analyzed the real estate market in eight neighborhoods in which community residences were located during the 1-year period beginning 6 months before a community residence was established and ending 6 months after it opened. After analyzing the sales of all homes in these neighborhoods that occurred during this time period, they concluded that there was neither a positive nor a negative impact of the community residence in terms of the number of days a house was on the market or its selling price as a per-

centage of its list price. In a similar study, Mambort, Thomas, and Few (1981) reported an analysis of seven neighborhoods in which community residences were located, and concluded that these facilities had no impact on market prices, market values, adjacent property values, or property turnover. Nevertheless, they also noted that an analysis of public opinion in these same neighborhoods revealed that as many as 46% of residents believed that the community residences had negatively affected property value when in fact no such impact had occurred. Finally, the Full Citizenship Task Force of the President's Committee on Mental Retardation (The President's Committee, 1980), which examined the problem of oversaturation in a northeastern U.S. city, concluded that, "despite concerns to the contrary, the proliferation of group living arrangements has not caused property values to decline nor has it increased the rate of property turnover. The establishment of such facilities may have stabilized the area by providing a market for homes no longer used by private families and by assuring a reliable tax base" (p. 1).

In conclusion, although fears about declining property values are reported to be the primary cause of community opposition to community residences, analyses of the real estate market have consistently found community residences to have no actual negative impact on property values. In light of this apparent inconsistency between beliefs about the negative impact of community residences and their real impact, it may be valuable to examine predictors of community opposition in order to enhance our understanding of this problem.

PREDICTORS OF COMMUNITY OPPOSITION

A review of the literature suggests that at least six hypotheses can be advanced to explain the occurrence and extent of community opposition to community residences. First, *client characteristics* can be hypothesized to be related to opposition. It is generally believed that younger adults, males, and more severely retarded clients with behavior problems will be viewed more negatively by the community than older persons, children, females, and less severely retarded persons. Second, *staff characteristics* have been hypothesized to be related to opposition. Lower staff-to-resident ratios, higher rates of staff turnover, and lower percentages of staff from the local area can all be thought to contribute to higher rates of community opposition. Third, *neighborhood characteristics* such as socioeconomic characteristics, housing stock, and residential stability can be hypothesized to be related to opposition, with higher rates of opposition believed to be more probable in wealthier, more stable neighborhoods. Fourth, the *relationship between the clients and the neighborhood* can be hypothesized to be related to opposition, with opposition believed to be less likely when clients originally came from the local area. Fifth, the *characteristics of the building in which the community residence is located* can be hypothesized to be related to community opposition, with well-maintained, inconspicuous buildings less apt to receive opposition. Sixth, the *entry strategy* utilized by the community residence may be related to opposition. Some have hypothesized that a "high-profile" entry strategy such as public education will minimize opposition (Lupacchino & Krishef, n.d.; Stickney, 1977), while others have hypothesized that a "low-profile" approach might be more successful (Sigelman, 1976; Willms, 1981).

The evidence for each of these hypotheses is as follows. First, regarding client characteristics, the level of retardation of the clients was found not to be related to extent of opposition in either the Baker et al. (1977) study or the Seltzer and Seltzer (1982) study. As noted earlier, Conroy (1980) reported that community members' attitudes toward hypothetical community residences were more negative when the community residence was said to contain severely retarded persons than when the hypothetical clients were said to be mildly retarded persons. However, these attitudes are not necessarily the same as the attitudes that would be expressed about real residences actually in operation. The age of clients was found to be

unrelated to community opposition by O'Connor (1976) and by Seltzer and Seltzer (1982). Johnson (1976) reported that community residences for children encountered the most opposition; his sample, however, included community residences for all types of clients, not just mentally retarded individuals. Finally, regarding the relationship between the proportion of males and females in the community residence and community opposition, no relationship was found by Johnson (1976) or by Seltzer and Seltzer (1982). However, one study (Community Acceptance of Group Homes in Ohio, n.d.) did report that community residences that had only male clients met more opposition than those that had only female clients or both male and female clients. Thus, the evidence regarding the relationship between client characteristics and community opposition suggests that the age, sex, and level of retardation of community residence residents are unrelated or weakly related to the likelihood that a community residence will experience opposition from the community.

Regarding the second hypothesis, Johnson (1976) reported no relationship between staff characteristics and community opposition. In contrast, Seltzer and Seltzer (1982) found that community residences with lower staff turnover encountered less opposition. Surprisingly, no relationship was found in this study between the likelihood of opposition and the number or proportion of staff who previously lived in the local community. Finally, a *higher* staff-to-resident ratio was more likely to be found in community residences that encountered *more* opposition. In explaining this unanticipated finding, Seltzer and Seltzer (1982) noted that when staff have more time, they may spend it on public education activities, which in that particular study were found to be associated with higher levels of opposition.

In terms of the third hypothesis (neighborhood characteristics), Lubin et al. (1982) reported no relationship between population density and amount of community support. Johnson (1976) found that opposition is more likely in high socioeconomic-status neighborhoods. Seltzer and Seltzer (1982) reported that U.S. Bureau of the Census tract indicators of residential stability suggested that opposition to community residences was more probable in more stable neighborhoods. Also, community support was more likely to be received in neighborboods in which there was a higher proportion of homeowners.

Regarding the fourth hypothesis (the relationship between the clients and the community), Seltzer and Seltzer (1982) reported the rate of opposition was no lower when clients originally came from the neighborhood of the community residence than when clients came from other areas. However, they did find that opposition tended to be lower when clients were more involved with the community, suggesting that current ties to the community may be more salient than past ties, although the causal direction of this relationship cannot be determined from the available data.

In relation to the fifth hypothesis (the characteristics of the building in which the community residence is located), O'Connor (1976) reported finding no relationship between the type of building and the likelihood of opposition. The location of a parking lot adjacent to the community residence was associated in another study with more opposition (Community Acceptance of Group Homes in Ohio, n.d.). Seltzer & Seltzer (1982) reported a trend-level finding in which community residences located in multiple family homes experienced less opposition than those located in single family homes.

To summarize the available evidence regarding predictors of community opposition to community residences, remarkably little has been consistently demonstrated. The characteristics of the residents, staff, and the building in which the community residence is housed were found to be weak predictors at best. Wealthier, more stable neighborhoods were found to oppose the establishment of a community residence more often than poorer, more transient neighborhoods. However, these findings provide only a limited understanding of the factors that are predictive of the problem of community opposition. An examination of the relationship between entry strategy and community opposition may provide greater under-standing of the factors associated with this phenomenon. The evidence regarding entry strategy is examined in the section following.

ENTRY STRATEGIES

Commonly Used Entry Strategies

Two categories of entry strategies have been discussed in the literature and used in the establishment of community residences: the "high-profile" approach and the "low-profile" approach. In the high-profile strategy, community members are informed of the intention to establish a community residence well in advance and are often invited to participate in the development of the facility. When strong opposition is encountered that cannot be resolved, the community residence frequently attempts to find another site for the proposed programs. The benefits of the high-profile approach are believed to be: 1) a positive and long-lasting impact on community attitudes and 2) the creation of a receptive environment for the clients.

In the low-profile approach, the community residence is established as inconspicuously as possible. Community members then have the opportunity to gradually become acquainted with clients and staff. Proponents of this approach believe that myths and prejudices can be dispelled more successfully through real interactions than through meetings and through abstract—and possibly inflammatory—public education techniques. The risks of public education and of possible site relocation in both time and money are believed to be greatly minimized by the low-profile approach.

Proponents of these two approaches have basic differences with respect to their beliefs about community receptivity to community residences, about the prospects for making an impact on existing attitudes, and about the effects of community attitudes on clients. Baron and Piasecki (1981) explain that the high-profile approach is based on the assumption that attitude change results in behavior change, while the low-profile approach assumes just the opposite.

Most of the literature describing entry strategies focuses on the high-profile approach. For example, the Massachusetts Department of Mental Health identified 30 options that could be pursued in building community acceptance, nearly all of which were consistent with the high-profile approach (Cornhill Associates, 1978). These options were classified into five activities: 1) provision of information to the community, 2) location of community residences so as to avoid oversaturation, 3) collaboration between state and municipal officials and provider groups, 4) citizen involvement, and 5) education of the general public about ongoing community residences. Stickney (1977) discussed similar high-profile strategies.

Several studies have reported the frequency with which various entry strategies were used. Meeting with neighbors was generally the most frequently used strategy (Baker et al., 1977; Lubin et al., 1982; Seltzer & Seltzer, 1982). Meetings held with other key groups (e.g., municipal officials, clergy, community leaders) were also commonly used entry strategies. It should be noted, however, that attempts at public education were not routinely conducted by all community residences. Baker et al. (1977) reported that 23% of the sample made no attempt to prepare community activities; Lubin et al. (1982) reported that 26% of the community residences in their sample maintained a low profile in response to community opposition; and Seltzer and Seltzer (1982) found that as many as 42% of the community residences did not conduct either formal or informal public education prior to or after the establishment of the facility.

Effectiveness of Entry Strategies

The weight of the evidence regarding the relative effectiveness of the high-profile approach versus the low-profile approach suggests that the low-profile approach is at least as effective and possibly superior to the high-profile approach in minimizing opposition. This finding is surprising in the context of the positive value placed by professionals in the field of mental retardation on public education, open communication, and broad participation in the planning process. Sigelman (1976) presented a strategic argument for what she termed the "Machiavellian approach."

> many administrators have decided to move in without informing neighbors or probing community attitudes in advance. This strategy of *fait accompli*, appealing to the Machiavellian, has the advantage of preventing moves to block the home's opening. And, if the present assessment of community attitudes is correct, it may be no less effective in the long run than more elaborate strategies involving advance attitude sampling (p. 28).

Ashmore (1975), in his review of the literature on attitude change, concluded that mass media campaigns are remarkably unsuccessful in achieving their goals because they reach primarily those who already agree with the position advocated. However, regarding actual contact between the general public and stigmatized groups, while at times this strategy has heightened prejudice, contact that meets certain conditions has been found to reduce stigma. Those conditions, identified by Ashmore (1975) in decreasing order of importance, are those that assure: 1) cooperative interdependence (shared means and goals); 2) equality of status; 3) norms favoring equality; 4) conclusion of contact on a successful note; 5) personal acquaintance; and 6) nonconformity of minority group members to stereotypes. Ashmore's conclusions thus favor a low-profile approach in which natural contacts between mentally retarded persons and community members occur once the community residence is established, as opposed to high-profile mass media campaigns.

Several studies have reported finding an unexpected positive relationship between community education and community opposition (Baker et al., 1977; Johnson, 1976; Seltzer & Seltzer, 1982). Baker et al. (1977) explained that

> This relationship may imply that some preparation efforts backfire, because they alert the community to the community residence's presence and spark opposition. An equally plausible explanation is that preparation is in response to incipient opposition (p. 217).

In determining the causal direction of the relationship between community education and community opposition, knowledge of the sequence of events is important. If education is found to precede opposition, evidence will be provided in support of a low-profile approach. Longitudinal experimental studies, yet unavailable, are needed to examine this issue directly and to provide solid conclusions about the effects of public education.

A related matter pertains to the point at which it is most advantageous to inform the community of the existence of the community residence. Seltzer and Seltzer (1982) examined the relative likelihood of community opposition when the community became aware of the community residence at various stages before and after the establishment of the community residence. The findings of this analysis suggest that community opposition is most likely when the community becomes aware of the intended existence of the community residence shortly before it opens. The lowest probability of opposition is when the community is informed after the residents have moved in. A moderate level of opposition is encountered when the community is made aware of the plan more than six months prior to the intended opening of the community residence. Thus, in order to minimize opposition, it would seem prudent to either inform the community very early (more than six months before opening) or, alternatively, after the residents have moved in.

The specific cause-and-effect relationships among the time at which a community becomes aware of the intended or actual existence of the community residence, the amount and types of public education activities engaged in by community residence staff, and the expression of opposition to the community residence cannot be clearly determined from the available studies. However, the findings of the research reported here raise significant questions about the benefits of public education in minimizing community antagonism. To determine more definitively whether public education has a positive or negative effect on community opposition, it would be necessary to compare community opposition in communities where public education was provided with opposition in comparable communities in which public

education was not provided. Such comparisons have not yet been done.

Seltzer and Seltzer (1982) also reported that community residences that encountered opposition were no less likely than community residences that did not experience opposition to have a site selection committee, to include local community members on this committee, to include members of the local community on the board of directors of the community residence, or to have staff members specially designated for public relations. Thus, while public education was more likely to be used by residences that faced community opposition, strategies designed to actually involve community members in the decision-making process and in the operation of the community residence were not found to be related to the likelihood of encountering opposition, even though it is commonly believed that these citizen-involvement strategies do have a positive effect. Lastly, Seltzer and Seltzer (1982) found no difference in the extent of community support received by community residences that encountered opposition and community residences that did not. This lack of a relationship between community opposition and community support is one of the most intriguing findings of this study and suggests that an understanding of the relationship between communities and community residences is far more complex than commonly assumed.

SUMMARY AND CONCLUSIONS
FOR RESEARCH AND POLICY

The attitudes held by community members toward community residences for mentally retarded persons can be placed along a continuum of attitudes and behavior, ranging from attitudes held in the abstract at one end of the continuum to attitudes expressed through behavior on the other. At the abstract extreme, attitudes are expressed through broad legal statements. These include zoning rules, legislation, and social policies that place limits on the development and location of community residences. Next along this continuum is public opinion about community residences, expressed not with respect to any particular facility but with regard to the general issue of community residential services for mentally retarded persons. Reactions to existing facilities elicited through interviews or other survey techniques come next on the continuum and are followed at the far end of the continuum by unsolicited opinions and actions taken in support of or in opposition to specific community residences.

The available knowledge about community attitudes toward community residences indicates that there are inconsistencies in these attitudes, with the same person likely to express more positive attitudes at one point along the continuum and more negative attitudes at some other point. Interestingly, attitudes tend to be most favorable near the extremes of the continuum. As noted earlier, some surveys have reported that over three-fourths of the general public say that they would not be opposed to the establishment of a community residence for mentally retarded persons in their neighborhood. Similarly, at the other end of the continuum, little opposition is expressed by neighbors after a facility has been in existence for a period of time. The estimates presented earlier indicate that fewer than 5% of community residences encounter continued opposition. Opposition tends to be most strongly expressed in the middle ranges of the continuum: in response to the ''threat'' of the establishment of a community residence or shortly after it begins operation. Opposition then diminishes, probably because the fears held by community members are not borne out by the reality of the situation. In addition, property values tend to remain as they were, perhaps further reducing the risk of continued opposition. Some have asserted that positive attitudes are built by increased contact between community members and mentally retarded clients. However, the research on the effects of integrating handicapped children in school settings has cast some doubt on this assumption.

Why does opposition diminish over time if increased contact may fail to promote positive feelings? A possible explanation might be found in an examination of the relationship be-

tween community opposition and community support. One study reported finding an absence of a relationship between these two phenomena; they are not opposite ends of the same continuum but instead two separate dimensions (Seltzer & Seltzer, 1982). What may happen is that over time opposition diminishes, but it may not be replaced by a concomitant degree of active support. Like relationships among many members of contemporary neighborhoods, passive support or indifference is descriptive of the attitudes held by most community members once a facility has been in operation for a period of time.

Two other broad issues were examined in this review: 1) the causes of community opposition, and 2) strategies for minimizing it. There is scant information about the underlying causes of opposition. The characteristics of both the neighbors and the neighborhood may be more predictive of opposition than the characteristics of the community residence itself or of the mentally retarded residents. The literature seems to indicate that wealthier and more stable neighborhoods may be more likely to express opposition to a community residence, and that the characteristics of the clients have little to do with the likelihood that a community residence will be opposed. Johnson (1976) made the following observation about the absence of concrete causes of community opposition:

> my own observations led me to believe that the fears expressed by opponents were not based primarily on experience. . . ; that they could not be justified by the record of community residence programs; that they could not be modified significantly by valid information; that the specific fears expressed seemed independent of the particular characteristics of the residents in question; and finally, that those most likely to be affected by the program were not always those who felt most threatened. All of this led me to the hypothesis that *neighbors who opposed community residence programs were not responding primarily to the actual characteristics of the program, its residents, or staff, but were responding to something else, still undefined, which the entry of the program into their residential neighborhood represented or symbolized* (pp. 19–20) (italics added).

According to Johnson, the intangible quality to

which neighbors were responding is the intrusion of the community residence into the neighborhood and the neighbors' fear that the neighborhood will be "contaminated" by foreign, unusual, or deviant persons. This reaction is very similar to that of community members who oppose the integration of racial or ethnic minorities into white neighborhoods. Moreover, according to Johnson, the mere expression of opposition may be a method for neighbors to publicly separate themselves from the deviant group, to reiterate to others and to themselves that the community residence is not a reflection of them. Once such a statement is made, its function may have been completed, and thus the need for strong continued opposition diminishes over time. Johnson's (1976) hypothesis is that the basic causes of community opposition have more to do with stigma and irrational fears than with rational reactions to the specific circumstances. This hypothesis may be useful in explaining why high-profile entry strategies tend to be associated with higher levels of community opposition than do low-profile strategies. The high-profile approach is intended to educate community members by appealing to them on a cognitive level. However, at times, this approach may have the effect of alerting community members to an event that they perceive to be a threat, and of provoking in them an irrational response. Subsequently, they may resist altering their opinions on the basis of new information or logical appeals. The low-profile entry strategy may be more successful because it mounts less of a direct assault on the community. It is important to reiterate that since the studies reported here neither longitudinally tracked the events that occurred prior to and following the establishment of community residences nor randomly assigned entry strategies to neighborhoods, the causal relationship between entry strategy and community opposition cannot be determined. However, the available evidence raises many questions about the efficacy of the high-profile approach.

The issue of community opposition to community residences is controversial because it raises the problem of rights in conflict: the right

of the community to determine its own makeup may be perceived to be in conflict with the right of mentally retarded persons to live in the community. When taken to extremes, the conflict is easily resolved. On the one hand, if a mentally retarded person threatens the integrity of a community by breaking the law, the usual legal sanctions are applied and the community is protected. On the other hand, the right of a family with a young handicapped child to live in the community of its choice cannot legally be limited by the larger community. However, the establishment of a group residence is clearly a more visible action than the integration of an individual family into a neighborhood. The community can make use of opportunities to place limitations on the establishment of the community residence, such as invoking zoning regulations, denying building permits for needed modifications, and overly zealous enforcement of health, building, and fire codes.

The problem of community opposition furthermore arouses dispute because of the various strategies that can be used to minimize it. Proponents of both the high-profile and the low-profile approach are firm in their views and question each other's approaches on moral and strategic grounds. Those who are high-profile advocates question the ethics of "sneaking in," while proponents of the low-profile approach assert that mentally retarded persons have as much right to live in a particular community as other citizens. Ideological arguments regarding the strategic superiority of one approach or the other have been very persuasive and appear to be held irrespective of the available evidence.

Because of the controversial nature of the issue under consideration and because of the limited amount of research that has been conducted, this review of the literature can productively suggest a number of new questions about the phenomenon of community opposition that warrant careful examination in future research. These are briefly enumerated here.

1. An in-depth analysis of the relationships among the following factors is needed: knowledge about mental retardation, de-

gree of public contact with mentally retarded persons, general attitudes toward mental retardation, and specific attitudes toward community residences. This analysis will be useful in determining the utility of public education efforts, as well as in enriching our understanding of the correlates of stigma in general.

2. An examination of the long-term effects of the community integration of mentally retarded persons on community attitudes is needed. Although mainstreaming may have only a limited impact on the attitudes of nonretarded youngsters in the short-run, the long-term impact of attending mainstreamed schools and of growing up in neighborhoods in which handicapped persons also live needs to be examined.

3. The actual effects of community opposition on mentally retarded persons should be examined. Since much of the opposition is expressed before the clients move into a community residence, to what extent are the clients aware of the sentiments expressed by the community? Also, what is the effect of community opposition on the extent to which mentally retarded clients are successful in integrating into the community?

4. A study is needed of the experiences of community residences that are prevented from opening due to community opposition. Most of the research reported in this review has focused only on those community residences that were successful in opening; these studies thus underestimate the magnitude of community opposition. A study of planned community residences that failed to open possibly could reveal entry strategies and types of neighborhoods to avoid and could also yield a picture of the true prevalence of community opposition.

5. Analyses of the effects of the various entry strategies should be conducted using both experimental and quasi-experimental techniques. Unless similar types of residences placed in similar types of communities are compared when different entry strategies are used, it will be difficult to determine with any degree of confidence the effect of the various entry strategies on community opposition. Although the literature suggests that the low-profile approach may be superior, the causal relationship between entry strategy and degree of opposition has yet to be firmly established.

In addition to these areas for future research, a social policy agenda is proposed here, based on this chapter's review of the literature, that maximizes the ease with which community residences become established in the communities of their choice. This policy agenda is as follows:

1. Groups that sponsor community residences should be helped by the appropriate state governmental agencies to minimize any conditions that may legitimately provoke community opposition. Sufficient staff and adequate maintenance of the physical facility are two obvious goals that should be met by providing the needed level of funding for the program. In addition, technical assistance should be provided to help staff of established community residences develop procedures to enable them to respond in the event of opposition.

2. Those state agencies that require high-profile approaches to be taken before a community residence is opened should relax this requirement. At best, the available research suggests that public education may not be warranted in all cases. At worst, public education may spark opposition that otherwise might not have occurred. Agenices should permit provider groups to attempt low-profile entry strategies.

3. State agencies should be prepared to help provider groups select sites for new community residences so as to minimize potential opposition. Information should include the higher likelihood of opposition in wealthier areas, the heightened publicity to be expected in areas that require obtaining a zoning variance, and density

of community residences for handicapped or otherwise-labeled groups of clients in different neighborhoods.

4. Provider groups that prefer to use high-profile entry strategies should begin their work substantially in advance of their expected date of entry—perhaps as much as 1 year before. This will, it is hoped, allow opposition to diminish if it is encountered. Start-up funding to support such advance planning may be needed from state agencies.

5. State and federal agencies and consumer groups should continue to advocate both the relaxation of zoning restrictions and the passage of legislation that facilitates the integration of residential programs into the community. Legal support of community integration efforts can productively assist in smoothing the movement of clients and community residences into otherwise-resistant neighborhoods.

There is, in addition, a present need to attempt to coordinate research and policy-making activities. In the past, the role of research in the formulation of social policies in this area has been rather restricted. Temporally, research has tended to follow rather than precede the development of policies concerning community opposition, and thus the policies often are already in place when research findings become available.

The unfortunate quality of this disjunction between policy development and research is that although policies usually reflect the best intentions of the policy makers, the actual effects of these policies often are different from what was originally intended. As Lakin, Bruininks, and Sigford (1981) have argued, *sheer belief* in the appropriateness of our policies and services has at times caused professionals in the field of mental retardation to adhere to counterproductive treatment models. Conversely, a change in the political or ideological climate has at times resulted in the dismantling of a social policy or service program that in fact was having desired effects on clients.

Although there are differences in perspective between policy makers and researchers, substantial cooperation between the two groups can occur because they generally share common goals. With respect to community residences for mentally retarded persons, both groups have been committed to maximizing the degree to which clients develop new functional abilities, grow personally, and integrate to the greatest extent possible with the larger community. With continued commitment to the ideals of the community residence movement, continued program innovation, and ongoing funding for needed services, the prospects for maximizing the community integration of mentally retarded persons appear promising.

REFERENCES

Ashmore, R.D. Background considerations in developing strategies for changing attitudes and behavior toward the mentally retarded. In: M.J. Begab & S.A. Richardson (eds.), *The mentally retarded and society: A social science perspective*. Baltimore: University Park Press, 1975.

Baker, B.L., Seltzer, G.B., & Seltzer, M.M. *As close as possible: Community residences for retarded adults*. Boston: Little, Brown & Co., 1977.

Baron, R.C., & Piasecki, J.R. The community versus community care. In: R.D. Budson (ed.), *Issues in community residential care*. San Francisco: Jossey-Bass, 1981.

Berdiansky, H.A., & Parker, R. Establishing a group home for the adult mentally retarded in North Carolina. *Mental Retardation*, 1977, *15*(4), 8–11.

Community acceptance of group homes in Ohio. Colum-

bus: Ohio Association for the Developmentally Disabled, n.d.

Conroy, J. *Attitudes toward the mentally retarded in selected communities. Technical report of selected findings*. Philadelphia: Temple University, 1980.

Cornhill Associates. *Elements of a community acceptance strategy for community programs for the mentally disabled*. Boston: Massachusetts Department of Mental Health, April 1978.

Gallup Organization. Report for the President's Committee on Mental Retardation. Public attitudes regarding mental retardation. In: R. Nathan (ed.), *Mental retardation: Century of decision*. Washington, D.C : U.S. Government Printing Office, 1976.

Gottlieb, J. Public, peer, and professional attitudes toward mentally retarded persons. In: M.J. Begab & S.A. Richardson (eds.), *The mentally retarded and society: A so-

cial science perspective. Baltimore: University Park Press, 1975.

Gottlieb, J. Mainstreaming: Fulfilling the promise? *American Journal of Mental Deficiency,* 1981, *86*(2), 115–126.

Heal, L.W., Sigelman, C.K., & Switzky, H.N. Research on community residential alternatives for the mentally retarded. In: N.R. Ellis (ed.), *International review of research in mental retardation,* Vol. 9. New York: Academic Press, 1978.

Hill, B.K., Lakin, K.C., Sigford, B.B., Hauber, F.A., & Bruininks, R.H. *Programs and services for mentally retarded people in residential facilities.* Minneapolis: University of Minnesota, Department of Psychoeducational Studies, 1982.

Johnson, G.R. *Sources of neighborhood opposition to community residence programs.* Unpublished doctoral dissertation, Harvard University, Cambridge, MA, 1976.

Kastner, L.S., Reppucci, N.D., & Pezzoli, J.J. Assessing community attitudes toward mentally retarded persons. *American Journal of Mental Deficiency,* 1979, *84,* 137–144.

Lakin, K.C., Bruininks, R.H., & Sigford, B.B. Deinstitutionalization and community-based residential adjustment: A summary of research and issues. In: R.H. Bruininks, C.E. Meyers, B.B. Sigford, & K.C. Lakin (eds.), *Deinstitutionalization and community adjustment of mentally retarded people.* Washington, D C : American Association on Mental Deficiency, 1981.

Lubin, R.A., Schwartz, A.A., Zigman, W.B., & Janicki, M.P. Community acceptance of residential programs for developmentally disabled persons. *Applied Research in Mental Retardation,* 1982, *3,* 191–200.

Lupacchino, R.W., & Krishef, C. H. *An analysis of barriers in establishing group homes for the mentally retarded.* Unpublished manuscript, Florida State University, n.d.

Mambort, T.T., Thomas, E.B., & Few, R.G. *Community acceptance.* Montgomery County, OH: Montgomery County Board of the Mentally Retarded and the Developmentally Disabled, 1981.

Moreau, F.A., Novak, A.R., & Sigelman, C.K. Physical and social integration of developmentally disabled individuals into the community. In: A.R. Novak and L.W. Heal (eds.), *Integration of developmentally disabled individuals into the community.* Baltimore: Paul H. Brookes Publishing Co., 1980.

O'Connor, G. *Home is a good place.* Washington, D C : American Association on Mental Deficiency, 1976.

Piasecki, J.R. *Community response to residential services for the psycho-socially disabled: Preliminary results of a national survey.* Paper presented at the First Annual Conference of the International Association of Psycho-Social Rehabilitation Service, Philadelphia, PA, November 15, 1975.

The President's Committee on Mental Retardation examines "over saturation" of community residential facilities. *Links,* 1980, *10*(1), 1–2.

Seltzer, M.M., & Litchfield, L.C. *Analysis of state policies regarding community opposition to community residences.* Unpublished manuscript, Boston University, Boston, 1983.

Seltzer, M.N., & Seltzer, G.B. *Community responses to community residences for mentally retarded persons.* Paper presented at the NICHD Conference on the Impact of Residential Environments on Mentally Retarded Persons, Lake Wilderness, WA, August 1982.

Sigelman, C.K. A Machiavelli for planners: Community attitudes and selection of a group home site. *Mental Retardation,* 1976, *14*(1), 26–29.

Stickney, P. (ed.), *Gaining community acceptance: A handbook for community residence planners.* White Plains, NY: Westchester Community Service Council, June 1977.

Wagner, C.A., & Mitchell, C.M. *The non-effect of group homes on neighboring residential property values in Franklin County.* Columbus, OH: Metropolitan Human Services Commission, August 1979.

Walbridge, R.H., & Conroy, J.W. *Changes in community attitudes.* Philadelphia: Temple University, 1981.

Walbridge, R.H., Whaley, A.M., & Conroy, J.W. *Models of change in community attitudes.* Philadelphia: Temple University, 1981.

Warren, D.I., & Warren, R.B. Six kinds of neighborhoods. *Psychology Today,* 1975, *9*(1), 75–80.

Willms, J.D. Neighborhood attitudes toward group homes for mentally retarded adults. In: P. Mittler (ed.), *Frontiers of knowledge in mental retardation.* Baltimore: University Park Press, 1981.

Wolpert, J. *Group homes for mentally retarded: An investigation of neighborhood property impacts.* Unpublished manuscript, Princeton University, Princeton, NJ, 1978.

Chapter 7

The Impact of Deinstitutionalization on Families

A Family Systems Approach

Ann P. Turnbull, Mary Jane Brotherson, and Jean Ann Summers

Families unquestionably play a critical role in the deinstitutionalization of handicapped children and youth. For the purpose of this chapter, the concepts of family and deinstitutionalization warrant an operational definition. *Family* is used here to refer primarily to the members of the natural parental family. As discussed later, this family is comprised of four subsystems: spouse, parental, sibling, and extrafamilial. The intervention approaches discussed are also applicable to foster and adoptive families. *Deinstitutionalization* refers to the integration of handicapped persons into the community, as opposed to their placement in institutional residences. There are two major strategies for achieving deinstitutionalization: 1) to maintain handicapped children and youth with their families or in other community settings so that institutionalization does not occur, and 2) to depopulate institutions by returning handicapped persons who have previously been institutionalized to live with their families or in community settings. This chapter focuses primarily (but not exclusively) on the former strategy. Emphasis on natural parental families and institutional prevention is consistent with demographic data indicating that the substan-

tial majority of handicapped children and youth live with their natural families rather than in institutional settings during the developmental period of their lives (Bruininks, 1979).

Institutional prevention requires that handicapped children and youth be integrated into their families, the educational system, and other community services and experiences. Successful family adaptation is necessary but not sufficient in preventing institutionalization. It is beyond the scope of this chapter to address educational and community integration; however, the complexity of successful deinstitutionalization in varied spheres of human interactions and services should not be minimized.

Considering the number of handicapped children and youth living with their families, it is disconcerting that family intervention models have not been more systematically developed and implemented. Numerous reasons account for this omission. First, the bulk of research conducted on deinstitutionalization has focused on the handicapped individuals rather than on the members in their family networks. When research has been extended to family members, it has typically focused on mothers. Too often, "mother" has been equated with "family" without adequate recognition of other family members. There has also been a failure to recognize the multiple realities within a given family; in other words, the needs and perspectives of one member may substantially differ from those of other members. Because deinstitutionalization of handicapped children and youth integrally involves all family members, interventions with handicapped individuals must consider the effects on the entire family. Second, researchers have largely ignored family systems theories from other disciplines, such as sociology and psychiatry. Thus, research has too often been devoid of a theoretical base. The absence of theory has tended to make data collection on family perspectives and their impact an end in itself rather than a means to future applications and interventions. Third, many researchers have failed to account for or even describe the structural characteristics and life cycle stages of the families from whom they collected data. There has been a generalization that families of handicapped children and youth are homogeneous; thus, normative intervention approaches rather than individualized intervention approaches have been the rule. Fourth, the frequent use of questionnaires that are narrowly defined and often not written in the language patterns of the parents has been a problem. Such questionnaires tend to seek sensitive information in a cursory way. Because of the need of stigmatized persons to present themselves as "well-adjusted" (Goffman, 1963), the validity of data collected through survey methodology is sometimes questionable. A fifth and final barrier to the development of family intervention models is the major lack of longitudinal research on family stress and coping. Data bases on life cycle needs of families with handicapped members are currently unavailable. The chronicity of handicapping conditions requires a far more systematic approach to life cycle support and planning than has occurred in the past.

This chapter presents the current formulation of a family systems model within which the impact of deinstitutionalization on families can be analyzed and future directions generated. This model is in the process of development at the Research and Training Center on Independent Living at the University of Kansas, Lawrence. The development of the model involves a two-tier approach: 1) a comprehensive review of the literature on families with handicapped children and the literature from related disciplines on family systems theory, and 2) intensive interviews with 12 family units (6 with mentally retarded members and 6 with physically handicapped members) using a naturalistic inquiry paradigm (Guba, 1981). Interviews have been conducted with mothers, fathers, nonhandicapped siblings, and the handicapped family member(s). Other family members (e.g., spouse, brother-in-law) were included when they were identified as playing a significant role in providing assistance to the handicapped family member. A future phase of this research will be the development of family assessment tools based on the family systems model that can be used to identify and place in order of priority the intervention needs of individual families.

FAMILY SYSTEMS MODEL

The family systems model is comprised of four family subsystems and three perspectives of family dynamics (illustrated in Figure 1). The four major subsystems include: the spouse subsystem (husband and wife interactions), the parental subsystem (parent-child interactions), the sibling subsystem (child-child interactions), and the extra-familial subsystem (nuclear family interactions with extended family and networks of social, community, and professional support) (Minuchin, 1974). In some families, the spouse subsystem is attenuated by having a single parent; in other families, the handicapped child may have no siblings. The extrafamilial subsystem varies greatly in its breadth and in the quality of its contribution to family members. Integrating a handicapped member into the family has implications for all four subsystems. Further, an intervention that

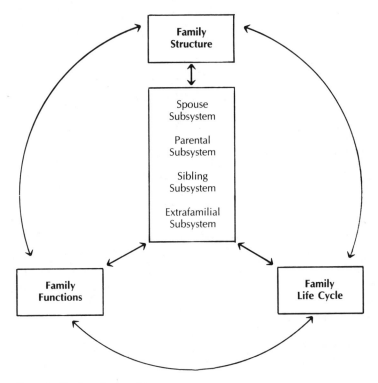

Figure 1. Family systems model.

may be specifically targeted to one of the sub-systems will invariably have spillover effects to the other three.

> Consider the case of a mother who has agreed to work on a home training program in the area of feeding. Allowing her child to feed himself triples the time involved in each meal. While the mother is working with the child on feeding, the dinner conversation with her husband and other children is substantially limited. After the other family members finish dinner, the father cleans the kitchen and the siblings proceed to their home-work, all feeling like some of their needs have been overlooked. Meanwhile, the mother is feel-ing harried and frustrated.

Healthy family life involves a complex balanc-ing of individual and group interests. Equal importance should be allocated to the well-being of every family member. Focusing ex-clusively on the needs of the handicapped member is far too narrow. Rather, a total fami-ly perspective accounting for the interactions represented in each of the four subsystems is

necessary when analyzing issues such as deinstitutionalization.

Family theorists have described family dy-namics from three different perspectives: struc-tural approaches (Minuchin, 1974; Stanton, 1981), functions assumed by families (Caplan, 1976), and family life cycle (Carter & McGoldrick, 1980; Duvall, 1977). Figure 2 outlines the components considered in each perspective. The remainder of this chapter dis-cusses family structure, functions, and life cy-cle as they relate to the integration of handi-capped children and youth within the family unit. For each perspective, information from three sources is presented: 1) a summary of sociological literature on family systems, 2) a summary of information from the developmen-tal disabilities literature on the impact of de-institutionalization on families, and 3) qualita-tive data from the previously described naturalistic study conducted by the authors. Se-lected future directions for research, interven-

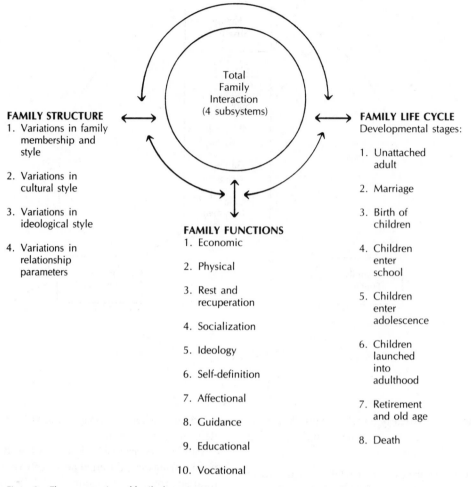

FAMILY STRUCTURE
1. Variations in family membership and style

2. Variations in cultural style

3. Variations in ideological style

4. Variations in relationship parameters

Total Family Interaction (4 subsystems)

FAMILY FUNCTIONS
1. Economic

2. Physical

3. Rest and recuperation

4. Socialization

5. Ideology

6. Self-definition

7. Affectional

8. Guidance

9. Educational

10. Vocational

FAMILY LIFE CYCLE
Developmental stages:

1. Unattached adult

2. Marriage

3. Birth of children

4. Children enter school

5. Children enter adolescence

6. Children launched into adulthood

7. Retirement and old age

8. Death

Figure 2.   Three perspectives of family dynamics.

tion, and policy are suggested as examples of how the model can be used to generate empirical, conceptual, and policy approaches to assisting families with deinstitutionalization.

FAMILY STRUCTURE

The structural characteristics of families can substantially influence their ability to keep handicapped members at home as opposed to placing them in an institution, as well as the degree of success they will experience in reincorporating members in the family after a period of institutionalization. The major components of family structure considered in the family systems model include:

1. Variations in family membership and style
2. Variations in cultural style
3. Variations in ideological style
4. Variations in relationship parameters

These components and their corresponding subcomponents are outlined in Table 1.

Variations in Family Membership and Style

Membership and style characteristics of families vary along many dimensions. Important factors to consider include number of parents, nature of kinship relationships, family size, primary versus reconstituted family status, and relationships of members to the labor force.

Table 1. Pluralistic family structures

1. Variations in Family Membership and Style
   a. Number of parents
   b. Nature of kinship relationships
   c. Family size
   d. Primary versus reconstituted family status
   e. Relationships of members to the labor force
2. Variations in Cultural Style
   a. Ethnic background
   b. Race
   c. Religious affiliation
   d. Socioeconomic status
   e. Location (urban/rural/suburban)
3. Variations in Ideological Style
   a. Instrumental versus expressive emphasis
   b. Child-rearing philosophy
   c. Attitudes toward disability
   d. Attitudes toward education
   e. Work ethic
   f. Attitudes toward independence and quality of life
4. Variations in Relationship Parameters
   a. Characteristics of individual and group members
   b. Power and hierarchy
   c. Role assignments
   d. Boundary definitions
   e. Communication style

Considering the fact that approximately 48% of the general population of preschool children have mothers working or seeking work (*Report on Preschool Education,* 1982), a clear implication is that many parents have less time for child-rearing than they have had in the past (Lieber, 1980). It has also been reported that 40% of all people now marrying will end their marriages in divorce, which has implications for the number of single-parent homes (Foster, Berger, & McLean, 1981). Whereas home training programs have been found to be a successful strategy for increasing the skills of handicapped children (Shearer & Shearer, 1977), an analysis of membership characteristics suggests that this option may not be feasible for a large number of families (for example, when only one parent is in the home, or when both parents are intensely involved in balancing the multiple responsibilities of work and family).

Another important membership consideration is family size. Trevino (1979) suggests that a larger number of children in the family contributes to an "atmosphere of normalcy" and decreases negative effects of having a handicapped child. Although such an outcome is certainly positive, larger numbers of children also create time, energy, and financial demands on parents. This point was borne out in a classic study by Bossard and Ball (1956), who studied 100 large families (6 or more children). They found that the increased workload had implications for the older children especially, who were regularly incorporated into the parental subsystem. The assumption of parental responsibilities had both positive (e.g., early maturity, greater sense of responsibility and belonging) and negative (e.g., sacrificing personal opportunities) effects. In the case of large families with a handicapped member, the pressures on the older, nonhandicapped siblings are even greater, and could place them at greater risk for emotional disturbance (Gath, 1977).

There are also positive and negative outcomes for small families. A mother of a severely handicapped son who had no other children stated during our interview:

> Over the years I have thought that if we had had other children, I might have had a built-in babysitter. As it is, Jim has advanced considerably, because I don't have to split my time. He is spoiled rotten being the only child and only grandchild.

In many ways, membership characteristics can influence the family's success with deinstitutionalization.

Variations in Cultural Style

The family culture consists of a variety of pluralistic features—ethnic background, race, religious affiliation, socioeconomic status, and location (urban/rural/suburban)—that can substantially influence family reactions and coping regarding deinstitutionalization. For example, Farber (1962) has reported that Jewish mothers and fathers show the greatest resistance to institutionalizing their retarded child. In our interviews with families, religion was mentioned with unanticipated frequency as an important coping strategy. The particular religious denomination seemed to be less important than the family's personal interpretations of religion. Interestingly, families demonstrated tremendous variability in their personal interpretations. Examples of this variance are illustrated in the following parent quotes:

> In the life hereafter, he'll have equal standing with everyone else. He won't be handicapped.

> I had to trust in the good Lord that things would turn out all right. I believe that God has a plan for that boy.

> I thought I would be helped [by God] if I helped others.

Thus, the family's general religious affiliation and its particular religious beliefs can influence the nature of its adaptation.

Socioeconomic style has also been identified as an important consideration. Farber (1962) characterizes two types of family crises in response to the birth of a mentally retarded child. The "tragic crisis" represents a frustration in the family's aims and aspirations and is generally associated with families having high socioeconomic status. The second type, associated with low socioeconomic families, is "role-organization crisis" resulting in a focus on major care burdens.

The location of a family can influence the availability of professional services and social support networks.

> The Bowers are a middle class farm family. Their social activities revolve around the church. Except for schools, which were described as extremely unhelpful, they had no agency or professional help in raising their mentally retarded son until he entered a sheltered workshop at the age of 20.

> The Johnston family live in a university community and have access to a wide array of educational, recreational, and respite care opportunities. They take advantage of many community services in meeting the needs of their handicapped daughter.

Research needs to be directed at matching deinstitutionalization interventions with particular cultural patterns of families.

Variations in Ideological Style

The family's ideology pertains to its beliefs about what is important for individual members and the group. These beliefs can be thought of as decision rules that provide the basis for a substantial degree of the family's behavior. Specific dimensions of ideological style include relative emphasis on instrumental or expressive activities, child-rearing beliefs, attitudes toward disability, attitudes toward education, work ethic, and attitudes toward independence and quality of life.

Although limited attention has been directed to family ideology in the literature, some data are available with respect to instrumental versus expressive emphases. Parsons and Bales (1955) characterize instrumental activities as those that interface the family with the outside world (e.g., work relationships, community "image"), while expressive activities are oriented toward the emotional well-being of family members (e.g., affection, developing a sense of belonging, and family cohesiveness). Parson and Bales (1955) have suggested that fathers tend to take an instrumental role in the family while mothers fulfill expressive functions. Subsequent research, however, has called this dichotomy into question (Aronoff & Crano, 1975; Gumz & Gubrium, 1972). It may be more accurate to characterize the family ideology on the whole as falling on an instrumental/expressive continuum with some families emphasizing one ideology more than the other, and other families striking a balance between the two. Birenbaum (1971) found that a sample of 103 mothers of retarded children tended to emphasize expressive mothering skills with their retarded children (e.g., love the child, don't be ashamed of the child), but emphasized instrumental skills with nonhandicapped children (e.g., teach him right from wrong, know his needs and wants). It is possible to speculate that achieving an appropriate balance in instrumental and expressive emphases might have important implications for the family's willingness to encourage independence in the handicapped child and thus reduce the risk for institutionalization.

All the dimensions of family ideology seem to be highly interdependent in shaping the family's response to disability. Furthermore, families in our study varied greatly along ideological dimensions, as illustrated in the following two quotes by fathers of handicapped males:

> George was our youngest child and he relied on his brothers and sisters. He wasn't able to go outside and work. We didn't want him to get hurt. My wife got along better with George than I did. I thought she babied him. I thought he should do more around the house. He just watched TV.

> I am a fairly rigid disciplinarian. I believe children should mind and be responsible. All of the children had chores, including Karl. I found tasks he could do like take out the garbage. I tried to insist he do whatever he could do and tried to challenge him with more. . . . A lot of people would want to do things for him. I would insist he would do it for himself. It was easy for him to think that his Dad was a big ogre.

Family ideology concerning the reactions to the handicapping condition can be largely influenced by professionals, or families can totally reject professional interpretations and create their own attitudes consistent with their value system. Whether or not professional opinions influence the family's beliefs is likely related to the personal characteristics of the parents, such as locus of control and autonomy. A demonstration of this point is provided by two different families in our research who were both from similar cultural backgrounds and were also highly consistent in membership style characteristics. They both had multiply handicapped children with similar levels of adaptive behavior and who were the same age. Both parents were advised by professionals when their children were infants that their children would always be totally dependent and that they should immediately initiate institutional placement. Both parents rejected this advice. The major difference in these families is found in their ideological style related to the prognosis of total dependency. The first mother described the approach taken as follows:

> We didn't have help. If that's it [child is handicapped] that's it. . . . I waited on him hand and foot. I did everything for him because the doctors told us he couldn't do for himself. . . . At 2, I tried to potty train him, but the doctor said to forget it. I went into shock when I was informed he could go to school. That was when he was 15. During those years of caring for him, I didn't feel cooped up. I have always been a homebody. I was

> an only child and was used to being alone. . . . I am also very big on home. I wouldn't have wanted to work. To me, a wife is supposed to be at home.

This ideology is in sharp contrast to the second family's approach, as shared by the mother:

> I am a questioning person. When the doctor said I think you ought to institutionalize Rachel for the best interests of your other children, I considered it a stupid statement from an intelligent man. . . . We enrolled her at the Institute of Human Development. We liked it from the very first. For 9 years it was sometimes hectic and sometimes a lot of fun. We had 72 to 76 volunteers coming into our home every week giving Rachel therapy for 8 hours per day—three shifts of volunteers. I lined them up in four towns. All the volunteers were a good influence and were really great about coming. Our house was the information exchange—people even posted signs on our bulletin board when there was something they wanted to sell or needed to buy. There was always a lot going on. . . . The great thing for us was the institute's philosophy of hope. There is always something you can do to improve the situation.

It is interesting to speculate on the ideological impossibility of these two mothers trading places with each other in terms of responding to a handicapped child with similar needs and a similar prognosis. To be maximally successful, deinstitutionalization interventions must be consistent with the ideological values of families.

The family's ideology regarding quality of life is a relatively overlooked area in the research literature and in intervention models. Yet, the data from our interviews suggest that this is an incredibly important domain. A wide range of basic beliefs about the criteria that constitute quality of life were identified. These included maximum development, independence, happiness and contentment, security, absence of stigma through competence, and absence of stigma through protection. Deinstitutionalization and normalization are frequently referred to as ideologies, but they are more correctly viewed as strategies for implementing a core set of beliefs. More attention needs to be directed to core ideological values, because it is these values that are at the base of many parents' negative or positive reactions to deinstitutionalization. Is it legitimate to value happiness over development? An interesting case in point is the data provided by Edgerton and Bercovici (1976). From the perspective of their sample of retarded adults living in the community, "competence appeared to be less important than confidence, with independence less vital than a subjective sense of well-being" (p. 494). Should mentally retarded persons have the option not to value development and independence? Do parents have that right? Research directed to these questions has tremendous policy implications. Far more attention needs to be directed to the ideological criteria upon which policy is based.

Variations in Relationship Parameters

The area of relationship parameters includes considerations of the characteristics of individual and group members, power and hierarchy, role assignments, boundary definitions, and communication style. The interaction of individual and group characteristics can produce a range of family reactions on a conflict/harmony continuum. Farber (1962) and Fowle (1968) report a greater maladjustment for brothers and lesser maladjustment for sisters when institutionalization occurs.

The precise nature of the role parameters within the family contributing to this differential outcome has not been identified. Characteristics of the handicapped individual important to consider in evaluating family stress include the type and severity of the condition, sex, temperament, physical appearance, predictability versus unpredictability of problems, time and effort required, and acceptance/rejection by the extrafamilial subsystem (Fotheringham & Creal, 1974). Bristol (1979) found that the majority of variance in predicting family stress could be accounted for by specific characteristics of autistic children and their environments.

The sex of the handicapped member seems to evoke a complex reaction on the part of families. Farber (1962) found that parents were more stressed by retarded sons than daughters. He speculated that daughters could more easily be taught "normal" sex-role activities such as

domestic chores, while there was little chance that retarded sons could achieve the more externally directed sex-role expectations for boys, such as success in sports or school. For families whose ideological style incorporates both traditional sex-role stereotypes and an attitude that a handicapped child should be protected, the effect of the sex of the child is even greater. As one mother put it: "I'm really lucky Carol is a girl. If she were a boy she would want to be out on the street." More recent research (Dailey, 1979; Saxton, 1980) has shown that stereotypical images of "disability" and "femininity" often work together to encourage passivity, dependence, reclusiveness, childishness, and helplessness. Thus, although a family's traditional sex-role stereotypes might make it easier to keep a handicapped daughter at home, such perceptions might also make it more difficult for that daughter to achieve successful integration into the community. Such sex-role expectations have implications for interventions with families and in service programs.

Other individual characteristics of the handicapped person also have an impact on the amount of stress experienced by the family. It is the interaction of the characteristics of the handicapped member with those of the rest of the family that likely determines the amount of stress produced.

> Tom is an adolescent who has been classified as both mentally retarded and autistic. The pervasive characteristic of Tom's temperament is an incredibly intense need for routine and structure. He is bothered by the position of closet doors and curtains; things out of place, such as phone books, cartons of milk, toothbrushes, shoes, newpapers, magazines, etc.; the timing of meals; and any change in the daily schedule. Holidays and vacations produce a particularly high level of tension and stress. The four other members in Tom's family value change, flexibility, and spontaneity. Both of Tom's parents work; both his siblings are involved in numerous extracurricular activities. The pace of the family is active and vibrant. Tom is stressed by the active and flexible life-style of his family. Other family members are stressed by Tom's compulsiveness and rigidity.

In this family, stress would be greatly eliminated if other family members had more of

Tom's characteristics or if he had more of theirs. Some families whose temperament might be more similar to Tom's would likely not experience the same level of stress as Tom's natural family.

Also called into question by this example is the simplistic criticism of institutions on the grounds that they provide a routinized environment and the inaccurate, normative assumption that routinization is "bad." An issue for many families who are attempting to integrate their handicapped children into the home environment is the incorporation of interventions to increase home routine and structure so that their handicapped children can tolerate living in that environment. This element of structure and routine has a major impact on the role parameters of all family members. Thus, research into family stress should focus on the *interaction* of individual and group characteristics of the members in a family unit. Interventions then need to be tailored to these interactions.

The resolution of conflicts related to individual and group characteristics is tied into the system of power and hierarchy within families. In molding the individual personalities of a family into a single unit, negotiation, power struggles, game playing, and decision making are involved. Limited information is available on how these power struggles might best be resolved. One influential factor is the family hierarchy, which is defined by the relative power and authority assigned to various members. Typically, family hierarchies are age-graded, with the greatest power resting with the parents (Foster et al., 1981). In considering the place of the handicapped child in the family hierarchy, there is typically a revision of age roles within the sibling subsystem (Farber & Ryckman, 1965). Regardless of birth order, the severely handicapped member eventually becomes the "youngest" child in the family's social hierarchy. Farber and Ryckman (1965) and Trevino (1979) state that female children, usually the eldest female child, are often expected to take the role of substitute parent in helping with the current and future management of the handicapped sibling. Many examples of this sibling expectancy were found in

our interviews as expressed by a comment from an elder female sibling:

> Very early my role was to take care of George. I was to be responsible for George for the rest of life. . . . Mother told me I would be responsible when I was about in the sixth grade. She was fearful he would have to be institutionalized and she didn't want that. Then it was fine. I chose my career with George in mind. I didn't think I would get married, partly because of George. Now I think it is unfair for Mom to expect me to take most of the burden when there are six children in the family.

The implication of family power and hierarchical positions of all family members, particularly those of siblings, warrants much greater attention in research and intervention programs.

Closely related to hierarchical issues are the role assignments within the family. Role assignments involve task allocation among family members, allocation that ranges on a continuum from traditional to egalitarian. In traditional arrangements, families tend to divide the family tasks, with various members responsible for carrying out various functions. Egalitarian arrangements involve sharing tasks so that all members contribute to carrying out all functions. Time efficiency and sex roles influence role allocation decisions. For many mothers who work outside the home, the result can be the expectation of completing two jobs—paid employment and housework. The relationship of role allocation to the family's success with deinstitutionalization should be investigated in future research. An important strategy for intervention may be assisting families in allocating roles equitably.

Another major dimension of role parameters is the definition of boundaries in a family. Boundaries exist across and within each of the four subsystems of the family. Boundaries can be considered the rules that define who participates and how he or she participates in carrying out family functions (Minuchin, 1974). Two concepts from the family therapy literature, *enmeshment* and *disengagement,* are particularly helpful in analyzing families with handicapped members. *Enmeshment* refers to the blurring of boundaries so that relationships become too intensive and exclusive of the needs of other members. *Disengagement* refers to rigid boundaries that result in the handicapped member being in a peripheral position separate from other family members. Institutionalization is most likely to occur when boundaries become disengaged. The boundary definitions vary widely across families; these definitions also vary within families, as demonstrated by the following description of a sibling subsystem:

> There were two camps in our family. One part of the family was embarrassed over having a retarded sibling [disengagement] and one part wanted to make him their life's project with missionary zeal [enmeshment].

This example is also relevant to the final element of relationship parameters, communication style. When asked whether the family just described had discussed their different approaches to establishing a relationship with the handicapped member, the response was, "Oh, no; the family doesn't work that way." Based on our interview data, a frequent approach to communication is to avoid it. Although such lack of communication may be found in families generally, this was a consistent finding across all family subsystems, as evidenced by the following comments from family members of mentally retarded persons.

> *Father:*   We didn't talk to our son about the fact that he's retarded. I presume he has figured it out. He never asked questions.
>
> *Mother:*   I have more or less worked out my adjustment on my own. My husband isn't communicative.
>
> *Sister:*   My brother's wife asked me about the genetic implications of Rachel's handicap before they got married. She didn't want to bring it up with my brother. I told her that, as far as we know, it is not genetic. It was probably caused by an outside influence, maybe a flu shot. She was relieved.

Other families talked about styles of communication that they have found important. Openness in discussing feelings and humor were both identified as helpful approaches. One sister of a cerebral palsied man described her family's use of humor to encourage her brother:

> Sure there were periods when he got a little depressed, but it never really got bad. We had a tendency to kind of poke fun at him and maybe make a certain noise or movement [imitating his spasticity], and it would put a stop to his bad feelings.

This entire conceptual area of relationship parameters is potentially rich in intervention approaches. A distinguishing characteristic of institutional and home environments appears to be the quality of personal relationships. Intervention strategies, to enhance the quality of relationships and the positive outcomes of such relationships for all family members, should be a high priority for future development.

Summary

Structural variations result in an infinite array of family characteristics and needs. The heterogeneity of families involved in the deinstitutionalization of their family member introduces tremendous complexity into the process of formulating future policy, research, and intervention. Family structure, however, is but one of the three perspectives on families that are important to consider in a comprehensive family systems approach. The next section considers the perspective of family functions; it should be recognized from the outset that the structural characteristics of families partially determine how families perform their functions. The precise relationships between structural and functional variations of families is a vital area for future research.

FAMILY FUNCTIONS

On the basis of our review of the sociological literature and qualitative analyses of interview data, 10 family functions have been identified for inclusion in the family systems model. These functions are listed in Table 2. Each family member has needs in each of these functional areas. The family unit has responsibility in meeting both individual and group needs. In this section the responsibilities of families in carrying out these functions is described and a summary of some of the special needs of handicapped children and youth according to each of

Table 2. Family functions serving individual needs

1. Economic
   a. Generating income
   b. Paying bills and banking
   c. Earning or dispensing allowance
2. Physical Needs
   a. Food purchasing and preparation
   b. Clothing purchasing and preparation
   c. Health care and maintenance
   d. Safety and protection
   e. Household maintenance
3. Rest and Recuperation
   a. Individual and family-oriented recreation
   b. Setting aside demands
   c. Developing and enjoying hobbies
4. Socialization
   a. Interpersonal relationships
   b. Developing social skills
5. Ideology
   a. Basic beliefs and values
   b. Religion
6. Self-Definition
   a. Establishing self-identity and self-image
   b. Recognizing strengths and weaknesses
   c. Expressing emotions
7. Affectional
   a. Nurturing and love
   b. Companionship
   c. Sense of belonging
   d. Intimacy
8. Guidance
   a. Problem solving
   b. Advice and feedback
9. Educational
   a. Developmental milestones
   b. Academic achievement
   c. Parent involvement at school
   d. Cultural appreciation
10. Vocational
   a. Career choice
   b. Development of work ethic
   c. Support for career interests and problems

these 10 functions is offered. In addition, suggestions are made on future directions for policy, research, and intervention.

Economic

One function of the family is to serve as a unit of economic consumption and production (Leslie, 1979), providing economic security to its members and coordinating the allocation of resources. The cost of providing necessary services and supports for handicapped family members may exceed the family income, thus causing the family to institutionalize their child for financial reasons. Because of the trend of federal expenditures to be directed at substitute rather than supportive family care (Moroney, 1981), the economics of maintaining handicapped children and youth in the home can create stress for some families. Although systematic economic data on the cost of home care are unavailable, the additional financial costs of handicapped children, as contrasted with nonhandicapped children, have consistently been identified (Boggs, 1979; McAndrew, 1976; Moroney, 1981). From interviews conducted with the parents of 116 orthopaedically handicapped children, McAndrew (1976) reported that 29% of the parents indicated that a financial hardship had been created for the family due to the associated costs of the handicap. With the current cutback of federal and state services for handicapped persons, the costs of home care may substantially increase in the future. Data are unavailable, however, on the economic impact of different child needs (e.g., need for extensive medical intervention, prosthetic equipment, specialized child providers). This is an important area for further research.

At the same time that a handicapped child increases the consumptive demands on the family, another effect can be a decrease in the family's productive power. Boggs (1979) reports that despite the same socioeconomic status and level of education, families of mentally retarded children are less upwardly mobile than others. She explains this in terms of "opportunity costs" when parents have invested all their psychic resources and other energies into family adaptation rather than career achievement. An orthopaedically handicapped adult from our study described such "opportunity costs" and the personal impact they had on him:

My dad turned down a promotional opportunity in another city because the school system did not have mainstreaming. He believed I should be in a regular school. He was very upfront about why he turned down the promotion, and I felt badly about it. It wasn't a really bad guilt trip, but those feelings were there.

Another consideration is the likely obstruction of some mothers' entrance into the job market because of the excessive physical care needs of their handicapped child. Such blocked opportunity can have strong economic ramifications.

Thus, both the cost of needed services and supports and the losses in "opportunity costs" lead to the assumption that institutionalization is more likely to occur when families must devote more energy to earning a living, yet have no available community resources to provide emotional and physical support. A strong need exists to review existing family policy and formulate new policy that will provide economic benefits and incentives to families who maintain their handicapped children at home rather than place them in institutions.

Physical Needs

Handicapped children and youth vary greatly in the degree to which they are able to attend to their own physical care needs as they advance in age during the childhood years. A consistent finding in the literature, however, is that the majority of handicapped children place greater physical caregiving demands on their parents over a substantially longer period of time than do nonhandicapped children (Birenbaum, 1971; Fotheringham & Creal, 1974; McAndrew, 1976). The parents in McAndrew's study (1976) estimated that attending to the physical needs of their orthopaedically handicapped children required an average of 2 hours per day. Time estimates varied widely, including one estimate of 10 hours per day. The overall emotional, time, and energy demands on some families with a severely handicapped child are enormous.

Families from our study mentioned several adaptations they had made to carry out what an outsider would view as extraordinary caregiving requirements. One adaptation was to establish a set routine of caregiving. In several families, the routine involved having an established time and a designated person to attend to bathing, toileting, dressing, and feeding needs. A couple of families continued to perform this routine for their late-adolescent children. They

gave every indication that they had incorporated this schedule into their family routine to the point that it had become a way of life, and they did not view it as a major source of stress. It is conjectured that for such families stress would be created by the introduction of home intervention programs to teach their severely handicapped children to be more independent in self-care skills. Such intervention would interrupt the family rhythms, create a need for a greater time investment of the parents, and once again pose the threat of failure for their children. As one sibling stated:

> My brother was always pampered by Mom, and I always thought she should allow him to do more for himself. But, when he came to live with me for a year, I realized I was not helping his independence either. I learned that it was easier and quicker to do things for him than to let him do for himself.

Another aspect of physical care is attending to housekeeping responsibilities. The presence of handicapped members can influence the family's responsibilities in this area in several ways: the delayed development of the handicapped member can create increased household maintenance responsibilities (e.g., washing wet sheets of adolescent or adult handicapped member); the time required to attend to the needs of the handicapped member can reduce the time to attend to the house; the extra costs of providing for the handicapped member can reduce the availability of money to purchase household assistance; and some handicapped individuals are not able to carry out chores consistent with the contributions of other family members that help with household maintenance. The inability of handicapped family members to assume responsibility for chores has implications for the family's role parameters, in that the handicapped member may possibly be given a reduced position in the family hierarchy. Time and stress management are major intervention needs for parents both in attending to the physical care demands of their children and in teaching their children to assume some of these responsibilities for themselves.

Rest and Recuperation

Caplan (1976) suggests that in a successfully functioning family, home is a place where family members can "let their hair down" and set aside the pressures and stresses of job and school. Recreation and the development of leisure time activities and hobbies are important aspects of this function.

Such rest and recuperation has been reported to be a major problem and source of stress in some families with handicapped children. Based on a survey of 400 families, Dunlap and Hollinsworth (1977) reported a preponderance of problems in this area (e.g., lack of trips, vacations, shopping, and going to movies). Thirty percent of the respondents in McAndrew's study (1976) reported restrictions on the number of their outings. Our interview results revealed these same trends. The parent of a 19-year-old mentally retarded son described their situation: "We haven't gone on a vacation since our honeymoon. It wouldn't be a vacation if we took our son." Furthermore, this middle class suburban family had never taken their son to a restaurant or a movie. Another family, however, who had a handicapped adolescent of a similar age and level of severity, frequently took their daughter on family outings.

Several factors seemed to influence a family's ability to initiate recreational activities in spite of the extra hassles involved. One factor was the family's own enjoyment of recreation. Some parents did not enjoy recreation themselves. As stated by one mother: "I'd rather stay home and cook than get dressed up and go out." A second factor is the ability of the parents to tolerate stress. Stress may be introduced by the unpredictability of the child's behavior in public, the stares of passersby, the extra energy required to transport appliances and equipment, and the extra time needed to plan an outing so that adequate support and structure can be provided for the child. When additional arrangements are necessary, it is understandable why the fun is taken out of recreational activities for some parents. A third factor is the availability of respite care services and the parents' comfort in using these services. Parents of handicapped children and youth, like other parents, need time away from home to pursue outside interests. The availability of respite care services may be a deciding factor for some families in making the decision to deinstitutionalize their handicapped child. Respite services, however, have been reported by Bruininks, Morreau, and Williams (1979) to be minimally available. Each of these factors related to recreational activities dictate the need for alternative intervention approaches depending upon the individualized needs of each family.

Socialization

The family has been identified as a key agent for the socialization of its members (Caplan, 1976; Leslie, 1979) and for instruction in socially desirable behavior (Schield, 1976). Interactions within the extrafamilial subsystem can provide opportunities for handicapped persons to develop interpersonal relationships.

Proponents of normalization and deinstitutionalization cite the importance of community placement as providing opportunities for handicapped persons to interact with nonhandicapped friends and neighbors (Center on Human Policy, 1979). Although this rationale sounds positive in theory, families can be faced with major obstacles in attempting to provide positive, social encounters for their handicapped children. McAndrew (1976) reported that 75% of the parents in her study had been "considerably disturbed" by behaviors such as people pointing and staring, tactless questions and comments, inappropriate pity, and being treated like an outcast. It is interesting to note that family ideology enters into this issue. Some of the family members in our interview study reported that they were not bothered by staring as illustrated in the following comment:

> Staring doesn't bother me. I don't care what other people think. I have always been rebellious. I only care about the reactions of people who I care about.

An important area of intervention is that of preparing parents and handicapped persons to handle public insensitivity constructively.

One could interpret the normalization principle to represent the placement of a higher value on the development of social interactions between handicapped children and youth and their nonhandicapped peers, as contrasted with exclusive contact with other handicapped children. As with all other functions, individual preferences of handicapped persons and their families should be considered.

Documentation exists that handicapped children and youth have reduced peer involvement, particularly with normal children (Fotheringham & Creal, 1974; Minde, Hackett, Killou, & Silver, 1972). In addition, Birenbaum and Re (1979) found that the socialization of mentally retarded adults in a group setting primarily revolved around the sheltered workshop. In time allocation outside the workshop, 83% of the residents settled into a routine of home recreation (e.g., television, records), attending to maintenance of their rooms, and engaging in personal hygiene. Their social contact with people outside the workshop and group was extremely limited, as was their involvement in community resources and activities.

When the peer contacts of handicapped persons are reduced, more demands are made on family members for social interaction and entertainment. In order to enhance socialization, family members may have to assume a high degree of responsibility for helping other people feel comfortable. The perspective of an adult sibling of a severely handicapped individual illustrates this point:

> I am more conscious of my sister's disability now than when I was younger. When some friend of mine is going to meet the family, I wonder how I should go about explaining the situation to them. Should I tell them beforehand or just be casual? I am never really sure.

Assuming the role of the handicapped individual's "socialization agent" may pay dividends in the long run; however, it is likely to increase stress for some family members in the short run.

Personal relationships can add enrichment, support, and joy to one's life. Evidence suggests that many handicapped children and youth are socially isolated. Interventions aimed at assisting parents and other service providers in enhancing the social integration of handicapped persons in neighborhoods, schools, and community settings need to be developed.

Ideology

The family is a vehicle for translating basic beliefs, values, and attitudes that shape an individual's understanding of life. For many families, religion is involved in this function by defining and strengthening ultimate values and beliefs.

As discussed in the previous section on family structure, the family's ideology plays a critical role in shaping their styles of problem solving and adjustment to their child's handicap. Gallagher (1979) studied a sample of "successful" and "average" parents of young handicapped children. His results indicated that the successful mothers had strong value systems enabling them to cope with crises and to maintain a positive perspective on life. Considering the important role of ideology, it is surprising that this topic has been given such scant attention in the literature. One interpretation of this gap is that professional emphasis on behavioral interventions has almost totally overshadowed the need to intervene concomitantly with families in helping them explore and clarify their core beliefs and personal philosophies.

In analyzing our interview data, a major ideological function of families was strikingly apparent—the development of a set of beliefs that helped families adjust to their child's handicap and turn what could be a very negative situation into a positive one. The values that were identified by family members as important in this regard included:

> "learning to love"
> "keeping a firm resolve"
> "looking past a lot to look inside"
> "finding strength from religion"
> "being more accepting of differences"

"taking a day at a time"
"being more patient"
"not taking life so seriously"
"being grateful for what we have"
"being able to be friends with the little person no one else wants to be friends with"

Interestingly, when we asked parents and siblings about the positive contributions their handicapped family member had made to them, these same values were mentioned. Essentially, the situation can be likened to the concept of supply and demand. Living with a handicapped child "demands" that the parents develop particular values that can serve as coping strategies. Parents and siblings are "supplied" these values through personal growth as they learn to come to grips with their family member's handicap. As one sibling of a mentally retarded adult said:

> She [my sister] is constantly teaching me things. Two things she has taught me are, to have more patience—accept people where they are at—and not to take life so seriously.

Every person we interviewed emphasized the important contribution their handicapped family member had made to the strengthening of their values; however, none mentioned the availability of counseling or support groups that helped them work through this process. The development of interventions based on values exploration and clarification is a promising area for future research and intervention.

The important role that religion plays in the lives of many parents suggests that churches can be valuable resources in providing ideological counseling and experiences for integration of handicapped children into church school programs. Churches, however, were reported to represent further barriers to integration because of architectual and programmatic features. Such barriers created stress for parents when they wanted to participate in church activities, yet the church had no programs to accommodate the needs of their children. Churches, as a support system for families with handicapped children and youth, may be one of the most underutilized intervention services. Research and development on the church's role in family support needs to be undertaken.

Self-Definition

A function of the family is to help members establish self-identity and a feeling of self-worth (Caplan, 1976). Self-definition is shaped through parental expectations and communication.

Establishing high expectations for a handicapped child can create stress for parents, since risk of failure is inherent; however, such expectations can lead to positive outcomes. Limited research has been devoted to this area of family intervention; again, its expressive rather than instrumental nature may have caused some professionals to discount its importance. An orthopaedically handicapped adult (quadriplegic amputee) described in our interview study how his father influenced his self-definition (his mother died when he was 1 year old):

> Dad talked about my disability a lot. I had a good self-image from the beginning. When I was 4 years old, I remember running up and down the block [using prostheses] in a cowboy outfit, boots, and all. There wasn't anything unique about me at all. When kids would tease me, I would come home crying and tell Dad what they said. His response was always that it was their problem and then he would go through a logical explanation.

This philosophy carried over to the nonhandicapped sibling in this family:

> People would ask me, "What's with your brother?" I couldn't relate to the question. I would say something like, "He has a cold." . . . Daddy as a parent had a controlling hand in not allowing us to see our brother as any different.

In other families, especially those with a mentally retarded member, the establishment of a clear self-definition is a difficult thing to accomplish. One family we interviewed expressed ambiguity about their nonverbal daughter's awareness of her retardation:

> Sometimes I think Carol understands she is different—she goes out of the room when we are talking about retarded people—and I think she is a little troubled by it.

Carol's sister also mentioned the ambiguity:

> I don't think Carol is aware of her disability. This is good because the borderline people are so sad.

But people do laugh and stare out in public. . . . I get angry if Carol notices it. She is very proud of her clothes and she doesn't understand why anyone would think she is different.

The parents' ideological style is a likely determinant of their ability to influence positively the self-definition of their handicapped child. The parents' positive view of the child is a precursor to translating these beliefs to the child. An unanticipated finding from our research is a coping strategy used by almost every family related to how they viewed their handicapped child. Parents consistently expressed their gratefulness that their handicapped child had the particular characteristics that he or she had. This comment was made by a mother of a nonambulatory adolescent:

> I'll take my own problem. I would not want to chase a kid around. We never had to pay for dancing lessons or Brownie uniforms. We never had to worry about her wearing out shoes.

This theme is also articulated by the mother of a moderately retarded adult:

> We are lucky because Carol doesn't seem to worry about getting married . . . or other things she can't do. . . . She's too handicapped to be hurt by her limitations.

The father of a severely orthopaedically handicapped adult:

> I want you to know Sheila's mind is very sharp . . . she could beat her teacher at chess six weeks after she learned. . . .

The father of an orthopaedically handicapped adolescent:

> We're lucky Denise has been healthy—she's never been sickly. The only real expense has been the electric wheelchair—otherwise she's been no more expensive than any other child.

We have entitled this coping strategy "the grass is always browner on the other side." It is a perspective that warrants careful consideration in the development of intervention programs.

Communication is an important component of the self-definition function. McAndrew (1976) reported that a third of the parents she interviewed avoided their child's questions about their own handicap. In our study, a mildly mentally retarded young adult commented: "I don't really understand my handicap. I wish people would tell me more about it." Family members need intervention assistance in developing effective communication strategies related to self-definition to use within and across the four family subsystems.

Self-definition can also be a major issue for siblings of handicapped persons, particularly in cases of mild handicaps where nonhandicapped siblings have a tendency to identify more with their handicapped brother or sister than they might otherwise. (Grossman, 1972). Severe handicaps also have implications for the development of self-definition in siblings. A sibling in our interview study described the initial negative impact of her sister's deinstitutionalization on her own self-definition:

> When she started coming home—that was a big shock. I had fantisized about my sister and then she couldn't play when she was at home and she wasn't fitting in. I was real embarrassed having her around my friends . . . I'd say, "This is my sister, she is retarded," wanting to explain that over very quickly before someone would look at her and say what's wrong.

Another sibling implication is that parents may expect their nonhandicapped children to have increased achievement to compensate for the limitations of the handicapped child (Cleveland & Miller, 1977; Trevino, 1979).

Finally, maintaining positive self-identity can also be a major issue for parents in feeling shared stigma with their child (Goffman, 1963). Without question, responsibilities associated with the self-definition function pose tremendous challenges for families. The development of family intervention in this area represents a vital need.

Affectional

An important function of the family is providing nurturing and love, companionship, a sense of belonging, and intimacy. Perhaps the most unique role of the family, when compared to other residential providers, is their expected affectionate relationship with their handicapped child.

Attachment formation between parents and handicapped children has been found to frequently be delayed, distorted, and in some cases absent (Blacher-Dixon, 1981). Many of the variables that have been identified as related to attachment in nonhandicapped children may be problematic for handicapped children. Variables were categorized by Blacher-Dixon (1981) into four categories including: 1) child variables—e.g., social and motor capabilities (Green, Gustafson, & West, 1980); 2) parent variables—e.g., sensitive responsiveness (Ainsworth, 1973); 3) parent-child variables—e.g., communicative behaviors (Kaye & Fogel, 1980); and 4) environmental variables—e.g., stability of caregiving environment (Anderson, 1980). More research is needed on the relationship of variables in each of these categories to the initial and long-term development of affectional relationships among families with handicapped members.

Featherstone (1981), the parent of a severely handicapped child, has written an eloquent book entitled *A Difference in the Family*. In this book, she discusses the parents' fear over their ability to love their child, especially in the case of severe handicaps. Lavelle and Keogh (1980) suggest that society's rejection of handicapped children and youth can influence the parent's ability to love and care for the child. A key determinant of successful deinstitutionalization may be the reciprocal affectional bonds established between handicapped persons and their families. These affectional bonds can enhance the family's ability to cope with stress and can provide handicapped individuals with emotional security and a positive self-definition. A family in our study had particularly emphasized the functions of affection and ideology in rearing their mentally retarded son. When the retarded individual was asked to identify the major contribution the members of his family had made to his adult development, he commented: "My parents gave me love, happiness, and peace." This family had not put equal emphasis on the development of social, educational, and vocational competence.

An often overlooked implication of having a handicapped child in the family is an improvement in the family's ability to foster a sense of belonging and cohesiveness (Klein, 1972). Many of the families in our study emphasized this benefit as illustrated by the following comment:

> Rachel has always been one factor all family members agreed on. Everyone thinks she's great. The other kids thought she was cute and smart. . . . She's been good for her siblings. She's helped them have compassion for people who are different.

Families also spoke about the impact that their handicapped child had had on their own ability to give and receive love. A father of a severely mentally retarded son commented: "The positive thing for me from this whole experience has been learning to love." Research has focused far more heavily on preparing parents to be teachers of their children than on preparing them to be providers and recipients of affection. The expressive functions of families, such as in the area of affection, warrant significantly greater attention.

Guidance

Families have been described as a control group for their members in providing feedback on behavior and assistance with daily problems (Caplan, 1976). Another aspect of the guidance function is that of teaching codes of behavior that one is expected to demonstrate within and outside the family. One difficulty for families with handicapped members is unpredictability of the handicapped member's future development (Birenbaum, 1971). Many parents do not know what they can reasonably expect of their handicapped child as he or she moves through the life cycle. The unreliability of expectations can result in some parents expecting too much achievement or development and other parents expecting too little. One sibling noted that her father's expectations resulted in considerable frustration for her retarded brother:

> He expects too much . . . he gets angry when Joey can't tie his shoes, and that doesn't help at all . . . Joey just gets upset.

But on the other hand when expectations are too low the response turns to overprotection:

My parents are always stressing that I shouldn't let people put a bunch of garbage in my head about the possibility of ever walking and so forth . . . I just have to keep on fighting. . . .

Family members need assistance in defining realistic expectations so that they, in turn, can walk the delicate balance between frustrating their child and overprotecting him or her, as they execute their guidance function.

Many families in our interviews expressed frustration over not knowing what degree of development to expect from their handicapped child in the future. This problem appeared to be exaggerated in families in which the handicapped member did not have language. In such cases, the family was cut off from many of their child's feelings and perspectives. Thus, family members did not have the benefit of being guided by the reactions and insights of the handicapped individual. As families described this void, it became increasingly apparent that guidance is stunted when the handicapped member is unable to engage in a reciprocal, interactive dialogue. One family pursued an effective intervention by developing a friendship with a handicapped adult who had a handicap of a similar type, but to a milder degree, as their daughter's. From this friend, the family reported that they gained considerable firsthand insight into what it is like to be a handicapped person. For example, their friend suggested to them that their daughter may not want to live with them for the rest of her life. The parents commented that they were able to accept this idea for the first time in their lives without defensiveness, because it came from another handicapped person rather than a relative or professional. An important area for research is the impact on family members and handicapped children and youth of mentors who are handicapped. The literature is replete with research and interventions based on the tutoring of handicapped children by their non-handicapped peers. Yet, it is conjectured that handicapped individuals can be tremendous guidance resources for parents, siblings, and handicapped children.

Another important point related to the family's role in the provision of guidance is the strong influence of each member's ideology. The basic beliefs of the family form the core for the provision of advice and feedback. One mentally retarded adult described the guidance provided to him by his parents:

> My parents taught me how to love people; not to get mad so easily; not to smoke and drink; to go out into the world and be kind and considerate to other people, and be a gentleman.

A severely cerebral palsied man described his parents as teaching him:

> to be honest, or try to, obey laws, pray, basically to be a good citizen . . . and to be myself. They basically provided support by encouraging me to do things and to not be ashamed if I failed.

Educational

As compared to other functions, the function of parents as teachers of their handicapped children has received greatest emphasis in the research and intervention literature (Baker, Heifetz, & Murphy, 1980; Karnes & Teska, 1980; Tjossem, 1976). Indeed, the belief in the importance of this function has pervaded national policy in early childhood intervention programs (Harvey, 1977) and in PL 94-142 (Turnbull & Turnbull, 1982; Turnbull, Turnbull, & Wheat, 1982) in the dual expectations that parents can advance skills development by working with their children at home and in holding schools accountable for the development of appropriate educational programs.

Although documentation exists for advances in child outcomes when parents assume the role of teacher at home (Boyd, 1980; Bricker & Bricker, 1976), some caution against overemphasizing this family function is in order. In research conducted with mothers of preschool handicapped children, Winton and Turnbull (1981) reported that 65% of the mothers expressed the need to turn their child's education over to competent professionals so that they could take a break from the educational problems and demands of their handicapped children. Moreover, the time and stress involved in being an active educational decision maker in holding the school system accountable is a responsibility that is gladly accepted by some parents and rejected by others. Extensive reviews of the literature on parent perspectives in this regard are provided elsewhere (Turnbull, 1983; Turnbull & Turnbull, 1982). A clear trend in this literature is the range of individual preferences of parents on the nature and degree of carrying out the family function of education. This trend was also evident in our interviews. One father expressed the point of view that his major job was to find a school that would accept his son after he was expelled from a parochial school. Another father described how he worked intensively with his son every evening to teach him motor and self-help skills. Another family's belief in the importance of their function in providing their mentally retarded daughter with an education led to their decision to institutionalize her:

> We believed the only thing of value we actually owed them [our children] was an education—we weren't worried about passing on money. But when Karin was young there was nothing available in the community. I have a lot of guilt involved—it's a hard thing to put into action— sending your child away to an institution for an education, even though we knew we were doing the right thing.

Often the assumption is made that parents institutionalize their handicapped children to be relieved of caregiving burdens; however, families often resort to institutionalization with the children's best interest in mind.

An unintended consequence of placing too much emphasis on the education function can be to overlook other important expressive functions of the family such as affection and self-definition. Tyler and Kogan (1977) reported on a significant decrease in warm and positive behaviors between mothers and orthopaedically handicapped children when the mother was involved in structured therapy sessions with the child. This point is clarified by Diamond (1981), a psychologist who is also orthopaedically handicapped. She shared insights on her own reaction to her parents' emphasis on therapeutic training at home:

> Something happens in a parent when relating to his disabled child; he forgets that they're a kid first. I used to think about that a lot when I was a kid. I would be off in a euphoric state, drawing or coloring or cutting out paper dolls, and as often as not the activity would be turned into an occupational therapy session. "You're not holding the scissors right," "Sit up straight so your curvature doesn't get worse." That era was ended when I finally let loose a long and exhaustive tirade. "I'm just a kid! You can't therapize me all the time! I get enough therapy in school every day! I don't think about my handicap all the time like you do" (p. 30).

In light of the strong expectation that parents assume an educational role, a worthwhile research study would be to investigate whether an increased emphasis on the function of education results in a decreased emphasis on other family functions. Both the positive and negative outcomes of parents as educators need to be documented and taken into account in planning intervention programs.

Vocational

Another valuable function of the family is the development of a work ethic in family members and assistance in a career choice. For families with handicapped members, this function takes on increased importance in light of the fact that employment services for handicapped persons have been reported to be inadequate (Bruininks, 1979).

Emphasis on vocational development is likely influenced by life cycle considerations. As discussed in the next section on life cycle, a major source of stress for families with handicapped children and youth is planning for the future (Birenbaum, 1971; Minde et al., 1972). Many families employ a coping strategy of maintaining a present rather than a future orientation to minimize this stress. Although a present orientation may reduce stress in the short range, it can increase long-term stress by postponing the development of vocational skills. Birenbaum (1971) reported that parents of handicapped youth and young adults rarely teach skills as their family member advances through the life cycle. An implication of this finding is that interventions are needed that can assist families in planning for the vocational development of their handicapped child during the developmental period.

One strategy for vocational training that can result in long-range time efficiency for the family is teaching handicapped children and youth to participate in household maintenance chores. A greater short-range time investment, however, will be needed on the part of parents to teach these skills to their children and to allow sufficient time for task completion. Our interviews revealed that a significant vocational contribution that some handicapped adults make to their families is companionship for elderly members. This point was made by an 81-year-old mother of a retarded adult when asked how she has benefited by her daughter: "I haven't been alone. I have friends who are widows and who are lonesome, but I have Carol." In such cases, the companionship of the handicapped member prevents the family from having, for example, to purchase live-in assistance or place the elderly member in a nursing home. An inherent conflict can occur when a handicapped adult's residence with an elderly family member results in the handicapped adult living in a more restrictive setting than necessary, despite the concomitant effect of maintaining the elderly family member in the least restrictive setting of the home.

Summary

A review of the 10 family functions clearly suggests that deinstitutionalization poses tremendous responsibilities for families. It must also be recognized that the health development of the handicapped family member is only one of the numerous other responsibilities that the family must concurrently assume. When these family responsibilities are combined with the work demands of the parents, it is strikingly clear that a challenge for families is the development of sufficient time and stress management skills so they can execute these functions in an efficient, systematic, and relaxed manner.

Just as family functions are highly influenced by the particular structural characteristics of families, functions are also intricately related to life cycle factors. A life cycle perspective of families with handicapped members is the third component of the family systems model. It is within this developmental cycle that priority is assigned to different family functions.

FAMILY LIFE CYCLE

The concept of family life cycle represents the collective process of evolution and change as individual family members move through various life stages. Eight stages of family development were originally suggested by Duvall in 1957. Since that time, family life cycle has been characterized in a variety of ways, including being expanded to encompass as many as 24 separate time frames (Rodgers, 1960). Typically, the sociological literature describes the eight stages listed in Table 3 (Carter & McGoldrick, 1980).

Applying the concept of family life cycle to research and intervention on the deinstitutionalization of handicapped children and youth is useful in two ways. First, it clarifies the divergent characteristics, needs, and functional emphases of families at various points in the life cycle. Second, it creates awareness of the sources of stress that occur in families as they move (or fail to move) through life cycle

Table 3. Developmental stages in family life cycle

1. Unattached Adult—accepting parent/offspring separation
2. Marriage—commitment to a new system and realignment of relationship with extended families and friends to include spouse
3. Birth of children—accepting new members into system; taking on parental roles
4. Children enter school—shifting parent/child relationship to permit the young child to gain extrafamily influence
5. Children enter adolescence—increasing flexibility of family boundaries to include children's independence
6. Children launched into adulthood—accepting exits and entries into the family system; renegotiation of marital subsystem
7. Retirement and old age—accepting the shift in generational roles
8. Death—dealing with loss of significant others; life review and integration

transitions. Family structure and functions undoubtedly influence both the needs of families during various developmental stages and the sources of stress arising during stage transitions. But family life cycle is another set of variables that must be considered in family research and intervention. Hill (1970) notes that "any researcher or clinician who seeks to generalize about families without taking into account variations resulting from the stage of development will encounter tremendous variance for which [he or she] will not be able to account" (p. 190).

Developmental Stages

Handicapped children and youth initially have an impact on the family life cycle at the time of birth. Particularly in the case of severe handicaps, this impact continues to influence the family life cycle in substantial ways even after the death of the parents (assuming a normal life span of the handicapped member). Based primarily on our interview data, examples of various needs of families at six of the eight life cycle stages are included in the following list:

Birth of children: Obtaining an accurate diagnosis, making initial emotional adjustments, informing siblings and the extrafamilial system, locating services, asking "ultimate" questions, clarifying a personal ideology to guide decision making, seeking to find meaning in the handicap, establishing new relationship parameters within the family, identifying priority family functions, establishing routines to carry out family functions

Children enter school: Adjusting emotionally to educational implications of the handicap, learning about educational options, clarifying personal ideology on mainstreamed versus specialized placements, learning about educational rights, participating in individualized education program (IEP) conferences, dealing with the reactions of the peer group, locating community resources, arranging for extracurricular activities, helping child identify personal strengths and weaknesses

Children enter adolescence: Adjusting emotionally to chronicity of the handicapping condition, helping youth understand physical and emotional changes associated with puberty, dealing with peer isolation and rejection, planning alternatives for expressing sexuality, clarifying personal ideology on independence, planning for vocational development, developing leisure time interests

Children launched into adulthood: Adjusting emotionally to the adult implications of the handicap, deciding upon an appropriate residence, establishing new relationship parameters, initiating vocational involvement, dealing with issues of sexuality, dealing with issues of marriage and childbearing, recognizing needs for continuing family responsibility, dealing with continued financial implications of dependency, encouraging socialization outside the family

Retirement and old age: Planning for care or supervision of the handicapped member after death, allocating family resources to secure the financial future of the handicapped member, clarifying personal ideology on the need for "permanent" (e.g., institution) versus "quasi-permanent" (e.g., group home) residences, transferring parental responsibilities to other family subsystems and/or service providers

Death: Dependent needs of handicapped family members are assumed by siblings, extended family, and/or service providers

The bulk of family research and intervention has focused rather narrowly on the developmental stages associated with the birth of the child and school entry. Further, the literature on emotional adjustment to handicapped children has implied an adjustment process both initiated and completed in the stage following the birth of the child (Wolfensberger, 1970). From our interviews it was strongly apparent that each life cycle stage requires new emotional adjustments on the part of family members. The impact of handicapped individuals on the family is chronic; thus, deinstitutionalization has lifelong implications for the family.

Stage Transitions

The stages of the family life cycle can be visualized as a series of relatively level plateaus, separated by transitional events that move the family to a new stage. The plateau periods represent periods of relative stability and low stress (Terkelsen, 1980). During plateau periods, many families establish a routine for attending to their functions. Just as routine characterizes plateau periods, change characterizes stage transitions. The nature of change at each transition varies according to the particular life cycle stage. Handicapped children and youth frequently experience the same transitional stresses as nonhandicapped peers; in some cases, however, the intensity of the stress may be greater. An orthopaedically handicapped male from our study commented:

> When I reached puberty it was the first time my disability really became a problem. The sexual scene was difficult. I didn't date and was frustrated by that. My date to the junior prom was the only other disabled person at another school. It was hard to be put in that class.

In this case, entering adolescence is a stressful event for everyone. The presence of a disability increased the natural stresses that one would anticipate. Such intensification of stress has implications, not only for the handicapped member but also for other family members. Neugarten (1976) emphasizes that stress is increased when normal life cycle events occur ''off-time''; consequently, the normal sequence and rhythm of life is disrupted. Thus, for many families with handicapped members, it is the delay or lack of transitions rather than the transitions themselves that create the most stress. Numerous examples of such delays were identified throughout interviews as illustrated by the following comment from the mother of a 19-year-old:

> Karl went to school for the first time when he was 15. That's when he learned to feed himself. Wetting is the most frustrating problem right now. Some days I want to give up and other times it goes well. In the morning, we do terrific. In the afternoons, he doesn't want to be bothered.

The readiness for transitions appears to be a crucial variable in the creation of stress. In some cases, parents are ready for their handicapped family member to move into the next life cycle stage; however, the handicapped member is not developmentally competent to do so, or is not motivated to break daily routines. The opposite situation also occurs when handicapped family members are eager to make transitions, and the parents hold back. An example of such a situation was provided by an orthopaedically handicapped adolescent who went away to college:

> I think they want me at home, but I just could not take it—there are things I want to do but they didn't want me to do them. My dad told me it's very hard to let go because he worries about me. I'm their only child and I'm handicapped.

Many factors contribute to delayed transition that are beyond the control of handicapped persons and their families. In some cases, however, such transitions may appear so stressful to the family that they solidify their routines established during plateau periods and actively avoid disruptions. A characteristic of almost every family in our study was a pronounced difficulty in planning for the future. This finding is consistent with literature suggesting a strong present rather than future orientation for families with handicapped members (Birenbaum, 1971; McAndrew, 1976; Minde et al., 1972). Comments from parents illustrate this stress:

> *Father of a 19-year-old:* I haven't really thought about my son's future in the last 6 months. I have a new job and I'm bushed when I get home. We've never spent much time discussing the future. We didn't think we had options.

> *Mother of a 17-year-old:* Parents of handicapped children have the right to live life one day at a time.

> *Mother of a 10-year-old:* With an autistic kid you just don't have time to think about the future. One minute things are fine, the next minute all hell breaks loose. . . . You don't live one day at a time. . . . It's more like one hour at a time. . . .

> *Father of a 22-year-old:* We have no [financial] trusts for Denise—mainly because of my lack of faith in investments and the business community. We say we should plan for economic security, but we don't.

Future planning is difficult for families for a variety of reasons. The family's ideological style and relationship parameters are most likely strong determinants of their ability to plan for the future in a systematic manner. Regarding ideological style, families who value security and protection will likely resist stage transitions. Many aspects of relationship parameters can also be influential, such as the degree of enmeshed versus disengaged boundaries of the various subsystems. Other factors in influencing future planning include the family's awareness of program options and their understanding of the adaptive behavior levels and needs of their handicapped family member. Future predictions are extremely difficult to make. This point was emphasized by Edgerton and Bercovici (1976) in interpreting the unreliable future predictions made several years earlier for the mentally retarded adults comprising their longitudinal research sample.

Because stage transitions and future planning are stressful, catalysts for change may be necessary in helping families move to a new stage. Numerous catalysts were mentioned in our interviews, including services (e.g., availability of sheltered workshop), equipment (e.g., purchase of new wheelchair), professionals (e.g., vocational instructors, group home parents), extended family members (e.g., brother-in-law), and friends (e.g., handicapped adult serving as mentor). Catalysts for change can essentially be thought of as outside energizers that can penetrate family routine to the point that change can occur. Thus, the initial introduction of the catylsts can be extremely stressful. For example, in one family we interviewed, a major change—the daughter's acquisition of a motorized wheelchair and her involvement with an independent living center—caused considerable stress in the family:

Handicapped adult: Good times are just starting for me [because] a year ago I got my chair. . . . Grandma threw a fit [about the wheelchair] . . . she's afraid I'll be hurt . . . she wants me to be her little girl. . . .

Sister: I think Grandma doesn't like it because she's been taking care of Sheila all these years and now she feels unappreciated. . . .

Father: We think Sheila has dreams that are unrealistic. . . .

Handicapped adult: But I just have to keep on fighting.

A major intervention goal with families is often to alleviate stress; however, the value of manageable levels of stress should be recognized. It is the presence of stress and disruption of routine that frequently lead to life cycle progression.

Stress management interventions aimed at stage transitions should be a high priority for intervention development. An important component for stress management is that of developing skill in forecasting and planning for the future. A related coping strategy needed by many families is the ability to tolerate uncertainty, ambiguity, and change.

Summary

Developmental stages and transitions have tremendous influences on the family's ability to maintain their handicapped member in home and community settings. Research and intervention efforts need to be directed to a full life cycle perspective. A major life cycle issue warranting systematic inquiry is family burnout. What are the variables contributing to family burnout and how can the negative impact of these variables be minimized?

DEVELOPING A FAMILY SYSTEMS POLICY AGENDA

The multiple subsystems of families—spouse, parental, sibling, and extra-familial—are all affected by the decision to deinstitutionalize a handicapped member. Successful family adaptation involves placing equal value on the well-being of every family member. The right to live in the least restrictive environment should apply to family members as well as handicapped individuals. Thus, the concept of least restriction should be considered in light of the needs of each family member. Placing many severely handicapped children and youth in the least restrictive environment of their families results in their family being required to live in a highly restricted manner. A total family perspective is thus necessary in planning for successful deinstitutionalization. A systematic analysis of current deinstitutionalization policies needs to be conducted to explicate the effects of these policies on each of the family subsystems. The development of future policy should take into account family needs, in addition to the specific needs of handicapped individuals. A supportive, well-adjusted family may be the most important factor in helping handicapped people live the most independent life possible.

The tremendous heterogeneity of the structural characteristics of families has vast implications for deinstitutionalization policy. The major implication is the need to formulate policy based on the criterion of choice. Because of the wide array of differences among families, equity can only be achieved when policy allows families options and alternatives based on their individual needs (Schodek, Liffiton-Chrostowski, Adams, Minihan, & Yamaguchi, 1980). An example of flexible family policy is the provision of service vouchers to families who maintain their handicapped member in the home or community. Such vouchers would entitle families to the purchase of services they need and prefer based on their structural composition (e.g., ideological beliefs, role allocation within the family), needs for assistance in carrying out particular family functions, and current life cycle stage.

Another policy implication is the need to offer supportive rather than substitute assistance to families (Moroney, 1981). In developing policy aimed toward family support, services should be available to assist families in carrying out the 10 previously described functions. Families can benefit from intervention assistance to identify the priority functions for which they will assume responsibility in light of their strengths, time availability, energy, and preferences. Community services are needed for the functions families cannot carry out on their own. The criterion of choice is a paramount issue, since each family has unique capabilities and gaps in meeting functional responsibilities.

It is likely that fear of the future and the concomitant need to make assumptions lead many families to decisions for institutionalization. Families should be provided with reasonable assurance of the availability of permanent community support; such assurance can only result from federal and state policy.

Finally, it should be recognized in family policy that placement of handicapped family members in the natural parental home is not always in the best interest of the handicapped individual and/or other family members. Again, the interests of all family members and the healthy functioning of all family subsystems must be considered. Provisions for a continuum of residential options should be addressed through policy development. This continuum should include the following options: natural parental family, foster family, adoptive family, group home, community-based care facility, and institutional placements. Families need a range of alternatives from which to choose the most appropriate placement for their handicapped member in consideration of the needs of all family members.

Just as handicapped individuals are entitled to normalization, so, too, are their families. A family systems approach to deinstitutionalization policy, research, and intervention can help ensure that the reality is equal to the promise.

REFERENCES

Ainsworth, M.D.S. The development of infant-mother attachment. In: B.M. Caldwell & H.N. Ricciuti (eds.), *Review of child development research,* Vol. 3. Chicago: University of Chicago Press, 1973.

Anderson, C.W. Attachment in daily separations: Reconceptualizing day care and maternal employment issues. *Child Development,* 1980, *51,* 242–245.

Aronoff, J., & Crano, W. A re-examination of the cross-cultural principles of task segregation and sex role differentiation in the family. *American Sociological Review,* 1975, *40,* 12–20.

Baker, B.L., Heifetz, L.J., & Murphy, D.M. Behavioral training for parents of mentally retarded children: One-year follow-up. *American Journal of Mental Deficiency,* 1980, *85*(1), 31–38.

Birenbaum, A. The mentally retarded child in the home and the family cycle. *Journal of Health and Social Behavior,* 1971, *12,* 55–65.

Birenbaum, A., & Re, M.A. Resettling mentally retarded adults in the community—Almost four years later. *American Journal of Mental Deficiency,* 1979, *83*(4), 323–329.

Blacher-Dixon, J. *Mother-child attachment in the severely handicapped.* Paper presented at the American Psychological Association 89th Annual Convention, Los Angeles, August, 1981.

Boggs, E.M. Allocation of resources for family care. In: R.H. Bruininks & G.C. Krantz (eds.), *Family care of developmentally disabled members: Conference proceedings.* Minneapolis: University of Minnesota, 1979.

Bossard, J.H.S., & Ball, E.S. *The large family system.* Philadelphia: University of Pennsylvania Press, 1956.

Boyd, R.D. Systematic parent training through a home based model. *Exceptional Children,* 1980, *45*(8), 647–650.

Bricker, W.A., & Bricker, D. The infant, toddler, and preschool research and intervention project. In: T.D. Tjossem (ed.), *Intervention strategies for high risk infants and young children.* Baltimore: University Park Press, 1976.

Bristol, M.M. *Maternal coping with autistic children: The effect of child characteristics and interpersonal support.* Unpublished doctoral dissertation, University of North Carolina, Chapel Hill, 1979.

Bruininks, R.H. The needs of families. In: R.H. Bruininks & G.C. Krantz (eds.), *Family care of developmentally disabled members: Conference proceedings.* Minneapolis: University of Minnesota, 1979.

Bruininks, R.H., Morreau, L.E., & Williams, S.M. *Issues and problems of deinstitutionalization in HEW Region V* (Project Report No. 2). Minneapolis: University of Minnesota, Information and Technical Assistance Project on Deinstitutionalization, 1979.

Caplan, G. The family as a support system. In: G. Caplan & M. Killilia (eds.), *Support systems and mutual help: Multidisciplinary explorations.* New York: Grune & Stratton, 1976.

Carter, E., & McGoldrick, M. The family life cycle and family therapy: An overview. In: E. Carter & M. McGoldrick (eds.), *The family life cycle: A framework for family therapy.* New York: Gardner Press, 1980.

Center on Human Policy. *The community imperative: The refutation of all arguments in support of institutionalizing anybody because of mental retardation.* Syracuse, NY: Center on Human Policy, 1979.

Cleveland, D.W., & Miller, N. Attitudes and life commitments of older siblings of mentally retarded adults: An exploratory study. *Mental Retardation,* 1977, *15*(3), 38–41.

Diamond, S. Growing up with parents of a handicapped child: A handicapped person's perspective. In: J.L. Paul (ed.), *Understanding and working with parents of children with special needs.* New York: Holt, Rinehart & Winston, 1981.

Dunlap, W.R., & Hollinsworth, J.S. How does a handicapped child affect the family? Implications for practitioners. *The Family Coordinator,* 1977, *26,* 286–293.

Duvall, E. *Marriage and family development* (5th ed.). Philadelphia: J.B. Lippincott, 1957.

Edgerton, R.B., & Bercovici, S.M. The cloak of competence: Years later. *American Journal of Mental Deficiency,* 1976, *80*(5), 485–497.

Farber, B. Effects of a severely mentally retarded child on the family. In: E.P. Trapp & P. Himeleston (eds.), *Readings on the Exceptional Child,* pp. 227–246. New York: Appleton-Century-Crofts, 1962.

Farber, B., & Ryckman, D. Effects of severely mentally retarded children on family relationships. *Mental Retardation Abstracts,* 1965, *2,* 1–17.

Featherstone, H. *A difference in the family.* New York: Basic Books, 1981.

Foster, M., Berger, M., & McLean, M. Rethinking a good idea: A reassessment of parent involvement. *Topics in Early Childhood Special Education,* 1981, *1*(3), 55–65.

Fotheringham, J., & Creal, D. Handicapped children and handicapped families. *International Review of Education,* 1974, *20*(3), 353–371.

Fowle, C.M. The effect of the severely mentally retarded child on his family. *American Journal of Mental Deficiency,* 1968, *73,* 468–473.

Gallagher, J.J. *Characteristics of successful parents of moderately/severely handicapped children.* Paper presented at the Handicapped Children's Early Education Conference, Washington, DC, December, 1979.

Gath, A. The impact of an abnormal child upon the parents. *British Journal of Psychiatry,* 1977, *130,* 405–410.

Goffman, E. *Stigma.* Englewood Cliffs, NJ: Prentice-Hall, 1963.

Green, J.A., Gustafson, G.E., & West, M. Effects of infant development on mother-infant interactions. *Child Development,* 1980, *51,* 199–207.

Grossman, F.K. *Brothers and sisters of retarded children: An exploratory study.* Syracuse, NY: Syracuse University Press, 1972.

Guba, E. Criteria for assessing the trustworthiness of naturalistic inquiries. *Educational Communication on Technology Journal,* 1981, *29,* 75–92.

Gumz, E.J., & Gubrium, J. Comparative parental perceptions of a mentally retarded child. *American Journal of Mental Deficiency,* 1972, *77,* 175–180.

Harvey, J. The enabling legislation: How did it all begin? In: J.B. Jordon, A.H. Hayden, M.B. Karnes, & M.M. Wood (eds.), *Early childhood education for exceptional children: A handbook of ideas and exemplary practices.* Reston, VA: Council for Exceptional Children, 1977.

Hill, R. *Family development in three generations.* Cambridge, MA: Schenkman, 1970.

Karnes, M.B., & Teska, J. Toward successful parent involvement in programs for handicapped children. In: J.J. Gallagher (ed.), *New directions for exceptional children: Parents and families of handicapped children,* Vol. 4. San Francisco: Jossey-Bass, 1980.

Kaye, K., & Fogel, A. The temporal structure of face-to-face communication between mothers and infants. *Developmental Psychology,* 1980, *16*(5), 454–464.

Klein, S. Brother to sister/sister to brother. *Exceptional Parent,* 1972, *3,* 1–3, 10–16, 24–27, 24–28.

Lavelle, N., & Keogh, B.K. Expectations and attributions of parents of handicapped children. In: J.J. Gallagher (ed.), *New directions for exceptional children: Parents and families of handicapped children,* Vol. 4. San Francisco: Jossey-Bass, 1980.

Leslie, G.R. *The family in social context* (4th ed.). New York: Oxford University Press, 1979.

Lieber, E.K. The professional woman: Coping in a two-career family. *Educational Horizons,* 1980, *58*(3), 156–161.

McAndrew, I. Children with a handicap and their families. *Child: Care, Health and Development,* 1976, *2,* 213–237.

Minde, K., Hackett, J.D., Killou, D., & Silver, S. How

they grow up: 41 physically handicapped children and their families. *American Journal of Psychiatry, 1972, 128,* 1554–1560.

Minuchin, S. *Families and family therapy.* Cambridge, MA: Harvard University Press, 1974.

Moroney, R.M. Public social policy: Impact on families with handicapped children. In: J.L. Paul (ed.), *Understanding and working with parents of children with special needs.* New York: Holt, Rinehart & Winston, 1981.

Neugarten, B. Adaptations and the life cycle. *Counseling Psychologist,* 1976, *6*(1), 16–20.

Parsons, T., & Bales, R.F. *Family, socialization and interaction process.* Glencoe, IL: Free Press, 1955.

Report on Preschool Education, 1982, 7, 14.

Rodgers, R. *Proposed modifications of Duvall's family life cycle stages.* Paper presented at the American Psychological Association meeting, New York, August, 1960.

Schield, S. The family of the retarded child. In: R. Koch & J.C. Dobson (eds.), *The mentally retarded child and his family: A multi-disciplinary handbook.* New York: Brunner/Mazel, 1976.

Schodek, K., Liffiton-Chrostowski, N., Adams, B., Minihan, P., & Yamaguchi, J. The regulation of family involvement in deinstitutionalization. *Social Casework: The Journal of Contemporary Social Work,* 1980, *61,* 67–73.

Shearer, M.S., & Shearer, D.E. Parent involvement. In: J.B. Jordon et al. (eds.), *Early childhood education for exceptional children.* Reston, VA: Council for Exceptional Children, 1977.

Stanton, M. An integrated structural/strategic approach to family therapy. *Journal of Marital and Family Therapy,* 1981, *7*(4), 427–440.

Terkelsen, K.G. Toward a theory of the family life cycle.

In: E. Carter & M. McGoldrick (eds.), *The family life cycle: A framework of family therapy.* New York: Gardner Press, 1980.

Tjossem, T.D. (ed.). *Intervention strategies for high risk infants and young children.* Baltimore: University Park Press, 1976.

Trevino, F. Siblings of handicapped children: Identifying those at risk. *Social Casework: The Journal of Contemporary Social Work,* 1979, *60*(8), 488–492.

Turnbull, A.P. Parent participation in the IEP process. In: S.A. Mulick & S.M. Pueschel (eds.), *Parent-professional participation in developmental disability services: Foundations and prospects.* Cambridge, MA: Ware Press, 1983.

Turnbull, H.R., & Turnbull, A.P. Parent involvement: A critique. *Mental Retardation,* 1982, *20*(3), 115–122.

Turnbull, H.R., Turnbull, A.P., & Wheat, M. Assumptions about parental participation. *Exceptional Education Quarterly,* 1982, *3*(2), 1–8.

Tyler, N.B., & Kogan, K.L. Reduction of stress between mothers and their handicapped children. *American Journal of Occupational Therapy,* 1977, *31,* 151–155.

Winton, P., & Turnbull, A.P. Parent involvement as viewed by parents of preschool handicapped children. *Topics in Early Childhood Special Education,* 1981, *1*(3), 11–19.

Wolfensberger, W. Counseling the parents of the retarded. In: A.A. Baumeister (ed.), *Mental retardation: Appraisal, education, and rehabilitation.* Chicago: Aldine Publishing Co., 1970.

[The authors wish to note that this chapter was written in the Fall of 1982. A review of the literature may provide more recent references for the interested reader.]

Chapter 8

Reactions to Deinstitutionalization among Parents of Mentally Retarded Persons

James W. Conroy

I n considering the impact and implications of deinstitutionalization, clinicians and researchers and decision makers must address the needs, feelings, and reactions of families. In 1978, 30.6% of residents released from institutions were children and approximately one-third of them returned to live with their families (Best-Sigford, Bruininks, Lakin, & Hill, 1982; Bruininks, Hauber, & Kudla, 1979). This chapter explores the attitudes of families toward deinstitutionalization, searches for special feelings among parents of children, reports new data on pre/post attitude changes, and explores the utility of one social psychological theory for understanding parent feelings and reactions.

WHAT IS KNOWN?

The literature has established several important points about the feelings of parents of mentally retarded persons. Olshansky (1962) suggests that chronic sorrow is natural, not neurotic, for parents of severely impaired children, and that

the feeling of sorrow may recur throughout the life cycle. Moreover, denial of one's own chronic sorrow may be as predictable as initial denial of the retardation itself. Regardless of controversy over Olshansky's position, it is certain that Olshansky tried to sensitize professionals to the depth and magnitude of distress that could barely be imagined by those who have not experienced it. Others have suggested (Weiss, 1979) that families pass through a sequence of reactions—denial, despair, guilt, frustration, and adjustment—and that these reactions may recur again and again at critical stages or events.

Efforts to study, comprehend, and measure these feelings have led to the understanding that initial institutionalization of a family member is an extremely stressful experience, often involving guilt, separation anxiety, and sorrow (Wikler, 1978; Wikler, Wasow, & Hatfield, 1978). Among 10 possible times of crisis and stress in the family life cycle, placement of the handicapped child (or adult) outside the home was found to be one of the most difficult.

The research reported here was supported by OHDS contract 130-81-0022, the Pennhurst Longitudinal Study.

Now the nation is involved in a process of drastic change in methods of caring for retarded citizens (Conroy, 1977; Hill & Bruininks, 1981). The population of public institutions for retarded citizens has fallen from a high of 195,000 in 1967 to about 120,000 in 1982 (Lakin, Krantz, Clumpner, Bruininks, & Hill, 1982; Scheerenberger, 1982). Over a decade ago, Klaber (1969) argued persuasively that the families of people in institutions are the true citizen consumers of the institutional system. But the trend toward deinstitutionalization has placed families in a difficult position. According to one parent (Gorham, 1975), "In the past, we were made to feel guilty when we did not institutionalize our children, and now, under the new normalization principle, we are made to feel guilty if we do" (p. 522).

Even more recently, Colombatto, Isett, Roszkowski, Spreat, D'Onofrio, and Alderfer (1980) surveyed superintendents of public institutions and asked, "In your opinion, have parents of mentally retarded persons been adequately polled regarding their views on deinstitutionalization?" The result was 78% no, 14% undecided, and only 8% yes.

A pattern of professional insensitivity to parental needs, like that documented eloquently by Turnbull and Turnbull (1978) regarding intervention in general, appears to have been replicated in the deinstitutionalization movement. As early as 1975, research had suggested that families were quite satisfied with institutional care and wished for it to continue (Brockmeier, 1975). This was later borne out by studies at other facilities (Keating, Conroy, & Walker, 1980; Meyer, 1980; Payne, 1976; Vitello & Atthowe, 1982). But during the 1970s, there was little effort to understand the reasons for the parental preferences. In fact, even in 1981, Vitello and Atthowe (1982) found that 68% of families whose relatives had been recommended for community placement felt that they did not have enough control over the decision; 71% were never even asked for consent. Yet 86% considered the institutional placement permanent, 91% found it adequate, and 54% expected no more than custodial care.

Given the known difficulty experienced by families in making the initial placement decision, it would appear obvious that deinstitutionalization could be extremely stressful and confusing. It is therefore amazing that so little attention is given to the feelings and needs of families in the process. It is surely true that the rights of mentally retarded persons and of their parents may conflict, as has been shown conclusively by Frohboese and Sales (1980), but this cannot justify ignoring the parents.

After a long delay, we now know that most families of institutionalized mentally retarded persons (72%–86%) oppose deinstitutionalization for their relatives, a fact we should have known when Brockmeier (1975) did his research in Nebraska in the early 1970s. Payne (1976) was the first to call attention to a "deinstitutionalization backlash" among families, but the warning seems to have been ignored. Stedman (1977) suggested clearly that discharge was stressful because it could force the family to question whether institutionalization was ever appropriate. Willer, Intagliata, and Atkinson (1981) showed in New York State that deinstitutionalization was a crisis event for 50% of familes, invoking guilt over the initial institutionalization and anxiety over the security and permanence of the new community placement.

At the same time that the feelings of families have been so systematically ignored, evidence has accumulated for the notion that deinstitutionalization can be quite beneficial for the mentally retarded persons themselves, in terms of developmental growth toward reduced dependence (Aanes & Moen, 1976; Conroy, Efthimiou, & Lemanowicz, 1982; Fiorelli & Thurman, 1979; Schroeder & Henes, 1978), reduction of maladaptive behavior (Sokol, Conroy, Feinstein, Lemanowicz, & McGurrin, 1983), and their own expressed happiness (Walsh & Conroy, 1982). There are further indications that benefits accrue in terms of variables related to quality, including individualized care practices (Balla, 1976), normalization (Eyman, Demaine, & Lei, 1979; Feinstein, 1982), and fostering of autonomy

(Bruininks et al., 1979; Feinstein, 1982). Finally, the most careful recent work suggests that community-based care is no more expensive, and may be less expensive, than institutional care (Intagliata, Willer, & Cooley, 1979; Jones, Conroy, Feinstein, & Lemanowicz, 1983; Mayeda & Wai, 1975; Nihira, 1979; Wieck & Bruininks, 1980).

WHAT ARE THE MAJOR GAPS IN KNOWLEDGE?

First, there has never been an adequate nationally representative survey of all families of institutionalized mentally retarded persons. This is a need that federal initiatives should address. There can no longer be any justification for failing to sufficiently poll families regarding deinstitutionalization and the related concerns it interjects into their lives.

Second, there is far too little understanding of the reasons for parental opposition to deinstitutionalization. In recent surveys of the families of residents of Pennhurst Center (an institution in Pennsylvania that is under federal court order to relocate all residents to group homes), Keating et al. (1980) found that most families opposed deinstitutionalization, that over 70% believed their relatives had no potential for further learning or skill acquisition, and that the initial placement decision was recalled as an extremely stressful event. The researchers composed a scale of attitudes toward deinstitutionalization, then explored the characteristics and feelings of families that were correlated with resistance to deinstitutionalization. Their analysis suggested that the family's perception of the resident's level of medical needs was the best predictor of resistance (more perceived needs, more resistance), followed closely by the age of the resident (families of older residents reported greater resistance). Race, education, and familiarity with the court order were significant, but relatively weak, predictors.

However, the resident's level of functioning, level of maladaptive behavior, and whether or not the family had ever visited a community residence were all unrelated to resistance to deinstitutionalization. The fact that these three variables were unrelated to family attitudes was surprising. The researchers had hypothesized that families of residents with advanced self-care abilities would be more optimistic about movement to a less restrictive setting, as would families of residents with few or no behavior problems, as well as those families of residents who had visited and learned about community placements for their children. These findings seem to demand a theoretical framework to understand how family attitudes developed and why they were unrelated to client behavior and family knowledge of alternatives. Such a framework could also lead toward realistic estimates of the likelihood of attitudinal change, as well as new ideas for methods of intervention.

Third, before the Pennhurst Longitudinal Study (see, in part, Conroy & Latib, 1982), there has never been a pretest/posttest study of family attitudes about deinstitutionalization. Only by investigating changes over time can we hope to comprehend the determinants of opposition and the amenability of attitudes to change.

Finally, the feelings of families of handicapped adults differ from those of families of handicapped children. It is possible that the two groups of families face qualitatively different histories and problems and hold correspondingly different attitudes about deinstitutionalization. Moreover, it follows that they might show different patterns of reactions to actual relocation of their relatives.

The following sections in this chapter address these gaps in knowledge, using data from the Pennhurst Longitudinal Study and the theoretical framework of cognitive dissonance. These preliminary explorations are not nationally representative but arise from a special situation of court involvement. Moreover, the theory is only an early attempt to gain insight and to generate new questions and new ways of understanding parental attitudes and attitude change in the field.

THEORIES OF ATTITUDE FORMATION AND CHANGE

Psychologists have devoted much effort toward developing theories to encompass the complexities of human attitudes. Himmelfarb and Eagly (1974) characterized four general varieties of theories: cognitive consistency theories, learning/reinforcement theories, social judgment theories, and functional theories. Within the cognitive consistency framework, which has generated the most interest over the years, they listed four approaches: balance, congruity, affective-cognitive consistency, and dissonance. All approaches share the idea that inconsistency is unpleasant and therefore leads to attempts to reduce the inconsistency; in other words, they are drive-reduction theories.

Among the cognitive consistency approaches, the dissonance theory has been by far the most controversial and influential (Greenwald & Ronis, 1978). In this chapter, the consistency framework is focused upon because the data from Keating et al. (1980) have suggested internal inconsistencies in the feelings of families; for example, families of higher-functioning residents were just as likely to oppose deinstitutionalization as were families of lower-functioning residents. Moreover, the dissonance theory is more fully explored because it appears to lend itself most readily to understanding of attitudes that, at first glance, may appear irrational and yet are resistant to change. For example, families of residents with extreme behavior problems were just as likely to favor deinstitutionalization as were families of residents with no behavior problems, and visiting a community setting made no difference in a family's attitude.

Cognitive Dissonance Theory

As already stated, cognitive dissonance theory (Festinger, 1957) has been the most influential of the attitude change models. Two cognitive elements, A and B, are said to be dissonant if one implies the negation of the other, i.e., if A implies not-B. They are consonant if A implies B. Festinger (1957) stated this core of the theory as follows:

1. There may exist dissonant or "nonfitting relations" among cognitive elements.
2. The existence of dissonance gives rise to pressures to reduce the dissonance and to avoid increases in dissonance.
3. Manifestations of the operation of these pressures include behavior changes, changes of cognition, and circumspect exposure to new information and new opinions (p. 31).

The most-often-cited example concerns smoking and health. Element A is "Smoking is bad for health" and element B is "I smoke." A implies not-B, thus assuring dissonance. The individual might relinquish B by quitting, or might attempt to read and hear only information contrary to A, or might gain social support from other smokers to tolerate the dissonant state. In more complex machinations, one might even be tempted to reject the implied proposition that health and long life are personally important.

The theory thus far is similar to the other consistency theories. It is the theory's extensions that have made it so powerful, explaining nonobvious, non–common-sense phenomena. Dissonance magnitude is related to the importance of the elements. The magnitude of dissonance is also greater as the original incentives (profits) for a decision are smaller; if a decision cannot be adequately accounted for by palpable gains, there is then a strong need to perceive the decision as correct, reasonable, and favorable. Conversely, the degree of hardship or unpleasantness (cost) associated with a decision affects dissonance. In Festinger's (1957) words, "people come to love the things for which they have suffered."

This formulation yields insight into people's postdecisional attitudes, particularly where profits from the decision were low and costs were high. Military service is a prime example. Consider an individual with two dissonant cognitive elements: A is "I enlisted for 3 years of service"; B is "That experience was totally valueless and painful for me." It is unpleasant to feel these two things. People often handle such problems by "discovering" later that the experience has, after all, conferred some benefits, although these benefits may be vague: "It made a man of me," "It helped me decide what I really wanted out of life," "It made me what I am today," "I made some of my greatest friendships," "I learned how to deal with authority." This approach may explain why surveys of the general population regarding happiness often reveal a large proportion of males who report that their military hitch was one of the happiest and most worthwhile times of their lives.

According to Deutsch, Krauss, and Rosenau (1962), postdecisional dissonance can be thought of as a form of "defensiveness," and dissonance reduction as a "mechanism of defense." They introduce the psychoanalytic term *rationalization* to refer to the processes of postdecisional dissonance reduction. When persons experience dissonance after making a choice, they are trying to defend themselves against a perceived implication of their choice that is contrary to their self-concept.

Over the years, dissonance theory has evolved toward a new formulation: "To the extent that dissonance theory has evolved since 1957, the evolution has been primarily due to the discovery that responsibility is a prerequisite for effects that we call dissonance reduction" (Wickland & Brehm, 1976). The newer formulation invalidates some of Festinger's (1957) original illustrations, such as dissonance in the sole survivor of an earthquake, because the survivor is not likely to feel responsibility for the earthquake itself.

Dissonance, Institutionalization, and Deinstitutionalization

Prior studies have shown that families of institutionalized mentally retarded persons often strongly resist the notion of deinstitutionalization, that they perceive little potential for learning among their relatives, and that they recall great stress at the time of initial institutionalization. Can dissonance theory explain these feelings? Can it be used to predict whether feelings differ between families of adults and those of children? Can it provide hypotheses about family stress at the time of deinstitutionalization, and about changes in feelings after deinstitutionalization of adults and of children?

The literature on initial institutionalization has established that it is an extremely upsetting event for the family, involving separation anxiety, chronic sorrow, and guilt; the cost is large. Conversely, we know that the quality of public institutions has often been severely questioned over the years in the public media and in professional literature, suggesting that the profit of the decision, with regard to the mentally retarded person's well-being, may have been presented to the families as dubious.

Given these premises, dissonance theory implies that families will be in a state of high postdecisional dissonance with regard to their relative's well-being: *A* is "We decided to place our child in a public institution," but *B* is "The institution seems unpleasant and may not be very helpful to our child's growth and development." Because cost is high and profit is low, dissonance is high. Because the crucial element of responsibility is present, the more recent formulation of dissonance theory applies. During the years following institutionalization, families may attempt to reduce dissonance by coming to believe that learning and development are not feasible and/or important goals by: selectively perceiving information supportive of the institution's quality, by rejecting new ideas or options, by emphasizing the medical aspects of the relative's needs, and by generally coming to a position that the institution is what the relative needs. These postdecisional resolutions should become stronger over time as defense mechanisms broaden and strengthen; hence, families of adults (who have been institutionalized longer) should show greater resistance to deinstitutionalization than families of children.

The dissonance approach does generate hypotheses, some of which are listed in Table 1. The research at Pennhurst provides an opportunity to test these hypotheses. Data reported are for parents only ($N = 321$), 291 being parents of clients over 21 years old and 30 being parents of children.

Indeed, parents are generally very satisfied with the institution (Hypothesis 1 in Table 1); 82.4% report that they are very or somewhat satisfied. Families of clients who have been

Table 1. Hypotheses derived from dissonance theory

1. Parents are very satisfied with the institution.
2. Parents of clients who have been institutionalized longer are more satisfied with the institution.
3. Parents of handicapped adults differ from parents of handicapped children in attitudes toward deinstitutionalization and related concepts, with parents of adults showing greater opposition.
4. Parents of handicapped adults perceive less developmental potential in their relatives than do parents of handicapped children.
5. Parents of handicapped adults and parents of handicapped children report similar levels of stress upon initial institutionalization.
6. Parents of handicapped children report less stress about the idea of deinstitutionalization.
7. Parents of handicapped children display less change in attitudes after relocation of their relatives than do parents of handicapped adults.

institutionalized longer are more satisfied with the institution (Hypothesis 2). The correlation between years institutionalized and the 5-point satisfaction scale is .14 (p = .005), a low but significant correlation. Similarly, 85.7% of parents of handicapped adults report satisfaction; the figure is 68.9% for parents of handicapped children. Dissonance theory would explain this as a function of parents of adults having had more time to activate and build dissonance-reduction strategies.

Parents of handicapped children display much less opposition to deinstitutionalization and related ideas than do parents of handicapped adults (Hypothesis 3), as is shown in Table 2 and suggested by the previous hypothesis. In Table 2, the scale of attitudes toward deinstitutionalization, composed of 25 related items, has excellent internal consistency (Cronbach's alpha = .94), and ranges from 1 (positive) to 5 (negative) toward deinstitutionalization. On the whole, parents of children are less opposed. This pattern is clearly shown in the individual survey items as well, with the important exception of community living ar-

Table 2. Attitudes toward deinstitutionalization: Parents of handicapped children and parents of handicapped adults

Attitudes about:	Percentage of negative attitudes			Mean satisfaction score	p^c
	1	50	100		
Agree with relocation	xxxxxxx[a] (34%)			2.4	.001
	oooooooooooooooo[b]	(74%)		4.3	
CLA[d] staff competence	xxxxxxxxx (43%)			3.0	.014
	oooooooooooo	(58%)		3.7	
CLA funding permanence	xxxxxxxxxxxx (57%)			3.5	.301
	oooooooooooo	(60%)		3.8	
CLA service availability	xxxxxxxx (43%)			3.1	.004
	oooooooooooooo	(68%)		4.0	
Normalization	xxxxx (27%)			2.6	.009
	oooooooooo	(50%)		3.5	
Least restrictive environment	xxxxxx (30%)			2.4	.001
	oooooooooooo	(54%)		3.5	
Deinstitutionalization	xxxxxxx (34%)				
	oooooooooooooooo	(74%)			
Total scale	Parents of children:			2.7	.001
	Parents of adults:			3.8	

[a]x = Parents of handicapped children; each x represents approximately 5%.
[b]o = Parents of handicapped adults; each o represents approximately 5%.
[c]p = Statistical significance of difference between responses of parents of children and parents of adults.
[d]CLA = Community Living Arrangement.

rangement (CLA) funding permanence; parents of children and adults are equally concerned about this issue.

Because part of the process of dissonance-reduction could be acceptance of labels and stereotypes about mentally retarded relatives, Hypothesis 4 (Table 1) was posed: that parents of handicapped adults perceive less potential for development toward basic skills than do parents of handicapped children. It supposes that, over the years, parents may come more and more to accept the discouraging statements made by professionals in prior decades: "He'll never be able to learn," "She'll always have the mental age of a 2-year-old," "He'll always need protection and separation from people who might hurt or make fun of him." This syndrome of counseling hopelessness may have become an integral part of parents' attempts to justify the initial institutionalization and the perceived need for permanent institutionalization.

Parents of handicapped children have not had as many years to absorb this kind of thinking, and therefore may be less pessimistic. Indeed, in response to the statement, "I believe my relative has reached his highest level of educational and psychological development and will not progress much beyond the level he is at now," 76% of parents of handicapped adults agreed, while only 27% of parents of handicapped children agreed (mean responses were 1.8 and 3.3, respectively, $p = .001$). This supports Hypothesis 4, but it is important to note that even the parents of children were only about neutral on this crucial item. The implications concerning the lack of substantial parental acceptance of the developmental model, which has become an integral part of professional practice and standards, are clear from these data.

The dissonance framework suggests no difference in parental stress at initial institutionalization between the two sets of parents; hence, Hypothesis 5 is that it was equally stressful whether it happened long ago or recently. In fact, 80% of parents of adults and 81% of parents of children recall extreme stress from that event.

The theory does, however, predict a difference in reactions to the idea of deinstitutionalization (Hypothesis 6). The parents of children have had less time to develop certainty about the necessity for the institution, and should therefore feel less stress in considering deinstitutionalization to a smaller, less-segregated residential setting. That is the case: 73% of parents of adults report extreme stress, but only 60% of parents of children report such stress (mean stress score = 1.5 for parents of adults, 2.3 for parents of children, $p = .022$). This does not de-emphasize the fact that most parents in both groups report great stress and concern about deinstitutionalization; it merely shows that parents of children feel somewhat less stress, as predicted by the theory.

Hypothesis 7 introduces the question of attitude change among parents of deinstitutionalized persons. The Pennhurst study surveys all families before actual deinstitutionalization of relatives, then surveys each family again, about 6 months after placement of the relative. The dissonance perspective has been shown to be useful in modeling the initial attitudes of parents; and it may be used to predict postrelocation reactions.

The dissonance model of initial attitudes implies a framework of defense mechanisms and rationalizations, built up and strengthened with each passing year. This framework probably includes the ideas that the relatives are as happy as they can be at the institution, that they have little or no chance of learning to be less dependent on others for daily living, and that the institution is the only proper, sensible, and safe way to care for such persons. If the actual placement of the relative in a new setting results in observable and unquestionable contradictions of this fabric of beliefs (i.e., increased client happiness, observable skill development, and success of the new setting), then dissonance theory would predict that the stronger the initial set of defenses (acquired via dissonance reduction), the greater the change in attitudes about the desirability of community living.

For a parent who has finally reached a stage of virtual certainty about the "rightness" of the institution for his or her relative, the direct experience of community living arrangement benefits might be comparable to an experience of conversion. An entire network of beliefs, carefully nurtured over the years, might be discarded entirely. Such a parent might express disbelief at his or her prior attitudes and might suddenly become as fervent a supporter of community services as he or she once was of the institution. The parent who has constructed a less-complete system of beliefs for dissonance reduction, in other words, is less convinced of the institution's necessity and would display less-drastic changes, because fewer beliefs have been shattered.

The data are consistent with this view of Hypothesis 7. Using the attitude scale as a general measure, the pretest/posttest findings for 19 parents of children and 29 parents of adults are shown in Table 3. The figures in the table show that parents of children were initially less opposed to deinstitutionalization than parents of adults ($p = .007$, group t-test), but at the 6-month follow-up, the two groups are about the same. This means that parents of adults changed *more* than parents of children (0.90 versus 0.40). Thus, while both groups became significantly more positive toward deinstitutionalization, the parents of adults seem to have experienced a more profound change.

In addition to the scale results, several items further illustrate this pattern. Families were asked what changes in their relatives' general happiness they expected if relocation occurred, and were later asked what changes they actually observed. Parents of adults showed much greater happiness than expected, while for parents of children the shift was significant but only half as large. This perceived increase in client happiness could be a primary reason for the overwhelming alterations in parents' belief structures. The item on "agreement with deinstitutionalization of the relative" showed a similar pattern. On this 5-point scale, 55% of parents of adults reported a 2 or more point change toward acceptance (21% went from strongly opposed to strongly in favor), but only 28% of parents of children reported such a large change. Moreover, parents of adults reported an increase in optimism about their relatives' potential that was twice as large as the increase among parents of children. The largest change of all was in the parents' own expected and actual happiness, and again this was twice as large for parents of adults.

Failures of the Theory

Having explored some of the hypotheses generated by dissonance theory and supported by certain data, it should be recalled that no social theory is complete. One of the more obvious predictions of dissonance theory would be that the amount of stress felt by a family at initial institutionalization (cost) should be related to current satisfaction with the institution. The higher the cost of a decision, the greater should be the efforts at dissonance reduction, in order to accept the situation and become satisfied with the institution. However, there was no linear relationship between reported initial stress and current satisfaction ($r = .01$, 305 df, $p = .441$).

Table 3. Preplacement and postplacement attitudes toward deinstitutionalization, based on scale of 1 (negative) to 5 (positive)

	Parents of handicapped children	Parents of handicapped adults	Difference	p^{1a}
Pre	2.67	3.37	.7	.007
Post	2.27	2.47	.2	.178
Change	.40	.90		
p^{2b}	.003	.001		

[a]p^1 = Statistical significance of preplacement and postplacement differences between the two groups of parents.

[b]p^2 = Statistical significance of change between pretest and posttest of each parent group.

Another strategy for dissonance reduction might involve the process of initial institutionalization; in the past, institutionalization was often advised and arranged by physicians, who justified it in the terminology of their profession, that is, in terms of the child's medical needs. If some parents took this to heart and gradually came to emphasize the intensity of their relative's medical needs as the reason for continued institutionalization, then they might tend to perceive greater medical needs than those that actually exist. Dissonance theory would suggest that parents who felt the most stress at initial institutionalization would be most likely to need and nurture such a justification. However, initial stress and current perception of the relatives' medical needs were not found to be related ($r = -.01$, 296 df, $p = .465$). This represents another shortfall of the theory.

DISCUSSION

This treatment of family attitudes and reactions to deinstitutionalization has attempted to show, above all, that families of handicapped persons have received woefully little attention from the research community. Furthermore, the research that has been done has not been heeded by professionals or decision makers. Theoretical analyses of parental attitudes and attitude change are potentially useful but need more work.

The dissonance theory is attractive to many because of its ability to explain behaviors and attitudes that seem to defy rationality. However, dissonance theory is only one approach to attitude formation and change. The other cognitive consistency theories (balance, congruity, affective-cognitive consistency) have not been explored or contrasted, nor have the various learning/reinforcement theories, social judgment theories, or functional approaches. Obviously, much theoretical analysis remains to be done in the field. The ultimate utility of the theories will only be settled with better data, with knowledge gained from competition among the theories, and with new insights and guidance provided by the parents themselves.

The major conclusions from the literature, supported by the Pennhurst work, are:

The majority of families of institutionalized persons are very satisfied with the institutional mode of care.

The majority of families of institutionalized persons oppose deinstitutionalization.

Consideration of deinstitutionalization is very likely to present a crisis for families, and this crisis is as intense as was the initial institutionalization.

Views and participation of families often are not solicited and treated with respect.

New conclusions from the Pennhurst Longitudinal Study must be viewed as tentative and not necessarily generalizable to other facilities or other states. According to the federal court order to close Pennhurst, every client is to be moved to a community residence or group home (maximum three clients, 24-hour staffing, with detailed individualized plans, day programs, special case managers, and ongoing monitoring required for each client). Clients *can* be relocated by court decree, even over the objections of parents; more often, parents finally accede to the multiple pressures from court, professionals, and state/county authorities. The Pennhurst deinstitutionalization process is unique. With this caution, the new contributions of the Pennhurst work involve the preplacement and postplacement findings and the identification of significant attitudinal differences between families of adults and of children. A few highlights are:

It is not only the highest functioning clients who have thus far been deinstitutionalized. Clients placed to date are remarkably similar (in adaptive and maladaptive behavior, medical status, and associated handicaps) to those remaining in the institutions.

Families of relocated clients were very satisfied with Pennhurst, but are now even more satisfied with the community living alternative arrangement.

Families of relocated clients display very large attitude changes, from initial resistance to postplacement support of deinstitutionalization and related concepts.

Despite the large, positive shifts, concern about the permanence and the security of the community living alternative system remains nearly as strong as ever.

Families of handicapped adults change attitudes to a greater degree than families of children, so that at posttest, the two groups are about equally positive toward deinstitutionalization.

RECOMMENDATIONS

The Pennhurst Longitudinal Study's pretest/posttest design is a significant contribution, but the case of court-ordered, "forced" deinstitutionalization cannot be considered representative of deinstitutionalization activities nationwide. Moreover, Pennsylvania's community living alternative system is different from those of other states. The single greatest priority in this area is a nationally representative baseline survey of parental feelings about deinstitutionalization and related issues.

Such a study is not difficult to design, via multistage sampling with adequate consent procedures, but the study must include pretest and postplacement measurement. Assuming that 5% of institutional clients are discharged to community living alternatives each year, the baseline must reach a large number of families (about 2,000) if we wish to obtain 100 pretest/postplacement interviews by the second year. Or, if we presume a 3-year study, we need 1,000 baseline responses to assure 100 complete observations. And 100 is a small number; although it would surely enhance our state of knowledge, multiple regression analyses would be limited in scope. Given such a study design, a large proportion of study resources should be devoted to theoretical analyses of attitude formation and change.

Future research should certainly explore the Keating et al. (1980) finding that the family's perception of the relative's level of medical need is the best single predictor of attitudes toward deinstitutionalization. In a small follow-up study, these family perceptions were compared to reports from the institutional staff who worked most closely with each resident on a day-to-day basis. There was little agreement between staff and families; families perceived far more intense medical needs than did staff (Conroy, Lemanowicz, & Feinstein, 1981). If the families had developed distorted impressions of medical needs, that should be relevant for any theoretical understanding of how the attitude of antideinstitutionalization developed and how it could change. While professionals in the field were battling the "medical model" and state "hospitals" were changing names to state "schools" and "centers," apparently no one was bringing the parents up to date on the reasons for such shifts in philosophy and practice.

A crucial final point is that, even in the Pennhurst situation, in which residents could be relocated over parental objections, the families of those who have moved thus far were less opposed to the idea than the average family with residents still living at Pennhurst. What we are observing is a process of relocating the residents whose families do not object too strongly. Hence, the remaining residents have families who object more strongly. This effect is cumulative; each year, the families of those who remain have a higher average level of opposition. This pattern is sure to be magnified in other facilities where no court order exists and where it is therefore far more difficult to transfer a resident over parental objections. It follows that the strength of the backlash to deinstitutionalization noted by Payne (1976) may intensify with each passing year.

Will the resistance eventually slow and halt deinstitutionalization? It could well be one of several powerful forces that together will do so, unless we work together with families to better understand their feelings, and also find ways to inform and educate them with sensitivity and without being threatening. Perhaps we will find that parents who have experienced the stress of deinstitutionalization of their sons and daughters will be effective resources to assist other families.

We professionals have heeded little the concerns of parents in our rush to deinstitutionalize and normalize living and learning environments for handicapped citizens. It is now time to listen carefully to the needs and feelings of families.

REFERENCES

Aanes, D., & Moen, M. Adaptive behavior changes of group home residents. *Mental Retardation,* 1976, *14,* 36–40.

Balla, D. Relationship of institutional size and quality of care: A review of the literature. *American Journal of Mental Deficiency,* 1976, *81,* 117–124.

Best-Sigford, B., Bruininks, R.H., Lakin, K.C., Hill, B.K., & Heal, L. Resident release patterns in a national sample of public residential facilities. *American Journal of Mental Deficiency,* 1982, *87,* 130–140.

Brockmeier, W.E. Attitudes and opinions of relatives of institutionalized mentally retarded individuals toward institutional and noninstitutional care and training. *Dissertation Abstracts International,* 1975, *35,* 5163A.

Bruininks, R.H., Hauber, F.A., & Kudla, M. *National survey of community residential facilities: A profile of facilities and residents in 1977.* Minneapolis: University of Minnesota, Department of Psychoeducational Studies, 1979.

Colombatto, J.J., Isett, R.D., Roszkowski, M., Spreat, S., D'Onofrio, A., & Alderfer, R. *Perspectives on deinstitutionalization: A survey of the National Association of Superintendents of Public Residential Facilities for the Mentally Retarded.* Philadelphia: Temple University, Woodhaven Center, 1980.

Conroy, J. Trends in deinstitutionalization of the mentally retarded. *Mental Retardation,* 1977, *15,* 21–26.

Conroy, J.W., Efthimiou, J., & Lemanowicz, J. A matched comparison of the developmental growth of institutionalized and deinstitutionalized mentally retarded clients. *American Journal of Mental Deficiency,* 1982, *86*(6), 571–587.

Conroy, J.W., & Latib, A. *Family impacts: Pre-post attitudes of 65 families of clients deinstitutionalized June 1980 to May 1982* (Pennhurst Study Report PC-82-1). Philadelphia: Temple University, Developmental Disabilities Center, 1982.

Conroy, J.W., Lemanowicz, J., & Feinstein, C. *Medical needs of clients: Perceptions of families and of staff* (Pennhurst Study Report BR-6). Philadelphia: Temple University, Developmental Disabilities Center, 1981.

Deutsch, M., Krauss, R.M., & Rosenau, N. Dissonance or defensiveness? *Journal of Personality,* 1962, *30,* 16–28.

Eyman, R., Demaine, G., & Lei, T. Relationship between community environments and resident changes in adaptive behavior: A path model. *American Journal of Mental Deficiency,* 1979, *83,* 330–337.

Feinstein, C. *Pennhurst class members in CLA's* (Pennhurst Study Report PC-82-3). Philadelphia: Temple University, Developmental Disabilities Center, 1982.

Festinger, L. *A theory of cognitive dissonance.* Evanston, IL: Row, Peterson, 1957.

Fiorelli, J., & Thurman, K. Client behavior in more and less normalized residential settings. *Education and Training of the Mentally Retarded,* 1979, *14,* 85–94.

Frohboese, R., & Sales, B. Parental opposition to de-

institutionalization: A challenge in need of attention and resolution. *Law and Human Behavior,* 1980, *4,* 1–83.

Gorham, K.A. A lost generation of parents. *Exceptional Children,* 1975, *3,* 521–525.

Greenwald, A.G., & Ronis, D.L. Twenty years of cognitive dissonance: A case study of the evolution of a theory. *Psychological Review,* 1978, *85,* 53–57.

Hill, B.K., & Bruininks, R.H. *Family, leisure, and social activities of mentally retarded people in residential facilities.* Minneapolis: University of Minnesota, Department of Psychoeducational Studies, 1981.

Himmelfarb, S., & Eagly, A.H. (eds.). *Readings in attitude change.* New York: John Wiley & Sons, 1974.

Intagliata, J., Willer, B., & Cooley, F. Cost comparison of institutional and community based alternatives for mentally retarded persons. *Mental Retardation,* 1979, *17,* 154–156.

Jones, P., Conroy, J., Feinstein, C., & Lemanowicz, J. *A matched comparison study of cost-effectiveness: Institutionalized and deinstitutionalized clients* (Pennhurst Study Report PC-82-2). Philadelphia: Temple University, Developmental Disabilities Center, 1983.

Keating, D.J., Conroy, J.W., & Walker, S. *Family impact baselines: A survey of the families of residents of Pennhurst* (Pennhurst Study Report PC-80-3). Philadelphia: Temple University, Developmental Disabilities Center, 1980.

Klaber, M.M. A study of institutions. In: S. Sarason & J. Doris (eds.), *Psychological problems in mental deficiency.* New York: Harper & Row, 1969.

Lakin, K.C., Krantz, G.C., Bruininks, R.H., Clumpner, J. L., & Hill, B. K. *Brief #13: One hundred years of data on populations of public residential facilities for mentally retarded people.* Minneapolis: University of Minnesota, Department of Psychoeducational Studies, 1982.

Mayeda, T., & Wai, F. *The cost of long term developmental disabilities care.* Pomona, CA: University of California–Los Angeles, Neuropsychiatric Institute, July, 1975.

Meyer, R.J. Attitudes of parents of institutionalized mentally retarded individuals toward deinstitutionalization. *American Journal of Mental Deficiency,* 1980, *85,* 184–187.

Nihira, L. *Costs for care of matched developmentally disabled clients in three settings.* Pomona, CA: University of California–Los Angeles, Neuropsychiatric Institute Research Group at Lanterman State Hospital, 1979.

Olshansky, S. Chronic sorrow: A response to having a mentally defective child. *Social Casework,* 1962, *43,* 190–193.

Payne, J.E. The deinstitutional backlash. *Mental Retardation,* 1976, *3,* 43–45.

Scheerenberger, R. C. *Public residential services for the mentally retarded: 1982.* Madison: Central Wisconsin Center for the Developmentally Disabled, 1982.

Schroeder, S., & Henes, C. Assessment of progress of

institutionalized and deinstitutionalized retarded adults: A matched-control comparison. *Mental Retardation,* 1978, *16,* 147–148.

Sokol, L., Conroy, J., Feinstein, C., Lemanowicz, J., & McGurrin, M. *Developmental progress in institutional and community settings* (Pennhurst Study Report PC-83-2). Philadelphia: Temple University, Developmental Disabilities Center, 1983.

Stedman, D.J. Introduction. In: J. Paul, D. Stedman, & G. Neufeld (eds.), *Deinstitutionalization: Program and policy development.* Syracuse, NY: Syracuse University Press, 1977.

Turnbull, A.P., & Turnbull, H.R. *Parents speak out: Views from the other side of the two-way mirror.* Columbus, OH: Charles E. Merrill Publishing Co., 1978.

Vitello, S.J., & Atthowe, J.M. *Deinstitutionalization: Family reaction and involvement.* Unpublished manuscript, College of Medicine and Dentistry of New Jersey, Rutgers Medical School, 1982.

Walsh, R., & Conroy, J.W. *Changes in client satisfaction after deinstitutionalization* (Pennhurst Study Report BR-16). Philadelphia: Temple University, Developmental Disabilities Center, 1982.

Weiss, A. *Parental and family perceptions.* Unpublished manuscript, University of South Carolina, Columbia, 1979.

Wickland, R. A., & Brehm, J. W. *Perspectives on cognitive dissonance.* Hillsdale, NJ: Lawrence Erlbaum Associates, 1976.

Wieck, C., & Bruininks, R.H. *The cost of public and community residential care for mentally retarded people in the United States.* Minneapolis: University of Minnesota, Department of Psychoeducational Studies, 1980.

Wikler, L. *Stress in families of mentally retarded children.* Unpublished manuscript, University of Wisconsin, Madison, 1978.

Wikler, L., Wasow, M., & Hatfield, E. *Chronic sorrow revisited: An empirical study of the adjustment of parents of mentally retarded children.* Unpublished manuscript, University of Wisconsin, Madison, 1978.

Willer, B.S., Intagliata, J.C., & Atkinson, A.C. Deinstitutionalization as a crisis event for families of mentally retarded persons. *Mental Retardation,* 1981, *19,* 28–29.

Part IV

ENVIRONMENTAL ISSUES
IN COMMUNITY INTEGRATION

The primary social principle underlying the term *least restrictive environment* is the commitment to finding and creating a place for handicapped individuals to live in settings that enhance their participation in society. The importance of this principle is tied not merely to basic social values but is also a powerful habilitation concept. Persons with severe handicaps must be immersed in normal social environments as much as possible if they are to be given the maximum opportunity to learn to participate in society.

Research and practice, legislation and litigation, and the achievements of handicapped persons themselves continue to confirm a place in the natural community for persons with severe handicaps. The findings of socially directed research, in particular, have had a major influence on contemporary service settings for handicapped persons.

The two chapters in this section focus on the contribution of research to our understanding of the environmental issues involved in community integration. In Chapter 9, Lisa L. Rotegard, Robert H. Bruininks, Julie Gorder Holman, and K. Charlie Lakin review the findings of existing research on residential placements. The authors describe the concepts and methods commonly employed in research measuring characteristics of environments and also review research on the relationships among environmental features and the behavioral functioning of the people in them. Suggestions are made for improving the specificity and ecological validity of factors studied in environmental research.

The recognition that learning occurs through direct experience with the environment has prompted considerable research interest on the effects of environmental factors. However, moving from this truistic level to an actual understanding of which characteristics of environments most elicit desired behavioral changes in people with various handicaps, of how those environmental characteristics can be identified and measured, and of how this information might be employed to improve processes and products of client-environment matching is considerably more problematic. In Chapter 10, Sharon Landesman-Dwyer discusses these issues, exploring lessons from and improvements needed in environmental studies to increase their usefulness in bringing about positive environmental impacts on clients. She notes that this process will involve greater specification not only of the characteristics of environments but also of the people in environments, whose individual characteristics interact with environmental features to produce a behavioral result.

Chapter 9

Environmental Aspects of Deinstitutionalization

Lisa L. Rotegard, Robert H. Bruininks,
Julie Gorder Holman, and K. Charlie Lakin

The movement toward implementing the philosophy of normalization in residential and educational programs has stimulated interest in the effects of environment on the development and behavior of handicapped persons. There is increasing evidence that many behaviors in children and adults are influenced by differences in the environments in which individuals have lived as well as by inherent differences in individuals themselves. In other words, there is a growing belief that environments have predictable social and psychological effects on individuals. This belief has fostered the demise of trait theories of personality, which emphasize the dominant and unchangeable influence of genes on an individual's behavior. What has developed concomitantly is the refinement of interactive theories that stress the interdependence between behavior and environment.

RELATIONSHIPS BETWEEN BEHAVIOR AND ENVIRONMENT

Kurt Lewin and Henry Murray were most influential in promoting environmental considerations in understanding human behavior and development. However, few theoretical approaches fully conceptualize a broad range of environmental variables and systematically relate them to behavior. Moos and Insel (1974), in a historical overview of systems for assessing and classifying human environments, reviewed six methodologies of environmental study: a) ecological variables, b) behavioral settings, c) organizational structure, d) average background characteristics of individuals, e) psychosocial characteristics, and f) organizational climate. This organization of methodologies provides a useful paradigm for conceptualizing environmental research on development and behavior.

Wohlwill (1970) described three forms of the relationship between behavior and environment from an interactionist's point of view. It was his contention that behavior necessarily occurred in particular environmental contexts that imposed major constraints on the range of behaviors permitted in them. These environmental contexts frequently served to determine particular aspects or patterns of behavior. This relationship can be understood in the study of behavior settings, which have been defined as ecological environments that are shared by several persons (Gump, 1971; Wicker, 1972). Each setting has an identity and viability of its own and can be distinguished in terms of intrinsic structural and dynamic properties. The concept of behavioral settings encourages study of how inhabitants, en masse, are actually interacting with their environments.

The second type of relationship between behavior and environment postulated by Wohlwill (1970) was that certain qualities associated with a particular environment may have a generalized effect on behavior and personality. This area of study includes the effects of institutionalization, crowding, and sensory deprivation on individuals. Severely handicapped persons, although possessing the same needs for variety and control of their physical space as other people do, may be even more affected by the physical environment than are nonhandicapped persons who have greater social abilities to alter situations.

In a third type of relationship described by Wohlwill (1970), behavior was seen as being instigated by and directed at particular attributes and characteristics of the physical environment. This relationship can be understood in the study of the motivational force of environmental stimulation. For example, people go to a favorite part of a room or house to engage in certain feelings or activities. Approach-avoidance and behavioral adaptation are other responses that may be determined by environmental attributes. The relationship of behavior to the physical environment, as postulated by Wohlwill (1970), suggests several questions including: How does the physical environment affect the psychosocial environment of institutions and community residential facilities? What kind of behaviors result from environmental features and arrangements? Answers to these questions may be too complicated to predict from available information, but they illustrate important, unresolved issues related to living in more normal environments.

Normalization is a heuristic concept for considering the interaction of environmental characteristics with the behavior of mentally retarded persons. In its broadest sense, normalization is the "utilization of means that are as culturally normative as possible in order to establish and/or maintain personal behaviors and characteristics which are as culturally nor-

mative as possible" (Wolfensberger, 1972, p. 28). In applying this principle to the severely handicapped population, both opportunity for independence in the physical environment and special assistance with skills (social, physical, economic, etc.) must be offered so that individuals learn to use the environment to satisfy their needs.

One result of normalization has been the removal of handicapped persons from large institutions and their subsequent placement in smaller facilities, which are assumed to provide more homelike environments not only by virtue of their architecture but also because of their proximity to services and normal community experiences. Although deinstitutionalization has been a national policy for nearly 20 years, it has not yet been wholeheartedly accepted. The reasons for this are varied and often complex (see, for example, Conroy, this volume) and their basis is not easily discredited by overwhelming amounts of data on the objectively certified achievements of community-based facilities. In fact most past decisions on the policy of deinstitutionalization have been made on the basis of deeply felt emotion, moral obligation, or financial necessity (see, for example, Bachrach, this volume).

Community-based residential care and other service programs offer a wide range of physical plants, types of supervision, and methods of care and training. Merely removing an individual from a large institution and placing him or her in a smaller unit does not necessarily ensure opportunities or experiences conducive to development or social integration (Balla, 1976, Tizard, 1975). Therefore, this chapter focuses on issues and research findings related to effects of residential environments on the behavioral functioning of severely handicapped persons. In the chapter following, Sharon Landesman-Dwyer critically discusses many important research and methodological issues in describing and evaluating environments and proposes suggestions for improving research regarding the impact of environmental factors upon development and behavior. Landesman-Dwyer (1984) also provides more extensive discussions of these issues.

PHYSICAL
CHARACTERISTICS
OF ENVIRONMENTS

Most research on the physical aspects of environments for severely handicapped persons is methodologically unsophisticated, having been based upon vague notions of how to translate normalization into design, with few specific desired behavioral outcomes in mind. Over the past 20 years there have been several attempts to determine objective characteristics of treatment milieus. For the most part this research has focused on residences for mentally ill individuals (Ellsworth, Maroney, Klett, Gordon, & Gunn, 1971; Jackson, 1969; Moos, 1970, 1972; Moos & Houts, 1968; Moos & Insel, 1974; Price & Moos, 1975).

Architecture and design have recently received increased emphasis because of the concept of normalization and the importance it places on establishing culturally normal living environments. The approach taken in studying architecture and design has been to operationalize aspects of built or human-modified settings and to attempt to relate the resultant variables to human behavior (Bednar, 1974, 1977; Craik, 1970; Dybwad, 1970; Gunzberg & Gunzberg, 1973; Proshansky, Ittelson, & Rivlin, 1970; Rapoport, 1982; Sommer, 1969). An example of this approach is a project by Robinson, Thompson, Graff, Emmons, & Franklin (1983) to develop design guidelines for residences for some able-bodied, severely and profoundly retarded adults. From a series of design principles (site/context, building, room/space), a preliminary checklist of 155 attributes characterizing institutional and homelike settings was developed to evaluate existing or proposed residences. Unlike already-existing instruments that are either very general in nature or quite selective and require extensive training to use reliably, the checklist created in this study contains a large number of items that can be easily assessed by a nonprofessional observer. While the authors confess that significant further study is required to make this a complete description and a reliable instrument, it is an architectural descriptor of

behavior settings with potential for becoming a reliable assessment tool. The long-term goal of this work is to develop a predictive model relating environment to behavior.

Built features of the environment have sometimes resulted in overcrowding, lack of sensory stimulation, and other undesirable consequences. In studying arousal and sensory stimulation, Kreger (1971) noted that many problems of severely retarded or behaviorally disturbed individuals result from functional retardation associated with environmental living conditions—conditions that produce more stress than residents are able to cope with. Kreger found bizarre behaviors of institutionalized people to be similar to those of normal individuals who have been sensorially deprived for a short time period. Similarly, Kahn (1974), in his research with institutionalized mentally retarded persons, suggested that a phyical setting can either support or hinder goal-directed activity. If motivation for reaching a goal is particularly strong, an individual will adapt the setting or his or her behavior to fulfill that need. If these options are impossible, however, as they are for many severely handicapped persons, a stressful situation will develop, often with resulting withdrawal or aggressive acts.

Altman (1975) has suggested that privacy is an important dimension for understanding the environment/behavior relationship. Privacy can be thought of as the central concept and regulatory process by which a person or group makes itself more or less accessible and open to others. Studies reviewed by Altman (1975, pp. 134–136) have shown that some behaviors (e.g., bedwetting and aggression) may decline once retarded persons are given identifiable territories such as private spaces, sleeping areas, or eating areas.

The term *crowding* can be used to describe social conditions in which privacy mechanisms have not functioned effectively, resulting in an excess of undesirable social contact. Spencer (1974) and James, Spencer, and Hamilton (1975) reported on the immediate effects of improved hospital environments on the behavior of mentally retarded patients in England.

Residents were moved from three extremely overcrowded hospitals with inadequate facilities and minimal staffing to a hospital affording more privacy, personal possessions, and habilitative activity. All patients improved in behavior after transfer to this improved physical environment.

In a series of experiments, Griffin, Landers, and Patterson (1974a, 1974b) examined whether changes in the behavior of retarded persons occur when social density is manipulated. Experimentation was done in a clear space with various numbers of retarded adolescents. Results implied that the critical factor was not how much living space was available but rather how many people occupied that space and their use of the space. The authors felt that normalization procedures that advocated a more secluded or private living environment were not necessarily producing therapeutic effects because fewer people in a given space did not always increase the positive social interactions among them.

Gunzberg (1973) discussed various therapeutic objectives to consider when designing physical environments. He suggested that if the physical environment is to support a habilitation program, it must be manipulated from the design stage through to the actual time of usage, in order to serve a particular training and educational philosophy. He expressed this philosophy as the interaction of three principles: *personalization, socialization,* and *normalization.*

Gunzberg (1973) called personalization the key to creating a suitable physical environment. In order to personalize a facility, said Gunzberg, the facility's management would have to select, from the wide range of "normal" ways of living, those aspects that offer the best opportunities for furthering independence in residents. Gunzberg defined socialization as the process of acquiring the skills that enable the handicapped person to participate more fully in ordinary life situations. In his scheme, the third principle, normalization is an active therapeutic action in which the environment is purposely manipulated to achieve defined objectives. Normalization is seen by Gunzberg as necessary for socialization. In his view, normalized physical environments offer residents the chance to learn concrete lessons from the more practical and meaningful experiences found outside of the institutional or abnormal environment. Gunzberg prepared a checklist containing 39 steps to normalizing the physical environment that could be used in facilities for mentally retarded people. The checklist was concerned with environmental aspects that were related directly to physical features.

Cleland and Sluyter (1973) proposed a design for an environment to humanize and provide motivating circumstances for residents and employees alike. The design, which aimed at normalizing the ward residence of bedfast retarded individuals, was based on the assumption that traditional ward homogeneity was out of the question for a bedfast population of many ages and functional levels. The residents were all immobile. Cleland and Sluyter capitalized on the positive aspects of immobility as a basis for programming for bedfast patients. The National Aeronautics and Space Administration (NASA) was consulted to explore the similarities of being an astronaut in space to being a relatively immobile ward patient. The authors' proposal, an exercise in creativity that included ideas such as mirrored ceilings, predicted that employee satisfaction would increase and that turnover would decrease by introducing a degree of visual variation to the ward.

Reizenstein and McBride (1977) evaluated the physical environment of a small community-based residential setting for retarded persons in order to discover if its design supported aspects implied by the principle of normalization. These researchers, who are an architect and a social scientist, respectively, supposed the major physical implication of normalization to be that retarded persons should live in homelike environments. The degree of social contact, the degree of activity support, and the symbolic expression of values, goals, and preferences were all used as indications of the effectiveness of the physical design in facilitating normalization. Reizenstein and McBride argued that normalized residential settings implied a continuum of physical spaces that allowed a range of interaction from that of being alone to being in a large group, as well as an environment that both promoted a range of normal activity and provided positive symbolic presentation for and about its residents and purpose. Interestingly, the authors concluded that the home studied portrayed three conflicting images: for residents it was a home only; for other people it was a model, or a showcase; possibly its best descriptor, from the point of view of staff, was as a congregate living facility. Reizenstein and McBride (1977) pointed out that service programs often describe themselves physically to reflect their idealized images, but that a program's defined life spaces must always be tested against actual experiences within the environment.

In another study, Levy and McLeod (1977) observed the social interaction patterns of residents and staff in one existing institutional facility and in the same facility redesigned to provide residents an enriched environment. Enrichment was defined as an environment that gives residents the freedom to choose to be part of a large group, a small group, or to be alone. This definition is similar to aspects of the operationalized definition of normalization of physical environments used in other studies. Levy and McLeod also provided developmental toys in their enriched environment. Results from a time-sampling observation system indicated that an enriched on-ward environment reduced neutral or stereotypic activity, increased purposeful movement, elicited new patterns of using space, and created an environment that could support and reinforce learning activities of severely retarded residents. Systematic observation of the use of space by the lowest-functioning residents supported the assumption that as intellect decreases, so does ability to perceive and manipulate the environment, and the importance of staff members in guiding interaction with the environment thus increases. Levy and McLeod concluded that therapeutic and supportive environments for profoundly retarded persons must provide both human and nonhuman qualities. They also stated that institutions should be designed with physically active rather than physically passive environments. It should be noted that Lewis and Baumeister (1982) have extensively reviewed literature on the effects of environment on stereotypic behaviors.

In an in-depth report of a four-year longitudinal study, Knight, Weitzer, and Zimring (1978) reported the effects of physical design and programmatic changes during a transfer of residents from traditional open-ward institutional facilities to renovated institutions and community placements. The study examined the effects of changing from a highly abnormal ward environment to one of three more home-like ones. Three designs were used in the renovation: modular, corridor, and suite. The modular-style renovation incorporated $4\frac{1}{2}$-foot high partitions placed in 30-foot-by-40-foot rooms that had formerly served as open dayhalls and sleeping wards. Partitions defined a small lounge and 12 modular units that each included a bed, a desk, and a dresser. The low height and the placement of the partitions offered limited privacy. At best, visual privacy was available when residents were seated or prone. The corridor-style renovation resulted in two large terrazzo-floored lounges furnished with couches, televisions, and other items. The lounges were flanked with two long corridors, one for men and the other for women. The corridors contained double and single bedrooms with locking doors, each bedroom provided beds and dressers. The suite-style renovation subdivided the dayhalls into three bedrooms, each for two to four persons, surrounding a common lounge area. Bedrooms were furnished with beds, dressers, and chairs. The lounges were carpeted and had televisions, chairs, couches, lamps, and so forth. Experts agreed that the suites were more attractive and homelike than were the corridor-style renovations, and that the modular-style design was the least normal and homelike.

The results of the experiment, based on thousands of behavior observations, indicated that the normalization principle, as it relates to physical designs, had limited usefulness in predicting the impacts of renovated environments.

A resident's use of newly provided personal or private space did not necessarily follow from its provision, nor did staff and other residents necessarily "keep out" of spaces designed for someone else's increased privacy. The implementation of modular renovation had little effect on resident and staff behaviors. The suite renovation, felt by most observers to be most homelike and attractive, had less positive impact on resident and staff behavior than did the corridor design. Overall, the renovated buildings did encourage staff and residents, even lower-functioning residents, to use and respect private/personal spaces.

Neither the claim that severely and profoundly retarded persons are too mentally deficient to respond differentially to various environments, nor the suggestion that normalized environments directly engender normal client behavior was supported by the research. The researchers found that even low-functioning residents (a group with an average IQ of 20.3) exhibited improved social and solitary behavior in the more homelike environments, but the effects of the homelike environments were primarily mediated by staff responses to the physical settings and by the extent to which residents were allowed to realize control over their environmental experience (e.g., over light, temperature, noise, choice of different activities, space, and kinds of social interactions).

ENVIRONMENTAL EVALUATION AND RESEARCH

PASS and PASSING

Increasingly, studies are conducted using specially designed environmental evaluation instruments. Two such devices are the Program Analysis of Service Systems (PASS 3), developed by Wolfensberger and Glenn (1975), and PASSING: Program Analysis of Service Systems Implementation of Normalization Goals, developed by Wolfensberger and Thomas (1983). These devices quantify the quality of a wide range of human management service projects, systems, and agencies. PASS 3 measures service quality in terms of the service's adherance to a) the principle of normalization, b) other service ideologies, and c) certain administrative desiderata, all believed to contribute to quality. PASSING, on the other hand, measures quality only in terms of a service's implementation of normalization. Quality in both measures is quantified by the degree of social, physical, and structural integration; developmental growth orientation; and the nature of the surroundings. An average rating of quality is given based on several rater scores derived from documentation, site visits, and interviews. One criticism of PASS 3 is that it was designed to measure the conformity of service systems to the normalization principle, whereas it has been suggested that the real issue is the effect of these systems on the individuals they are designed to serve (see Wolfensberger, 1980, for a rebuttal of this and other criticisms of normalization). Shorter versions of PASS 3 have been developed for use in studies designed to link various behaviors to environments differing along one or more dimensions implied by normalization.

ALERT

The Alternative Living Environments Rating and Tracking System (ALERT) is another method for evaluating major aspects of physical settings (Budde, 1976). ALERT uses two continua to match residents and environments. The first continuum includes four general service delivery models that range from least restrictive to most restrictive. Restrictiveness is determined by the amount of independence allowed to clients. The second environmental continuum includes nine specific service delivery models. Placement into one of the nine models depends on the apparent degree of physical and social integration within the system. This rating refers to the normalizing or institutionalizing aspects of an environment.

ALERT was developed for use by service system administrators, advocacy groups, and parent organizations. It can also be used to describe and compare services for mentally retarded persons within a state, although it does not provide the means for evaluating service processes or the behavioral characteristics of residents. ALERT is intended to describe improvement in an individual's life-style over time by characterizing the environments through which he or she progresses.

Management Practices
Scale, Index of the Physical
Environment, and Other Scales

Raynes, Pratt, and Roses (1979) have also developed techniques for evaluating the environments and quality of care in residential settings. They identified four dimensions of care that included the management of daily events, staff-resident verbal interaction, community contact of residents, and the physical environment. These four dimensions were found to vary relatively independently, which suggested that global measures of the quality of care are of limited value. Pratt, Luszcz, and Brown (1980) modified these techniques to measure the quality of care in seven small community-based homes. The management of daily events in a facility was assessed by the Management Practices Scale, originally developed by King, Raynes, and Tizard (1971) as the Child Management Scale. This instrument characterizes the management of daily life in a facility as either resident-oriented or institution-oriented. It was based conceptually on Goffman's (1961) description of four characteristics of total institutions: rigidity of routine, block or group treatment of residents, social distance between staff and residents, and depersonalization of the residents. Pratt et al. (1980) also used the Index of the Physical Environment, an observational checklist of physical amenities (Gunzberg & Gunzberg, 1973; Morris, 1969). This index was designed to characterize the stimulation provided by the physical environment throughout a residence and consisted of a checklist of furnishings and physical facilities available in each room in a residence. Both the Management Practices Scale and the Index of the Physical Environ-

ment significantly discriminated between small community homes and large institutions.

The findings of studies presented previously indicate that living in the community does not alone have inherently normalizing effects on the behavior or competency of mentally retarded persons in residential facilities. Various authors/researchers have found the essence of normalization of the environment to be in the opportunity for control of personal space, the chances for positive social interaction, the personalization of the physical setting, and/or the encouragement of socialization. It is problematic, however, to develop a set of attributes on which to characterize facilities, to accurately measure those characteristics, and to develop a taxonomic classification based on those measurements (Frederiksen, 1972; Landesman-Dwyer, this volume). Furthermore, while environmental attributes have been researched extensively in educational, correctional, and psychiatric settings, very little work has been done in facilities for severely handicapped individuals.

Moos (1973) assumed that environments have unique personalitites that can be measured. Moos and Insel (1974) studied nine types of environments (psychiatric treatment programs in the community, psychiatric wards, correctional institutions, military companies, university residences, secondary schools, group environments, work environments, and families) and developed perceived social climate scales for each. Social climate can be thought of as an indicator of the interaction between physical and social environments. Three dimensions were developed to discriminate among different subunits in each of the nine environments: a) relationship dimensions measured the extent to which individuals were involved in the environment and the extent to which they tended to support and help each other; b) personal development dimensions assessed opportunity afforded by the environment for self-enhancement and the development of self-esteem (i.e., autonomy, practical orientation, personal problem orientation); and c) system maintenance and system change measured degree of order, organization, clarity, and control. Information about these three dimensions was generally obtained from the perceptions of participants in the system but could have been obtained from outside observers.

WAS

Moos and Houts (1968) developed a Ward Atmosphere Scale (WAS) to assess the social environments of psychiatric wards. This scale, which was standardized on a national sample of 160 psychiatric wards (Moos, 1971), was shown to empirically differentiate among inpatient psychiatric wards and showed high profile stability over several months. Items for the WAS were derived from several sources, including observations of ward differences made by trained observers, popular and professional books about psychiatric wards, and interviews with patients and staff who had spent time on different wards.

COPES

In order to compare directly the perceived environmental characteristics of in-hospital and out-of-hospital psychiatric programs, the *Community-Oriented Programs Environment Scale* (COPES) was developed (Moos & Otto, 1972). This scale assesses the psychosocial environments of transitional community-oriented psychiatric treatment programs in a manner parallel to the WAS used in psychiatric wards. COPES is also used to assess the social climate of facilities for mentally retarded persons.

The choice of items used in COPES was guided by the general conceptualization of "environmental press" (Stern, 1970). The press of an environment, as the individual perceives it, defines what he or she must adapt to. Press can be objective or subjective and generally indicates the direction a person's behavior must take in order to remain adequately satisfied within the environment. Operationally, press is a characteristic demand or feature of the environment as perceived by those who live in it. COPES was designed to measure the features of press. For example, an emphasis on "program involvement" (one of 10 scales) is

inferred from the following items: "Members put a lot of energy into what they do around here" and "This is a lively place." Autonomy is inferred from these items: "Members are expected to take leadership here" and "Members here are very strongly encouraged to be independent." The 102-item COPES Form C (Moos, 1972) has 10 subscales: Program Involvement (measures how active members are in the day-to-day functioning of their program), Support (measures the extent to which members are encouraged and supported by staff and other members), Spontaneity (measures the extent to which the program encourages members to act openly and express their feelings openly), Autonomy (assesses how self-sufficient and independent members are encouraged to be in making their own decisions), Practical Orientation (assesses the extent to which the member's environment orients him or her toward preparing himself or herself for release from the program), Personal Problem Orientation (measures the extent to which members are encouraged to be concerned with their personal problems and feelings and to seek to understand them), Anger and Aggression (measures the extent to which a member is allowed and encouraged to argue with members and staff, to become openly angry, and to display other aggressive behavior), Order and Organization (measures how important activity planning and neatness is in the program), Program Clarity (measures the clarity of goal expectations and rules), and Staff Control (assesses the extent to which the staff determines rules).

Pankratz (1975) administered the COPES to residents and staff in two halfway houses for retarded persons. The houses were similar in physical aspect as well as in general organization. Both were large, older homes whose residents were mildly and moderately retarded. One house was for men and the other house was for women. The study attempted to determine whether mildly and moderately retarded persons could respond meaningfully to the scale and whether the results would be meaningful in relationship to existing norms. COPES items were read individually to each resident.

Results of the study indicated that residents and staff were in agreement about the nature of their programs. People who were well acquainted with the program felt that the results described the programs for mentally retarded persons well and accurately. It was apparent to Pankratz (1975) that COPES allowed valid feedback by the retarded individuals themselves as to the nature of their treatment environment.

McGee and Woods (1978) administered a slightly modified version of the Ward Atmosphere Scale to staff and students at a residential center for mildly and moderately retarded adolescents. The results of administering this scale similarly provided evidence for the applicability and usefulness of the instrument with this population. Differences between staff perceptions of the environment and their image of an ideal environment, and between staff's and students' perceptions of the school environment were regarded by the school director as accurate. These differences in perception pointed to problems in the school's organization that had not previously been well articulated.

Characteristics of the
Treatment Environment (CTE)

Another scale that has been used in assessment/treatment environments was designed by Jackson (1969) after successive attempts to objectify the theoretical concepts of M. Schwartz concerning the attributes of treatment environments for mentally ill persons. The original scales of Schwartz (1957) were described in terms of patients' pathologies or symptoms that would be alleviated by the appropriate environmental state. Jackson conducted a factor-analytic study based on responses of 840 staff members of four large mental hospitals, resulting in a new scoring system for Schwartz's scale. Five factors composed of 72 items were identified: Active Treatment (the degree of staff activity directed toward patient welfare and improvement), Social-Emotional Activity (the degree to which the environment permits or encourages normal socioemotional relations or activity among patients), Patient Self-Man-

agement (the degree to which the environment permits or encourages patient responsibility for the management of self or other patients), Behavior Modification (the degree to which staff attempts to influence, demand, or control specific behaviors of patients), and Instrumental Activity (the degree to which the environment permits or encourages normal choice or rational problem-solving activity by patients).

The factor-based scales were oriented not toward patients and their symptoms (as were the earlier ones) but toward the treatment environment and its characteristics. Jackson, after quantifying Schwartz's theoretical notions, concluded that the Characteristics of the Treatment Environment (CTE) could not be interpreted as an indication of how therapeutic the environment was but only as an objective measure of various treatment environment characteristics.

A more recent factor analytic study of the CTE was undertaken by Silverstein, McLain, Hubbell, and Brownlee (1977), who wished to adapt the scale for use in residential facilities for mentally retarded individuals. A series of factor and cluster analyses led to the decision to accept an oblique solution, with two factors identified as Autonomy and Activity. The Autonomy factor included items such as, "Patients are encouraged to make their own decisions in spending their personal money," "Patients are encouraged to start projects with other patients to improve the physical environment of the ward," and "The staff encourages patients to take over management of their own affairs whenever possible." The Activity factor included items such as, "Patients are kept busy on the ward by frequent social, intellectual, or recreational activities, conducted by members of the staff," "Patients have many opportunities to express themselves in music, painting, hobby-work, or other creative activities," and "Members of the staff are constantly seeking ways of expanding patients' freedom of movement (about the hospital, grounds, and community)."

On two different occasions, McLain, Silverstein, Hubbell, and Brownlee (1975) administered the CTE and the Residential Management Survey (a version of the Child Management Scale, discussed earlier), to 195 staff on selected wards of a hospital serving 1,800 mentally retarded persons. Respondents received scores on both the CTE factors and a total Residential Management Survey score. In each case high scores were associated with desirable treatment practices and low scores with undesirable practices.

The results of the study led to three conclusions concerning the discriminative power of the instruments, the stability of the treatment environment, and the relationship of the results to staff characteristics. First, the CTE and the Residential Management Survey differentiated not only among treatment programs with varying therapeutic goals but among wards within programs as well. Second, the responses of staff to the questionnaires were only minimally related to their length of employment at the hospital and on the ward. There was no significant relationship found between staff response and their age, sex, or job classification. Third, the two scales' mean scores for individual wards were relatively stable over a 10-month period.

McLain, Silverstein, Hubbell, and Brownlee's most recent study (1977) was a further attempt to test the discriminative power of the CTE and the Residential Management Survey to differentiate among staff management practices in treatment programs and living units of 19 state hospitals and 3 family residential facilities that differed in size, organization, and resident characteristics. The results lent support to the position that treatment practices employed with retarded persons differ in various types of residential settings. Those differences could be viewed along the dimension of activity, autonomy, and staff orientation. The results further suggested that in attempting to account for the differences among management practices in various facilities, one was not able to point to staff demographic characteristics or employment history. Just as in previous studies, staff responses to the questionnaires were only minimally related to these background variables.

Brown and Guard (1979) administered the CTE to 130 employees of eight nursing homes serving retarded persons. The authors found that all eight homes fell short of the levels of patient autonomy and activity that the studies by McLain et al. (1975, 1977) had predicted for a therapeutic community. No direct relationship was found between the size of the facilities and either autonomy or activity levels, consistent with the findings of Balla (1976) and Zigler and Balla (1977). Brown and Guard (1979) discovered that autonomy and activity correlated strongly with each other and that both levels were greater in homes with larger proportions of supervisory staff, in homes that included the family in planning treatment goals, in homes where staff expressed greater approval of the policy of admitting retarded persons, and in privately owned homes as opposed to corporation-owned homes.

A revision of Jackson's (1969) CTE was used by Rotegard, Hill, and Bruininks (1983) to measure levels of autonomy and activity afforded to residents in a national sample of 75 public (state-operated facilities with a mean of 596 residents and a median of 446 residents) and 161 community residential facilities (private facilities with a mean of 17 residents and a median of 6 residents) selected to be representative in size and geographic location of all such facilities in the United States. Community facilities showed a significantly more positive treatment environment than did public facilities (generally institutions) on all measures, although the difference was less pronounced on the Activity subscale. Similarly, the characteristics of facilities' physical environments were assessed on a five-item measure that rated the dining room, living room, bedroom, bathroom, and yard. Scores ranged from one to five, with one denoting a very homelike environment and five reflecting a less homelike environment. An average score was derived for each facility. Not surprisingly, data from this portion of the analysis indicated that community residential facilities were generally more homelike than public residential facilities.

Applications of Psychosocial Assessment Scales

Although assessments employing psychosocial assessment scales have only begun to be used in facilities for mentally retarded persons, there are several possible applications of the scales. For example, direct comparisons can be made of the psychosocial environments of institutions and of a variety of community-based residences, or among facilities of each type and the changes in the perceived psychosocial characteristics of the same environments over time. For example, Pierce, Trickett, and Moos (1972) successfully used the WAS to help staff alter the treatment environment in an inpatient psychiatric ward. The change was consistent with staff goals but retained the overall direction and ideology of treatment.

Assessments using psychosocial climate scales can serve as a valuable "quality control" function. Congruence between idealized views of a treatment program and perceptions of its actual operation, as well as the extent of agreement between members and staff and/or among various groups of staff and administrators, can be determined.

Analysis of the psychosocial environment may also come to be used in research to identify environmental factors related to favorable or unfavorable treatment outcomes, and to predict outcomes based on the differential impact of milieu settings on specific groups of residents. When the psychosocial elements of treatment environments are reliably dimensionalized and adequately validated, their differential effects on different people or types of people can be more adequately studied (Moos, Shelton, & Petty, 1973). Along these lines, Jelinek (1974) devised a new instrument to measure the quality of long-term care facilities. This instrument assessed care independently of compliance to state regulations by matching the characteristics of the facility with characteristics of individual residents. This match was an indicator of the appropriateness of placement. Using the *Community-Oriented Programs Environment Scale,* along with a number of other instruments, a hierarchical system was developed to combine scores to create a global index of characteristics of facilities. Criterion scores were reduced into three general objective areas: psychosocial environment, physical plant, and professional services. These three areas ultimately formed a single quality index that was shown to discriminate among facilities

in ways that could be used to identify individual strengths and weaknesses of each facility.

Finally, such assessments may serve to identify those clients or staff who have deviant perceptions of their environment. Different types of people react differently to different milieus. There may be an important interaction effect between staff and environment or between residents and environment that in part determines treatment outcomes (Penk & Robinowitz, 1975).

Size of Residential Facilities

One significant environmental feature that has generated extensive research and policy discussion is size of or number of residents living in residential facilities.

Size patterns of residential facilities have changed dramatically in the past 20 years. In the 1960s, residential services for retarded citizens consisted primarily of large publicly operated institutions and a small number of privately operated facilities. Available statistics in 1967 reported 195,000 people residing in state institutions. The average size of these facilities has declined steadily, from 1,516 residents in 1960, to 1,201 in 1967, to 648 in 1968, and to 478 in 1982 (Lakin, 1979; Lakin, Bruininks, Doth, Hill, & Hauber, 1982). Paralleling these changes and substantial reductions (about 40%) in residents since 1967 in public institutions has been the increase in smaller, privately operated residential programs (includes specialized foster care). The mean size of private facilities was 47 residents in 1969 (34 of whom were retarded persons), less than 17 in 1977 (nearly 15 of whom were retarded persons), and about 9 residents (8 of whom were retarded persons) in 1982. The vast majority of over 14,000 private facilities reported in a 1982 survey were small and had opened within the previous 10 years (Hauber, Bruininks, Hill, Lakin, & White, 1984; Lakin et al., 1982).

Given such dramatic changes in size and ownership of facilities, it is not surprising that the effects of size have been the focus of research studies, court cases, and policy debates. Past investigators have questioned the notion that a critical size exists, after which a community facility becomes, for all practical purposes, no different than a large institution. The effects of facility size on resident care practices have been noticeable when the size difference was very large. Considerable variation has been reported among small community-based facilities and between living units in the same institution (Balla, 1976; King et al., 1971; Mc-Cormick, Balla, & Zigler, 1975; Tizard, 1975; Zigler & Balla, 1977).

The results of the study by Rotegard et al. (1983) support the premise that meaningful differences exist among environmental characteristics in facilities of various sizes. Generally, as the size of a facility increased, its Physical Environment Scale score increased, denoting less homelike surroundings. Facilities with less than 16 residents were the most homelike and differed significantly from facilities with 16 or more residents. Residents of facilities housing 5 to 8 persons were encouraged to be more autonomous and active than were residents of smaller or larger facilities. Bjaanes and Butler (1974) found that very small facilities showed less-positive treatment environments than slightly larger facilities and speculated that small homes may hinder autonomy because of overprotective staff. Treatment environments encouraging resident autonomy in facilities with less than 9 residents were significantly more positive than in facilities with more than 63 residents. In addition, residents in facilities with 5 to 8 persons were significantly more active than were residents in facilities with more than 15 residents. When a series of regression analyses were conducted to determine the amount of variance in the dependent environmental measures explained by size and several other facility resident and staff characteristics, it was found that size made a difference even after controlling for resident ability. In addition, no other variables contributed significantly to the explained variance in the two treatment measures, with the possible exception of staff job satisfaction. (The relationship between staff job satisfaction and characteristics of the treatment environment could not be explained, owing to dependency between measures used in the study.)

The literature on size and environmental qualities is not sufficient in either amount or rigor to permit unequivocal conclusions (see, for instance, Balla, 1976; Baroff, 1980). It does appear that smaller size is generally correlated with more normalized environmental qualities, but the relationships among these variables is far from uniform. Furthermore, little can be currently said about the effects of size and organization of settings upon staff performance or client behavior and development. As Landesman-Dwyer notes in Chapter 10, environments are multivariate and complex, suggesting that little can be learned about these questions without more careful study of specific environmental features and precise behavioral outcomes. In the past, facilities for severely handicapped persons were usually compared in terms of readily observable indices such as number of clients, number of staff, staff/client ratio, average age or average IQ of residents, type of ownership, or size and location of facility. It can now be shown that a whole range of less-observable dimensions can also be used to differentiate environments. Treatment environment may be at least as important as more easily observed indices, and is probably more meaningful as a measure of facility differences, as a predictor of resident outcome, or as a program descriptor.

PHYSICAL SETTINGS, PSYCHOSOCIAL CLIMATES, AND ADAPTIVE BEHAVIOR

The design of physical plants for handicapped persons has traditionally been based on considerations of durability, ease of maintenance, cost, and building patterns prevalent in comparable facilities (Griffin et al., 1974a). The construction of these facilities has been predicated on building codes and on voluntary guidelines for which no empirical justification is available (Zeisel, 1970). More recently, with the advent of the philosophy of normalization, physical environments have been selected or designed with respect to the opportunities provided residents to satisfy their needs and to live more normalized lives. However, a facility's physical characteristics may only be understood when viewed as part of a larger context.

Because actors and their relative influence in any specific system may vary, every physical setting can be conceptualized as having a psychosocial character or climate as well.

One outgrowth of the principle of normalization is the expectation that more normal physical and social environments will result in parallel changes in resident behavior (MacEachron, 1983; Wolfensberger, 1972). Two major types of research have examined relationships between adaptive behavior skills and placement in the less-restrictive environments. The first group of studies focused on the adaptive behavior skills associated with successful adjustment in the community. In these studies, successful community adjustment is generally described as remaining in a particular living environment, for example, a family or group home setting, without returning to a more restrictive setting such as a highly supervised large state institution. The second type of studies examined increases and declines in adaptive behavior skills occurring after placement in less-restrictive environments in which more specific environmental qualities are measured and researched. Findings from studies of both types are reviewed in this section.

Adaptive Behavior Skills and Community Adjustment

Identification of the adaptive behavior skills that lead to personal independence and social competence are particularly crucial when dealing with deinstitutionalization and community integration of handicapped persons. The major goals of deinstitutionalization are increased personal independence and social integration (Crnic & Pym, 1979; Tjosvold & Tjosvold, 1983); hence, assessment and training efforts for individuals released from institutions should focus on those skills that will allow greater independence and integration. The research evidence, however, has not clearly identified those particular adaptive behavior skills that most facilitate successful community integration and maximum personal independence. Although the majority of studies have found some adaptive behavior skills to be related to successful community adjustment, the particular skills identified as important have

varied considerably from study to study. A summary of the adaptive behavior skills identified in more recent studies as related to aspects of community adjustment is provided in Table 1.

In a series of studies by R.L. Schalock and his colleagues, many of the adaptive behavior skills originally identified as predictive of successful community adjustment remained significant over a 5-year period of community placement. Schalock and Harper (1978) provided training in independent living skills to 79 clients residing in group, family, and foster homes, and then placed them in supervised or independent apartments and houses. Clients had been referred initially from state institutions, state mental health facilities, and natural homes. Sixty-nine of the 79 residents remained in the semi-independent or independent living arrangements after 2 years. Successful clients exhibited strengths in symbolic operations, personal maintenance, clothing care and use, socially appropriate behavior, and functional academics. Clients who returned to the more restrictive settings (i.e., group homes or institutions) had adaptive behavior deficits in money management, cleanliness, social behavior, and meal preparation. When Schalock, Harper, and Carver (1981) studied the same group of individuals 3 years later, 55 of the 69 remained in supervised or independent housing. The successful clients demonstrated significantly more adaptive behavior skills in the areas of personal maintenance, clothing care and use, social behavior, community utilization, and functional academics (time and money use). Major reasons in the later follow-up study for return to more restrictive living facilities included nutritional problems, inadequate home maintenance, bizarre behavior, and legal difficulties. The adaptive behavior skills that were found to be the most significant predictors of success over the 5-year period were personal maintenance, communication, food preparation, community use, and clothing care.

In a similar study, Schalock, Harper, and Genung (1981) provided training in independent living skills over a 9-year period to 166 mentally retarded adults living in group homes. Upon completion of training, they moved into

Table 1. Adaptive behavior skills predictive of successful placement in less-restrictive community residential facilities

Adaptive Behavior Skills	Literature Reference							
	Schalock & Harper, 1978	Schalock, Harper, & Carver, 1981	Schalock, Harper & Genung, 1981	Intagliata & Willer, 1982	Sternlicht, 1978	Thiel, 1981	Crnic & Pym, 1979	Sitkei, 1980
Self-help skills	x	x			x	x	x	
Motor development								
Communication							x	
Social-emotional development	x	x	x	x			x	x
Cognitive functioning	x	x					x	
Health care and safety								
Consumer skills	x	x						x
Domestic skills	x	x					x	x
Community orientation		x					x	
Vocational skills				x				x

supervised or independent apartments. The 140 successful clients who remained in community placements were significantly more proficient than unsuccessful clients in the areas of social-emotional behavior and work skills. The 26 unsuccessful clients who returned to state institutions or who were admitted to state mental health facilities demonstrated more high-frequency behavior problems that tended to occur in community settings.

The adaptive behavior characteristics of 49 mentally retarded persons currently living in the community but previously reinstitutionalized (returnee group) were compared with 255 people who remained in the community continuously (nonreturnee group) in a study by Intagliata and Willer (1982). All residents lived either in family-care homes (private homes owned and operated by a family who provides living accommodations for an average of 3 mentally retarded persons) or in group homes (facilities serving an average of 10 mentally retarded individuals). Returnees had significantly poorer social relations skills, less regular contact with friends in the community, and less behavior control in terms of destructiveness and disobedience than the nonreturnee comparison group. Although there were no significant differences between the groups in terms of their self-care skills, community living skills, or use of community resources, returnees were more likely to travel independently in the community than were nonreturnees. To explain this unusual finding, the authors speculated that the same characteristics leading to increased behavior problems may also result in more independence in the community.

Ability to perform self-care skills has most often been found to be positively related to successful community adjustment. Sternlicht (1978) summarized research related to the success of foster care placement for previously institutionalized mentally retarded residents. He concluded that independence in self-care skills was the most significant factor required for successful placement. Unacceptable behavior and poor health were found to be the two most common causes of failure of foster care placement. The subjects used in these studies were generally more handicapped than those studied by either Schalock and his associates (1981) or by Intagliata and Willer (1982).

Using the AAMD Adaptive Behavior Scale (Nihira, Foster, Shellhaas, & Leland, 1974),

Thiel (1981) compared the adaptive and mal-adaptive behavior of 25 successful and 24 un-successful clients placed in community facili-ties. Unsuccessful clients who returned to the institution within 12 months after their place-ment were more likely to demonstrate behavior problems and a lack of self-help skills. Al-though the personal independence factor (i.e., self-help) scores were higher for the residents that were successfully placed, there were no significant differences between the two groups in terms of self-help or other adaptive behavior skills.

Studies by Crnic and Pym (1979) and Sitkei (1980) used reports of residence staff rather than actual measures of adaptive behavior skills to ascertain the perceived importance of particular adaptive behavior skills to successful community adjustment. Nine behavioral skill areas (personal maintenance, clothing care, food preparation, home maintenance, time management, social behavior, community uti-lization, communication, and functional aca-demics) were the focus of training for 17 group home residents in the study by Crnic and Pym. Following training, residents were placed in semi-independent living settings. Fourteen of the 17 residents were considered successful in the transition. Ratings by staff in the semi-in-dependent living facility indicated that skills in the adaptive behavior areas just listed were necessary, but not sufficient, to ensure suc-cess. Respondents felt that resident motivation and coping skills, as well as environmental support factors (e.g., social interaction, ser-vice agency support), were also required to fa-cilitate a successful transition to semi-indepen-dent living. Although adaptive behavior skills were measured and trained in this study, analy-ses were not conducted to identify the specific types of adaptive behavior skills that were important for successful semi-independent living.

Over a 2-year period, Sitkei (1980) surveyed 105 operators of group homes for mentally re-tarded persons regarding the education, voca-tional training, social interaction, community involvement, and mobility of their residents. Of the 1,804 persons living in the group homes

at the start of the study, 731 transferred from the group homes to other settings in the course of the 2 years. Most (30.8%) of the transferring residents moved to independent living arrange-ments. Operators reported that the residents moving to independent living settings appeared to assume more responsibility in adaptive be-havior tasks such as cleaning house, helping with laundry, cooking, and shopping. Accord-ing to the operators, independent living was also facilitated by obtaining a job in the com-munity. A major limitation in this investigation and in the study by Crnic and Pym (1979) is the reliance on subjective reports of facility oper-ators and staff rather than on direct assessment of behavioral functioning of residents. The adaptive behavior skill levels of transferring residents were not reported or analyzed sys-tematically in these studies, thus limiting the confidence with which conclusions can be drawn about the relation of adaptive behavior skills to community placement success.

An inverse relationship between adaptive behavior and successful community placement was found by Sutter, Mayeda, Call, Yanagi, and Yee (1980). They compared the self-help skills, social skills, and maladaptive behaviors of a group of 60 mentally retarded residents who had remained in small community homes for 3 years with a group of 17 residents who had returned to the institution within the 3-year pe-riod. The small community homes were pri-vately owned and licensed to provide support and care for 1 to 5 mentally retarded residents. The results of this study are unusual in that the unsuccessful clients demonstrated signifi-cantly more self-help and social skills but more maladaptive behavior than the successful cli-ents. It is probable that the severity of behavior problems for the unsuccessful clients masked the beneficial effects of the adaptive behavior skills they possessed.

Comparisons of Behavior before and after Placement

The relationship of adaptive behavior to living in less-restrictive environments has been eval-uated in another body of literature by measur-ing adaptive behavior prior to and after placement. The purpose of these studies is to determine whether changes in adaptive behavior occur in conjunction with changes in living settings. It is generally assumed that less-restrictive environments will facilitate progress on adaptive behavior skills (Intagliata, Crosby, & Neider, 1981). Improvements in adaptive behavior functioning over time are regarded as indicators of successful community adjustment and as evidence supporting placement in less-restrictive environments.

Kleinberg and Galligan (1983) measured the adaptive behavior of 20 mentally retarded clients who were transferred from large living units (housing 350 residents with about 25 residents per unit) to small community facilities (housing 8 to 10 residents). The community facilities were either single-family homes or a unit of an apartment building. The AAMD Adaptive Behavior Scale and the Minnesota Developmental Programming System (Bock & Weatherman, 1979) were administered to the residents shortly before release from the institution and 4, 8, and 12 months after community placement. Several areas of adaptive behavior (language development, domestic activity, responsibility, and social interaction) showed initial increases upon community placements and were sustained over the 1-year period in the community; however, the initial improvements made in grooming and vocational skills were not maintained.

In a study by Aanes and Moen (1976), the adaptive behavior of 46 residents in group homes housing 3 to 8 residents was measured using the AAMD Adaptive Behavior Scale. The previously institutionalized residents were evaluated shortly after their move to the group homes and then again 1 year later. Six areas of adaptive behavior revealed significant increases over the 1-year period: eating, cleanliness, appearance, socialization, kitchen duties, and clothing care. In the area of language development, marked improvements occurred in speaking, writing, and general language (i.e., politeness and sociability). However, comprehension skills, including reading and following complex instructions, significantly decreased over the 1-year period. There were

no major changes in the areas of toileting, dressing, occupation, self-direction, physical development, locomotion, economic activity, numbers and time concepts, and general independent functioning. Ratings in the dressing, toileting, and physical development areas were near the top end of the scale during the initial testing; thus, substantial improvement in the second administration was probably quite limited. Providing more training and increased opportunity to practice those skills in which no significant differences were obtained may be necessary to achieve greater gains in adaptive behavior.

Thompson and Carey (1980) studied the adaptive behavior change of eight mentally retarded women who were moved from an institution to a small group home. The Minnesota Developmental Programming System was administered at the time of admission to the group home and again 2 years later. After 2 years of individualized behavioral programming, the mean score had risen from 29.7 points to 39.6 points. The areas in which scores improved most dramatically were social skills, language development, domestic activities, and use of community leisure-time resources. Domestic skills increased most rapidly, possibly owing to the increased opportunities for practice of those skills in the group home.

The adaptive behavior skills of 38 mentally retarded individuals were maintained, and in some cases increased, after release from an institution to group homes in a study by Soforenko and Macy (1977). Several adaptive behavior skills trained prior to release from the institution were maintained after placement in the community (e.g., money management, grooming, interpersonal relationships, communication, time skills, and knowledge of community services). Improvements after transfer to the community were noted in the areas of vocational skills, transportation, independent living skills, and general community adjustment.

Changes in the adaptive behavior skills of 403 individuals released from institutions for mentally retarded persons and placed in natural homes, halfway houses, or group homes were measured in studies by Bell, Schoenrock, and Bensberg (1981). Data were collected at five time periods during the first 2 years of placement in community settings. Basic skills (i.e., writing name and address), homemaking activities, social network, and self-esteem improved over the 2-year period, but not all changes were statistically significant. For example, basic skills did not change markedly during the first 20 months, but did increase significantly after the 20th month. Although there was a gradual decline over time in the amount of community involvement in activities such as church, movies, and Young Men's Christian Association–type organizations, that decrease may have been offset by the increases in the number of close friends, amount of visiting with neighbors, and number of telephone calls made to friends.

More Specific Environmental Measures

A number of studies have assessed placement in various settings and more specific environmental qualities on changes in adaptive behavior. Eyman, Demaine, and Lei (1979) designed a study to investigate the relationship of factor-analyzed scores derived from PASS 3 with changes in adaptive behavior of residents placed in the community. A path analysis was used to relate resident characteristics—including age, IQ, and initial scores on adaptive behavior—to six PASS 3 environmental ratings. Each resident's average annual change in adaptive behavior over a 3-year period was analyzed.

Eyman et al. (1979) found that PASS 3 subscores, which related to the degree of normalcy apparent in the physical environment and surroundings of a facility, were significantly associated with positive change in adaptive behavior for specified types of residents. In general, it was shown that older, less-retarded residents improved in overall adaptive behavior regardless of where they resided. Significantly contributing to growth in adaptive behavior, however, were the four PASS 3 ratings factors: Administrative Policies, Environmental Blending of the Facility with the Neighborhood, Location and Proximity of Services,

and Comfort and Appearance of the Home. These results suggested the importance of a homelike facility where supportive encounters with adults and nonretarded individuals in the community were available. The results also suggested that factors such as Service Proximity and Neighborhood Harmony were more complicated than just geographical location, because post-hoc comparisons between rural and urban locations indicated that the reported results generalized to both types of settings. Finally, it was noteworthy that the Application of Normalization Principles factor was not related to developmental change in any of the adaptive behavior domains, suggesting that a merely prescriptive application of the normalization principle to facilities does not guarantee the improvement of adaptive behavior scores of individuals residing in them.

In a subsequent longitudinal study Eyman and Borthwick (1984) used an even shorter version of PASS 3 to measure the environment in a sample of California's small family homes. The measurement consisted of four PASS 3 subscales: Normalization of Program (19 items), Normalization of Setting (12 items), Administration (8 items), and Proximity and Access (4 items), developed by Flynn and Nitsch (1980) from a factor analysis and item analysis of 256 PASS 3 evaluations. PASS 3 factors found to be significant predictors of adaptive behavior growth in an earlier study (Eyman et al, 1979) were found to be associated with client development in this study. Younger clients, regardless of level of retardation, seemed to have benefited significantly on their adaptive competence in connection with positive PASS 3 ratings on administrative and service policies. Moreover, proximity and access to community services as well as harmony with the neighborhood had a significant relationship with gains in adaptive behavior regardless of either age or level of retardation of the residents.

A primary objective of a study by Bjaanes and Butler (1974) was to distinguish between facilities that encouraged behavior leading to normalization and competency as opposed to those that did not. Their study included two board-and-care and two home-care facilities. The environment of each facility was considered to be a total entity made up of attitudinal, supportive, physical, and behavioral components that were assumed to be measurable. The attitudinal and supportive aspects were measured by questionnaires and interviews, the physical component was measured by inspection, and the behavioral environment was measured by coding all activities observed during four 2–3-hour sessions per subject. Activities were coded as independent or dependent; spontaneous, planned, or routine; structured or not; obligatory or discretionary; and "passing" (an attempt by the retarded person to conceal his or her incompetency or history of institutionalization) or "natural." The frequency and proportion of time spent in each major activity, as well as the characteristics of the behaviors, were analyzed for the four categories.

In this study, facilities were tentatively divided into three kinds of environments: therapeutic, maintaining, and custodial. A therapeutic environment was conceptualized as one that actively enhanced the normalization process and the development of social competence. In maintaining facilities, residents tended to remain at about the same level of competence. Custodial residences were those in which little or nothing was done to achieve normalization, and in which a lack of organized and structured activities could lead to regression by facility residents.

The tentative study conclusions were that social competence and independence were greater in the two large board-and-care settings than in the two small homes. Furthermore, Bjaanes and Butler (1974) noted that the geographic location of the facility and the involvement of the caregiver in the ongoing stream of behavior appeared to relate to the development of independent functioning and social competence in residents. Exposure to the community was seen as important to normalization. Of greatest importance was the conclusion that different community facilities were associated with different outcomes and that these differences appeared to be functions of variations in the facilities' psychosocial climates.

The objective of a second study by Butler and Bjaanes (1978) was to gather data on effective habilitative programs to provide guidelines to help place mentally retarded persons in settings that enhanced their potential and opportunity for more normal living experiences. The study used time-sampling techniques, observation, in-depth interviews, questionnaires, data from official records, and statistical analyses to abstract information from 160 facilities. Facility type was determined by including eight factors: Habilitative Programs, Community Interaction, Recreational Activities, Sheltered Workshop Participation, Social Activities Participation, Resident Participation in Chores, Active Caretaker Involvement and Daily Routine, from which a profile of each facility was formulated. Each facility was then determined to be one of the three types: therapeutic, maintaining, or custodial. This study utilized the concept of life space or total environment, which was delineated into temporal space, physical space, and social space. Social space was thought of as having behavioral, attitudinal, and supportive components.

General conclusions of this study indicated that to provide a normalizing environment, community care facilities must be activity-enriched with both internal programs and external contact and exchange. That is to say that the facility must be therapeutic as opposed to being a custodial or maintaining facility. Community facilities that had few or no internal and external programs were shown to resemble many features of traditional institutions.

An ethological observational study by Landesman-Dwyer, Stein, and Sackett (1976) described the group home program in Washington State according to the behavior of residents and staff, as well as to group home resources. The results showed that there was no inherent improvement in behavior or normalizing influence associated with small facilities or specially designed facilities. In their sample of group homes serving 6 to 20 residents (mostly mildly to moderately retarded young adults Landesman-Dwyer et al. (1976) found that more positive social behaviors occurred in larger facilities, that specially designed new group homes were related to decreased community interaction, and that more homogeneous groupings of residents were associated with more positive social behavior. Of course, causal relationships could not be determined. Longitudinal follow-up studies could be conducted to support the reliability and validity of this study and other similarly designed studies. In this study, for example, comparisons made between data from observations of resident behaviors and interviews about resident behavior with staff and administration showed sizable discrepancies.

In a subsequent longitudinal study involving a large number of observational and measurement techniques, Landesman-Dwyer (1984) described the effects on individuals of moving from large institutional group settings to smaller settings (new duplexes) or of continuing to live in groups modified socially. The subject populations consisted of adults whose functional and cognitive abilities were comparable to that of preschool children. Each of 37 living units was characterized in terms of its a) physical space and resources, b) degree to which the environment was institutionally oriented versus resident-oriented according to King et al's. (1971) revised Child Management Scale, and c) amount of cognitive stimulation provided, as reflected on scores on the Caldwell Home Observation for Measurement of the Environment (Caldwell, 1978). In addition, data pertaining to staffing patterns and attitudes, staff perceptions of their responsibilities, as well as detailed documentation of resident characteristics and activities were collected.

Analysis of the possible person-environment interactions showed that certain clusters of subjects, based on their baseline patterns of behavior, were differentially affected by their environments. A general lack of large behavioral changes among residents was not surprising given the fact that the environments, whether old or new, were relatively unstimulating; however, the new duplexes offered residents considerably more private spaces and normalized surroundings as well as significantly greater resident-oriented management practices.

Fiorelli and Thurman (1979) selected four institutionalized residents for placement in a supervised apartment building. The community living setting was defined as more normalized than the institutional setting on the basis of environmental ratings using an instrument that combined items from PASS 3 (Wolfensberger & Glenn, 1975) and the short form of PASS 2 (Wolfensberger & Glenn, 1973). The ratings of the two environments were significantly different, indicating that the apartment setting was more normalized than the institutional setting. The adaptive behavior skills of the residents were measured by direct observation occurring 5 to 6 weeks prior to discharge from the institution and 5 to 6 weeks after community placement. Target behaviors being observed were personal maintenance skills (e.g., eating, cleaning own room, dressing, hygiene), group maintenance skills (e.g., preparing food for the group, cleaning of group living areas and grounds) and recreational activities. Significant increases were shown in the areas of personal appearance and hygiene, preparation of food/drink for the group, maintenance of group objects and rooms, and participation in passive recreational games and tasks.

An explanation sometimes cited for improved adaptive behavior skills in community settings is that residents have greater opportunity to participate in such activities. In a study by O'Neill, Brown, Gordon, Schonhorn, and Greer (1981), the activity level of 26 mentally retarded adults moved from an institution into supervised apartments was examined. The activity level of the residents was assessed with the Activity Pattern Indicators (Brown, Diller, Fordyce, Jacobs, and Gordon, 1980) prior to leaving the institution, 8 months later, and again $2\frac{1}{2}$ years after moving into the supervised apartments. The major categories of activity level assessed by the Activity Pattern Indicators were Self-Care, Family Role (i.e., cooking, shopping, paying bills), Vocation/Education/Rehabilitation, Recreational/Social, and Quiet activities. Self-care activity level remained unchanged after 8 months in semi-independent living settings. The frequency and diversity of all other activities was substantially increased after 8 months in the community, and those increases were maintained after $2\frac{1}{2}$ years. Recreational/Social activities increased significantly after living in supervised apartments, but the most dramatic increases occurred in Family Role activities, an area in which activity was nearly nonexistent in the institutional setting. This study indicates that the opportunity to engage in certain adaptive behavior skills may, indeed, increase in less-restrictive living settings.

Forty-two mentally retarded persons released from institutions who had remained in a community residential facility for approximately 4 years were interviewed in a study by Birenbaum and Re (1979). The purpose of the study was to determine whether changes had occurred in their interpersonal relationships, work experience, self-image, personal decision making, and social competency since their move to the community. Because of staff-imposed consequences, personal decision making was found to be more restricted than it had been earlier in the residents' tenure. Over the 4-year period, the number of community leisure activities in which the residents were involved decreased greatly. The sheltered workshop, at which most of the residents were employed, seemed to have replaced community leisure activities as the central focus of their social lives. Conversations and interaction with others at the sheltered workshop had increased dramatically. Although this study did not measure adaptive behavior per se, it does provide some information regarding the social adjustment of individuals placed in community residential facilities. Since data in this study were obtained through interviews directly with the mentally retarded persons, the reliability and validity of the results may be somewhat questionable (see, for example, Nathan, Millham, Chilcutt, & Atkinson, 1980; Sigelman, Schoenrock, Winer, Spanhel, Hromas, Martin, Budd, & Bensberg, 1981).

Findings from an investigation by Aninger and Bolinsky (1977) are at variance with most other studies of changes in adaptive behavior after community placement. These authors studied 18 mentally retarded adults who were transferred from an institution to a supervised apartment complex situated next to the institution. The AAMD Adaptive Behavior Scale and Burk's Behavior Rating Scales were among the instruments used to measure the adaptive behavior of residents prior to and 6 months after release from the institution. Although slight improvements were noted between the pretest and posttest scores of the criterion measures, statistically significant differences were not obtained. Living in a less-restrictive environment for 6 months did not appear to appreciably increase independent functioning, but residents were able to function successfully in the more independent setting. Perhaps a longer period of time is required to obtain significant improvements in adaptive behavior.

A study conducted by Hemming, Lavender, and Pill (1981) examined the adaptive behavior of 38 subjects moved from large custodial institutions to smaller nearby living units and 33 subjects who continued to reside in institutions. The smaller living units contained three to four attached bungalows, with each bungalow housing eight residents. Quality of life in the two settings was compared by using King and Raynes's (1968) Scale of Management Practices and Butler and Bjannes's (1978) Criteria for Therapeutic Environments, which measures participation in activities within the residence and community. Large institutions were found to engage in more institution-oriented practices, while the small bungalows were more resident-oriented. Staff-resident interaction increased with the move to smaller units, but participation in activities decreased for higher-functioning residents. Overall, Hemming et al. (1981) concluded that the quality of life improved for the majority of residents when they moved to smaller living units.

Adaptive behavior change occurring after the move to smaller units was also assessed in this study. A revised version of the AAMD Adaptive Behavior Scale was administered to all subjects prior to the release of the experimental group from the institution and at four additional time periods within the 2 years after their transfer. Most adaptive behavior skills of residents transferring to bungalows improved significantly over the 2-year period, with the majority of improvements occurring 9 months after the move. Areas in which improvements were most notable included language development, responsibility, and domestic activity. The residents of small bungalows more frequently engaged in informative and sociable conversations than they had while living in the institutions. Decreases in vocational activity were evidenced, however, particularly after the first 4 months of placement. When the adaptive behavior of transferred residents was compared with that of the contrast subjects who remained in the institution, few significant differences emerged. To a large extent, the gains in adaptive behavior made by the institutionalized residents kept pace with the gains made by the group in the smaller living units. Although the transferred residents demonstrated greater increases in domestic activity and responsibility, they also showed greater declines in vocational activity than did the contrast subjects. Scores on the remaining areas of adaptive behavior did not yield any significant differences between the experimental and control subjects.

This study by Hemming et al. (1981) demonstrates the importance of the use of control groups in studies of this nature. When viewed in isolation, the overall increases in adaptive behavior by the experimental subjects may lead to the conclusion that placement in less-restrictive settings produces gains that are attributable to the new placement. However, when the adaptive behavior gains of experimental subjects are compared to those of control subjects, such a conclusion may not be supported. Improvements in performance of individuals remaining in more restrictive environments must be compared with improvements in performance of similar individuals moving to less-restrictive environments, in order to conclude that adaptive behavior changes were due to the change in living setting rather than the effects of maturation and history

(Seltzer, Sherwood, Seltzer, & Sherwood, 1981).

Adaptive Behavior Gains in Institutions versus Less-Restrictive Settings

Few studies exist in which the adaptive behavior gains of subjects remaining in institutions have been compared with those of residents transferring to less-restrictive environments. Studies that have utilized such controls have generally obtained results favoring the subjects in less-restrictive settings. An exception, however, is an investigation by Eyman, Silverstein, and McLain (1975) in which the adaptive behavior gains of three groups of mentally retarded individuals were compared: a) residents of an institution who received standard care, b) residents who received special training in the institution, and c) previously institutionalized residents who were placed in the community. Of the 360 total subjects, 49 participated in an in-house sensory-motor training program; 86 attended school programs in the living unit of the institution; 120 received standard care at the institution; and 105 were placed in foster homes. Gains in ambulation over the 3-year period were significantly greater for the sensory-motor training program than for any of the other groups. Similarly, the gains in toileting were significantly greater for those in the sensory-motor training program and in the school program than for those in standard care, but not significantly greater than for those in foster care. The results of this study indicate that mere change of placement to a more homelike living environment is not sufficient to guarantee increases in adaptive behavior skills. The type of training provided in each setting must also be taken into account. Unfortunately, the type of training provided has not been controlled in any of the studies to ensure that both experimental and control groups receive the same type and amount of training.

In some studies, the type of training provided to residents in community-based facilities was intentionally different from the training provided in institutions. In a study by Close

(1977), 8 of 15 residents of an institution were randomly selected for placement in a community vocational program and group home. The Developmental Record (Hutton & Talkington, 1974) and the Community Living Observational System (Taylor & Close, 1976) were used to assess the adaptive behavior of residents, and particular emphasis was placed on self-help skills, domestic skills, and social skills. Individualized training programs focused on these skills and on the reduction of inappropriate behavior. After the first year of programming, the residents of the group home had made significantly greater gains in the areas of eating, toileting, personal hygiene, and social interaction in comparison with the group of residents who remained in the institution. That the subjects were randomly selected for community placement lends credence to the results of this study. In this study, as in most studies, it is impossible to determine whether the gains in adaptive behavior were due to the change in placement, to the change in training program, or to other factors.

Schroeder and Henes (1978) used the Progress Assessment Chart. (Gunzberg, 1976) to assess the adaptive behavior of 19 deinstitutionalized group home residents and 19 matched subjects who remained in institutions. Pretest scores on the Progress Assessment Chart were not significantly different for the two groups. After approximately 1 year of placement in the group homes, the communication scores of the experimental subjects showed significant improvements beyond those of their counterparts who remained in the institution. Although there were no significant differences between the two groups in terms of gains in the areas of self-help and socialization/occupation, the residents of the group homes had gained more in those areas than had those in the institution. Similar findings were reported by Kushlick (1975) on the progress of adaptive behavior of two groups of severely retarded children in England. The 18 children who moved to smaller community-based residential units (housing 20–25 residents) made significantly more progress in the areas of eating, dressing, and appropriate social behavior

than the 20 children who remained in the institution that had units containing 40 children. In nearly all adaptive behavior areas, the scores of residents in community-based facilities increased more over the 4-year period than those of residents in the institution.

In a related study, Campbell (1971) studied 37 matched pairs of institutionalized mentally retarded adults. At the time of the study, half of the subjects resided in institutions and half had lived in hostels in the community for at least 6 months (average length of residence was $16\frac{1}{2}$ months). The residents of the two types of facilities were compared on 10 self-care skills, including bathing, dressing, grooming, eating, and use of money. The residents of hostels were found to be significantly more independent in self-care skills than the institutionalized residents. In a follow-up study conducted a year later, the self-care skills of the hostel group had not significantly increased, while the self-care skills of the institutionalized group had improved. However, the residents of the hostels still scored significantly higher in self-care skills than the residents of the institution in both assessments.

In a study by Witt (1981), the adaptive behavior of 64 institutionalized residents who were transferred from large (30–35 residents) to smaller (14 residents) living units was compared with the adaptive behavior of 31 residents remaining in the large living unit. Other than size, the two types of living units were judged to be very similar. The Vineland Social Maturity Scale (Doll, 1965) was administered annually from 3 years prior to the move until approximately 1 year after the move. Over the 4 years, the residents remaining in a large living unit increased in adaptive behavior, with small increments in performance each year. The group that moved to the small living units, by contrast, demonstrated significant increases when tested approximately 1 year after the move. Skills in the areas of self-help, socialization, and occupation improved more dramatically than other adaptive behavior skills after the transition to the smaller living units. It is particularly unfortunate that environmental attributes were not measured in this study. If, indeed, the two living settings were virtually the same except for size, the improvements in adaptive behavior might more reliably be related to size of facility.

One additional investigation focused on the effects on adaptive behavior of smaller size and more normalized living environments while staying within the context of an institutional setting. MacEachron (1983) randomly assigned adult mentally retarded residents who had been stratified according to gender and intellectual level to treatment and control groups. Subjects in the control group remained in older, custodial living units in the institution that housed an average of 55 persons, while the treatment subjects were placed in smaller, more normalized cottages that housed approximately 15 residents. Although MacEachron (1983) expressed the view that cottages were more normalized than traditional institutional buildings, the physical environments of both cottages and custodial living units were measured using three environmental measures. Size was measured by the number of clients living in a building. The extent to which a client's residential environment contained normal or homelike features was measured by the Physical Environment Index (Gunzberg and Gunzberg 1973; Morris, 1969). Finally, the extent to which building staff members allowed residents to use or manage the physical environment at the residents' discretion rather than the staff's discretion was measured by the Accessibility of the Physical Environment Index (Gunzberg and Gunzberg, 1973).

The treatment variable was very strongly associated with the three physical environment indicators of normalizing care. The Resident Management Practices Scale (King et al., 1971) was used to measure the treatment environment in this study. Resident-oriented practices were found to strongly correlate with cottage living. Thus, cottage living did consist of both physical and psychosocial normalizing features. After 1 year of residence, the AAMD Adaptive Behavior Scale was used to measure the adaptive behavior of the 129 subjects in the control group and the 160 subjects in the treatment group. All of the groups living in the cottages had higher adaptive behavior scores than their comparison groups in the custodial units, and the differences were statistically significant for about half of the comparison groups. The major differences between control and treatment groups were in the areas of Domestic Activity, Adult Socialization, and Independent Functioning. The social and physical aspects of the living environments that were found to be the strongest predictors of adaptive behavior were the availability of physical environments for residents to use at their discretion, the use of resident-oriented management practices, and participation in programs. In this study, as in the study by Witt (1981), the residents of smaller, more normalized living units exhibited adaptive behavior skills that were superior to those of their counterparts in the larger custodial settings. Apparently, normalizing some portions of the living environment has favorable results, even without integrating residents more fully into the community.

Seventy residents of community-based facilities who had previously lived in institutions were matched with 70 residents remaining in the institution in a study by Conroy, Efthimiou, and Lemanowicz (1982). Adaptive behavior functioning was assessed with the Behavior Development Survey (1979), a shortened version of the AAMD Adaptive Behavior Scale, both while all subjects resided in the institution and 2 years after the experimental group had been placed in the community. No significant differences were found in adaptive behavior scores during the initial testing, but the adaptive behavior of the residents of community facilities was significantly higher than that of their matched partners in the institution at the time of the second testing. The adaptive behavior scores of the individuals who remained in the institution did not change significantly over the 2-year period. Environmental quality was also measured in this study, and partial correlations were calculated between adaptive behavior gain and environmental measures. Three measures were used: a) the shortened version of PASS 3 (Flynn & Heal, 1981), b) Resident Management Survey (King et al., 1971) and c) a measure of the physical quality of living settings derived from the standards of the Accreditation Council for Services for Mentally Retarded and Other Developmentally Disabled Persons. Adaptive behavior gain was negatively correlated with ratings obtained from each of these measures on the clients' former institutional cottages. Presumably, clients who came from cottages with lower environmental ratings gained more when they were transferred to community-based facilities.

Interpreting Effects of Environmental Change on Adaptive Behavior

In the vast majority of studies, adaptive behavior skills improved, or at least remained stable, after placement in less-restrictive environments. A word of caution is in order, however, in interpreting research on the effects of environmental change on adaptive behavior. Although adaptive behavior skills generally improved in the less-restrictive environment, the results of these studies indicate that changes in adaptive behavior may not occur immediately following placement in community living facilities. Despite findings by Fiorelli and Thurman (1979) in which positive changes occurred within 5 to 6 weeks after placement, most other studies have indicated that changes may be delayed. Aninger and Bolinksy (1977), for example, studied residents after 6 months of community residence and found no significant improvements in adaptive functioning. Hemming et al. (1981) found that improvements in adaptive behavior skills were most noticeable after 9 months of placement in less-restrictive environments.

Any number of factors may be responsible for the changes in adaptive behavior that frequently occur after a move to a community-based residential facility. Among the possible explanations, it is reasonable to hypothesize that improvements may be due to Hawthorne effects (mere change of physical environment), to greater opportunity to practice adaptive behavior skills, to the increased emphasis on training, or to more rapid acquisition of adaptive behavior skills in the new environment. In order to isolate the effects that may be due to

Hawthorne effects, Sokol-Kessler, Conroy, Feinstein, Lemanowicz, and McGurrin (1983) measured the rate of developmental growth that occurred in two groups of clients over a 2-year period. Clients in one of the groups had resided in small community-based facilities for several years (an average of 2.5 years at the beginning of the study), and thus, had not recently undergone a change of residence. Those subjects were matched on adaptive and problem behavior scores, on gender, and on age with 104 residents of an institution. Using the Behavior Development Survey, adaptive and maladaptive behaviors of the two groups were compared at Time 1 and 2 years later at Time 2. Although the two groups were relatively homogeneous, the group in the community received considerably more day programming time than the group in the institution (31.2 hours per week compared with 19.4 hours per week).

Despite the increased programming time and living in small community-based facilities, there were no statistically significant differences between the two groups in terms of adaptive behavior skills at Time 2. Nevertheless, the adaptive behavior scores of individuals living in the community had increased slightly over the 2 years, while the scores of the institution residents had declined slightly. The most notable differences occurred in the area of maladaptive behavior. The community group displayed significantly fewer behavior problems at Time 2 than did the institution group. Although the changes in adaptive behavior were minimal, improvements in both adaptive and maladaptive functioning appeared to occur more rapidly for residents of community-based facilities than for residents of institutions. This study lends support to the notion that improvements in functional abilities are due to factors other than simply Hawthorne effects resulting from a mere change of living environment.

Three major adaptive behavior skills have been identified most frequently as predictive of successful community adjustment and as areas in which gains are likely to occur after placement in the community: domestic skills, social behavior, and self-help skills. Residents who possess adequate skills in these areas are more likely to succeed in the community, possibly because domestic, social, and self-help skills are frequently performed and needed in community settings. Moreover, changes in the focus of adaptive behavior training in community-based facilities may lead to significant improvements in these particular adaptive behavior skills. Given the wide array of other adaptive behavior skills that have also been identified as important, however, it is still not possible to state unequivocally that particular adaptive behavior skills merit more emphasis than other skills in the assessment and training of skills required for successful placement in less-restrictive living environments.

Limits of Adaptive Behavior Research

The studies reviewed in this section are limited by the instruments that were used to assess adaptive behavior, as well as by inadequate assessments of environmental qualities. If the scales did not assess consumer skills or health care, for example, it was not possible to ascertain the impact of those skills on successful community placement. Given the wide array of other adaptive behavior skills that have also been identified as important, however, it is still not possible to state unequivocally that particular adaptive behavior skills merit more emphasis than others in the assessment and training of skills required for successful placement in less-restrictive living environments. Perhaps even more serious is the absence of environmental measures in nearly all studies. Most studies merely report general attributes of placements such as size or location but generally provide no information on the physical, social, or habilitative qualities of environments. Without more information on environmental features, activities of daily living, and other salient features of the treatment environment, it cannot be assumed that a home in a neighborhood represents a less-restrictive environment than a larger facility in a nonneighborhood setting. These conceptual and measurement issues are discussed more thoroughly by Landesman-Dwyer in Chapter 10.

The interaction of client characteristics with community adjustment and with effects of training is still relatively unexplored. It is possible that higher-functioning individuals may be more likely to fail in community placements as a result of problem behaviors, while severely handicapped persons may more often fail due to inadequate adaptive behavior skills. These results suggest that the adaptation of people in environments is not a simple, straightforward matter of placement in different settings. Further evaluation is clearly needed of the interaction effects of client characteristics, placement, and training strategies before definitive conclusions can be drawn regarding relationships between behavioral functioning and adjustment in different environments.

CONCLUSION

With the promulgation of deinstitutionalization and normalization, there has been increased interest in evaluating the qualities of environments; the differentiation and typing of various kinds of environments using physical, behavioral, and psychosocial criteria; and the assessment of individual adaptive growth as it relates to environmental qualities. One manifestation of these concerns has been a rapidly expanding literature aimed at the refinement and validation of instruments used to measure characteristics of the environment. Another area of inquiry has arisen from research in designing physical environments and the assessment of effects of environmental qualities upon development and behavior of handicapped persons.

The evidence is somewhat mixed regarding whether there is any inherent improvement in behavior or normalizing influence associated with small facilities or specially designed facilities. From the results of research in these areas, it appears that the provision of a variety of living spaces in a facility does not ensure their use and, also, that mediation is often necessary by staff in the form of training residents to manipulate and exercise control over aspects of their environments. Physical space must be designed with concern for increasing the amount of individual control of the environment exercised by each resident. Intrafacility factors (such as activity levels and involvement of caregivers) and extrafacility characteristics (such as geographic location) interact to produce more or less normalizing effects on individuals. In other words, there are psychosocial, behavioral, and physical interactions of environmental variables at work in each setting that probably differentially influence behavior of personnel and clients in treatment settings.

On a more global level, the literature on the relationship between adaptive behavior and living in less-restrictive environments tends to support the notion of deinstitutionalization and community integration of handicapped individuals. The large majority of handicapped persons placed in the community remain there successfully, as reported in most studies during the past several years. Although adaptive behavior skills of individuals placed in less-restrictive environments do seem likely to improve after movement to less-restrictive living settings, still too little is known regarding the precise contribution of environmental influences and training methods in supporting community adjustment.

A vast array of instruments exists to measure characteristics of individuals. Environmental assessment, however, has just begun to be utilized, particularly in facilities for mentally retarded persons. Few instruments that assess characteristics of the treatment environment have been used more than once in facilities for mentally retarded individuals. From these studies, it has been determined that there is a great variation in treatment environments between community and public residential facilities, as well as among facilities of each type. More positive treatment environments do not necessarily correlate with smaller facilities, with facilities located in the community, or with any other variable that has been manipulated in the past. Research has shown correlations between staff approval of facility admission policy, privately owned facilities, and homes where families participate in planning treatment goals with higher levels of client autonomy (Brown & Guard, 1979). However, these findings have not been replicated. The literature reflects the complexity of the interaction between behavior and environmental characteristics in programs for severely handicapped persons.

The studies in this chapter do illustrate that the labels ascribed to residential environments do not, ipso facto, convey reliable information on environmental qualities. This particular problem makes the study of environmental effects upon behavior and development problematical. There is a need for more precise environmental measurement that can differentiate among facilities and predict behavioral outcomes from various environments. (These issues are elaborated upon extensively by Landesman-Dwyer in the next chapter.)

Client outcomes of community care have often been predicated upon three types of variables: preplacement factors (i.e., degree of retardation), facility characteristics (i.e., size or location), and facility type (e.g., room and board, supervised living). Ultimately, the aim of further research would be to show that certain adaptive behaviors are predictable from these characteristics and more precisely defined treatment environment characteristics. Relationships might be found between staff/resident ratios; family involvement in the planning of treatment goals; staff satisfaction; and facility ownership; or a number of other variables defining the characteristics of living and treatment environments.

The deinstitutionalization process has promoted the development of alternative residential environments for increasing numbers of severely handicapped persons, and this trend is expected to continue. It is believed that environmental attributes, more psychosocial than physical, contribute to handicapped citizens' happiness, learning ability, and morale. However, if the aim is to scientifically translate behavior/environment relationships into living spaces, and then into desired outcomes for individuals, some greater understanding of our motives and refinement of our methodologies are necessary.

Research focusing on the environmental assessment of service program facilities has usually emphasized discrete components of the psychosocial or physical environment. It has seldom assessed complex interactions among environmental features and behavioral outcomes or assessed means by which environments can be experimentally manipulated to improve functioning of service personnel and severely handicapped clients. Through further research, it is possible that environmental assessments can be refined and combined through appropriate intervention programs to improve the quality of life for severely handicapped clients.

REFERENCES

Aanes, D., & Moen, M. Adaptive behavior changes of group home residents. *Mental Retardation,* 1976, *14*(4), 36–40.

Altman, I. *The environment and social behavior.* Monterey, CA: Brooks/Cole, 1975.

Aninger, M., & Bolinksy, K. Levels of independent functioning of retarded adults in apartments. *Mental Retardation,* 1977, *15*(4), 12–13.

Balla, D.A. Relationship of institution size to quality of care: A review of the literature. *American Journal of Mental Deficiency,* 1976, *81,* 117–124.

Baroff, G.S. On size and the quality of residential care: A second look. *Mental Retardation,* 1980, *18,* 113–117.

Bednar, M.J. *Architecture for the handicapped in Denmark, Sweden, and Holland: A guidebook to normalization.* Ann Arbor: University of Michigan, Architectural Research Laboratory, 1974.

Bednar, M.J. *Barrier free environments.* Stroudsburg, PA: Dowden, Hutchinson & Ross, 1977.

Behavior Development Survey User's Manual. Pomona, CA: University of California, Los Angeles, Neuropsychiatric Research Group at Lanterman State Hospital, 1979.

Bell, N.J., Schoenrock, C., & Bensberg, G. Change over time in the community: Findings of a longitudinal study. In: R.H. Bruininks, C.E. Meyers, B.B. Sigford, & K.C. Lakin (eds.), *Deinstitutionalization and community adjustment of mentally retarded people.* Washington, D.C.: American Association on Mental Deficiency, 1981.

Birenbaum, A., & Re, M.A. Resettling mentally retarded adults in the community—Almost four years later. *American Journal of Mental Deficiency,* 1979, *83,* 323–329.

Bjaanes, A.T., & Butler, E.W. Environmental variation in community care facilities for mentally retarded persons. *American Journal of Mental Deficiency,* 1974, *78,* 429–439.

Bock, W.H., & Weatherman, R.E. *The assessment of behavioral competence of developmentally disabled individuals: The Minnesota Developmental Programming System.* Minneapolis: University of Minnesota, 1979.

Brown, J.S., & Guard, K.A. The treatment environment for retarded persons in nursing homes. *Mental Retardation,* 1979, *17,* 77–82.

Brown, M., Diller, L., Fordyce, W., Jacobs, D., & Gordon, W. Rehabilitation indicators: Their nature and uses for assessment. In: B. Bolton & D.W. Cook (eds.), *Rehabilitation client assessment.* Baltimore: University Park Press, 1980.

Budde, J.F. *Analyzing and measuring deinstitutionalization across residential environments with Alternative Living Environments Rating and Tracking System (ALERT).* Lawrence: University of Kansas, Affiliated Facilities Publications, 1976.

Butler, E.W., & Bjaanes, A.T. Activities and the use of time by retarded persons in community care facilities. In: G. Sackett (ed.), *Observing behavior: Theory and application in mental retardation,* Vol. 1. Baltimore: University Park Press, 1978.

Caldwell, B., & Bradley, R. *Home Observation for Measurement of the Environment (HOME).* Unpublished manuscript, University of Arkansas, Little Rock, 1978.

Campbell, A.C. Aspects of personal independence of mentally subnormal and severely subnormal adults in hospital and local authority hostels. *International Journal of Social Psychiatry,* 1971, *17,* 305–310.

Cleland, C.C., & Sluyter, G.V. The heterobedfast ward: A model for translating normalization into practice. *Mental Retardation,* 1973, *11*(1), 44–46.

Close, D.W. Community living for severely and profoundly retarded adults: A group home study. *Education and Training of the Mentally Retarded,* 1977, *12*(3), 256–262.

Conroy, J., Efthimiou, J., & Lemanowicz, J. A matched comparison of the developmental growth of institutionalized and deinstitutionalized mentally retarded clients. *American Journal of Mental Deficiency,* 1982, *86,* 581–587.

Craik, K.H. Environmental psychology. In: K.H. Craik (ed.), *New directions in psychology,* Vol. 4. New York: Holt, Rinehart & Winston, 1970.

Crnic, K.A., & Pym, H.A. Training mentally retarded adults in independent living skills. *Mental Retardation,* 1979, *17,* 13–16.

Doll, E.A. *Vineland Social Maturity Scale.* Circle Pines, MN: American Guidance Service, 1965.

Dybwad, G. Architecture's role in revitalizing the field of mental retardation. *British Journal of Mental Subnormality,* 1970, *16*(30), 45–48.

Ellsworth, R., Maroney, R., Klett, W., Gordon, H., & Gunn, R. Milieu characteristics of successful psychiatric treatment programs. *American Journal of Orthopsychiatry,* 1971, *41,* 427–441.

Eyman, R.K., & Borthwick, S.A. A longitudinal study of foster care placement. In: S. Landesman-Dwyer (ed.), *The social ecology of handicapped people.* Baltimore: University Park Press, 1984.

Eyman, R.K., Demaine, G.C., & Lei, T. Relationship between community environment and resident changes in adaptive behavior: A path model. *American Journal of Mental Deficiency,* 1979, *83,* 330–338.

Eyman, R.K., Silverstein, A.B., & McLain, R. Effects of treatment programs on the acquisition of basic skills. *American Journal of Mental Deficiency,* 1975, *79,* 573–582.

Fiorelli, J.S., & Thurman, S.K. Client behavior in more and less normalized settings. *Education and Training of the Mentally Retarded,* 1979, *14,* 85–94.

Flynn, R., & Heal, L. A short form of PASS 3—A study of

its structure, interrater reliability, and validity for assessing normalization. *Evaluation Review,* 1981, *56,* 357–376.

Flynn, R.J., & Nitsch, K.E. (eds.). *Normalization, social integration and community services.* Baltimore: University Park Press, 1980.

Frederiksen, N. Toward a taxonomy of situations. *American Psychologist,* 1972, *27,* 114–123.

Goffman, E. *Asylums: Essays on the social situation of mental patients and other inmates.* New York: Doubleday & Co., 1961.

Griffin, J.C., Landers, W.F., & Patterson, E.T. *Behavioral architecture: Effects of the physical environment on the behavior of the retarded.* Unpublished manuscript, Texas Technical University, Research and Training Center in Mental Retardation, Lubbock, TX, 1974a.

Griffin, J.C., Landers, W.F., & Patterson, E.T. *Toward behavioral architecture: Effects of crowding on the behavior of the retarded.* Unpublished manuscript, Texas Technical University, Research and Training Center in Mental Retardation, Lubbock, TX, 1974b.

Gump, P.V. The behavior setting: A promising unit for environmental designers. *Landscape Architecture,* 1971, *61,* 130–134.

Gunzberg, H. C. The physical environment of the mentally handicapped, VII: 39 steps toward normalizing living practices in living units for the mentally retarded. *British Journal of Mental Subnormality,* 1973, *19*(37), 91–99.

Gunzberg, H.C. *Progress assessment chart of social and personal development* (4th ed.). England: SEFA, 1976.

Gunzberg, H.C., & Gunzberg, A.L. *Mental handicap and physical environment: The application of an operational philosophy to planning.* New York: Macmillan Publishing Co., 1973.

Hauber, F.A., Bruininks, R.H., Hill, B. K., Lakin, K.C., & White, C.C. *1982 national census of residential facilities: Summary report, Brief #19.* Minneapolis: University of Minnesota, Center for Residential and Community Services, 1984.

Hemming, H., Lavender, T., & Pill, R. Quality of life of mentally retarded adults transferred from large institutions to new small units. *American Journal of Mental Deficiency,* 1981, *86,* 157–169.

Hutton, W., & Talkington, L. *Developmental record.* Corvallis, OR: Continuing Education Publications, 1974.

Intagliata, J., Crosby, N., & Neider, L. Foster family care for mentally retarded people: A qualitative review. In: R.H., Bruininks, C.E. Meyers, B.B. Sigford, & K.C. Lakin (eds.), *Deinstitutionalization and community adjustment of mentally retarded people.* Washington, D C : American Association on Mental Deficiency, 1981.

Intagliata, J., & Willer, B. Reinstitutionalization of mentally retarded persons successfully placed into family-care and group homes. *American Journal of Mental Deficiency,* 1982, *87,* 34–39.

Jackson, J. Factors of the treatment environment. *Archives of General Psychiatry,* 1969, *21,* 39–45.

James, F.E., Spencer, D.A., & Hamilton, M. Immediate effects of improved hospital environment on behavior patterns of mentally handicapped patients. *British Journal of Psychiatry,* 1975, *126,* 577–581.

Jelinek, R. *A methodology for the evaluation of quality of life and care in long term facilities.* Springfield, VA: U.S. Department of Commerce (NTIS), 1974.

Kahn, L. Fundamental processes of environmental behavior. In: J. Long, C. Burnelle, W. Moleski, & D. Vachon (eds.), *Designing for human behavior.* Stoudsburg, PA: Dowden, Hutchinson & Ross, 1974.

King, R., & Raynes, N.V. An operational measure of inmate management in residential institutions. *Social Sciences and Medicine,* 1968, *2,* 41–53.

King, R.D., Raynes, N.V., & Tizard, J. *Patterns of residential care: Sociological studies in institutions for handicapped children.* London: Routledge & Kegan Paul, 1971.

Kleinberg, J., & Galligan, B. Effects of deinstitutionalization on adaptive behavior of mentally retarded adults. *American Journal of Mental Deficiency,* 1983, *88,* 21–27.

Knight, R.C., Weitzer, W.H., & Zimring, C.M. *Opportunity for control and the built environment: The ELEMR project.* Amherst: University of Massachusetts, Environment and Behavior Research Center, 1978.

Kreger, K. Compensatory environment programming for the severely retarded behaviorally disturbed. *Mental Retardation,* 1971, *9,* 29–32.

Kushlick, A. Epidemiology and evaluation of services for the mentally handicapped. In: M.J. Begab & S.A. Richardson (eds.), *The mentally retarded and society: A social sciences perspective.* Baltimore: University Park Press, 1975.

Lakin, K.C. *Demographic studies of residential facilities for the mentally retarded.* Minneapolis: University of Minnesota, Department of Educational Psychology, 1979.

Lakin, K.C., Bruininks, R.H., Doth, D., Hill, B.K., & Hauber, F.A. *Sourcebook on long-term care for developmentally disabled people.* Minneapolis: University of Minnesota, Department of Educational Psychology, 1982.

Landesman-Dwyer, S. The changing structure and function of institutions: A search for optimal group care environments. In: S. Landesman-Dwyer (ed.), *The social ecology of handicapped people.* Baltimore: University Park Press, 1984.

Landesman-Dwyer, S., Stein, J., & Sackett, G.P. Group homes for the developmentally disabled: A behavioral and ecological description. In P. Mittler & J. DeJong (eds.), *Research to practice in mental retardation: Care and intervention,* Vol. 1. Baltimore: University Park Press, 1976.

Levy, E., & McLeod, W. The effects of environmental design on adolescents in an institution. *Mental Retardation,* 1977, *15,* 28–32.

Lewis, N.H., & Baumeister, A.A. Stereotyped mannerisms in mentally retarded persons: Animal models and theoretical analyses. In: N.R. Ellis (ed.), *International review of research in mental retardation,* Vol. 11. New York: Academic Press, 1982.

McCormick, M., Balla, D., & Zigler, E. Resident-care practices in institutions for retarded persons. *American Journal of Mental Deficiency,* 1975, *80,* 1–17.

MacEachron, A.E. Institutional reform and adaptive functioning of mentally retarded persons: A field experiment. *American Journal of Mental Deficiency,* 1983, *88,* 2–12.

McGee, M.G., & Woods, D.J. Use of Moos' Ward Atmosphere Scale in a residential setting for mentally retarded adolescents. *Psychological Reports,* 1978, *43,* 580–582.

McLain, R.E., Silverstein, A.B., Hubbell, M., & Brownlee, L. Comparison of the residential environment of a state hospital for retarded clients with those of various types of community facilities. *Journal of Community Psychology,* 1977, *5,* 282–287.

McLain, R.E., Silverstein, A.B., Hubbell, M., & Brownlee, L. Comparison of the residential environment of a state hospital for retarded clients with those of various types of community facilities. *Journal of Community Psychology,* 1977, *5,* 282–287.

Moos, R. The generality of questionnaire data ratings by psychiatric patients. *Journal of Clinical Psychology,* 1970, *26,* 234–236.

Moos, R. *Revision of the Ward Atmosphere Scale (WAS).* Palo Alto, CA: Stanford University, Department of Psychiatry, Social Ecology Laboratory, 1971.

Moos, R. Assessment of the psychosocial environments of community oriented psychiatric treatment programs. *Journal of Abnormal Psychology,* 1972, *79,* 9–18.

Moos, R. *Conceptualizing educational environments* (Seaday Papers: On problems of development in Southeast Asia). New York: 1973.

Moos, R., & Houts, P. Assessment of the social atmospheres of psychiatric wards. *Journal of Abnormal Psychology,* 1968, *73,* 595–604.

Moos, R., & Insel, P. (ed.). *Issues in social ecology: Human milieu.* Palo Alto, CA: National Press Books, 1974.

Moos, R., & Otto, J. The community-oriented programs environment scales: A methodology for the facilitation and evaluation of social change. *Community Mental Health Journal,* 1972, *8*(1), 28–37.

Moos, R., Shelton, R., & Petty, C. Perceived ward climate and treatment outcome. *Journal of Abnormal Psychology,* 1973, *82,* 291–298.

Morris, P. *Put away: A sociological study of institutions for the mentally retarded.* New York: Athesson, 1969.

Nathan, M., Millham, J., Chilcutt, J., & Atkinson, B. Mentally retarded individuals as informants for the AAMD Adaptive Behavior Scale. *Mental Retardation,* 1980, *18,* 82–84.

Nihira, K., Foster, R., Shellhaas, M., & Leland, H. *AAMD Adaptive Behavior Scale.* Washington, D.C.: American Association on Mental Deficiency, 1974.

O'Neill, J., Brown, M., Gordon, W., Schonhorn, R., & Greer, E. Activity patterns of mentally retarded adults in institutions and communities: A longitudinal study. *Applied Research in Mental Retardation,* 1981, *2,* 367–379.

Pankratz, L. Assessing the psychosocial environment of halfway houses for the retarded. *Community Mental Health Journal,* 1975, *11,* 341–345.

Penk, W., & Robinowitz, R. *Interrelations among measures of environment and personality: COPES and the MMPI.* Dallas: Psychology Service, VET Administration Hospital, 1975.

Pierce, W.D., Trickett, E.J., & Moos, R.H. Changing ward atmosphere through staff discussion of the perceived ward environment. *Archives of General Psychiatry,* 1972, *26*(1), 35–41.

Pratt, M.W., Luszcz, M.A., & Brown, M.E. Measuring dimensions of the quality of care in small community residences. *American Journal of Mental Deficiency,* 1980, *85,* 188–194.

Price, R.H., & Moos, R.H. Toward a taxonomy of inpatient treatment environments. *Journal of Abnormal Psychology,* 1975, *84,* 181–188.

Proshansky, H., Ittelson, W., & Rivlin, L. (eds.). *Environmental psychology: Man and his physical setting.* New York: Holt, Rinehart & Winston, 1970.

Rapoport, A. *The meaning of the built environment: A nonverbal communication approach.* Beverly Hills, CA: Sage Publications, 1982.

Raynes, N., Pratt, M., & Roses, S. *Organizational structure and the care of the mentally retarded.* London: Croon-Helm, 1979.

Reizenstein, J.E., & McBride, W.A. Design for normalization: A social environmental evaluation of a community for mentally retarded adults. *Journal of Architectural Research,* 1977, *6*(1), 10.

Robinson, J.W., Thompson, T., Graff, M., Emmons, P., & Franklin, E. *Architecture parameters of normalization: An exploratory study.* Unpublished manuscript, Department of Architecture, University of Minnesota, 1983.

Rotegard, L.L., Hill, B.K., & Bruininks, R.H. Environmental characteristics of residential facilities for mentally retarded people in the United States. *American Journal of Mental Deficiency,* 1983, *88,* 49–56.

Schalock, R.L., & Harper, R.S. Placement from community-based MR programs: How well do clients do? *American Journal of Mental Deficiency,* 1978, *83,* 240–247.

Schalock, R.L., Harper, R.S., & Carver, G. Independent living placement: Five years later. *American Journal of Mental Deficiency,* 1981, *86*(2), 170–177.

Schalock, R.L., Harper, R.S., & Genung, T. Community integration of mentally retarded adults: Community placement and program success. *American Journal of Mental Deficiency,* 1981, *85,* 478–488.

Schroeder, S.R., & Henes, C. Assessment of progress of institutionalized and deinstitutionalized retarded adults: A matched control comparison. *Mental Retardation,* 1978, *16,* 147–148.

Schwartz, M. What is a therapeutic milieu? In: M. Greenblatt, D.J. Levinson, & R.H. Williams (eds.), *The patient and the mental hospital.* Glencoe, IL: Free Press, 1957.

Seltzer, M.M., Sherwood, C.C., Seltzer, G.B., & Sherwood, S. Community adaptation and the impact of deinstitutionalization. In: R.H. Bruininks, C.E. Meyers, B.B. Sigford, & K.C. Lakin (eds.), *Deinstitutionalization and community adjustment of mentally retarded people.* Washington, D.C.: American Association on Mental Deficiency, 1981.

Sigelman, C.K., Schoenrock, C.J., Winer, J.L., Spanhel, C.L., Hromas, S.G., Martin, P.W., Budd, E.C., & Bensberg, G.J. Issues in interviewing mentally retarded persons: An empirical study. In: R.H. Bruininks, C.E. Meyers, B.B. Sigford, & K.C. Lakin (eds.), *Deinstitutionalization and community adjustment of mentally retarded people.* Washington, D.C.: American Association on Mental Deficiency, 1981.

Silverstein, A.B., McLain, R.E., Hubbell, M., & Brownlee, L. Characteristics of the treatment environment: A factor-analytic study. *Educational and Psychological Measurement,* 1977, *37,* 367–371.

Sitkei, E.G. After group home living—What alternatives? Results of a two year mobility follow-up study. *Mental Retardation,* 1980, *18,* 9–13.

Soforenko, A.Z., & Macy, T.W. *A study of the charac-*

teristics and life status of persons discharged from a large state institution for the mentally retarded during the years 1969–1977. Columbus: Ohio State University, Monograph, Vol. 1, 1977.

Sokol-Kessler, L.E., Conroy, J.W., Feinstein, C.S., Lemanowicz, J.A., & McGurrin, M. Developmental progress in institutional and community settings. *Journal of the Association for the Severely Handicapped,* 1983, *8*(3), 43–48.

Sommer, R. *Personal space: The behavioral basis of design.* Englewood Cliffs, NJ: Prentice Hall, 1969.

Spencer, D.A. Redevelopment of a hospital for the mentally handicapped. *Nursing Times,* 1974, *70*(30), 1172–1173.

Stern, G. *People in context: Measuring person-environment congruence in education and industry.* New York: John Wiley & Sons, 1970.

Sternlicht, M. Variables affecting foster care placement of institutionalized retarded residents. *Mental Retardation,* 1978, *16,* 25–28.

Sutter, P., Mayeda, T., Call, T., Yanagi, G., & Yee, S. Comparison of successful and unsuccessful community placed mentally retarded persons. *American Journal of Mental Deficiency,* 1980, *85,* 262–267.

Taylor, V., & Close, D.W. *Community living observational system.* Eugene: University of Oregon, Rehabilitation Research and Training Center in Mental Retardation, 1976.

Thiel, G.W. Relationships of IQ, adaptive behavior, age, and environmental demand to community-placement success of mentally retarded adults. *American Journal of Mental Deficiency,* 1981, *86,* 208–211.

Thompson, T., & Carey, A. Structured normalization: Intellectual and adaptive behavior changes in a residential setting. *Mental Retardation,* 1980, *18,* 193–137.

Tizard, J. Quality of residential care for retarded children. In: J. Tizard, I. Sinclair, & R.V.G. Clarke (eds.), *Varieties of residential experience.* London: Routledge & Kegan Paul, 1975.

Tjosvold, D., & Tjosvold, M.M. Social psychological

analysis of residences for mentally retarded persons. *American Journal of Mental Deficiency,* 1983, *88,* 28–40.

Wicker A. W. Processes which mediate behavior: Environment congruence. *Behavioral Science,* 1972, *17,* 265–277.

Witt, S. Increase in adaptive behavior level after residence in an intermediate care facility for mentally retarded persons. *Mental Retardation,* 1981, *19,* 75–79.

Wohlwill, J. The emerging discipline of environmental psychology. *American Psychologist,* 1970, *25,* 303–312.

Wolfensberger, W. *The principle of normalization in human services.* Toronto: National Institute on Mental Retardation, 1972.

Wolfensberger, W. Research, empiricism, and the principle of normalization. In: R.J. Flynn & K.E. Nitsch (eds.), *Normalization, social integration, and community services,* 117–132. Baltimore: University Park Press, 1980.

Wolfensberger, W., & Glenn, L. *PASS 2: A system for the quantitative evaluation of human services.* Toronto: National Institute on Mental Health (sponsored by Canadian Association for the Mentally Retarded), 1973.

Wolfensberger, W., & Glenn, L. *PASS 3: A method for the quantitative evaluation of human services.* Toronto: National Institute on Mental Retardation, 1975.

Wolfensberger, W., & Thomas, S. *PASSING, Program Analysis of Service Systems Implementation of Normalization Goals: Normalization criteria and ratings manual* (2nd ed.). Downsview, Ontario, Canada: National Institute on Mental Retardation, 1983.

Zeisel, J. Behavioral research and environmental design: A marriage of necessity. *Design and Environment,* 1970, *1*(1), 50–51, 64–66.

Zigler, C., & Balla, D. Impact of institutional experience on the behavior and development of retarded persons. *American Journal of Mental Deficiency,* 1977, *82,* 1–11.

Chapter 10

Describing and Evaluating Residential Environments

Sharon Landesman-Dwyer

The concept of "least restrictive environment" involves three key assumptions: a) that environments can be clearly defined, b) that individuals are significantly affected by their environments, and c) that there are standards for judging the degree to which environments restrict or enhance the development of individuals. This chapter explores these assumptions, considers what is known about the relationship between environmental variables and "quality of life," and proposes a general approach to "person-environment match" in providing services for severely handicapped persons.

DEFINING "ENVIRONMENT"

The notion of "environment" is complex and multidimensional. In the broadest sense, environment is defined in *Webster's New World Dictionary* as "all the conditions, circumstances, and influences surrounding and affecting the development of an organism or group of organisms" (Guralnik, 1974, p. 468). This definition acknowledges that environments incorporate many diverse features; yet to encompass *all* of the factors that impinge upon and influence the course of an individual's life, a unique or idiographic environment would have to be delineated for each person.

Conventionally, environments are thought of in a narrower sense, based on naturally occurring combinations of variables circumscribed in time and space. In addition to their external boundaries and physical features, environments often distinguish themselves by their prescribed societal purposes. For example, homes and schools represent conventionally defined types of environments. Each of these environments may be characterized in terms of certain key features, both inanimate and animate, as well as by the functions they serve for society. It is important to mention that these distinguishing environmental variables theoretically are independent of their actual impact on individuals.

For purposes of this chapter, the more restricted and commonplace definition of environments has been adopted. That is, environments have geographical boundaries, contain certain objective physical and social resources, and serve a recognized purpose or role. This definition focuses primarily on objective elements or characteristics but is not intended to

Preparation of this manuscript was supported in part by grants from the National Institute of Child Health and Human Development (HD02274 and HD00346).

I extend special thanks to Katherine Mabbatt for her careful technical assistance.

minimize the significance of subjective aspects of environments. Individuals clearly assume an active part in perceiving and responding to selected elements in their environments. Indeed, both environmental and developmental psychologists (e.g., Lewin, 1935; Magnusson, 1981; Pervin & Lewis, 1978; Russell & Ward, 1982; Stokols, 1982) have written extensively about the distinctions between objective, geographical, or "actual" environments and behavioral, immediate, subjective, or "perceived" environments.

Another important quality of environments is that they are perceived as a whole, rather than a mere collection of independent features impinging on all the senses (Ittleson, 1978; Lewin, 1935). Moreover, given the rich and constant exchange between people and environments, environments must be defined in dynamic terms rather than static ones. Although the key characteristics that identify a particular environment may persist over time, other aspects—perhaps of equal or greater significance to the individuals who experience those environments—may change dramatically.

Environments represent as great a challenge to scientific inquiry as does human behavior itself. This challenge is underscored by the fact that environments may be conceptualized, described, and analyzed at many levels and from divergent perspectives (see Magnusson, 1981). As Bronfenbrenner (1977) recognized,

> Human environments and—even more so—the capacities of human beings to adapt and restructure these environments are so complex in their basic organization that they are not likely to be captured, let alone comprehended, through simplistic unidimensional research models that make no provision for assessing ecological structure and variation (p. 518).

CLASSIFICATION AND TERMINOLOGY

Identifying a single environment and its boundaries is not difficult. In contrast, reliably grouping environments into "types" is more problematic. Although there are no a priori reasons why environments should be classified differently solely on the basis of who uses them, such segregation by population frequently occurs. In the field of developmental disabilities, a terminology has evolved to describe and classify environments. The origin of this population-specific classification of environments is linked, in part, to the fact that many of the places where developmentally disabled persons live, learn, work, and play have been separated from other community environments that serve the general population. Furthermore, these environments are controlled largely by public policies (connected with the expenditure of public funds) that are enforced by local or state agencies. In addition, there has been a prevailing philosophy that specialized settings are essential to meet the individual needs of handicapped children and adults.[1] Frequently, special technologies have been advocated as the best means for enhancing the development of a "special needs" population. Many of these techniques rely on a combination of prosthetic aids, physical modifications or accommodations, and specially trained individuals who in turn design and maintain uniquely programmed environments. Given such historical, social, and political conditions, the creation of a separate vocabulary to label these environments for developmentally disabled individuals is scarcely surprising.

Distinctive jargon often helps professionals, particularly those in minority fields or emerging subdisciplines, to define their turf in a seemingly exclusive way. Some of the terms

---

[1]This widespread belief that specialized programs are needed appears to be fundamentally in conflict with the ideology of normalization. In practice, however, developmental disabilities advocates are likely to defend their dual stance on the basis of political and social realities. That is, they believe that advocates and professionals must control these programs initially—even those that foster community integration and maximize the use of culturally "normative" means of achieving desired goals for individuals. The numerous negative experiences encountered by developmentally disabled individuals seeking access to generic services are cited as further justification for this transitory period of continued segregation in the service delivery system.

characterizing the residential and educational environments for developmentally disabled persons illustrate this vividly—such as developmental centers, learning resource rooms, intermediate care facilities for the developmentally disabled (ICF/DDs), family care homes, residential habilitation centers, mainstreamed classrooms, extended sheltered workshops, developmental maximation units, specialized group homes, core cluster–individual placement concept, and so forth. Although these terms may elicit certain common images among specialists, their meanings are not apparent to "outsiders." In fact, the terms frequently are misleading. Furthermore, some of the environmental labels merely reflect shifts in jargon (i.e., not necessarily connected to functional changes within the program) or attempts to destigmatize environments that have acquired negative connotations. The most obvious example is the renaming of state hospitals and institutions, which now are labeled variously as schools, developmental centers, central core facilities, and residential habilitation centers.

There are potential dangers, however, in utilizing a set of distinctive terms to describe environments for special populations. The first is simply that communication becomes severely restricted; that is, researchers and professionals interested in certain environments may ignore relevant findings from closely related fields, simply because they are unfamiliar with the words used to characterize the environments in these fields. This contributes to an unfortunate situation in which important principles about person-environment interaction may be missed because of arbitrary divisions in program administration, in professional identities, and in special interest groups that do not want to align themselves with other populations or services. For instance, many nursing homes, hospitals, and institutions share important environmental features and serve similar types of individuals. In actuality, some of these environments may be indistinguishable from one another, despite differences in their official or administrative labels. Yet a review of the literature concerning

these kinds of environments indicates that cross-referencing of relevant work seldom happens (e.g., findings about staff-resident interactions in nursing homes are not cited by researchers interested in institutions, and vice versa).

The use of special terms for various populations further implies that these environments are tailored or specialized in some way for the individuals. Although this condition may be so, this assumption needs empirical validation. All too often professionals and service recipients passively accept the new terms as evidence that the programs are "special," without seeking further confirmation.

Finally, the ability to analyze major social and historical trends over time will be obliterated by haphazard labeling of environments in ways that defy objective identification. Because classification of people, as well as of environments, is vulnerable to popular trends and political realities, the difficulties are compounded. Understanding what the real criteria are for identifying a child as "multiply handicapped" or "severely impaired" or "behaviorally disturbed," for example, is impossible without carefully reviewing the operating procedures of a clinic or agency or region at a particular time. Similarly, knowing what comprises a "family care home" or a "developmental center" or a "board and care home" is impossible given the current ambiguities in terminology.

Why Classify Environments?

One major reason for classifying environments is to enhance our understanding of their impact on various individuals at different times in their lives. To accomplish this objective, two minimal conditions must be met: a) the classification scheme must be conceptually well grounded in terms of predicted functional or dynamic organization of the environments; and b) all environments must be classifiable on the basis of a reliably measured set of features that are independent of their actual effects on people.

At present, there is no primary classification scheme in use for the residential environments of developmentally disabled persons. There are, however, a number of frequently used terms, and a few investigators have suggested ways to conceptualize different residential settings. Interestingly, there has never been a *typology* of natural family settings for normally developing children, although there has been extensive research on the effects of early environments and the relationships among quality of home stimulation, parenting styles, and subsequent child development. Instead, researchers studying the effects of home environments typically have focused on one or a few variables at a time, essentially ignoring the entire constellation of social and nonsocial characteristics that combine to create the functional milieu for a developing child. Such a segmented empirical approach often has yielded results that highlight the *interactional* nature of variables—essentially, pointing out that when variables are combined within a real life setting, their effects are not necessarily additive but often produce surprising and/or complex results (e.g., Stokols, 1982).

An alternative to the conventional approach of viewing environments as a collection of separate characteristics is to acknowledge the fundamentally multidimensional and codetermined nature of environments and to develop a useful typology to guide inquiry. Such a typology would need to be based on a set of fundamental assumptions, the first being *that important environmental variables seldom occur or operate in isolation.* Accordingly, because of the highly intercorrelated nature of environmental characteristics, specifying precise cause-effect relationships between single variables and outcomes is not realistically possible or even theoretically necessary. Rather, the collective group of naturally occurring variables (both static and dynamic ones) is likely to comprise a more meaningful index of an environment. This postulate is particularly important if the goal is to predict how different environments affect individuals. Of course, assessing the *relative* contribution of separately measured variables is not precluded by select-

ing this approach, but the primary emphasis is shifted from a segmented view of environments to a more integrated conceptualization of the environment as a functional whole. Ideally, studying the natural variability of environments (even within the same class or category) and manipulating select components within them will help to solve the mystery of what matters most and in what ways, as well as for whom and at what time in their lives.

Existing Typologies of Residential Environments

Baker, Seltzer, and Seltzer (1977) developed a classification scheme of community residential facilities. The 10 categories they used to characterize 381 community residences throughout the United States were:

1. Small group homes for 10 or fewer retarded adults
2. Medium group homes for 11 to 20 retarded adults
3. Large group homes for 21 to 40 retarded adults
4. Mini-institutions for 41 to 80 retarded adults
5. Mixed group homes for retarded adults and former mental hospital patients and/or ex-offenders
6. Group homes for older retarded adults, often with other nonretarded adults living there
7. Foster family care for five or fewer retarded adults in a family's own home
8. Sheltered villages that are segregated and self-contained communities (usually in rural locations) for retarded adults and live-in staff
9. Workshop-dormitories where the residential and vocational programs are administratively and often physically linked
10. Semi-independent units that provide less than 24-hour supervision of retarded adults.

This typology was useful for further elaboration and description of Baker et al.'s (1977) subsample of 17 residences selected for visitation. Whether this system was the most effective way to characterize the major kinds of residential facilities was not evaluated. This classification scheme was not intended, however, to be exhaustive, definitive, or theoretically grounded. At the time, it provided a useful handle for acquainting others with the diversity of residential models operating in 1973. As the investigators noted, actual practices and ideological commitment *even within a given type of residence* differed widely— which prevented them from making simple generalizations about the effectiveness of different models or the degree to which a given model fostered "normalization" of the residents' lives.

A radically different kind of typology was suggested by Butler and Bjaanes (1977), who proposed three major categories for community care facilities: custodial, maintaining, and therapeutic. In this system, the key variables that differentiate facilities are a) the presence of habilitation programs, b) the degree of community contact, c) the level of activity within the facility, and d) the intensity of caregiver involvement with residents. The actual typology assumes that "habilitative" programs have vigorous training programs, a great deal of community contact, high levels of activity, and very involved caregivers. In contrast, custodial programs are low in all four of these areas (i.e., they provide no habilitation programs or community contact, have extremely low activity levels, and feature minimal caregiver involvement). The central axiom is that client outcomes—notably, social competence and satisfaction—are directly related to these variables.

There are two fundamental flaws in the evaluative typology of Butler and Bjaanes (1977). The first is that a large number of programs will not fit neatly into one of the three categories. This is because facilities often are uneven in their provision of services across the domains of habilitation, community contact, home activity, and caregiver involvement. Moreover, a change in one of these four variables can occur easily (e.g., habilitation programming could be stopped temporarily for factors outside the facility's control, or staff turnover could alter

caregiver involvement). Would this necessitate classifying the home as a different "type"? At the pragmatic level, we need to recognize that the standards for judging what comprises "no," "minimal," or "intensive" habilitation, community contact, activity level, and so forth are subject to constant revision and dispute. This means that a facility that qualifies as "therapeutic" according to one set of standards may be considered to be a "maintainance" facility by another set of standards. In fact, the "custodial" institutions of today would appear quite "habilitative" if the standards of the mid-1950s were applied (Berkson & Landesman-Dwyer, 1977). Second, this typology relies on the premise that the more intensive is each of these four variables, the more positive is the influence on the individual. That is, individuals in therapeutic environments are expected to show the greatest number of positive changes, while those in custodial facilities are predicted to show no progress or even to regress developmentally. According to this typology, in the event that discrepancies were noted between client progress and the type of program, one would have to assume that the program was incorrectly classified. Accordingly, no program could be classified without ongoing monitoring of client progress. Of course, given what we already have learned from studying residential environments, we know they are not likely to have uniform effects on all residents. Would this mean that each facility should be classified on the basis of its success rate? Although this is a provocative idea and undoubtedly would be informative to pursue, this is a very different task from that of initially classifying facilities for purposes of meaningful comparisons or of endeavoring to understand the impact of environments on individuals. Despite this critique of Butler and Bjaanes's (1977) typology, admittedly still embryonic by their own standards, they performed a valuable service by identifying some important facility characteristics to consider and a conceptual framework for relating program activities to client adjustment.

Another system of classifying residential programs derives from the ENCOR (Eastern

Nebraska Community Office of Retardation) system (ENCOR, 1977). The programs are intended to be graded developmentally and originally included three types of hostels (for children, adolescents, and adults), adult room-and-board homes, apartment clusters, supervised living units, co-resident apartments, behavioral development residential hostels, and developmental maximation units. When such a system is planned and then implemented by a public agency, then obviously all facilities "fit" into one of the categories. Whether the administrative categories actually represent the best means for understanding the major differences among types of residential settings remains undetermined. Indeed, when the classification is based primarily on characteristics of the clientele, such as age, degree of mental retardation, medical needs, or behavioral problems, rather than on environmental features, few meaningful conclusions can be reached about the *differential impact* of these various models on clients.

Interestingly, when other states have adopted the Nebraska service delivery format, they typically report a need to make significant changes (e.g., Knowlton, 1980). This suggests that ENCOR is not necessarily comprehensive or all-purpose, and that the categorization of its various residential programs may be more system-specific or administratively oriented than indicative of important treatment or environmental characteristics. Given the guiding philosophical tenets of ENCOR, however, any grouping of environmental settings may be viewed as somewhat arbitrary. Indeed, ENCOR advocates repeatedly emphasize the flexible nature of their service delivery system. For example:

The core cluster–individual placement concept was adopted to allow more individualized, integrated modes of service. There has been movement from reliance on a "couple" houseparent role to a more professional staff approach, and the

introduction of a more complex geographical regionalization-cluster approach to system management. The system also now serves more severely handicapped clients than in its early years (Hitzing, 1980, pp. 84–85).

Such comments indicate that even trying to use a single state's categorization system to analyze residential programs may be extremely difficult. This is especially true if the system frequently undergoes changes in whom it serves, the type of people with primary program responsibility, or philosophical modifications.[2]

In the state of Washington, as in many other states, administrators view residential environments as representing an array rather than a developmental continuum per se. Although the programmatic objectives do vary across different administrative categories of residences, bureaucrats, service providers, and consumers recognize that what actually happens is the result of many historical, political, and practical influences as well as ideological objectives. Despite the fact that certain residential programs have been designed for target populations, often there is significant overlap in the types of clients served within such programs (Landesman-Dwyer & Brown, 1976; Landesman-Dwyer & Mai-Dalton, 1981). Similarly, the observed variation in practices and activities in facilities within a single administrative type sometimes is as great as that across different categories (e.g., Landesman-Dwyer & Butterfield, 1983), similar to earlier findings of Baker et al. (1977), Bjaanes and Butler (1974), and Edgerton (1975).

Across different states, the actual number and types of major residential programs for developmentally disabled citizens vary remarkably. In some instances, the same terms may be used to identify totally different types of programs. For example, a number of states refer to their former state institutions, hospitals, and residential schools as "developmental cen-

---

[2]Frankly, those of us who have been participant-observers in the past decade of residential programming cannot help remarking on the inconsistencies in practitioners' reports on the same system and the nature of various "types" of residences within that one system. Further documentation of these impressions is readily available in courtroom testimony in which professionals within the same system, especially the Nebraska ENCOR, have provided different stories about who is served in which types of settings.

ters,'' while in other states this term is used to denote day training programs for individuals who are not eligible for vocationally oriented workshop programs. Two other labels that may be misleading if not interpreted carefully within a given state's definition are ''foster care'' and ''group homes.'' In California, for instance, ''foster care'' frequently involves a single nonwhite female providing some care for four or five mentally retarded individuals (Lei, Nihira, Sheehy, & Meyers, 1981). Foster care is likely to be the primary means of income for the caregiver in this situation. In contrast, the term *foster care* is reserved in many states for describing natural families (almost always with two parents) that choose to have one, or at most two, mentally retarded individuals join them as additional family members. Similarly, the term *group home* has been applied in some states to facilities that serve as many as 150 to 200 mentally handicapped persons, while other states set size limits at much lower levels (typically 6, 10, or 20). Also, ownership and operation of residential facilities may be public or private, or in some situations, facilities may be owned by the state and operated by a private organization. Moreover, some states require staff training and special licensing for facilities that serve mentally retarded clients, while other states do not. Thus, simply knowing that someone lives in a foster home or a group home may convey virtually no meaningful information about the physical or functional qualities of his or her environment. If the nature of these programs is not carefully investigated in each locality, erroneous conclusions could be drawn about the impact of these environments on individuals. In fact, the majority of empirical studies about different types of residential programs fail to provide enough descriptive information to determine reliably what the program itself is like.

Even when general descriptions of the residential categories are provided, as in a large-scale study of more than 6,000 people receiving services in three states (Borthwick, Meyers, & Eyman, 1981), it may be virtually impossible to compare findings with data gathered in other studies. In this study, resi-

dents' adaptive behavior skills were compared across five types of facilities, described as follows:

> Institutions are state facilities providing a comprehensive array of services primarily to severely mentally retarded residents. Convalescent hospitals are generally skilled nursing facilities, caring for nonambulatory severely and profoundly retarded persons. Board and care homes consist primarily of group homes and residential schools, usually providing such services as nursing care and schooling. Family care homes are licensed to care for six or fewer developmentally disabled persons of all ages and levels of retardation, although profoundly retarded persons are seldom found in them. Clients who reside with their own parents are provided services other than out-of-home placement by the service agency (Borthwick et al., 1981, p. 352).

Such a five-fold division of residential facilities would be inapplicable to many states' service delivery systems. For example, in Washington State, this scheme would require combining several vastly different residential programs into single categories (e.g., under the rubrics of board and care homes and convalescent hospitals) and excluding a number of other residential services that do not fit into any of these five categories. Moreover, nursing care and schooling are not provided by board and care facilities or group homes in Washington.

Toward a Systematic Language of Environments

The need for a uniform classification scheme and for a common terminology in the field is obvious. Given the present diversity of services and program models, plus the exceedingly cumbersome local, state, and federal regulations pertaining to almost all out-of-home and training environments for retarded individuals, it is highly unlikely that a single classification system will be accepted by both social scientists and service providers. In fact, such efforts to systematize the field have occurred sporadically, although none to the author's knowledge has resulted in specific recommendations for a common classification scheme and descriptive terminology. Ideally, a guide analogous to the American Association on Mental Retardation's *Manual on Terminology and Classification in Mental Retardation* (Grossman, 1983) should be prepared. This would provide the groundwork for more precise and valid descriptions of environments. In essence, there is a need to develop a systematic method for identifying a set of salient environmental characteristics even if state or local agencies continue to rely on their own labels for programs. A standardized set of terms, once adopted and used to describe all residential environments, would allow useful and explicit comparisons of programs (regardless of their administrative labels) and evaluations of their impact on residents, families, staff, and the surrounding community. The development of standardized nomenclature not only could serve the objective of encouraging a more uniform scientific literature but also could meet the urgent need for an empirical basis to inform decision makers about how best to make individual placements and to modify their service delivery systems.

HOW ARE RETARDED INDIVIDUALS AFFECTED BY THEIR ENVIRONMENTS?

The question of how developmentally disabled individuals are affected by their environments implicitly assumes that retarded individuals are aware of and responsive to their environments. The extent of definitive literature about the effects of residential environments on development and on adjustment is singularly disappointing and severely constrained scientifically (see Butterfield, 1967, in press; Windle, 1962). Even those studies that demonstrate changes in individuals over time and/or across different residential facilities have not been adequately designed to demonstrate the actual contribution of the environment per se to the reported changes. On the other hand, the large collection of anecdotal evidence and the collective experiences of many parents and dedicated service providers constitute a sufficiently strong basis for accepting the basic tenet that *residential settings can be and often are critical influences on individuals.*

To glean precisely which environmental variables are among the most significant for individuals or groups, however, is a risky business. Any straightforward collation of the findings from the research literature is likely to be very misleading. Alternatively, one can review selectively those studies that meet one's standards of scientific rigor and objectivity. Historically, the best examples in this category have tended to assess relatively small sets of variables or a single variable—largely because such investigations were guided by theory or designed to test selected hypotheses. For example, the pioneering work of Berkson and his colleagues (Berkson, 1964; Berkson & Mason, 1963, 1964; Davenport & Berkson, 1963) demonstrated that high rates of aberrant stereotypic behavior occurred in relatively deprived environments and that either sensory (object) or social stimulation could serve to reduce these rates. This clearly confirms that certain characteristics of the environment significantly affect behavior; yet these findings cannot readily be used to scale the amount of stimulation provided within a given environment. Indeed, the notion of estimating the total stimulation available within an environment may be far too simplistic, since there are many different types of stimulation, and the direction or extensiveness of effects may not be the same for various kinds. What is even more likely is that "environmental stimulation," like the primitive, undifferentiated form of "reinforcement," may require person-specific evaluation, such as demonstrating that particular individuals actually notice and respond favorably to particular aspects of their environment. If anything, the multiple sensory and cognitive impairments of mentally retarded persons would accentuate the variability in individual responses to their environments (Berkson, 1966; Landesman-Dwyer & E. Butterfield, 1983). Moreover, Suedfeld (1980) provides empirical support that the negative aspects of severely restricted environmental stimulation are not uniform across subjects—in fact, some individuals appear to enjoy or prefer conditions that are perceived by others as very oppressive or intolerable.

It is interesting to consider that the extensive literature on stereotypy (see Lewis & Baumeister, 1982, for an excellent review) and its relationship to environmental parameters is rarely cited in the new wave of social ecology research on developmental disabilities. Indeed, there are many experimental demonstrations about the influence of various forms of stimulation on retarded individuals, but because these studies originally were couched in terms of a particular theory or orientation (e.g., learning theory, motivation, memory) and the variables were not necessarily evaluated where or when they "naturally" occurred, their findings are excluded from most reviews about the impact of environments on handicapped people. Although a detailed review of the entire psychological literature in mental retardation is not possible here, Landesman-Dwyer and E. Butterfield (1983) recently highlighted what were judged to be the major conclusions that could be drawn from that research. Concerning the social ecology of retarded children, four important conclusions were made:

1. *The quality of environments cannot be judged without reference to the specific characteristics and needs of the children in those environments* (p. 499);
2. *It is important to consider a child's mental or developmental age when evaluating his or her social environment* (p. 502);
3. *Environmental variables account for much of the behavior of retarded children* (pp. 502–503);
4. *To assess the impact of environmental variables, the child's total social repertoire and behavior in many situations should be considered. . . . . First, a change in the environment is seldom singular. . . . Second,* an individual's behavior is complex and multidimensional. . . . *Third,* positive changes in a given behavior are not necessarily correlated with positive changes in closely related behaviors (pp. 504–506).

These four conclusions are based on extensive empirical findings. Failure to heed these fundamental facts will result in a biased or incomplete view of developmentally disabled individuals and of their adaptation to environments. More importantly, when designing and evaluating residential (or any other) programs,

the significance of the basic principle of person × environment interaction must be acknowledged in operational terms. This principle has been discussed at length by environmental psychologists (e.g., Bem & Allen, 1974; Cronbach, 1975; Stokols, 1981), has surfaced in several placement studies (Landesman-Dwyer, 1981), and recently has been confirmed in a large-scale prospective study of retarded individuals randomly assigned to alternative living arrangements (Landesman-Dwyer, 1983, in press). Accordingly, instruments that purport to evaluate the quality of an environment in absolute terms—such as PASS 3 (Flynn, 1980)—rather than ones specific to the individuals, will not be very useful. Similarly, obtaining outcome measures in only one domain, such as brief caregiver ratings on adaptive behavior, is not likely to yield a valid picture of an environment's important influences. It is disturbing that many researchers and service providers readily acknowledge the severe limitations in their choice of measures, yet they continue to rely on them to judge a program's effectiveness. Their rationalization is that there are no other readily available, easy-to-obtain measures. Unfortunately, the conclusions from such research are very likely to be misleading rather than merely incomplete.

CAN "QUALITY" OF ENVIRONMENTS BE MEASURED RELIABLY?

It is clear that the quality of environments can be measured reliably, even though there is no consensus on what characteristics are most important. Of course, reliability must be separately established for any instrument designed to capture either qualitative aspects of environments or individuals' subjective impressions. However, it is necessary to underscore that the fact that different people have different opinions about the same environment is *not* synonymous with unreliability. Indeed, the author has been involved in two recent studies of deinstitutionalization and community adjustment (Landesman-Dwyer, Sulzbacher, Edgar, Keller, Wise, & Baatz, 1980; Landesman-Dwyer

& G. Butterfield, 1983) in which a central design premise was that *multiple perspectives* or ratings were essential to estimate the quality of each residential program. By combining these ratings, all of which were related to the degree of match between facility and individual residents, it was possible to evaluate how consistently a facility's programs were perceived and to focus on the nature of the discrepant judgments and their probable sources. Although there was fairly high reliability for programs rated as extremely high quality or low quality, the overall lack of consensus regarding individual-program fit was impressive.

Ideally, one would like to offer a straightforward alternative to the use of the present environmental assessment instruments such as Program Analysis of Service Systems (PASS 3) (Wolfensberger & Glenn, 1975), the Caldwell Home Observation for Measurement of the Environment (Caldwell, 1968), the Moos scales (Moos, 1974), the King and Raynes Resident Management Scale (King & Raynes, 1968), or the various quality of environmental measures adapted from the psychiatric literature. Although the authors and others have struggled for years to do this, a final product and set of guidelines for this area have not yet emerged. In the absence of a commonly accepted environmental assessment tool that meets psychometric standards, researchers and program evaluators alike should be urged to follow a common set of general procedures, as follows:

1. *Objective environmental features believed to have an effect on program integrity and success should be listed.* These variables do not need to be limited to those hypothesized to have direct effects on residents, but may include parameters associated with staff morale and behavior, parental responses, community acceptance, and so forth. Care must be taken that the description of these variables is not contaminated by judgments about their actual influence or outcome.

2. *Key informants believed to be able to provide insights into a residential facility should be asked to provide both objective and subjective accounts.* Individuals who have had close contact with the program, including service providers and recipients themselves, should be included but supplemented by the use of some neutral viewers such as outside professionals or researchers. Clearly, one informant's evaluation never represents the entire truth or a completely unbiased account of what an environment is like. Rather, collectively these informants provide viewpoints that warrant consideration in developing a composite impression of the environment.

3. *If standardized tools are used, investigators should consider analyzing the individual items for their relevance to the particular types of environments under assessment.* Standardized instruments should be examined to see how many of the items are appropriate to the settings and the populations in them, and how many responses are predetermined by formal licensing procedures, practical conditions, program location, and so on. In many cases, the instruments would be more informative if those items hypothesized to relate significantly to the ongoing program or to the residents' adjustment were specified and the results for these items presented separately. Too often only total scores or factor-derived scores are presented, preventing further interpretation of the actual program qualities or characteristics that were most important.

4. *To the extent possible, indicators of program "success" or "outcome" should be selected that can be separated from the description of the environment per se.* Ideally, these indicators should reflect what is expected as a function of particular environmental variables. For example, if an evaluator wanted to assess how "normalized" an environment was according to PASS 3 criteria, then the outcome measures could include actual aspects of staff and resident behavior judged to be more or

less normalized. Of course, what is normal behavior for individuals varies markedly depending on their developmental level, even more so than on their chronological age (Landesman-Dwyer & E. Butterfield, 1983). Similarly, if one hypothesizes that staff-to-resident ratios and staff training are important indices of program quality, then the outcome measures should include amount and appropriateness of staff attention to residents. Other measures could include staff morale, presence of special staff-resident relationships, sophistication of staff programming, and so forth. In all studies, the initial or baseline performance of residents must be taken into account, as well as the residents' primary service needs. In many situations, this means that a single direction of change cannot be assumed to be "good" or "bad." For instance, some residents may need to spend more time interacting with staff members, while others may need to spend less time with staff (e.g., they may need to learn to spend more time alone or

with peers). This task of adjusting environmental evaluations to the needs of particular residents is not as overwhelming as it initially appears. More importantly, this is the only way to prevent making overgeneralized or inappropriate evaluations of environments.

Those of us engaged in describing and evaluating residential environments need to communicate with one another and to share failures, as well as advances. Data bases need to be broadened and strengthened, especially by developing more sensitive measures that build on what is already known about person-environment interaction. There is a continuing need to provide adequate details about the environments studied, so that others may obtain a rich and valid picture of these environments. Such activities, coupled with creative programming efforts and adequate fiscal and social support within this society, will help achieve the important objective of "revitalizing residential settings" (Wolins & Wozner, 1982).

REFERENCES

Baker, B.L., Seltzer, G.B., & Seltzer, M.M. *As close as possible: Community residences for retarded adults.* Boston: Little, Brown & Co., 1977.

Bem, D.J., & Allen, A. On predicting some of the people some of the time: The search for cross-situational consistencies in behavior. *Psychological Review,* 1974, *81,* 506–520.

Berkson, G. Stereotyped movements of mental defectives: V. Ward behavior and its relation to an experimental task. *American Journal of Mental Deficiency,* 1964, *69,* 253–264.

Berkson, G. When exceptions obscure the rule. *Mental Retardation,* 1966, *4,* 24–27.

Berkson, G., & Landesman-Dwyer, S. Behavioral research on severe and profound mental retardation (1955–1974). *American Journal of Mental Deficiency,* 1977, *81,* 428–454.

Berkson, G., & Mason, W.A. Stereotyped movements of mental defectives: III. Situation effects. *American Journal of Mental Deficiency,* 1963, *68,* 409–412.

Berkson, G., & Mason, W.A. Stereotyped movements of mental defectives: IV. The effects of toys and the character of acts. *American Journal of Mental Deficiency,* 1964, *68,* 511–524.

Bjaanes, A.T., & Butler, E.W. Environmental variation in community care facilities for mentally retarded persons. *American Journal of Mental Deficiency,* 1974, *78,* 429–439.

Borthwick, S.A., Meyers, C.E., & Eyman, R.K. Comparative adaptive and maladaptive behavior of mentally retarded clients of five residential settings in three western states. In: R.H. Bruininks, C.E. Meyers, B.B. Sigford, & K.C. Lakin (eds.), *Deinstitutionalization and community adjustment of mentally retarded people.* Washington, D C : American Association on Mental Deficiency, 1981.

Bronfenbrenner, U. Toward an experimental ecology of human development. *American Psychologist,* 1977, *32,* 513–531.

Butler, E.W., & Bjaanes, A.T. A typology of community care facilities and differential normalization outcomes. In: P. Mittler (ed.), *Research to practice in mental retardation,* Vol. I. *Care and intervention.* Baltimore: University Park Press, 1977.

Butterfield, E.C. The role of environmental factors in the treatment of institutionalized mental retardates. In: A.A. Baumeister (ed.), *Mental retardation: Appraisal, education, and rehabilitation.* Chicago: Aldine Publishing Co., 1967.

Butterfield, E.C. The consequences of bias in studies of living arrangements for the mentally retarded. In: D. Bricker & J. Filler (eds.), *The severely mentally retarded: From research to practice.* Reston, VA: Council for Exceptional Children, in press.

Caldwell, B. *Instruction manual: Home Observation for*

Measurement of the Environment. Unpublished manuscript, 1968.

Cronbach, L.J. Beyond the two disciplines of scientific psychology. *American Psychologist,* 1975, *30,* 116–127.

Davenport, R.K., Jr., & Berkson, G. Stereotyped movements of mental defectives: II. Effects of novel objects. *American Journal of Mental Deficiency,* 1963, *67,* 879–882.

Edgerton, R.B. Issues relating to the quality of life among mentally retarded persons. In: M.J. Begab & S.A. Richardson (eds.), *The mentally retarded and society: A social science perspective.* Baltimore: University Park Press, 1975.

ENCOR [Eastern Nebraska Community Office of Retardation]. *Residential specific training.* Omaha: ENCOR, 1977.

Flynn, R.J. Normalization, PASS, and service quality assessment: How normalizing are current human services? In: R.J. Flynn & K.E. Nitsch (eds.), *Normalization, social integration, and community services.* Baltimore: University Park Press, 1980.

Grossman, H.J. (ed.). *Manual on terminology and classification in mental retardation.* Washington, D C : American Association on Mental Deficiency, 1983.

Guralnik, D.B. (ed.). *Webster's new world dictionary of the American language* (2nd college ed.). Cleveland: William Collins & World, 1974.

Hitzing, W. ENCOR and beyond. In: T. Apolloni, J. Cappuccilli, & T.P. Cooke (eds.), *Achievements in residential services for persons with disabilities: Toward excellence.* Baltimore: University Park Press, 1980.

Ittleson, W.H. Environmental perception and urban experience. *Environment and Behavior,* 1978, *10,* 193–213.

King, R.D., & Raynes, N.V. An operational measure of inmate management in residential institutions. *Social Science and Medicine,* 1968, *2,* 41–53.

Knowlton, M. The Pennsylvania system. In: T. Apolloni, J. Cappuccilli, & T.P. Cooke (eds.), *Achievements in residential services for persons with disabilities: Toward excellence.* Baltimore: University Park Press, 1980.

Landesman-Dwyer, S. Living in the community. *American Journal of Mental Deficiency,* 1981, *86,* 223–234.

Landesman-Dwyer, S. Residential environments and the social behavior of handicapped individuals. In: M. Lewis (ed.), *Beyond the dyad.* New York: Plenum Publishing Corp., 1983.

Landesman-Dwyer, S. The changing structure and function of institutions: A search for optimal group care environments. In: S. Landesman-Dwyer & P. Vietze (eds.), *Living with retarded people.* Baltimore: University Park Press, in press.

Landesman-Dwyer, S., & Brown, T.R. *A method for subgrouping mentally retarded citizens on the basis of service needs.* Olympia, WA: Department of Social and Health Services, 1976.

Landesman-Dwyer, S., & Butterfield, E.C. Mental retardation: Developmental issues in cognition and social

adaptation. In: M. Lewis (ed.), *Origins of intelligence* (2nd ed.). New York: Plenum Publishing Corp., 1983.

Landesman-Dwyer, S., & Butterfield, G. *Specialized group homes: Evaluation of a new residential program.* Olympia, WA: Department of Social and Health Services, 1983.

Landesman-Dwyer, S., & Mai-Dalton, R. *A statewide survey of individuals receiving case management services from the division of developmental disabilities.* Olympia, WA: Department of Social and Health Services, 1981.

Landesman-Dwyer, S., Sulzbacher, S., Edgar, E., Keller, S., Wise, B., & Baatz, B. 1979 *Rainier School placement study.* Olympia, WA: Department of Social and Health Services, 1980.

Lei, T., Nihira, L., Sheehy, N., & Meyers, C.E. A study of small family care for mentally retarded people. In: R.H. Bruininks, C.E. Meyers, B.B. Sigford, & K.C. Lakin (eds.), *Deinstitutionalization and community adjustment of mentally retarded people.* Washington, D C : American Association on Mental Deficiency, 1981.

Lewin, K. *A dynamic theory of personality.* New York: McGraw-Hill Book Co., 1935.

Lewis, N.H., & Baumeister, A.A. Stereotyped mannerisms in mentally retarded persons: Animal models and theoretical analyses. In: N.R. Ellis (ed.), *International review of research in mental retardation,* Vol. 11. New York: Academic Press, 1982.

Magnusson, D. *Toward a psychology of situations: An interactional perspective.* Hillsdale, NJ: Lawrence Erlbaum Associates, 1981.

Moos, R.H. *The social climate scales.* Palo Alto, CA: Consulting Psychologists Press, 1974.

Pervin, L.A., & Lewis, M. (eds.). *Perspectives in international psychology.* New York: Plenum Publishing Corp., 1978.

Russell, J.A., & Ward, W. Environmental psychology. *Annual Review of Psychology,* 1982, *33,* 651–688.

Stokols, D. Group × place transactions: Some neglected issues in psychological research on settings. In: D. Magnusson (ed.), *Toward a psychology of situations: An interactional perspective.* Hillsdale, NJ: Lawrence Erlbaum Associates, 1981.

Stokols, D. Environmental psychology: A coming of age. In: A. Kraut (ed.), *G. Stanley Hall Lecture Series,* Vol. 2. Washington, D C : American Psychological Association, 1982.

Suedfeld, P. *Restricted environmental stimulation.* New York: John Wiley & Sons, 1980.

Windle, C. Prognosis of mental subnormals. *American Journal of Mental Deficiency* (Monograph Supplement), 1962, *66,* 1–180.

Wolfensberger, W., & Glenn, L. *PASS 3, a method for the quantitative evaluation of human services.* Toronto: National Institute on Mental Retardation, 1975.

Wolins, M., & Wozner, Y. *Revitalizing residential settings.* San Francisco: Jossey-Bass, 1982.

Part V

PERSPECTIVES ON METHODOLOGY IN RESEARCH AND EVALUATION

Throughout this book there has been a heavy emphasis on using research to validate practices. This is not because the volume's contributors feel there is no "art" in providing care and services to handicapped persons, but because they realize that one generation's state-of-the-art has often become the next generation's most visible abuses. Until relatively recently, systematic scrutiny of the effects of programs and/or specific practices did not greatly interest researchers. Practices were credited with being effective based solely on the belief, often largely conditioned by hope, that they must be worthwhile. More recently, however, with the increasing emphasis on program accountability and outcomes, researchers have been propelled into the arena of service provision with pressures to demonstrate the relevance of scientific research principles to the daily lives of persons touched by various social and educational programs.

The use of scientific (or quasi-scientific) principles to evaluate and improve social practices and public policies has been referred to as "policy research" (Coleman, 1972). In conducting such research it is acknowledged that outcomes of social practices are often not of the type or magnitude expected (i.e., they may be better, worse, or different). The commitment in such research is to provide information that will make service outcomes better understood, more beneficial to clients and to the larger society, and that will contribute to decisions about how best to allocate limited resources. The history of care and treatment for handicapped persons provides many examples of how programs continued for decades to isolate handicapped persons in segregated housing, education, and social leisure activities, without systematic evaluation of the practices and theories upon which these programs were based. Such adverse practices persisted and still persist, with no empirical evidence that such treatment was or is justified on any grounds.

Given this volume's concentration on the need to look to research for guidance in providing services to handicapped persons, it is appropriate to devote a chapter to methods of applying research to evaluate the residential developmental, social/leisure, and support programs described throughout this book. In Chapter 11, Laird W. Heal discusses systematic approaches to studying the effects of community-based programs for handicapped persons. The discussion is structured around the major considerations facing the researcher: Who or what will be the subject(s) of research? Who will provide and collect the data? What subject, setting, and intervention variables will be studied or controlled? How will data be analyzed and interpreted? Although these questions seem straightforward, Heal notes that the research designer, in conducting his or her research in the real world, must make a number of decisions—and frequently concessions.

The author points to major methodological pitfalls that researchers face as they respond to these questions, illustrating these dilemmas with reference to actual research projects. The chapter also discusses the ethics of conducting research in this area and emphasizes the scientist's obligation to encourage increased citizen participation.

Heal's thorough treatment of the effect of policy research design on program outcomes is complemented by Craig Thornton's discussion in Chapter 12 of research on the cost-effectiveness of programs. In recent years there has been an increasingly perceived need to assist policy makers in allocating scarce resources among alternative programs and activities, each of which has a wide range of effects and may require a variety of resources. The techniques of benefit-cost analysis were designed specifically to deal with this type of problem but have been adopted slowly in the social services and education evaluation areas. In large measure, this is because different social programs often have diverse goals and outcomes and present difficulties in measuring effects precisely. Nevertheless, the framework discussed by Thornton illustrates how benefit-cost analysis can deal with the problems of evaluating social programs, by providing a means of systematically comparing values of a single program's multiple effects; of comparing the value of the effects to their costs; and of comparing the effects and costs of alternative programs. Because benefit-cost analysis is an applied technique, the chapter summarizes a case-study application of the conceptual framework to an evaluation of a specific social program, Job Corps. It also makes recommendations for improving the use of benefit-cost analysis in other social programs.

Although the first two chapters in this section focus primarily on evaluating the effects of programs and policies with large numbers of clients, an evaluative focus on the daily changes in individuals is also important. Two related perspectives on the care and habilitation of handicapped persons have been found particularly applicable in day-to-day evaluation of the effects of programs. In Chapter 13, Janis G. Chadsey-Rusch discusses the theoretical and practical value of the behavioral and ecological perspectives in providing and evaluating skill-training activities for handicapped persons. Chadsey-Rusch outlines the relative strengths and weaknesses of each perspective and notes major similarities in the approaches in terms of assessment of training programs. Among those similarities Rusch stresses the emphasis of each approach on observable behavior in natural environments. Both models also have generally been applied to interventions that have direct relevance to the daily lives of clients. Both furthermore view behavior as manipulated by environmental stimuli and, consequently, are based on the belief that the most effective way of changing client behavior is to modify the relationship between the individual and environment. Chadsey-Rusch notes how these two perspectives are being melded for program purposes and provides examples of the kinds of assessment activities that make the "eco-behavioral perspective" a particularly compelling conceptual model for the evaluation of program effects.

REFERENCES

Coleman, J.S. *Policy research in the social sciences*. Morristown, NJ: General Learning Press, 1972.

Chapter 11

Methodology for Community Integration Research

Laird W. Heal

The scientific method begins with the observation and recording of empirical events. These events are then collected and organized in order to establish empirical regularities, called laws. Logical minds then deduce implications from these laws and invent experiments designed to demonstrate the generality of the empirical laws and the correctness of the experimenters' logic. This chapter discusses the implications of this elegant ritual for studying the integration of handicapped citizens into the mainstream of society.

At the outset it is necessary to point out that many issues in applied social science are ideological rather than empirical. For example, the decision that all citizens, regardless of handicap, have a right to be educated in the public schools is an ideological decision that may or may not have empirical support in terms of the amount of return on the taxpayer's investment, the amount of additional satisfaction accorded the handicapped student, or the loss of educational resources available to other students. On the other hand, each of these presumed effects

of universal education is a plausible result that can be examined empirically.

This chapter avoids ideological comments except those related to the value of applying the scientific method to questions of social moment. The focus here is instead on those issues that are amenable to scientific inquiry. These issues are explored in the context of the universal questions of empirical research:

1. Who or what is the subject of the study?
2. Who provides the data?
3. What are the inherent status characteristics of the subject?
4. What setting and ideological conditions impinge upon the subject, if any?
5. What interventions are imposed upon the subject?
6. What inferences can be made on the basis of the research?

This chapter (see also Heal & Fujiura, in press) deals with research issues in community placement research. There are numerous sources of more general instruction on social

This chapter is a companion to: Heal, L.W., & Fujiura, G.T. Toward a valid methodology for research on residential alternatives for developmentally disabled citizens. In: N.R. Ellis & N.W. Bray (eds.), *International review of research in mental retardation,* Vol. 13. New York: Academic Press, 1982. Whereas the present chapter is organized according to the universal steps of a research project, Heal and Fujiura advance the discussion to issues of design validity (Campbell & Stanley, 1963; Cook & Campbell, 1979)—external validity (including population and setting), internal validity, referent validity (i.e., validity of measurement), and social validity—as they apply to research on community integration.

science research methodology. Especially recommended are Campbell and Stanley (1963) and Cook and Campbell (1979), for their classic analyses of threats to the validity of socially relevant research; Isaac and Michael (1971), for synopses of a large number of published approaches to addressing methodological dilemmas; Selltiz, Wrightsman, and Cook (1976), for a readable text on the major social science methodologies; and Williamson, Korp, Dalphin, and Gray (1982), for a more general, philosophical discussion of various methodologies.

SUBJECT OF STUDY

Among the most perplexing challenges in the study of community integration are the definition, location, and sampling of the subjects of study. Although epidemiological studies (see Conley, 1973, for an excellent review) set the prevalence of mental retardation at least 1% of the total population (i.e., 2 million individuals), the number of mentally retarded persons among institutionalized individuals has never reached 200,000 (Lakin, Krantz, Bruininks, Clumpner, & Hill, 1982), and the number in both public and community facilities is well under 250,000 (Bruininks, Hauber, & Kudla, 1980; Krantz, Bruininks, & Clumpner, 1980). Thus, the population of developmentally disabled citizens that is studied in the community integration literature is about 10% of that which is assumed to exist nationally. Presumably, the other 90% have been successfully integrated into the community, either as independent citizens or as adult dependents on relatives and friends. Nevertheless, it is possible that some fraction of this 90% simply has not been sampled because of inferior research procedures. This section deals with three issues in selecting subjects: a) defining the study population, b) establishing the population registry, and c) sampling individual units.

Defining the Study Population

Community placement research has focused on three major subject populations, the developmentally disabled individual, the caregiver for the developmentally disabled individual, and the facility in which the individual resides. In addition, occasional studies use the state (e.g., Hanley-Maxwell & Heal, 1980; Sigelman, Roeder, & Sigelman, 1980) or parents (see chapter by Turnbull, Brotherson, & Summers, in Lakin & Bruininks, in press).

The first procedural step in residential placement research is defining what is meant by public and/or community residential facilities. Based on their review of all the major national studies of community integration, Heal, Novak, Sigelman, and Switzky (1980) developed the following taxonomy of community residential facilities (CRFs):

1. *Independent Living* refers to a site where an individual lives with a roommate, a spouse, or alone; usually an apartment or duplex, but occasionally a house.
2. *Natural or Adoptive Home* refers to the home of one's parents, usually natural parents, since Gollay, Freedman, Wyngaarden, and Kurtz (1978) found a negligible proportion of adoptive homes. Studies do not always discriminate between homes of parents and those of relatives, so this category occasionally includes both. The largest number of discharges [from public residential facilities—PRFs], nearly a quarter . . . of the total, are made to these natural homes.
3. *Other Relatives' Home* refers to the home of a resident's sibling, grandparent, aunt, uncle, or offspring.
4. *Friend's Home* refers to the home of someone who has befriended the resident or the resident's family.
5. *Foster Home* refers to a home whose "parents" accept the discharged individual in return for a stipend. The stipend is usually insufficient to provide a monetary incentive for the placement. These placements are often called family care placements, and are often made to homes that are approved by the institution rather than by the state's department responsible for family services.
6. *Group Homes* are homes that house as few as two or as many as 100 developmentally disabled children or adults. Typically, the number residing in one home is six to eight. Residences in several other categories are often called group homes.
7. *A Community ICF* (intermediate care facility) is licensed as a nursing home, making it eligible for federal Medicaid support (Title

XIX of the Social Security Act and its Amendments). Two classes are distinguished according to size: 15 and under, and 16 and over. The larger homes must have a nurse (LPN) on duty at all times, whereas the smaller homes need only have one on call. ICFs, especially the smaller ones, often refer to themselves as group homes, and are usually classified as such in research on residential alternatives.

8. *A Convalescent Home* is a nursing home whose residents are expected to stay for a reasonably short period of time for rehabilitation before they return to the community.

9. *Nursing Homes* include a variety of residential alternatives, all providing continuing medical care for anyone who needs it. The convalescent home and intermediate care facility are specially licensed nursing homes. Nursing homes are nearly always privately owned and are expected to make a profit for their owners.

10. *The County Home* is another type of nursing home, usually for the elderly who are unable to afford private nursing home care. It was a much more common institutional alternative for the elderly before Medicaid made nursing homes more readily affordable.

11. *Public Residential Facilities (PRFs)* are state institutions. Until recently these were very large, typically having about 1500 residents and occasionally having over 5000, but today they average only about 500 residents each, and many have fewer than 50.

12. *Private Residential Facilities* are a variety of privately owned and foundation-owned residential alternatives. Some of these are expensive, highly visible, multiple-treatment centers; some are largely custodial facilities; and some are communes that feature an idyllic life for handicapped and nonhandicapped co-residents.

13. *Work Placement* refers to placement where room and board are provided as a condition of employment. Presumably this category includes the "workshop dormitories" studied by Baker, Seltzer, and Seltzer (1977).

14. *Boarding Homes* are homes where the resident is provided room and board for a fee, but no other services are contracted. These homes house individuals of varying abilities. They are usually not classified as group or family care homes.

15. *A Mental Hospital* is an institution for mentally ill individuals. Although many placements were made to these facilities in the past, Scheerenberger's data (1978a, 1978b) indicate that they are [currently] about 5% of total placement.

16. Other alternatives including *Prisons*, account for less than 0.2% of the discharges from institutions for developmentally disabled persons (pp. 48–50).

An important refinement in the definition of group home is to distinguish between those that have 15 or fewer residents and those that have 16 or more. The reason for this refinement is twofold. First, the category as it now exists is too coarse in that it includes both small, familylike facilities and large mini-institutions. Second, states are increasingly exercising the option to fund the smaller group homes as ICFs with Medicaid monies. Until recently, nearly all states applied these monies to the support of public residential facilities, skilled nursing homes, and large intermediate care nursing homes.

After defining facility type, the next task is to ensure that the facility population is representative of those that are so categorized. The problems of establishing this representativeness are discussed in the next two parts of this section.

Study Population Registry

At least two dimensions define study population: *geographical scope* and *comprehensiveness*. Geographically, studies have been national in scope (e.g., Baker et al., 1977; Gollay et al., 1978; Hauber, Bruininks, Wieck, Sigford, & Hill, 1981; O'Connor, 1976); regional (e.g., Edgerton & Bercovici, 1976; Eyman, Silverstein, McLain, & Miller, 1977; Heal & Daniels, 1978; Intagliata & Willer, 1982; Willer & Intagliata, 1981; Wolpert, 1978); or confined to a single facility (e.g., Birenbaum & Re, 1979; Conroy, Efthimiou, & Lemanowicz, 1982; Soforenko & Macy, 1977, 1978). In terms of comprehensiveness, studies have sampled every member of the defined population, a representative sample, or an accidental sample.

Restricted geography and/or limited comprehensiveness can seriously compromise the validity of research conclusions. A study of regional or idiosyncratic scope cannot logically produce results of national generality. Similarly, a population must be comprehensive to yield credible results. When populations are loosely defined, experimenters' preferences or acquaintances can result in the overrepresentation of certain facility types. Such biases are further exacerbated by the characteristics of the facilities that are accidentally overlooked in the development of a facility roster. The unidentified facilities are likely, for example, to be smaller, to be less visible in the community, and to have fewer staff per resident than the facilities that are identified.

To date, only studies of public residential facilities (PRFs) (Krantz, Bruininks, & Clumpner, 1978, 1979, 1980; Scheerenberger, 1978a, 1982) can boast objective and comprehensive definition of the study population. In the study of community residential facilities, Bruininks et al. (1980), Hauber et al. (1981), and O'Connor (1976) made commendable efforts to be comprehensive and specific in the definition of their populations, but the goal of building a comprehensive registry of CRFs is likely to be unattainable in the foreseeable future. Thus, biases in the development of a registry of residential facilities for developmentally disabled persons have inevitably undermined all of the national studies of community residential facilities to date, since the most careful sampling cannot correct for a biased registry. And, as we shall see, facility sampling may be even more challenging than facility definition and location.

Sampling

This subsection treats issues in the sampling of facilities and experimental units within facilities.

Sampling of Facilities Once the facility roster has been developed for a certain research project, facilities are ordinarily sampled from all of those that are defined as eligible. The sample characteristics should reflect those of its population to the maximum extent possible. The safest and most conventional approach to accomplishing this representativeness is to sample experimental units randomly. The term *randomly selected* is probably misused more

than any other in social science research. Its only meaning is that experimental units have an equal probability of being selected from their population. The names or numbers of experimental units must be selected blindly from a well-shuffled deck of cards bearing the names of all members of the population, or by some analogous procedure. Because the truly random sample puts the experimenter at risk of missing certain critical types completely, most random samples have some constraints. For example, Hauber et al. (1981) constrained their sample so that four regions of the country were represented in proportion to their populations, and size classes of facilities were represented disproportionately, with rarer facilities having larger sampling weights (see Groves and Hess, 1975, for a complete discussion of probability sampling.)

Once a facility has been sampled, the scientist's next task is to enlist its participation. Universal participation is crucial to ensure the generalizability of results from the sample to the targeted study population. For example, Bruininks et al. (1980) made three follow-up mailings and a follow-up telephone call to nonrespondents on their original questionnaire. Similarly, Scheerenberger (e.g., 1978a, 1982) routinely telephones his nonrespondents to obtain answers to a short form of his large questionnaire, in order to assure a 100% response rate, at least for selected items.

The same sampling biases that were listed for unidentified facilities are likely to occur among the nonrespondents who have actually been selected for study. A nonrespondent may fear comparison with other similar facilities, may be short of staff, may have residents with serious behavior problems, may have a shortage of staff time for administrative tasks, and so forth.

Sampling of Units within Facilities Once the facility has been selected, the scientist may want to sample residents or caregivers within the facility. Again, a truly random sample or a stratified random sample is essential (Groves & Hess, 1975). As with the sampling of facilities, the biases associated with nonrespondents are severe and are to be avoided at all costs. At the resident level, refusal to participate is often, paradoxically, an indication of normalized integration into the community. As Edgerton noted in 1967, developmentally disabled persons exert extreme efforts to "pass" as nonhandicapped persons. Soforenko and Macy (1977) could find only 48% of the residents released from Orient State Hospital in Ohio over a 9-year period. Similarly, a resident who is too busy with activities to find the time to participate in interviewing and testing should get high marks for social development. On the other hand, many reasons for nonparticipation might be associated with poor adjustment to residential living; for example, a resident might be too sick or too uncontrollable to participate. Thus, missing information has an indeterminate but deleterious effect on the interpretability of a study regarding its study population.

Sampling problems do not end with the selection of a resident. Often information about a resident is obtained from respondents who know the resident well. Scientists must discipline themselves to define explicitly which respondents are to be selected. For example, Hauber et al. (1981) used respondents who had known the subject for at least 2 months and who worked with the subject regularly. Such explicit definitions are essential to the replicability of respondent-provided data.

Sampling of Measures Finally, attention must be paid to the sampling of measures, or what Snow (1974) calls referent generality. Just as subjects are sampled from a population of those possible, so are questions, observations, and responses sampled from their respective referent populations. Sampling the substantive content of a study is crucial for its interpretation. The problems of defining abstract constructs in terms of concrete observables and of controlling response biases that influence the validity of these observables are discussed below.

THE RESPONDENT

Respondents for studies on community integration have included the mentally retarded residents themselves (e.g., Gollay et al., 1978; Sigelman, Budd, Winer, Schoenrock, & Mar-

tin, 1982), nonretarded peers of mentally retarded students (e.g., Gottlieb & Switzky, 1982; Voeltz, 1980), the caregivers or teachers of the developmentally disabled individuals (e.g., Gollay et al., 1978; Lakin, Bruininks, Hill, & Hauber, 1982; Zaharia & Baumeister, 1979), the facility, with no specific respondent identified (e.g., O'Connor, 1976; Wieck & Bruininks, 1980), the experimenters themselves (e.g., Gollay et al., 1978; Heller, Berkson, & Romer, 1981; Romer & Berkson, 1980a, 1980b), state administrative officers for developmental disabilities (e.g., Hanley-Maxwell & Heal, 1980; Hill, Sather, Kudla, & Bruininks, 1978), and resident records (e.g., Ellis, Moore, Taylor, & Bostick, 1978; Landesman-Dwyer & Sulzbacher, 1981).

Response Biases

Sudman and Bradburn's (1974) massive meta-analysis of inadvertent response biases in survey research covered no less than 935 references to methodological studies from 95 different social science journals, as well as numerous dissertations, monographs, and books. They classified dependent variables according to a) behavior (e.g., Did you buy any milk last week?) or b) attitude (e.g., Should the United States supply England with warships to fight Nazi Germany?). They classified their 46 independent variables as a) task variables (e.g., home versus out-of-home, face-to-face versus self-administered, importance of the interview question for the respondent, deliberate deception), b) interviewer roles and characteristics, and c) respondent roles and characteristics. They reported that attitudes covaried with virtually every independent variable investigated, whereas "behavior" covaried only with method of questionnaire administration: respondents tended to underreport behaviors that they were asked to recall in self-administered questionnaires relative to reporting rates in interviews and other forms of query.

Although no studies reviewed by Sudman and Bradburn (1974) used mentally retarded respondents, there is every reason to believe that they, too, are affected by task, interviewer, and respondent characteristics. There are serious methodological problems in gathering data from any respondent. Sigelman, Schoenrock, Spanhel, Hromas, Winer, Budd, and Martin (1980) have confirmed that mentally retarded respondents, especially those who are more severely impaired, are somewhat unreliable and are prone to the "acquiescence" bias, i.e., the disposition to say yes to whatever question is asked of them (Sigelman, Budd, Spanhel, & Schoenrock, 1981; Sigelman et al., 1982). In order to neutralize the acquiescence bias, Sigelman et al. (1982) recommended the use of either-or questions instead of yes-no questions even though the former were less reliably answered. Another approach was used by Heal, Rusch, and Novak (1983). They used yes-no questions, but included a subscale to assess acquiescence directly. The degree of acquiescence of each subject was assessed, and covariance adjustments for it were made in all other subscales.

Triple-Blind Procedures

The task of respondents is to describe reality as closely as possible, not as they would like it to be or think someone else would like it to be. One of the most important procedures to ensure sound logical interpretation of data is to blind respondents (that is, to withhold from them information about the expectations of the research), so that they are not influenced by their preconceptions or their desire to please or displease the experimenter. The highest-quality research employs triple-blinding procedures: the subject, the respondent, and the interviewer are instructed in a way that blinds them from any anticipated results of the investigator. Furthermore, the investigators protect themselves to the maximum extent possible by leaving all judgments about the scoring of variables to their respondents. Respondent biases are especially likely when the experimenter is also the interviewer or the observer in a research study. Ample evidence exists to demonstrate that even in the case of very simple, very objective responses, data tend to agree with the expectations of the experimenter when they are gathered by unblinded observers (McGuigan, 1963; Sudman & Bradburn, 1974).

Respondent Accuracy

A crucial procedure in gathering data that require respondent judgments is to establish the degree to which different respondents agree on these data. (Respondent agreement is discussed in detail below.) However, Kazdin (1982) cites evidence that agreement does not guarantee accuracy. All respondents who check one another's scores for interrespondent agreement are likely to influence one another's subsequent scores. Furthermore, respondents are notorious for conforming to investigator expectations (McGuigan, 1963). Special precautions—notably blinding and respondent agreement procedures—must be taken to assure respondents' disinterested objectivity.

Unfortunately, these procedures have been overlooked by the vast majority of investigators in community integration research. While it could be argued that most investigators lack the resources to employ and train two fleets of interviewers, even the well-funded national projects have failed to employ elementary blindness and reliability procedures. Two notable exceptions are Ellis et al. (1978) and Landesman-Dwyer and Sulzbacher (1981). In both of these studies subjects were facility residents, and the respondent's task was to complete a data form from information that was gleaned from the subjects' facility file folders. In both cases folders were scored by two different respondents and their agreement was reported. While accuracy is not guaranteed by this procedure, there seems to be little room for rater bias.

An interesting study by Halpern, Irvin, and Landman (1979) demonstrates a methodology that could be much more broadly applied in assessing respondent accuracy. The purpose of this study was to compare the direct testing of mentally retarded subjects with the assessment of these subjects via informants. These two measures were used to predict three subtests from the *Social and Prevocational Information Battery* (SPIB) (Halpern, Raffeld, Irvin, & Link, 1975). In predicting the three SPIB subtests, it was found that direct testing with true-false and multiple choice questions addressed to the mentally retarded respondents was "substantially superior" to informant assessment made using author-developed rating forms. Although it is impossible to generalize these results beyond the specific materials used in the study, the procedure demonstrates that it is possible to assess the accuracy of different respondents in an empirical investigation of community integration.

MEASUREMENT OF ABSTRACT ATTRIBUTES

The observations with which a scientist starts are not so simple as one might expect. In the first place, observations are merely *a sample* of events, but they are assumed to be typical of situations and populations that lie far beyond those that are specifically observed. Furthermore, scientists have found it necessary to develop many conventions in measuring and describing observations in order to communicate among themselves and with the public at large.

The Dilemma of Operationism

The scientific method described at the beginning of this chapter has lost much of its simple elegance in the social sciences. The major complication is the disposition of social scientists to study abstractions such as anxiety, emotion, motivation, learning, and productivity instead of more concrete observables such as the latency, duration, and frequency of the salivation response to sour flavors. For example, an adaptive behavior test score is taken to be the operational definition of adaptation to the environment (Hill & Bruininks, in press; Nihira, Foster, Shelhaas, & Leland, 1974); the abstract attribute of normalization is defined operationally as a PASS score (Wolfensberger & Glenn, 1975a, 1975b); self-report of satisfaction is taken as an index of happiness (Gollay et al., 1978; Heal & Daniels, 1978; Hull & Thompson, 1980; Seltzer, 1981; Seltzer & Seltzer, 1976); frequency of conversations is taken as an index of affiliation (Heller, Berkson, & Romer, 1981; Romer & Berkson, 1980a, 1980b); proportion of compliances to coworkers' requests for assistance is taken as

an index of on-the-job social competence (Rusch & Menchetti, 1981); and number of bicycle brakes assembled per unit time is taken as an index of production (Gold, 1973). While some of these measures are less abstract than others, they all share the property of operationism (Bridgeman, 1927): they are all intended to index an attribute of the subject that is far more general than that actually observed. While Skinner (1953) and many others (see, especially, Johnston & Pennypacker, 1980, for a compelling, scholarly analysis) have argued that these abstractions lie outside the realm of science, the tradition of defining them in terms of events that can be observed and recorded has become the foundation of contemporary social science.

The first methodological concern of the social scientist is to realize that every measured variable has a more or less tenuous correspondence to the construct that it purports to index. This analog approach to measurement of constructs in deinstitutionalization parallels that in social science generally. Because these variables are the foundation of all social science inquiry, the properties are discussed in detail as a preface to the remainder of this chapter.

Properties of Variables

Every variable possesses three elementary properties: its *nature,* its *function,* and its *scale.* It is useful to define these characteristics explicitly in order to discuss more clearly many of the nuances of research methodology.

The Nature of a Variable Regardless of its function, a variable can be *status* or *interventional* in nature. A *status variable* is one that resides in the subject of study and can be "manipulated" only by sampling. For instance, IQ, height, weight, adaptive behavior, and facility size are status variables. An *interventional variable* is manipulated directly by the intervention of the experimenter. For example, hours of practice, training method, and feedback procedure can be interventional variables.

Because a status variable is manipulated by sampling, it is impossible to assure that samples are random with regard to status variables other than the one that is manipulated. For instance, groups that differ on IQ also tend to differ in socioeconomic level, history of rewards and punishments, education, number of siblings, color of skin, and so forth. It is very difficult to control all of these variables simultaneously and rule out their influence in an experimental situation.

An interventional variable, on the other hand, is one that is manipulated by some operation imposed on the environment by the experimenter. As with the status variable, it is necessary to be concerned with subtle side effects (correlates) of an interventional variable. For instance, the specified intervention might consist of material presented via flip chart (Martin, 1982). However, many collateral, unspecified interventions could also occur. For example, perhaps the trainer nods his head at critical times; perhaps the subject believes that good performance will get him a job or some other reward; perhaps the subject thinks the trainer has some divine powers. Any number of intervention correlates could influence an intervention group but not a control group. Nevertheless, *it is much easier to control the variables that tend to correlate with an interventional variable than those that tend to correlate with a status variable.*

The Function of a Variable   The second aspect of a variable is its *function*. A variable can function as an independent variable, a dependent variable, or a control variable. The *independent variable* is the one that is systematically manipulated by the experimenter, who hopes to observe some correlated change in the *dependent variable*. The *dependent variable* is always status in nature; it is some observable measurement of the subject of the investigation. All other variables (*control variables*) that might affect the dependent variable are held constant in some way so that the relationship between the independent and dependent variables can be separately and unambiguously assessed. Independent and control variables can be either interventional or status in nature.

The following example helps to clarify these three functions. Conroy et al. (1982) compared a group of residents who had been discharged

from a large state residential facility with matched residents who had not been discharged. Thus, the primary independent variable was discharge condition (yes-no). Unfortunately, subjects were not randomly selected for discharge, so the independent variable was status rather than interventional in nature. Primary dependent variables were changes in adaptive behavior and maladaptive behavior during the period of the study. Sophisticated statistical procedures addressed the issues inherent in the use of gain scores (Cronbach & Furby, 1970; Linn & Slinde, 1977).

Several variables were presumably controlled (held constant) by selecting control subjects who matched the placed subjects: sex, level of retardation, age (within 5 years), length of institutionalization in three categories (0–10 years, 11–30 years, 31–plus years), and preplacement adaptive behavior. Many other variables were presumably controlled by this design. First, a single releasing facility was employed, holding constant a host of geopolitical and experiential factors. Second, many pretest variables were held constant by having the same research team gather, analyze, and interpret the results for each subject. Finally, the matching variables (e.g., sex, age, preplacement adaptive and maladaptive behavior) were plausible proxies for a number of other abilities and experiences. It should be noted that control achieved by matching intact groups is undermined by the statistically inevitable regression of control subjects' scores on matching variables to lower values (Heal & Fujiura, in press).

The finding that the average adaptive behavior score of the placed residents increased from 67.6 to 75.8 in 2 years, while that of the unplaced residents rose only from 64.4 to 65.0 in the same time period, indicated that placement facilitated the development of adaptive behavior. The difference in gains was statistically significant. Because of the control inherent in the matching strategy, a large number of alternative conclusions can be ruled out: group differences could not be attributed to sex, level of retardation, or preplacement adaptive behavior. Age and length of institutionalization were controlled more coarsely, but it is unlikely that more refined measurement would have provided greater control. Furthermore, these control variables were of demonstrated reliability, and, in addition, were proxies for a number of other theoretically important constructs that are known to covary with them. Nevertheless, the fact that the independent variable, residential placement, was status in nature undermines the conclusion that placement fostered differential growth in adaptive functioning. Many subtle unspecified criteria could have been used in the selection of placement subjects (e.g., physical appearance, parental support for placement, personal advocates in the community and in the institution, and other factors). Thus, there are many plausible alternatives to the argument that community placement was the cause of the increase in adaptive functioning. Furthermore, there are many concomitants of placement itself that could have undermined the valid comparison of placed and unplaced residents *even if they had been randomly assigned*. Thus, once a person has been selected for placement, he or she might be judged by a rater to be more competent ipso facto. Furthermore, parents might take more interest in placed children because they are concerned for their safety or because they are closer geographically. None of these effects can reasonably be seen as a component of the placement intervention itself; all must be ruled out as possible explanations before placement per se can be seen as the sole cause of adaptive improvement.

This simple example dramatizes the challenge of conducting valid research on community placement. Control of extraneous variables is virtually impossible, and the scientist is always at the mercy of these variables and of the critic who points them out.

The Scale of a Variable The third aspect of a variable is its *scale*. Ordinarily a variable can be measured along an *interval* (additive) scale (e.g., height, weight, or examination score) or a *nominal* (categorical) scale (e.g., sex or teaching method). A third type of scale, *ordinal,* is less frequently used in social science. Ordinal scales consist of ordered but not equal-interval values. Many measures used in the social sciences can more justifiably be called ordinal than interval, but the statistical treatment of ordered scales is more difficult, and so it has become conventional to make interval assumptions about such scales as socioeconomic status, age, grade level, ratings, and test scores. The rationalization for this practice, which is not so preposterous as it may seem, is beyond the scope of this chapter. The reader is referred to Baird and Noma (1978), Edwards (1957), or Guilford (1954) for additional instruction on scaling.

The scale of a variable is the chief determinant of the statistical analysis applied to it. For example, when a variable is nominal, its distribution is succinctly described by reporting the mode and the index of variation. The mode is a figure that represents the most typical members of the distribution, and the index of variation represents the proportion of cases not at the mode, or the extent to which there is deviation from what is typical. When a variable can be measured on an interval scale, then its typical member is taken to be at the mean of all those sampled, and variability of scores about the mean is indexed by the standard deviation. The typical case measured on an ordinal scale is indexed by its median, and variability is indexed by the range between the top and bottom scores or the range between the top and bottom when a certain percentage (e.g., 50%) of the extreme scores is ignored.

Sources of Measures for Community Integration Research

Several excellent reviews and compendia of scales and tests, which students of community integration should find useful, have appeared in the recent literature. Doucett and Freedman (1981) have reviewed critically many of the popular published instruments that have been used or proposed for research and evaluation in this area. Coulter and Morrow (1978), Meyers, Nihira, and Zetlin (1979), chapters by Holman & Bruininks and by Morreau in Lakin & Bruininks (in press) focus specifically on adaptive and maladaptive behavior. Menchetti, Rusch, and Owens (1983) review the vocational literature from the assessment perspective. Chun, Cobb, and French (1975), Johnson (1976), and Johnson and Bommarito (1971) have compiled summaries of tests and scales, mostly unpublished, that are referenced in the social science literature. Heal and Laidlaw (1980) suggest measures in each of the six domains that are important to monitor in the integration process: approximation to normalization (Wolfensberger & Glenn, 1975a, 1975b), social and self-care competence, the individual's satisfaction, others' satisfaction, residential climate, and cost. Finally, Berkson (1978) and Landesman-Dwyer, Stein, and Sackett (1978) present excellent observation systems for social behavior.

Conclusions

The properties of variables just described form a foundation for understanding their use in assessing the residents (e.g., age, weight, adaptive behavior), settings (e.g., facility type, day program, caregiver characteristics), and the variations in conditions (e.g., training interventions or some status variable that is manipulated by judicious sampling of different subject types) that are found in community integration research. These three classes of variables are discussed in turn in the next three sections.

SUBJECT VARIABLES

Measures of individual residents can be classified into two categories: status variables that are usually reported for descriptive purposes and status variables that are ordinarily used as outcome measures to assess the results of some intervention.

Descriptive Status Variables

Descriptive status variables include the age, sex, weight, and similar characteristics of the individual mentally retarded client. Some of these characteristics, such as age, are deceptive in that they appear to be on an interval scale but are probably not. That is, movement through the years of one's life is probably not linearly related to other variables. Instead, life presumably consists of several stages: infancy, pre-

school years, school years, young adult years, middle age, and old age. It is usually wise to categorize such a variable when the investigator wants to assess its relationship with other variables. Occasionally, however, the problem of a nonlinear relationship can be addressed by calculating the square and cube of such a predictor variable (see, for example, Heal, Lakin, Bruininks, Hill, & Best-Sigford, 1984). These new derived variables can be entered into a multiple correlation in order to assess the degree of *linear and nonlinear* relationship between the status variable and some outcome measure.

Intelligence (Fisher & Zeaman, 1970), adaptive behavior (Conroy et al., 1982; Coulter & Morrow, 1978; Hill & Bruininks, in press; Isett & Spreat, 1979; Meyers et al., 1979; Nihira, 1976; Spreat, 1980), and maladaptive behavior (Arndt, 1981; Borthwick, Meyers, & Eyman, 1981; Clements, DuBois, Bost, & Bryan, 1981; Eyman & Call, 1977; Sutter, Mayeda, Call, Yanagi, & Yee, 1980) are status variables that have been thoroughly investigated. While IQ measurement has become a whipping boy of practitioners in both education and habilitation circles, it remains one of the best predictors of other status variables, including adaptive behavior. It holds despite the variation in standards faced by scientists when they attempt to use IQ scores from subjects' records. For scientific purposes, it seems most advisable to improve the quality of intelligence testing in order to control maximally for general intelligence in the study of variables that are more amenable to intervention; the fact that an IQ score is of little help to the practitioner in programming for a resident habilitation does not eliminate its value to the scientist in understanding relationships among important variables.

Outcome Measures

Any status variable may be employed as an outcome measure, especially if the researcher is interested in resident change. For example, Carsrud, Carsrud, Henderson, Alisch, and Fowler (1979) used weight change as a measure of residents' psychological dysfunction following relocation from one cottage to another. Similarly, the changes in the adaptive-behavior scale factors just described were the dependent variables employed by Eyman et al. (1977). The use of change scores has been criticized in the measurement literature on two grounds. First, change scores tend to be less reliable than measures made at any single time. Second, change scores tend to be correlated with the first of the two scores. Ordinarily, the correlation is negative because of the ceiling of the measure involved. However, it is also possible for change scores to be positively correlated with initial scores. The reader is referred to Cronbach and Furby (1970) and Linn and Slinde (1977) for insightful reviews of the issues involved in measuring change, which suggest that research questions should be framed in terms of posttest scores and, occasionally, in terms of deviations of observed posttests from those expected on the basis of individuals' pretests. Simple gain scores are mathematically reasonable only in *one-sample* studies when the absolute size of the change is the outcome of interest.

The most common outcome measure used in the community integration literature has been some index of the individual's success in the community (e.g., Bell, Schoenrock, & Bensberg, 1981; Gollay et al., 1978; Heal, Sigelman, & Switzky, 1978; Rosen, Kivitz, Clark, & Floor, 1970; Schalock, Harper, & Genung, 1981; Seltzer, 1981; Windle, Stewart, & Brown, 1961; see Sigelman, Novak, Heal, & Switzky, 1980, for a recent review). Most-often used is a simple dichotomous result: such as, remained in the community or returned to the institution (e.g., Gollay et al., 1978; Schalock, Harper, & Genung, 1981; Windle et al., 1961). Other outcome measures include competence in community survival skills (Schalock, 1982, in press), movement through the continuum of human services (Schalock, 1982, in press), affiliation, as indexed by proximity to others and extent of conversations (e.g., Heller et al., 1981), acceptance, as indexed by an acceptance scale (Voeltz, 1980) or by certain patterns of responses on an adjective checklist (Gottlieb &

Switzky, 1982), satisfaction with one's community, job, or residential arrangement (Novak, Heal, Pilewski, & Laidlaw, 1980; Seltzer & Seltzer, 1976), staff-resident interactions (Hemming, Lavender, & Pill, 1981; Repp & Barton, 1980), critical incidents (Nihira & Nihira, 1974)—especially those that would tend to jeopardize the placement of the individual, anthropological observations (Edgerton & Bercovici, 1976), and cost (Heal & Daniels, 1978; Wieck & Bruininks, 1980). All of these outcome measures, except cost, are reviewd in this chapter. (Discussion of cost is intentionally omitted here because of its excellent treatment by Thornton in Chapter 12 in this volume).

SETTING VARIABLES

In any research it is important that the context be specified in sufficient detail to permit the reader to infer the limits of its replicability. Thus, studies in this area delineate their settings extensively. This specification includes such variables as facility type (Baker et al., 1977; Bruininks, Hauber, Hill, Lakin, Sigford, & Wieck, 1981; Gollay et al., 1978; O'Connor, 1976), facility size (Balla, 1976; Baroff, 1980; McCormick, Balla, & Zigler, 1975), domiciliary unit size (McCormick et al., 1975), staff-to-resident ratio (Balla, Butterfield, & Zigler, 1974; Bruininks et al., 1981), administrator-to-direct-care ratio (Lakin, Bruininks, Hill, & Hauber, 1982), degree of normalization (Eyman, Demaine, & Lei, 1979; Flynn, 1980b; Heal & Daniels, 1978; Novak et al., 1980), enriching "characteristics of the treatment environment" (Eyman, Silverstein, & McLain, 1975; Eyman et al., 1977; King, Raynes, & Tizard, 1971; Willer & Intagliata, 1981), and social climate (Jackson, 1969; Moos, 1968, 1975; Moos & Moos, 1976; Pratt, Luszcz, & Brown, 1980).

In addition to the facility itself, the persons responsible for the direct care of residents have often been studied. Variables include age, sex, education, and relationship to owner (Bruininks et al., 1981; Gollay et al., 1978; Wyngaarden, Freedman, & Gollay, 1976), and job satisfaction (George & Baumeister, 1981; Lakin et al., 1982; Zaharia & Baumeister, 1979).

Finally, resident variables can be aggregated and used to describe facilities. For example, a facility can house a group having a certain age (e.g., Flynn, 1980b; O'Connor, 1976), or a certain level of disability (e.g., Baker et al., 1977; McCormick et al., 1975).

INDEPENDENT VARIABLE(S)

As noted above, an independent variable may be either interventional or status in nature. Thus, many of the status characteristics of the residents, their caregivers, and their facilities have been used to predict resident changes (see McCarver & Craig, 1974, and Novak & Heal, 1980, for reviews). Another independent variable that is certainly status in nature is the simple passage of time. A number of studies have monitored resident changes over time, with no explicit intervention imposed (e.g., Bell et al., 1981; Eyman & Arndt, 1982; Fisher & Zeaman, 1970; King, Soucar, & Isett, 1980; Lakin, Krantz, Bruininks, Clumpner, & Hill, 1982). Facility type has been used as an independent variable (e.g., Bjaanes, Butler, & Kelly, 1981; Conroy et al., 1982; Gollay et al., 1978; Heal & Daniels, 1978; Hill & Bruininks, in press; Rudrud, Ferrara, & Ziarnik, 1980; Willer & Intagliata, 1982). Finally, the relocation from one public residential facility building to another has been taken as an independent variable (Carsrud et al., 1979).

Occasionally, independent variables in the research on community integration have been genuinely interventional in nature. For example, Close (1977) and Tizard (1964) compared randomly selected residents who had been placed with those who remained in institutions. Similarly, Townsend and Flanagan (1976) randomly assigned parents of waiting-list clients to an anti-institutionalization training program. Also, particular treatment packages have been quantified and varied systematically to observe their effects (see Martin, Rusch, & Heal, 1982, for a recent review).

ANALYSES AND INFERENCES

Many, probably most, scientific advances have been accomplished by sound observation and measurement and nothing more: many status variables are held constant (controlled), some theoretically critical independent variable is changed in a publicly describable way, and changes, if any, in the dependent variable are measured and reported.

However, ambiguities often exist in this process. First, as measured constructs become more abstract, the best operations to index them are not always clear. Second, theoretical predictions are frequently impossible to make; thus, it is efficient to investigate a large number of variables simultaneously, in order to reveal relationships that may become the basis for integrated theoretical laws. Third, and most critically, it is often difficult to decide whether changes that occur in the dependent variable are larger than would occur in the natural fluctuation in scores. Over the years statistical strategies have been developed to address these three ambiguities: measure development, hypothesis discovery, and hypothesis confirmation. *Measure development* is the construction or selection of variables to index the constructs studied in hypothesis discovery and hypothesis confirmation research. *Hypothesis discovery* involves the observation of natural events in whose interrelationships the observer has interest but little knowledge. *Hypothesis confirmation* involves a systematic attempt to confirm one's suspicions about the interrelationships among variables.

Just as these three strategies differ conceptually, so do they also differ in terms of their statistical analysis strategies. Measure development involves some variation of clustering of items that have a common dimension, usually via item intercorrelations. Hypothesis-discovery research emphasizes descriptive analysis with the reporting of means, standard deviations, and frequencies. The discovery of interrelationships typically uses factor analysis with its many variations (Gorsuch, 1974) or stepwise multiple regression (e.g., Kerlinger

& Pedhazur, 1973; Pedhazur, 1982). Hypothesis confirmation, on the other hand, tends to use some form of controlled regression analysis, especially the analysis of variance, to predict a clearly identified outcome variable from one or more independent variables (Kerlinger & Pedhazur, 1973; Pedhazur, 1982).

It is usually explicit or clearly implicit from the type of study what statistical model, if any, would enhance the meaning of the study data. The paragraphs following discuss this correspondence briefly.

Measure Development

As already indicated, the necessary tradition of employing operational measures to index abstract attributes constitutes a logical flaw that threatens the validity of most social science research. Scientists have responded to this threat by developing certain logical and conventional procedures that are designed to maximize the correspondence between the measurements and their constructs.

The two statistical workhorses of instrument construction are factor analysis (e.g., Gorsuch, 1974), and item analysis (e.g., Guilford, 1954). Factor analysis is applied when an instrument builder is uncertain of the latent structure in his conceptual arena. For example, Nihira (Nihira 1969a, 1969b) and Lambert (Lambert & Nicoll, 1976) applied factor analysis to different versions of the American Association on Mental Deficiency's (AAMD) Adaptive Behavior Scale (ABS), in order to establish the three basic factors of adaptive behavior (Personal Self-Sufficiency, Community Self-Sufficiency, and Personal-Social Responsibility) and the two factors of maladaptive behavior (Intrapunitive and Extrapunitive). Similarly, Demaine, Wilson, Silverstein, and Mayeda (1978), Eyman et al. (1979), Flynn (1980b), and Flynn and Heal (1981) factor analyzed the major index of normalization, PASS 3 (Wolfensberger & Glenn, 1975a, 1975b), in order to discover its latent factor structure. Using PASS scores from a broad array of human-disability services, Flynn (1980b) identified two major factors (Normalization of

Place and Normalization of Program) and two minor ones (Administration, and Proximity and Access). Using a more homogeneous sample of facilities, Demaine et al. (1978) and Eyman et al. (1979) found a somewhat different factor structure. Once the factor structure of an instrument has been identified, individual subjects can be given factor scores according to a sophisticated weighting system or more simply by the formation of separate subscales from the items that are the most potent correlates of each factor.

The other common strategy for developing separate subscales from a body of items in a large multidimensional domain is called item analysis. In contrast to factor analysis, item analysis requires the investigator to determine the conceptual groupings of his or her items before completing any statistical procedures. These conceptual groupings become trial subscales. Each item is then correlated with all of the other items in its own grouping and all of the items in the other subscales. Items are retained only if they have both a high conceptual relationship *and* a high empirical relationship with their subscales. Ideally, items will have low correlations with subscales other than their own. Item-analysis procedures have been employed by Heal, Hill, and Bruininks (1983), and Heal, Rusch, and Novak (1983) in the development of a maladaptive behavior scale and a life-style satisfaction scale, respectively.

While both factor analysis and item analysis have their place in the development of psychometric scales, it seems that the latter is to be preferred: the conceptual development of psychological constructs should precede, not follow, statistical decision making; statistics are properly the slave, not the master, of the social scientist. Nevertheless, either approach requires considerable judgment on the part of the scientist, and this artistry should be exercised without apology and with several iterations, if necessary, until the scale has the best correspondence possible to the construct that it purports to index.

Cross-Validation Cross-validation is the calculation of reliability and validity statistics for a scale using a second, independent sample from the same population of subjects used to select and refine items for the scale. Whichever approach is applied to the development of a measurement instrument, cross-validation is mandatory. The use of either item analysis or factor analysis to select items inevitably capitalizes on chance, because some items have high correlations with their subscales solely due to accidental errors of measurement. It is unlikely that the same accidents will occur in two independent samples, however, and so the summary statistics from a cross-validation sample are credible estimates of the true values in the population, whereas those in the original sample, which was used to select "good" items, are not.

Reliability   Reliability is the consistency or stability of measuring the same variable on two or more occasions. Reliability of measurement is especially important in the social sciences because of the lack of objectivity or abstractness of many of our measures. There are three major types of reliability: repeatability of a measure over time, called *test-retest reliability;* stability among raters or judges of the attribute being assessed, called *interrater agreement;* and the extent to which the various items

on a test tend to agree with one another, called *internal consistency.*

These three reliability types are sensitive to three different sources of measurement error. Test-retest reliability assesses time errors—the extent to which scores vary simply with the passage of time. Interrater agreement assesses the extent to which observers of the same events vary in their reporting of what these events are. Internal consistency assesses content-sampling errors—the extent to which scores are likely to vary as the result of a broadness or multivariateness of the items that are presumed to index the same construct. Heal and Fujiura (in press) discuss in detail the optimal statistics to be applied to each type of reliability. Their analysis is summarized in Table 1. Berk (1979) and Hollenbeck (1978) provide excellent reviews of the interobserver agreement and reliability literature.

Validity   Conventional measurement texts (e.g., Nunnally, 1978) describe three types of validity, in addition to *face* ("apparent" or "appearance") *validity. Content validity* refers to the representative sampling of items from the content domain that is being assessed by an instrument. *Empirical validity* refers to the extent to which a measure predicts some

Table 1.   Optimal reliability statistics[a]

| | **Type of reliability** | | |
	Test-retest	Interrater agreement	Internal consistency
Type of error	Time-related changes in examinees	Individual differences in raters' perceptions	Variations in sampling of items from the content domain
Preferred statistic(s)			
a. Nominal scale	Phi (binary *r*)	Cohen's Kappa[b]	
b. Interval scale (items may be yes-no)	Pearson's *r*	Robinson's *A*[c]	Cronbach's alpha[d]

[a]Adapted from Heal and Fujiura, in press.
[b]Cohen (1968).
[c]Robinson (1957).
[d]Cronbach (1970).

criterion, which itself has credibility as an index of the construct being measured. For example, an adaptive behavior scale is seen to be empirically valid if those who are successfully placed in the community achieve high scores and those who fail in their community placements achieve low scores. An empirically valid test need not have face validity. *Construct validity* is the joint occurrence of content validity and empirical validity. A measure is said to have construct validity if its items are representative of the content domain being measured and if it consistently predicts, according to some theoretical position, criterion behaviors that are associated with the construct.

Hypothesis-Confirmation Analyses

The model for all hypothesis-confirmation research is the simple, true experiment in which subjects are randomly assigned to either of two groups, an experimental group (which gets a critical intervention), and a control group (which is treated exactly the same as the experimental group except for the absence of the critical intervention or, better, the substitution of a placebo intervention). Random assignment is critical in this definition, for only random assignment assures that the backgrounds of the two groups are logically equated. It is not surprising that few hypothesis-confirmation studies in the community integration literature conform to this model, but, as indicated earlier under "Independent Variables," some do exist (Close, 1977; Landesman-Dwyer, in press; Tizard, 1964; Townsend & Flanagan, 1976). Kiesler (1982) reports 10 other studies with mentally ill persons. Butterfield's (in press) excellent discussion of the importance of random assignment for community research indicates that nearly all designs for testing hypotheses about community integration are quasi-experimental: the independent variables are manipulated by the judicious sampling of subjects, whose status with regard to the independent variable has been determined by forces that are external to the investigation. He notes that few studies in this area have employed random assignment to experimental and control groups before the onset of interventions.

In applying statistical analyses it is convenient to separate these designs into two major classes, those that have a single outcome measure and those that have multiple outcome measures.

Designs with Single Outcome Measures

Probably the most common design in community integration research is that in which a single outcome can be identified and in which a number of independent variables are proposed as precursors of the outcome. This is a classical regression situation in which a multiple correlation is calculated between the single dependent variable and the multiple predictors (e.g., Flynn, 1980a). If all the predictors are categorical, the model is called an analysis of variance.

Several decisions must be made in the application of this procedure. First, if some of the predictors are categorical and some are continuous, it is necessary to transform the categorical variables into binary predictors. This can be accomplished in a number of ways (see, for example, Pedhazur, 1982). The second decision is to determine the order in which predictor variables are entered into the prediction picture. If predictor variables are correlated, then their prediction of the dependent variable involves some overlap among them, and overlap (called multicolinearity) must be assigned to one predictor or another. Regression programs automatically assign overlapping variance to the variables that are entered earlier in the prediction process. The experimenter's task, then, is to make certain that the variables chosen earlier are those with which he or she wants to associate overlapping variance. Three procedures are especially recommended: controlled stepwise regression, uniqueness analysis, and path analysis. Each has its optimal applications.

Controlled Stepwise Regression In controlled stepwise regression analysis, every variable or conceptually linked group of variables is entered in sequence according to an order explicitly specified by the investigator. For example, in a study of occupational success, Flynn (1980a) used a temporal order: educational aspirations came before educational accomplishment, and vocational knowledge before vocational accomplishment. In the case of Heal, Hill, and Bruininks (1983), variables that were conceptually defined as control variables were inserted early and variables that were conceptually defined as independent variables were inserted later. For example, region of the country and socioeconomic status of the local county were entered early; resident psychometric characteristics were entered in the middle of the sequence; and facility characteristics were entered near the end. These were entered in order, so that any overlapping variance was captured by the variables entered earlier. Thus, regional characteristics functioned as covariates (statistical control variables) for all other variables in the list; these and resident status variables functioned as covariates for all variables below them in the list. As in any analysis of covariance, the capture of overlapping variance (statistical control) has two effects: first it removes from the residual individual differences (i.e., from error variance) any variance in the dependent variable that is predicted by covariates; and second, it partially equates subjects on the dependent variable for any reliable advantage or disadvantage that they might have on the covariates. For example, subjects in the Heal, Hill, and Bruininks (1983) paper were statistically equated regarding the region of the country from which they had come before the correlation of facility characteristics and resident maladaptive behavior was assessed. This equating is quite imperfect when the control variables are unreliable and when the subsequent independent variables are status characteristics (e.g., age or adaptive behavior), rather than interventional variables (e.g., membership in randomly constituted experimental and control groups).

It is crucial that the experimenter specify the order of variables' entry a priori rather than ask a computer program to order the variables according to the variance that they capture on an a posteriori basis. The probability of the replication of one's results by chance are reasonably close to nominal levels of statistical significance in the former case but not in the latter.

Uniqueness Analysis   In uniqueness analysis every variable in turn is entered into the prediction process last so that its unique prediction (i.e., that which does not overlap with other predictors) of the dependent variable can be established. This procedure is most useful when the intercorrelations among predictors are very small, for if the overlap among predictors is very large, none will uniquely predict the dependent variable appreciably. For example, Romer and Berkson (1980a) presented a sophisticated analysis of the prediction of three social-affiliation factor scores: extensity (i.e., the number of friends), intensity (i.e.,, intensity of friendship regardless of the number of friends), and aggregation (i.e., amount of affiliation without actual interaction). In their analysis Romer and Berkson entered four individual difference variables (sex, IQ, age, and diagnostic category) in step 1; workshop of the observation in step 2; individual difference by workshop interactions in step 3; and theoretically important "mediators" of affiliation (attractiveness ratings, peer sociometric ratings, time in setting [log (years + 1)], medication category, disability category, and years of institutionalization) in step 4. Using a separate controlled stepwise regression analysis for each affiliation score, they found, among other things, that after controlling for individual differences and workshop characteristics, attractiveness and sociometric ratings were statistically significant predictors of all three affiliation indices.

Path Analysis   The path-analysis application of multiple regression appears to have great promise for social science generally and community integration in particular. For this analysis the investigator constructs a chain of predictors, which may be linear or may have some parallel links. The chain is usually organized temporally but may be organized logically as well. Once the causal path or chain of predictors has been organized so that each one is clearly conceptualized as to its precursors and effects, it is a fairly simple matter to identify path coefficients that index the extent of presumed causation. These coefficients may be tested for significance to determine whether or not the presumed causation meets a statistical criterion of reliability. Pedhazur (1982) provides an excellent introduction and overview of this topic.

Eyman et al., (1979) and Flynn (1980a) provide highly refined applications of this technique. Eyman et al. (1979) performed three separate regression analyses, one for each of Nihira's (1976) three factor-analytically derived dimensions of the AAMD Adaptive Behavior Scale, (Personal Self-Sufficiency, Community Self-Sufficiency, and Personal-Social Responsibility). For each analysis, the dependent variable was gain in adaptive behavior over a 3-year study period. Again, for each analysis, independent variables were entered in two steps. Step 1 featured the resident characteristics of age, IQ, and initial ABS score. Step 2 featured the factor scores of normalization as measured by PASS 3, assigned to residents' facilities on each of six dimensions (Wolfensberger & Glenn, 1975a, 1975b). ABS improvement was very predictable, with R^2 of .40, .39, and .54 between the nine predictors and the respective ABS variables of Personal Self-Sufficiency, Community Self-Sufficiency, and Personal-Social Responsibility. While not reported directly, it was clear from the results that the personal characteristics accounted for most of the ABS improvement: older, higher-level subjects made greater gains. Nevertheless, some normalization dimensions—notably, proximity of support services and environmental beauty and comfort—added significantly to the prediction of improvement. Especially valuable for the present discussion were the diagrams of "path coefficients," amply interpreted by Eyman et al. (1979), and Flynn (1980a), which quantified the extent to which each predictor contributed to or mediated the explanation of the variance in adaptive behavior improvement.

Designs with Multiple Outcomes The research questions associated with community integration are almost certainly multivariate in complexity, and there can be little doubt that studies with single outcomes are guilty of over-simplifying reality. But analyses involving multiple outcomes are extremely challenging. The simplest way to deal with multiple outcomes is to construct a *regression model for each one*. There are numerous examples of this approach in the literature. The analyses by Eyman et al. (1979) and Romer and Berkson (1980a), reported earlier, provide examples. Unfortunately, the separate-treatment-of-dependent-variables approach fails to identify the dimensions of intercorrelations among them. The mathematical generalization of simple regression to multivariate dependent variables is called *canonical correlation* (e.g., Eyman et al., 1979). When all predictors are categorical, this procedure is called the *multivariate analysis of variance* (e.g., Vitello, Atthowe, & Cadwell, 1983). The special case where there is only one categorical predictor is called *discriminant analysis* (e.g., Bartnik & Winkler, 1981; Gully & Hosch, 1979). The interpretation of the canonical correlation is similar to that of other least-squares-correlation coefficients (e.g. Harris, 1975). The "first canonical correlation" is a correlation of an optimized linear combination of the independent variables with a similar linear combination of the dependent variables. Its square is interpreted as the proportion of variance that these two sets of variables have in common. The residuals remaining after calculation of the first canonical correlation are then used in a new calculation to obtain a second, statistically independent canonical correlation coefficient. This procedure is continued until the degrees of freedom for either the dependent variables or the independent variables are exhausted, each canonical coefficient requiring one degree of freedom from each set.

Hypothesis-Discovery Analyses

Hypothesis discovery takes many forms. The most obvious is the descriptive analysis that is frequently applied when an unknown area is studied. A number of questions are asked, and descriptive analyses are completed in an effort to discover associations among variables. The associations that are discovered are then interpreted and hypotheses of causation proposed. The national surveys of Baker et al., (1977), Bruininks et al. (1981), Gollay et al. (1978), and O'Connor (1976) are all examples of hypothesis-discovery research.

Another major class of descriptive hypothesis-discovery research originated in the fields of anthropology and ethnology and involves observing, as unobtrusively as possible, the natural environment. Much recent work (e.g., Berkson, 1978; Butler & Bjaanes, 1978; Heller et al., 1981; Landesman-Dwyer et al., 1978; Romer & Berkson, 1980a, 1980b) falls into this tradition. This approach differs from surveys and direct observations in that the measures used are often developed as part of the observation procedure. Sackett (1978a, 1978b) presents an excellent overview of this method.

When the goal of hypothesis discovery is to describe relationships among constructs, any of the procedures described in this chapter under "Hypothesis-Confirmation Analyses" may be applied. However, a certain amount of confusion is generated by the failure to separate the process of hypothesis discovery from hypothesis-confirmation goals. For example, regression analysis and its variations (e.g., the analysis of variance, and the multivariate analysis of variance) are statistical procedures in which it is possible to establish an explicit and appropriate probability that the observed data could have occurred by chance (i.e., an explicit level of statistical significance). These statistical procedures have often been misinterpreted through the use of stepwise regression procedures (e.g., Hull & Thompson, 1980; Schalock, Harper, & Carver, 1981; Seltzer, 1981), which significantly reduce the probability of the chance occurrence of the data. Yet, the results are reported and inappropriately interpreted as hypothesis confirmations with true significance levels.

Principal-components analysis, factor analysis, and their many variations (Gorsuch, 1974) were developed primarily for their hypothesis-discovery function. These procedures permit the investigator to determine which of a large number of variables cluster together to form a much smaller number of dimensions. The application by Nihira (1969a, 1969b, 1976), who completed large factor analyses of the AAMD Adaptive Behavior Scale in order to discover the interrelationships among items, was cited earlier as an example of measure development. Nihira found that the items generally measured three more-or-less independent aspects of adaptive behavior: personal independence, community orientation, and social appropriateness. He had no a priori hypothesis that these three factors would emerge, but operated in a hypothesis-discovery mode.

Another family of procedures, especially useful in the development of typologies, is cluster analysis. These procedures assist in the identification of clusters of subjects that have similar profiles on a number of characteristics. The basic strategy is to identify profiles that are as similar to one another as possible and, simultaneously, are as different as possible from those of other clusters. Using such an approach Mink, Nihira, and Meyers (1983) identified five types of families from homes of trainable mentally retarded children based on their social and physical environments and child-rearing practices. Mink et al. (1983) then validated their clusters by demonstrating that different types of families varied significantly and meaningfully with regard to fathers' participation in child care, mothers' out-of-home employment, and rate of stressful family events. It appears that this approach could be much more broadly applied to the chronically frustrating task of defining types of residential alternatives.

Other Nonexperimental Methodologies

This chapter's discussion has been limited to the experimental and quasi-experimental methodologies that have dominated research on residential alternatives for developmentally disabled children and adults. It is by no means exhaustive, a number of methodologies are conspicuous by their absence here and in the community integration literature; the reader is directed to Borg and Gall (1983), Selltiz et al. (1976), or Williamson et al. (1982) for well-rounded introductions to research methodology. Two recent methodological developments—benefit-cost analysis (discussed in depth in Chapter 12) and meta-analysis—are especially useful. Meta-analysis is described briefly here.

Meta-Analysis Meta-analysis is even more foreign to community integration research than benefit-cost analysis. The strategy of meta-analysis is to combine the results of all studies that have tested essentially the same hypothesis (i.e., in our terms, the same tentative empirical law). A serious disadvantage of using this technique is the great difficulty in maintaining internal and external validity. Suppose one wants to do a meta-analysis of all studies that have tested the hypothesis that community placement from an institution brings about improvement in adaptive behavior. Regarding external validity, the meta-analyzer must identify the population of studies that have tested a particular hypothesis. Published studies are almost certainly biased in favor of those that have found a significant effect, and the extent of this bias cannot be estimated. Regarding internal validity, the meta-analyzer must combine the results from studies whose procedures varied greatly from one another. Glass, McGaw, and Smith (1981) have addressed these and other questions. Their admittedly imperfect solution to the problem of external validity is to include all locatable studies—if they meet a minimum standard of quality regarding their internal validity. Their similarly flawed solution to the problem of combining the results of varying types and qualities is to use the meta-statistic, effect size. This score, calculated for each comparison between an experimental and control group, is the difference between the scores of the two groups divided by the standard deviation of the control group.

Even from this brief explanation, it is clear that meta-analysis has apparently insurmountable problems as a scientific method. Nevertheless, it must be seen as a more objective and more public procedure than the integrative literature review, which is the social scientist's current tool for combining information from a number of studies having a common hypothesis. Thus, application of meta-analysis to the study of the community integration of handicapped citizens would probably result in some valuable syntheses of information.

Applied Behavior Analysis (ABA)

Applied behavior analysis presents an entirely different and refreshing approach to the application of science to behavior. It has features of both hypothesis discovery and hypothesis confirmation. As defined by Birnbrauer, Peterson, and Solnick (1974), research in this tradition is defined by four characteristics: a) repeated measures on the same subject(s) under controlled conditions; b) the use of reliable measures that consist of directly observable behaviors; c) the use of interventions that are defined in sufficient detail to allow their replication; and d) the demonstration of repeatable behavioral effects of those interventions. In their seminal article, Baer, Wolf, and Risley (1968) included two important additional features: ABA is to have "applied" content and to have the significance of its outcome evaluated on the basis of its value for individual members of its target population. Although a number of statistical procedures have been proposed to assist applied behavior analysts in making decisions on this last point (e.g., Kazdin, 1982), most prefer to base their judgments of socially useful effects on visual inspection of their data.

There are two popular strategies for demonstrating a functional (i.e., presumed causal) relationship between an independent variable and a dependent variable. The first, feasible only for performance (i.e., temporary) measures, is the *reversal* procedure. In this procedure baseline measures (scores) are gathered on repeated occasions until the investigator is satisfied that the scored behavior is stable and predictable over time in the absence of any intervention that he or she might impose. Then, while the same measures are gathered in the same manner as before, an intervention is applied. This intervention may be praise for good performance, a tangible reward for good performance, or some other manipulation of the environment that is under the experimenter's control. After the measured behavior has stabilized in its response to the intervention, the intervention is withdrawn. If the performance of the measured behavior changes in a desirable direction and degree during intervention and then reverts to its baseline level when the intervention is removed, it is said to be under experimental control. The second strategy for demonstrating experimental control is the *multiple baseline* strategy, in which several behaviors are monitored simultaneously. After baselines stabilize for all behaviors, an intervention is applied to them one at a time, ideally in a random order. The procedure continues until the experimenter is satisfied that the intervention and not some accidental event in the environment is responsible for the behavior changes. These behaviors need not necessarily be different behaviors in the same subject. They may be the same behavior assessed and intervened upon at different times of the day or in different environments; they may be the same behavior intervened upon by different agents; or they may be the same behavior in different and independent subjects. The multiple baseline design is suitable for studying permanent changes in the subject, such as learning changes or the results of other irreversible operations.

The applied behavior analysis strategy has many advantages in the study of handicapped populations:

1. Because changes are observed in individual subjects, it is not necessary to wonder if an intervention that has been found to raise a group average will be effective in the individual case.
2. Because the strategy deals with individual subjects, it is not necessary to find groups of subjects who have similar characteristics or pathologies in order to control for individual differences. Thus, ABA is especially useful with handicapped populations, which often have only a few cases and pose difficult sampling problems.
3. Because the strategy focuses on behavioral changes that have practical significance, investigators are unlikely to be seduced by trivial or ephemeral, but statistically significant, behavior changes.
4. Because the procedures deal with individual cases, procedures can be modified at will when they are seen to have no effect, and then can be replicated in other subjects or settings in order to demonstrate that behavioral changes, when they finally do occur, are not accidental.

In a typical study Vogelsberg and Rusch (1979) applied several procedures before succeeding in teaching three severely retarded young adults to cross partially controlled intersections on their way to work as kitchen laborers at a university. The six training phases included: a) preinstruction and instructional feedback, b) preinstructional feedback and five trials of repeated practice on the looking response, c) instructional feedback alone, d) no instruction at all, e) instructional feedback and rehearsal of the proper procedures, and f) simple observation. The researchers found appropriate street-crossing behavior was associated with the original interventions (*b* and *c*) but did not sustain itself (in *d*) until rehearsal of the procedures was implemented (in *e*). Because this special training procedure was replicated over the three subjects, it was viewed to be a necessary and powerful component of the total training intervention. This study demonstrates the utility of ABA procedures to document the effect of an intervention package on a problem of practical importance. Only three subjects were available, and two would have been sufficient (see earlier-noted advantages 1 and 2); the problem was significant, its solution being essential for employment and perhaps for survival as well (see advantage 2); and procedures were modified when they were seen to be ineffective, without threatening the validity of the final conclusion (see advantage 4).

The technology of applied behavior analysis has developed substantially in the past two decades. Kazdin (1982) provides a complete and readable text on these procedures. Chadsey-Rusch discusses the use of this methodology within an ecological perspective elsewhere in this volume.

ETHICS OF APPLIED SCIENCE

The foregoing sections demonstrate that social scientists have a vast arsenal of research tools at their disposal. Furthermore, it is clear that these scientists are addressing pressing, current social problems. Understanding the conditions necessary to support developmentally disabled individuals in settings that are the least restrictive possible is a fundamental objective in American society, for it has become increasingly clear that civil liberties denied to one individual represent a threat to the civil liberties of all.

Yet, society's support of this research falls incredibly short. Only rarely can surveys report responses from 100% of their target sample. Of all the studies known to this author that relate to the integration of developmentally disabled citizens into the community, Scheerenberger (1978a, 1982) and Krantz, Bruininks, and Clumpner (1978, 1979, 1980) alone have accomplished this feat. Scientists must have privileged access to their target populations if their studies are to be relevant. A second major flaw in the research reported here is the almost complete absence of true experiments. Only a handful of studies reported the random assignment of subjects to the levels of their independent variable. Still, it is only through random assignment of subjects to conditions that the unambiguous evaluation of interventions can proceed.

Scientists are remiss to tolerate the present state of affairs. Science and its practitioners are charged with the responsibility of providing society with information that it needs to make decisions about its social progress. With this responsibility comes the obligation to advocate the best methodology known. There has been a clear failure to meet this obligation.

REFERENCES

Arndt, S. A general measure of adaptive behavior. *American Journal of Mental Deficiency*, 1981, *85*, 554–556.

Baer, D.M., Wolf, M., & Risley, T.R. Some current dimensions of applied behavior analysis. *Journal of Applied Behavior Analysis*, 1968, *1*, 91–98.

Baird, J.C., & Noma, E. *Fundamentals of scaling and psychophysics*. New York: John Wiley & Sons, 1978.

Baker, B.L., Seltzer, G.B., & Seltzer, M.M. *As close as possible*. Cambridge, MA: Little, Brown & Co., 1977.

Balla, D.A. Relationship of institution size to quality of care: A review of the literature. *American Journal of Mental Deficiency*, 1976, *81*, 117–124.

Balla, D., Butterfield, E.C., & Zigler, E. Effects of institutionalization on retarded children: A longitudinal cross-institutional investigation. *American Journal of Mental Deficiency*, 1974, *78*, 530–549.

Baroff, G. On "size" and quality of institution care: A second look. *Mental Retardation*, 1980, *18*, 117–119.

Bartnik, E., & Winkler, R.C. Discrepant judgments of community adjustment of mentally retarded adults: The contribution of personal responsibility. *American Journal of Mental Deficiency*, 1981, *86*, 260–266.

Bell, N.J., Schoenrock, C.J., & Bensberg, G.J. Change over time in the community: Findings of a longitudinal study. In: R.H. Bruininks, C.E. Meyers, B.B. Sigford, & K.C. Lakin (eds.), *Deinstitutionalization and community adjustment of mentally retarded people*. Washington, D C : American Association on Mental Deficiency, 1981.

Berk, R.A. Generalizability of behavioral observations: A clarification of inter-observer agreement and inter-observer reliability. *American Journal of Mental Deficiency*, 1979, *83*, 460–472.

Berkson, G. Social ecology and ethology of mental retardation. In: G.P. Sackett (ed.), *Observing behavior, Vol. 1: Theory and applications in mental retardation*. Baltimore: University Park Press, 1978.

Berkson, G., & Romer, D. Social ecology of supervised communal facilities for mentally disabled adults: 1. Introduction. *American Journal of Mental Deficiency*, 1980, *85*, 219–228.

Birenbaum, A., & Re, M.A. Resettling mentally retarded adults in the community—almost four years later. *American Journal of Mental Deficiency*, 1979, *83*, 323–329.

Birnbrauer, J., Peterson, C.R., & Solnick, J. Design and interpretation of studies of single subjects. *American Journal of Mental Deficiency*, 1974, *79*, 191–203.

Bjaanes, A., Butler, E., & Kelly, B. Placement type and client functional level as factors in provision of services aimed at increasing adjustment. In: R.H. Bruininks, C.E. Meyers, B.B. Sigford, & K.C. Lakin (eds.), *Deinstitutionalization and community adjustment of mentally retarded people*. Washington, D C : American Association on Mental Deficiency, 1981.

Borg, W.R., & Gall, M.D. *Educational Research: An introduction* (4th ed.). New York: Longman, 1983.

Borthwick, S.A., Meyers, C.E., & Eyman, R.K. Comparative adaptive and maladaptive behavior of mentally retarded clients of five residential settings in three western states. In: R.H. Bruininks, C.E. Meyers, B.B. Sigford, & K.C. Lakin (eds.), *Deinstitutionalization and community adjustment of mentally retarded people.* Washington, D C : American Association on Mental Deficiency, 1981.

Bridgeman, P.W. *The logic of modern physics.* New York: MacMillan Co., 1927.

Bruininks, R.H., Hauber, F.A., Hill, B.K., Lakin, K.C., Sigford, B.B., & Wieck, C.A. *Brief #5. 1978–1979 in-depth national interview survey of public and community residential facilities for mentally retarded persons.* Minneapolis: University of Minnesota, Department of Psychoeducational Studies, September, 1981.

Bruininks, R.H., Hauber, F.A., & Kudla, M. National survey of community residential facilities: A profile of facilities and residents in 1977. Minneapolis: University of Minnesota, Department of Psychoeducational Studies, 1979. Also available in *American Journal of Mental Deficiency,* 1980, *84*(5), 470–478.

Butler, E.W., & Bjaanes, A.T. Activities and the use of time by retarded persons in community care facilities. In: G.P. Sackett (ed.), *Observing behavior,* Vol. I: *Theory and applications in mental retardation.* Baltimore: University Park Press, 1978.

Butterfield, E.C. Why and how to study the influence of living arrangements upon the mentally retarded. In: S. Landesman-Dwyer & P. Vietze (eds.), *Living with retarded people.* Baltimore: University Park Press, in press.

Campbell, D.T., & Stanley, J. *Experimental and quasi-experimental designs for research.* Chicago: Rand McNally & Co., 1963.

Carsrud, A.L., Carsrud, K.B., Henderson, D.P., Alisch, C.J., & Fowler, A.V. Effects of social and environmental change on instutionalized mentally retarded persons: The relocation syndrome reconsidered. *American Journal of Mental Deficiency,* 1979, *84,* 266–272.

Chun, K.T., Cobb, S., & French, J.R.P., Jr. *Measures for psychological assessment.* Ann Arbor, MI: Survey Research Center, 1975.

Clements, P.R., DuBois, Y., Bost, L., & Bryan, C. Brief reports: Adaptive Behavior Scale, Part Two: Predictive efficiency of severity and frequency scores. *American Journal of Mental Deficiency,* 1981, *85,* 433–434.

Close, D.W. Community living for severely and profoundly retarded adults: A group home study. *Education and Training of the Mentally Retarded,* 1977, *12,* 256–262.

Cohen, J. Weighted kappa: Nominal scale agreement with provision for scaled disagreement or partial credit. *Psychological Bulletin,* 1968, *70,* 213–220.

Conley, R.W. *The economics of mental retardation.* Baltimore: Johns Hopkins University Press, 1973.

Conroy, J., Efthimiou, J., & Lemanowicz, J. A matched comparison of the developmental growth of institutionalized and deinstitutionalized mentally retarded clients. *American Journal of Mental Deficiency,* 1982, *86,* 581–587.

Cook, T.D., & Campbell, D.T. *Quasi-experimentation design and analysis issues for field settings.* Boston: Houghton-Mifflin Co., 1979.

Coulter, W.A., & Morrow, H.W. *Adaptive Behavior:*

Concepts and measurements. New York: Grune & Stratton, 1978.

Cronbach, L.J. *Essentials of psychological testing* (3rd ed.). New York: Harper & Row, 1970.

Cronbach, L.J., & Furby, L. How we should measure "change"—or should we? *Psychological Bulletin,* 1970, *74,* 68–80.

Demaine, G., Wilson, S., Silverstein, A., & Mayeda, T. *Facility ratings based on a tested organizational nomenclature and a validated PASS 3.* Paper presented at the annual meeting of the American Association on Mental Deficiency, Denver, May, 1978.

Doucett, P., & Freedman, R. *Review and evaluation of instrumentation utilized by programs for the developmentally disabled.* Cambridge, MA: Abt Associates, 1981.

Edgerton, R.B. *The cloak of competence: Stigma in the lives of the mentally retarded.* Berkeley: University of California Press, 1967.

Edgerton, R.B., & Bercovici, S.M. The cloak of competence: Years later. *American Journal of Mental Deficiency,* 1976, *80,* 485–497.

Edgerton, R.B., & Langness, L.L. Observing mentally retarded persons in community settings: An anthropological perspective. In: G.P. Sackett (ed.), *Observing behavior,* Vol. 1: *Theory and applications in mental retardation.* Baltimore: University Park Press, 1978.

Edwards, A.L. *Techniques of attitude scale construction.* New York: Appleton-Century-Crofts, 1957.

Ellis, N.R., Moore, S.A., Taylor, J.J., & Bostick, G.E. *A follow-up of severely and profoundly retarded children after short-term institutionalization.* Tuscaloosa: University of Alabama, February, 1978.

Eyman, R.K., & Arndt, S. Life-span development of institutionalized and community-based mentally retarded residents. *American Journal of Mental Deficiency,* 1982, *86,* 342–350.

Eyman, R.K., & Call, T. Maladaptive behavior and community placement of mentally retarded persons. *American Journal of Mental Deficiency,* 1977, *82*(2), 137–144.

Eyman, R.K., Demaine, G.C., & Lei, T. Relationship between community environments and resident changes in adaptive behavior: A path model. *American Journal of Mental Deficiency,* 1979, *83,* 330–338.

Eyman, R.K., Demaine, G.C., & Lei, T. Relationship between community environments and resident changes in adaptive behavior: A path model. *American Journal of Mental Deficiency,* 1981, *85,* 473–477.

Eyman, R.K., Silverstein, A., & McLain, R. Effects of treatment programs on the acquisition of basic skills. *American Journal of Mental Deficiency,* 1975, *79,* 573–582.

Eyman, R.K., Silverstein, A.B., McLain, R., & Miller, C. Effects of residential settings on development. In: P. Mittler (ed.), *Research to practice in mental retardation.* Baltimore: University Park Press, 1977.

Fisher, M.A., & Zeaman, D. Growth and decline of retardate intelligence. In: N.R. Ellis (ed.), *International review of research in mental retardation,* Vol. 4. New York: Academic Press, 1970.

Flynn, R.J. Mental ability, schooling, and early career achievement of low-IQ and average-IQ young men.

American Journal of Mental Deficiency, 1980a, *84,* 431–443.

Flynn, R.J. Normalization, PASS, and quality assessment. In: R.J. Flynn & K.E. Nitsch (eds.), *Normalization, social integration and community services.* Baltimore: University Park Press, 1980b.

Flynn, R.J., & Heal, L.W. Short form of PASS #3. *Evaluation Review,* 1981, *5,* 357–376.

George, M.J., & Baumeister, A.A. Employee withdrawal and job satisfaction in community residential facilities for mentally retarded persons. *American Journal of Mental Deficiency,* 1981, *85,* 639–647.

Glass, G.V., McGaw, B., & Smith, M. *Meta-analysis in social research.* Beverly Hills, CA: Sage Publications, 1981.

Gold, M.W. Research on the vocational habilitation of the retarded: The present, the future. In: N.R. Ellis (ed.), *International review of research in mental retardation,* Vol. 6. New York: Academic Press, 1973.

Gollay, E., Freedman, R., Wyngaarden, M., & Kurtz, N.R. *Coming back: Community experiences of deinstitutionalized mentally retarded people.* Cambridge, MA: Abt Books, 1978.

Gorsuch, R.L. *Factor Analysis.* Philadelphia: W.B. Saunders Co., 1974.

Gottlieb, J., & Switzky, H.N. Development of school-age children's stereotypic attitudes toward mentally retarded children. *American Journal of Mental Deficiency,* 1982, *86,* 596–600.

Groves, R.M., & Hess, I. An algorithm for controlled selection. In: I. Hess, D.C. Riedel, & T.B. Fitzpatrick (eds.), *Probability sampling of hospitals and patients,* (2nd ed.). Ann Arbor, MI: Health Administration Press, 1975.

Guilford, J.P. *Psychometric methods.* New York: McGraw-Hill Book Co., 1954.

Gully, K.J., & Hosch, H. Adaptive behavior scale: Development as a diagnostic tool via discriminant analysis. *American Journal of Mental Deficiency,* 1979, *83,* 518–523.

Halpern, A., Irvin, L.K., & Landman, J.T. Alternative approaches to the measurement of adaptive behavior. *American Journal of Mental Deficiency,* 1979, *84,* 304–310.

Halpern, A., Raffeld, P., Irwin, L., & Link, R. *Social and prevocational information battery.* Monterey, CA: Publishers Test Service, 1975.

Hanley-Maxwell, C., & Heal, L.W. Legislative constraints and facilitations for community integration. In: A.R. Novak & L.W. Heal (eds.), *Integration of developmentally disabled individuals into the community.* Baltimore: Paul H. Brookes Publishing Co., 1980.

Hauber, F.A., Bruininks, R.H., Wieck, C., Sigford, B.B., & Hill, B.K. *1978–1979 in-depth national survey of public and community residential facilities for mentally retarded persons: Methods and procedures.* Minneapolis: University of Minnesota, Department of Psychoeducational Studies, 1981.

Heal, L.W., & Daniels, B.S. *A cost-effectiveness analysis of residential alternatives for selected developmentally disabled citizens of three northern Wisconsin counties.* Paper presented at the 1978 meeting of the American Association on Mental Deficiency, Denver, May, 1978.

Heal, L.W., & Fujiura, G.T. Toward a valid methodology for research on residential alternatives for developmentally disabled citizens. In: N.R. Ellis & N.W. Bray (eds.), *International review of research in mental retardation,* Vol. 12. New York: Academic Press, in press.

Heal, L.W., Hill, B.K., & Bruininks, R.H. Maladaptive behavior in a national sample of public and community residential facilities. Unpublished report, University of Illinois at Urbana-Champaign, 1983.

Heal, L.W., & Laidlaw, T.J. Evaluation of residential alternatives. In: A.R. Novak & L.W. Heal (eds.), *Integration of developmentally disabled individuals into the community.* Baltimore: Paul H. Brookes Publishing Co., 1980.

Heal, L.W., Lakin, K.C., Bruininks, R.H., Hill, B.K., & Best-Sigford, B. Placement of mentally retarded residents from public residential facilities in the United States. In: J.M. Berg (ed.), *Perspectives and progress in mental retardation,* Vols. 1 & 2. Baltimore: University Park Press, 1984.

Heal, L.W., Novak, A., Sigelman, C.K., & Switzky, H.N. Characteristics of community residential facilities. In: A.R. Novak & L.W. Heal (eds.), *Integration of developmentally disabled individuals into the community.* Baltimore: Paul H. Brookes Publishing Co., 1980.

Heal, L.W., Rusch, J.C., & Novak, A.R. *The lifestyle satisfaction scale.* Unpublished report, University of Illinois at Urbana-Champaign, 1983.

Heal, L.W., Sigelman, C.K., & Switzky, H.N. Research on community residential alternatives for the mentally retarded. In: N.R. Ellis (ed.), *International review of research in mental retardation,* Vol 9. New York: Academic Press, 1978.

Heller, T., Berkson, G., & Romer, D. Social ecology of supervised communal facilities for mentally disabled adults: VI. Initial social adaptation. *American Journal of Mental Deficiency,* 1981, *86,* 43–49.

Hemming, H., Lavender, T., & Pill, R. Quality of life of mentally retarded adults transferred from large institutions to new small units. *American Journal of Mental Deficiency,* 1981, *86,* 157–169.

Hill, B.K., & Bruininks, R.H. Maladaptive behavior of mentally retarded people in residential facilities. *American Journal of Mental Deficiency,* in press.

Hill, B.K., Sather, L.B., Kudla, M.J., & Bruininks, R.H. *A survey of the types of residential programs for mentally retarded people in the United States in 1978.* Unpublished report, Department of Psychoeducational Studies, University of Minnesota, 1978.

Hinkle, D., Wiersma, W., & Jurs, S. *Applied statistics for the behavioral sciences.* Chicago: Rand McNally & Co., 1979.

Hollenbeck, A.R. Problems of reliability in observational research. In: G.P. Sackett (ed.), *Observing behavior,* Vol. 2: *Data collection and analysis methods.* Baltimore: University Park Press, 1978.

Hull, J.T., & Thompson, J.C. Predicting adaptive functioning of mentally retarded persons in community settings. *American Journal of Mental Deficiency,* 1980, *85,* 253–261.

Intagliata, J., & Willer, B. Reinstitutionalization of mentally retarded persons successfully placed into family-care and group homes. *American Journal of Mental Deficiency,* 1982, *87,* 34–39.

Isaac, S., & Michael, W.B. *Handbook in research and evaluation*. San Diego: Robert R. Knapp, 1971.

Isett, R., & Spreat, S. Test-retest and interrater reliability of the AAMD Adaptive Behavior Scale. *American Journal of Mental Deficiency*, 1979, *84*, 93–96.

Jackson, J. Factors of the treatment environment. *Archives of General Psychiatry*, 1969, *21*, 39–45.

Johnson, O.G. *Tests and measurements in child development: Handbook II*. San Francisco: Jossey-Bass, 1976.

Johnson, O.G., & Bommarito, J.W. *Tests and measurements in child development: Handbook I*. San Francisco: Jossey-Bass, 1971.

Johnston, J.M., & Pennypacker, H.S. *Strategies and tactics of human behavioral research*. Hillsdale, NJ: Lawrence Erlbaum Associates, 1980.

Kazdin, A.E. *Single-case research designs: Methods for clinical and applied settings*. New York: Oxford University Press, 1982.

Kerlinger, F.N., & Pedhazur, E.J. *Multiple regression in behavioral research*. New York: Holt, Rinehart & Winston, 1973.

Kiesler, C. Mental hospitals and alternative care. Noninstitutionalization as potential public policy for mental patients. *American Psychologist*, 1982, *37*, 349–360.

King, R.D., Raynes, N.V., & Tizard, J. *Patterns of residential care: sociological studies in institutions for handicapped citizens*. London: Routledge & Kegan Paul, 1971.

King, T., Soucar, E., & Isett, R. Brief reports: An attempt to assess and predict adaptive behavior of institutionalized mentally retarded clients. *American Journal of Mental Deficiency*, 1980, *84*, 406–410.

Krantz, G.C., Bruininks, R.H., & Clumpner, J.L. *Mentally retarded people in state-operated residential facilities: Year ending June 30, 1978* (2d ed.). Minneapolis: University of Minnesota, Department of Psychoeducational Studies, 1978.

Krantz, G.C., Bruininks, R.H., & Clumpner, J.L. *Mentally retarded people in state-operated residential facilities: Year ending June 30, 1979*. Minneapolis: University of Minnesota, Department of Psychoeducational Studies, 1979.

Krantz, G.C., Bruininks, R.H., & Clumpner, J.L. *Mentally retarded people in state-operated residential facilities: Year ending June 30, 1980*. Minneapolis: University of Minnesota, Department of Psychoeducational Studies, 1980.

Lakin, K.C., & Bruininks, R.H. (eds.). *Strategies for achieving community integration of developmentally disabled citizens*. Baltimore: Paul H. Brookes Publishing Co., in press.

Lakin, K.C., Bruininks, R.H., Hill, B.K., & Hauber, F.A. Turnover of direct-care staff in a national sample of residential facilities for mentally retarded people. *American Journal of Mental Deficiency*, 1982, *87*, 64–72.

Lakin, K.C., Krantz, G.C., Bruininks, R.H., Clumpner, J.L., & Hill, B. One hundred years of data on populations of public residential facilities for mentally retarded people. *American Journal of Mental Deficiency*, 1982, *87*, 1–8.

Lambert, N., & Nicoll, R. Dimensions of adaptive behavior of retarded and nonretarded public school children. *American Journal of Mental Deficiency*, 1976, *81*, 135–146.

Landesman-Dwyer, S. The changing structure and function of institutions: A search for optimal group care environments. In: S. Landesman-Dwyer & P. Vietze (eds.), *Living with retarded people*. Baltimore: University Park Press, in press.

Landesman-Dwyer, S., Stein, J., & Sackett, G. A behavioral and ecological study of group homes. In: G.P. Sackett (ed.), *Observing behavior*, Vol. 1: *Theory and applications in mental retardation*. Baltimore: University Park Press, 1978.

Landesman-Dwyer, S., & Sulzbacher, F. Residential placement and adaptation of severely and profoundly retarded individuals. In R.H. Bruininks, C.E. Meyers, B.B. Sigford, & K.C. Lakin (eds.), *Deinstitutionalization and community adjustment of mentally retarded people*. Washington, D C : American Association on Mental Deficiency, 1981.

Linn, R.L., & Slinde, J.A. The determination of the significance of change between pre- and posttesting periods. *Review of Educational Research*, 1977, *47*, 121–150.

McCarver, R.B., & Craig, E.M. Placement of the retarded in the community: Prognosis and outcome. In: N.R. Ellis (ed.), *International Review of Research in Mental Retardation*, Vol. 7. New York: Academic Press, 1974.

McCormick, M., Balla, D., & Zigler, E. Resident care practices in institutions for retarded persons: A cross-institutional, cross-cultural study. *American Journal of Mental Deficiency*, 1975, *80*, 1–17.

McGuigan, F. The experimenter: A neglected stimulus object. *Psychological Bulletin*, 1963, *60*, 421–428.

Martin, J.E. *Assessing maintenance of acquired self-control in completing complex tasks through withdrawal of training components and trainers*. Unpublished doctoral dissertation, University of Illinois, 1982.

Martin, J.E., Rusch, F.R., & Heal, L.W. Teaching community survival skills to mentally retarded adults: A review and analysis. *Journal of Special Education*, 1982, *16*, 243–268.

Menchetti, B.M., Rusch, F.R., & Owens, D.M. Assessing the vocational training needs of mentally retarded adults. In: J.L. Matson & S.E. Breuning (eds.), *Assessing the mentally retarded*. New York: Grune & Stratton, 1983.

Meyers, C., Nihira, K., & Zetlin, A. The measurement of adaptive behavior. In: N.R. Ellis (ed.), *Handbook of mental deficiency, psychological theory and research* (2d ed.). Hillsdale, NJ: Lawrence Erlbaum Associates, 1979.

Mink, I.T., Nihira, K., & Meyers, C. Taxonomy of family life styles: I. Homes with TMR children. *American Journal of Mental Deficiency*, 1983, *87*, 484–497.

Moos, R.H. A situational analysis of a therapeutic community milieu. *Journal of Abnormal Psychology*, 1968, *73*, 49–61.

Moos, R.H. *Evaluating correctional and community settings*. New York: John Wiley & Sons, 1975.

Moos, R.H., & Moos, B.S. A typology of family social environments. *Family Process*, 1976, *15*, 357–371.

Nihira, K. Factorial dimensions of adaptive behavior in adult retardates. *American Journal of Mental Deficiency*, 1969a, *73*, 868–878.

Nihira, K. Factorial dimensions of adaptive behavior in mentally retarded children and adolescents. *American Journal of Mental Deficiency*, 1969b, *74*, 130–141.

Nihira, K. Dimensions of adaptive behavior in institutionalized mentally retarded children and adults: Developmental perspective. *American Journal of Mental Deficiency,* 1976, *81,* 215–226.

Nihira, K., Foster, R., Shellhaas, M., & Leland, H. *AAMD Adaptive Behavior Scale, 1975 revision.* Washington, D C : American Association on Mental Deficiency, 1974.

Nihira, L., & Nihira, K. Jeopardy in community placement. *American Journal of Mental Deficiency,* 1974, *79*(5), 538–544.

Novak, A.R., & Heal, L.W. (eds.). *Integration of developmentally disabled individuals into the community.* Baltimore: Paul H. Brookes Publishing Co., 1980.

Novak, A.R., Heal, L.W., Pilewski, M.B., & Laidlaw, T. *Independent apartment settings for developmentally disabled adults: An empirical analysis.* Paper presented at the annual meeting of the American Association on Mental Deficiency, San Francisco, May, 1980.

Nunnally, J. *Psychometric theory.* New York: McGraw-Hill Book Co., 1978.

O'Connor, G. *Home is a good place.* Albany, NY: American Association on Mental Deficiency: Boyd Printing Co., 1976.

Pedhazur, E. *Multiple regression in behavioral research* (2d ed.). New York: Holt, Rinehart & Winston, 1982.

Pratt, M.W., Luszcz, M.A., & Brown, M.E. Measuring dimensions of the quality of care in small community residences. *American Journal of Mental Deficiency,* 1980, *85,* 188–194.

Repp, A.C., & Barton, L.E. Naturalistic observation of institutionalized retarded persons: A comparison of licensure decisions and behavioral observations. *Journal of Applied Behavior Analysis,* 1980, *13,* 333–341.

Robinson, W.S. The statistical measurement of agreement. *American Sociological Review,* 1957, *22,* 17–25.

Romer, D., & Berkson, G. Social ecology of supervised communal facilities for mentally disabled adults: II. Predictors of affiliation. *American Journal of Mental Deficiency,* 1980a, *85,* 229–242.

Romer, D., & Berkson, G. Social ecology of supervised communal facilities for mentally disabled adults: III. Predictors of social choice. *American Journal of Mental Deficiency,* 1980b, *85,* 243–252.

Romer, D., & Berkson, G. Social ecology of supervised communal facilities for mentally disabled adults: IV. Characteristics of social behavior. *American Journal of Mental Deficiency,* 1981, *86,* 28–38.

Rosen, M., Kivitz, M.S., Clark, G.R., & Floor, L. Prediction of postinstitutional adjustment of mentally retarded adults. *American Journal of Mental Deficiency,* 1970, *74,* 726–734.

Rudrud, E., Ferrara, J., & Ziarnik, J. Living placement and absenteeism in community-based training programs. *American Journal of Mental Deficiency,* 1980, *84*(4), 401–404.

Rusch, F.R., & Menchetti, B.M. Increasing compliant work behaviors in a non-sheltered work setting. *Mental Retardation,* 1981, *19,* 107–111.

Sackett, G.P. (ed.), *Observing behavior,* Vol. 1: *Theory and applications in mental retardation.* Baltimore: University Park Press, 1978a.

Sackett, G.P. (ed.), *Observing behavior,* Vol. 2: *Data collection and analysis methods.* Baltimore: University Park Press, 1978b.

Schalock, R.L. *Services for the developmentally disabled:* *Development, implementation, and evaluation.* Baltimore: University Park Press, 1982.

Schalock, R.L. Untying some Gordian knots in program evaluation. *Journal of Rehabilitation Administration,* in press.

Schalock, R.L., Harper, R.S., & Carver, G. Independent living placement: Five years later. *American Journal of Mental Deficiency,* 1981, *86,* 170–177.

Schalock, R.L., Harper, R., & Genung, T. Community integration of mentally retarded adults: Community placement and program success. *American Journal of Mental Deficiency,* 1981, *85,* 478–488.

Scheerenberger, R.C. *Public residential services for the mentally retarded.* Madison, WI: National Association of Superintendents of Public Residential Facilities for the Mentally Retarded, Central Wisconsin Center for the Developmentally Disabled, 1976. Also available in N.R. Ellis (ed.). *International review of research in mental retardation,* Vol. 9. New York: Academic Press, 1978a.

Scheerenberger, R.C. *Public residential services for the mentally retarded.* Madison, WI: National Association of Superintendents of Public Residential Facilities for the Mentally Retarded, Central Wisconsin Center for the Developmentally Disabled, 1978b.

Scheerenberger, R.C. Public residential services, 1981: Status and Trends. *Mental Retardation,* 1982, *20*(5), 210–215.

Selltiz, C., Wrightsman, L.S., & Cook, S.W. (eds.). *Research methods in social relations.* New York: Holt, Rinehart & Winston, 1976.

Seltzer, G.B. Community residential adjustment: The relationship among environment, performance, and satisfaction. *American Journal of Mental Deficiency,* 1981, *85,* 624–630.

Seltzer, G.B., & Seltzer, M.M. *The Community Adjustment scale.* Cambridge, MA: Educational Projects, 1976.

Sigelman, C.K., Budd, E.C., Spanhel, C.L., & Schoenrock, C.J. When in doubt, say yes: Acquiescence in interviews with mentally retarded persons. *Mental Retardation,* 1981, *19,* 53–58.

Sigelman, C.K., Budd, E.C., Winer, J.W., Schoenrock, C.J., & Martin, P. Evaluating alternative techniques of questioning mentally retarded persons. *American Journal of Mental Deficiency,* 1982, *86,* 511–518.

Sigelman, C.K., Novak, A.R., Heal, L.W., & Switzky, H.N. Factors that affect the success of community placement. In: A.R. Novak & L.W. Heal (eds.), *Integration of developmentally disabled individuals into the community.* Baltimore: Paul H. Brookes Publishing Co., 1980.

Sigelman, L., Roeder, P.W., Sigelman, C.K. *Social service innovation in the American states: Deinstitutionalization of the mentally retarded.* Unpublished manuscript, University of Kentucky, Lexington, 1980.

Sigelman, C.K., Schoenrock, C.J., Spanhel, C., Hromas, S., Winer, J.W., Budd, E.C., & Martin, P.W. Surveying mentally retarded persons: Responsiveness and response validity in three samples. *American Journal of Mental Deficiency,* 1980, *84,* 479–484.

Skinner, B.J. *Science and human behavior.* New York: Free Press, 1953.

Snow, R.E. Representative and quasi-representative designs for research on teaching. *American Educational Research Journal,* 1974, *44,* 265–291.

Soforenko, A.Z., & Macy, T.W. *A study of the characteristics and life status of persons discharged from a large state institution for the mentally retarded during the years 1969–1977.* Orient, OH: Orient State Institute, 1977.

Soforenko, A.Z., & Macy, T.W. Living arrangements of MR/DD persons discharged from an institutional setting. *Mental Retardation,* 1978, *16*(3), 269–270.

Spreat, S. The Adaptive Behavior Scale: A study of criterion validity. *American Journal of Mental Deficiency,* 1980, *85,* 61–68.

Sudman, S., & Bradburn, N.M. *Response effects in surveys: A review and synthesis.* Chicago: Aldine Publishing Co., 1974.

Sutter, P., Mayeda, T., Call, T., Yanagi, G., & Yee, S. Comparison of successful and unsuccessful community-placed mentally retarded persons. *American Journal of Mental Deficiency,* 1980, *85,* 262–267.

Thompson, M.S. *Benefit-cost analysis for program evaluation.* Beverly Hills, CA: Sage Publications, 1980.

Tizard, J. *Community services for the mentally handicapped.* London: Oxford University Press, 1964.

Townsend, P.W., & Flanagan, J. Experimental preadmission program to encourage home care for severely and profoundly retarded children. *American Journal of Mental Deficiency,* 1976, *80,* 562–569.

Vitello, S.S., Atthowe, J.M., Jr., & Cadwell, J. Determinants of community placement of institutionalized mentally retarded persons. *American Journal of Mental Deficiency,* 1983, *87,* 539–545.

Voeltz, L.M. Children's attitudes toward handicapped peers. *American Journal of Mental Deficiency,* 1980, *84,* 455–464.

Vogelsberg, R.T., & Rusch, F.R. Training severely handicapped students to cross partially controlled intersection. *AAESPH Review,* 1979, *4,* 264–273.

Whatmore, R., Durward, L., & Kushlick, A. Measuring the quality of residential care. *Behavior Research and Therapy,* 1975, *13,* 227–236.

Wieck, C., & Bruininks, R.H. *The cost of public and community residential care for mentally retarded people in the United States.* Minneapolis: University of Minnesota, Department of Psychoeducational Studies, 1980.

Willer, B., & Intagliata, J. Social-environmental factors as predictors of adjustment of deinstitutionalized mentally retarded adults. *American Journal of Mental Deficiency,* 1981, *86,* 252–259.

Willer, B., & Intagliata, J. Comparison of family-care and group homes as alternatives to institutions. *American Journal of Mental Deficiency,* 1982, *86,* 588–595.

Williamson, J.B., Korp, D.A., Dalphin, J.R., & Gray, P.S. *The research craft* (2d ed.). Boston: Little, Brown & Co., 1982.

Windle, C.D., Stewart, E., & Brown, S.J. Reasons for community failure of released patients. *American Journal of Mental Deficiency,* 1961, *66*(2), 213–217.

Wolfensberger, W., & Glenn, L. *PASS 3. Program Analysis of Service Systems field manual.* Toronto: National Institute on Mental Retardation, 1975a.

Wolfensberger, W., & Glenn, L. *PASS 3. Program analysis of service systems handbook.* Toronto: National Institute on Mental Retardation, 1975b.

Wolpert, J. *Group homes for the mentally retarded: An investigation of neighborhood property impacts.* Study prepared for the New York State Office of Mental Retardation and Development Disabilities, August, 1978.

Wyngaarden, M., Freedman, R., & Gollay, E. *The community adjustment of deinstitutionalized mentally retarded persons. Vol. 4. Descriptive data on the community experiences of deinstitutionalized mentally retarded persons.* (Contract Number OEC-0-74-9183, U.S. Office of Education.) Cambridge, MA: Abt Associates, 1976.

Zaharia, E.S., & Baumeister, A.A. Cross-organizational job satisfactions of technician-level staff members. *American Journal of Mental Deficiency,* 1979, *84,* 30–35.

Chapter 12

Benefit-Cost Analysis
of Social Programs

Deinstitutionalization and Education Programs

Craig Thornton

Efforts to deinstitutionalize and educate handicapped children and young adults face severe resource constraints. Even as President Gerald Ford signed Public Law 94-142, a legislative cornerstone of these efforts, he noted that "unfortunately, this bill promises more than the federal government can deliver." Federal expenditures to educate handicapped persons have fallen consistently below the levels specified in the law; in fiscal year (FY) 1981 federal expenditures were less than half the prescribed amount, with little expectation of future growth. These resource constraints are mirrored at the local level, where deinstitutionalization and education policies are actually implemented and where funding sources are often more restricted.

These limitations force national and local policy makers to make difficult trade-offs between alternative programs that have diverse goals, methods of operation, client populations, effects, and resource needs. Efficient decision making requires accurate program assessments, which in turn require that all these features be measured and, at least implicitly, assigned relative values.

The need to make these assessments and comparisons has created interest in techniques for program evaluation, particularly the techniques of benefit-cost analysis that deal specifically with the problems of cross-program comparisons. However, these techniques have been adopted slowly in many areas of social policy because of a lack of useful paradigms for conducting such analyses of social programs. Also, considerable controversy has resulted from difficulties in estimating dollar values for program effects and in incorporationg intangible effects that are often a central concern of social programs such as deinstitutionalization and special education.

This chapter responds to these difficulties by presenting a benefit-cost accounting model for social programs. This framework provides a means for organizing data on program effects and costs to facilitate their use in policy discussions and decision making. The analysis recognizes the humanitarian aspects of social programs while also assessing the economic efficiency of particular programs. It takes into account that from the start many benefits are difficult to appraise and quantify precisely.

However, by using a standard procedure for valuing as many effects and costs as possible, it provides a convenient and useful basis for comparing multiple program effects with each other and with program costs, for evaluating qualitative benefits and costs, and for comparing one program's benefits and costs with those of other programs.

This model draws on several benefit-cost evaluations performed on employment and training programs including the Job Corps (Long, Mallar, & Thornton, 1981; Thornton, Long, & Mallar, 1982), the national Supported Work demonstration (Kemper, Long, & Thornton, 1981), and the Structured Training and Employment Transitional Services (STETS) demonstration for mentally retarded young adults (Thornton, 1981). This chapter is organized in four parts. The first part outlines the goals and objectives of benefit-cost analysis and provides an overview of the approach presented here. The second part presents the accounting framework and discusses how it could be applied to a hypothetical vocational education program for mentally retarded youths. The third part discusses an application of the framework to the assessment of the Job Corps. The final section reviews the strengths and weaknesses of benefit-cost analysis, as well as the need to coordinate benefit-cost efforts with other evaluation activities, and recommends policies for facilitating the use of benefit-cost analysis in assessing programs for severely handicapped persons.

OVERVIEW OF BENEFIT-COST ANALYSIS

Social programs generally use a variety of resources to produce a wide range of effects. For example, a vocational education program for mentally retarded youths that focuses on its participants' employability may affect the participants' employment, residential situation, use of other service programs, transfer program dependence, and, it is hoped, the quality of their lives. In addition, to produce these effects a program requires administrative, professional, and operational personnel; classroom and office space; books; testing and

evaluation materials; and numerous other supplies and services.

The primary issue addressed in a benefit-cost analysis is whether the various outcomes justify their costs in terms of economic efficiency. In other words, does society have more goods and services at its disposal as a result of funding a particular program, or would society have more goods and services if the resources devoted to the program were used for alternative purposes? The basic technique used to determine economic efficiency is to assign dollar values to all estimated effects and costs. These values are then summed together to yield an estimate of the program's *net present value* (i.e., the difference between the benefits and costs where all dollar values are adjusted to reflect their value in a specific base period). This process is called *discounting* and is used to adjust the value of benefits or costs that accrue over several time periods to reflect their value at a specified base period (for example, the time during which program participants were enrolled in the program). (For a more detailed review of discounting and other benefit-cost concepts and methods, see Gramlich, 1981, or Warner & Luce, 1982.) A positive net present value indicates that resources are being used efficiently. A negative net present value indicates that (at least at its current scale) the program's resources could be used more efficiently elsewhere.

While the net present value criterion is easy to define, a high degree of uncertainty surrounds its actual estimation: program effects are measured imperfectly and some cannot be estimated at all; uncertainties surround the values to be placed on specific program effects or resources; and the appropriate techniques needed to aggregate individual benefits and costs inherently involve numerous approximations. As a result, it is difficult to apply the criterion and judge the economic efficiency of the program.

Because of the potential error associated with any single estimate of net present value, much of the usefulness of benefit-cost analysis relates to its comprehensiveness. The processes of integrating measures of various inputs and outcomes and of identifying the general patterns that emerge from the attempts to assign relative values are often more useful than any specific estimate of net present value. For this reason, the analysis design proposed here does not focus on a single net present value estimate but, instead, on a set of estimates. This set includes 1) a benchmark estimate that incorporates the assumptions and estimates with which the researchers feel most comfotable and 2) several estimates based on sensitivity tests, each illustrating the effect of changing one or more of the estimates, approximations, or assumptions used in the benchmark calculations while holding the others constant.

Thus, the findings do not rely on a single set of assumptions and estimates, but, instead, on a range of plausible conditions and estimates. By examining the different assumptions, the underlying outcome estimates, and the techniques used to value outcomes, it is possible to identify those aspects of the program and of its evaluation that are most vital and those about which there is the greatest uncertainty. Such an understanding of the program and of its performance is crucial to the ability to make good cross-program comparisons and decisions regarding funding trade-offs.

A benefit-cost accounting model imposes a logical rigor on the analysis and serves as a guide for interpreting the results. The *accounting framework* defines the scope of the analysis, the criteria by which benefit-cost comparisons will be made, the analytical perspectives to be used, and the specific program inputs and effects to be examined. A part of this framework is a consistent means of valuing diverse sets of effects. The approach proposed here is based on concepts similar to those underlying the estimation of gross national product (GNP). It focuses on the net resource gain or loss to society that results from the program under study. Essentially, this is done by estimating the change in resources available to society owing to the program and then valuing those resources at their market cost. Thus, if a program caused participants to reduce their use of transfer-benefit programs (e.g., Food

Stamps or Supplemental Security Income [SSI]), it would allow society to reallocate some of the resources that would have been used to administer those programs. The market value of the saved resources is used as a measure of the value resulting from the reduction in transfer program use. In general, this valuation procedure is convenient to use and does not require attempts to measure the willingness of society to pay for the various outcomes.

Of course, the resource cost approach implicitly assumes that social demand is accurately reflected in the cost of commodities (i.e., that market prices equal marginal costs and demands). Economic theory clearly indicates that this need not be the case if the economy is not competitive, if there is imperfect information about social programs and their effects, if important external factors are operating, or if governments do not accurately translate social demands for public goods into policy. Furthermore, many social programs are designed to protect or foster individual rights and liberties or to influence public attitudes and perceptions. In any of these instances, the resource cost approach will exclude some key benefits and costs.

Most of these excluded benefit-cost components cannot be valued monetarily. In some cases, a social willingness-to-pay can be estimated (see, for example, Rowe & Chestnut, 1982). In other cases, the preferences implicit in government budget allocation decisions or public opinion polls can be used to assign relative values to social outcomes (see, for example, Weisbrod, 1978). However, in most cases, the analyst can only qualitatively incorporate intangibles into the analysis. This can be done by including measures of the intangible program outcome without assigning a specific dollar value. For example, a vocational education program may increase its participants' ability to live independently. Indicators of moves to more independent residential situations or scales showing increases in adaptive behavior can be presented along with estimated values of the net change in resource use. Together, the qualitative and quantitative information can be used to assess accurately the full range of program outcomes—that is, to evaluate economic efficiency without losing track of the less-easily-quantified program goals and outcomes.

In summary, the approach described here begins with a comprehensive listing of benefits and costs and then proceeds to value as many components as possible on the basis of resources used, saved, or created. Those components not valued are then assessed using available qualitative measures. The final product is a comparison of the net value of those benefits and costs that are explicitly valued with the indexes of the intangible outcomes (which may be benefits or costs). In many cases, the valued benefits and costs can be assumed to predominate, and the net present value estimates based on resource costs can be used to make program assessments. In other cases, if measured costs are found to exceed measured benefits, the program evaluation will depend on whether the intangible benefits exceed the intangible costs by at least that difference.

ACCOUNTING FRAMEWORK

In developing a benefit-cost accounting framework there are five major tasks: 1) defining the program and the standard against which it will be compared, 2) specifying the analytical perspectives to be adopted, 3) listing the specific benefits and costs, 4) estimating the shadow prices—the prices used to value the various outcomes, and 5) determining the appropriate techniques for assessing benefits and costs that occur at different times. These tasks are discussed in turn below for a benefit-cost analysis of a hypothetical vocational education program.

Program Definition
and the Counterfactual

Before any benefit-cost assessments can be made, it is necessary to define the program under study. This requires specifying what the program is, who it will serve, what its intended (and unintended) effects will be, and how it operates. In the case of a vocational education program, the program definition would delineate, for example, the specific curricula, types of materials and staff to be used, and how the program is expected to change its students' skills and work activities.

Along with the program definition, it is necessary to specify the alternative with which the program will be compared. This alternative, called the *counterfactual,* can be of several types, depending on the program comparisons of interest and the environment in which the program operates. Returning to the example of a vocational education program, the counterfactual could be another specific vocational education program, a sheltered workshop, or a group of transitional employment programs. Another counterfactual that is particularly useful and is adopted for this chapter is the set of programs and treatments participants would have used if they had not been given the opportunity to participate in the vocational program under study. This counterfactual results in a benefit-cost study that assesses the net benefit of switching from the current set of programs actually in use to the specific program under study.

Typically, a control or comparison group is needed to estimate the counterfactual. The behavior of such a group, if accurately measured, is a good indication of what would have happened to the program participants if they had received the comparison treatment instead. In very small evaluations, where it is not possible to observe a valid comparison group, the counterfactual must be based on conjecture. For example, Hill and Wehman (1983) estimated for each participant in their transitional employment program the probable program alternative, including day activity program, sheltered workshop, and public school, as well as the possibility of participating in no program at all. The effects of the transitional employment program were then estimated relative to these alternatives. Similarly, a counterfactual for a deinstitutionalization program could be that in the absence of the program, participants would have spent their entire lives in the institution. All effects would then be estimated in relation to the experiences of persons in institutions. In either case, the counterfactual, its policy relevance, and its estimation should be specified explicitly.

Efficiency, Equity, and Analytical Perspectives

While countless questions can be asked about a social program, only a few of these can be addressed by benefit-cost analysis. In particular, benefit-cost analysis (and economic analysis in general) is concerned with two types of questions: Was the program efficient? Was it equitable? *Efficiency* typically has to do with a program's effect on the total value of the goods and services available to society (i.e., Is the value of those goods and services greater because of the program under study?). *Equity* concerns the distribution of goods and services among groups in society, how that distribution is affected by the program, and whether a specific group of individuals benefits or loses.

In many program evaluations (particularly of programs for disadvantaged groups), equity considerations may dominate efficiency considerations in determining the program's social desirability. However, regardless of the equity aspects of the program, an evaluation of the program's economic efficiency is important for determining the best means for achieving any particular equity goal. Examining the resource efficiency of programs should improve policy makers' ability to identify which program provides a given level of benefit for lowest cost. Equity questions are more difficult to answer. The benefit-cost analysis can determine (to some extent) a program's effect on the distribution of resources, but it has no special criteria for judging whether a distributional change is desirable. Thus, the analysis of equity questions is more descriptive, with conclusions based in the broader and more uncertain context of public policy.

The issues of efficiency and equity can be addressed by examining benefits and costs from several perspectives. Typically, there are three perspectives of interest: those of society as a whole, of program participants, and of

taxpayers. Society's perspective ignores all the redistributional aspects of the program and focuses on its efficiency.[1] Thus, only the use of resources is analyzed. Transfers of income between groups are assumed to cancel each other—i.e., a dollar of benefit or cost to one person is assumed equivalent to a dollar of benefit or cost to all others. (Of course, any resources consumed in making such transfers would be counted as costs from the social perspective.) The perspectives of participants and nonparticipants facilitate analysis of distributional consequence. For each group, the question regarding net present value is the same as it was for society as a whole: Does net present value (as seen from that perspective) exceed zero? This perspective permits an assessment of the net impact of the program on the income of the two groups, participants and nonparticipants. The evaluation asks: Do participants gain from the program and can they therefore be expected to enroll voluntarily? Do taxpayers receive a net benefit or must the program justification be based on equity and other value concerns?

Other perspectives could also be used. In previous benefit-cost evaluations it has been useful to disaggregate the taxpayer perspective to assess the impact of specific funding sources—for example, a state program using state and federal funds might disaggregate the taxpayer perspective into in-state taxpayers and out-of-state taxpayers. Also, there may be interest in focusing on specific groups of participants, and results could be calculated for each group. However, the analytical complexity of the analyses increases rapidly with the number of perspectives, and it is usually preferable to use only the three major perspectives presented in the preceding paragraph.

When defining perspectives it is important for the perspectives to be distinct and yet include everyone in society. Thus, the taxpayer perspective would include all persons in society who are not given the opportunity to enroll

---

[1]This abstraction is not necessary. It is possible to combine the analysis of efficiency and equity by specifying the *social marginal rate of substitution* between output growth and the redistribution of income (i.e., the rate at which society is willing to trade off growth in production and income redistribution). This rate can then be used to evaluate the program's relative effect on the income distribution and production. This procedure is not proposed here because of the difficulty and arbitrariness associated with estimating this marginal rate of substitution.

in the program (even though some of these persons may not pay any taxes). One analytically useful feature of defining perspectives in this way is that, under the stated assumptions, the *social net present value* will equal the sum of the net present values calculated from the other perspectives. This results from the assumptions that transfers between the groups cancel out each other. Thus, when the net present values are summed, only benefits or costs that accrue to one group with no offsetting cost or benefit to another group (i.e., those involving the use rather than the redistribution of resources) will remain in the net present value calculation. This adding-up feature imposes a logical rigor on the analysis, which is helpful when analyzing the distributional implications of program effects.

Listing Benefits and Costs

The next step in developing the benefit-cost framework is to specify the benefits and costs of the program. This step follows directly from the program definition and analysis of its expected effects and resource needs. The typical procedure is to determine how each effect will be perceived from each analytical perspective.

Table 1 presents a listing of expected benefits and costs for a hypothetical vocational education program for mentally retarded youths, along with an indication of how these program components are viewed from the three perspectives. In this case, the program is expected to increase postprogram employment. This creates direct benefits in the form of higher earnings (some of which are redistributed through the tax system), as well as indirect benefits in the form of reduced use of alternative programs, moves to less-expensive and less-restrictive residential situations, reduced use of transfer programs, and a variety of psychological benefits. The costs are those associated with operations, management, and participant

labor. A potentially important offset to costs is the value of output produced by participants while they are enrolled in the vocational program.

An attempt should be made to make the list of benefits and costs as comprehensive as possible. While it is clear that all effects cannot be estimated (particularly if the evaluation budget is modest), a comprehensive framework allows the analysis to assess the relative magnitudes of measured and unmeasured benefits and costs. In this way, if measured costs exceed benefits (i.e., if estimated net present value is negative) the analyst can assess qualitatively whether unmeasured net benefits are likely to be valued by at least the amount of that difference.

Valuing Program Effects and Costs

After listing the benefits and costs, the analysis proceeds by estimating the program's effects on participant behavior. The changes in various behaviors are then valued by multiplying the estimated effects by the appropriate estimated dollar values. These dollar values, called shadow prices, reflect the average dollar value of the resources saved or used as a result of a unit change in the relevant behavior.[2] For example, the average administrative cost per case month on Supplemental Security Income (SSI) could be used to value changes in months of SSI dependence. Shadow prices are generally not directly observable; they are estimated from published data, from special studies of program operation, or from program accounting records. To give the reader a sense of how these prices are estimated and some of the problems associated with valuing specific benefits and costs, each major benefit-cost component is examined briefly.

Postprogram Output[3]   Increasing postprogram employment and earnings is often a principal objective of vocational education programs. It is clearly a benefit to participants and

---

[2]Shadow prices are used when market prices are nonexistent or inappropriate and can be defined so that they incorporate demand and psychological aspects as well as the resource costs (see Mishan, 1982). In the framework developed here they reflect only resource costs.

[3]This sub-section includes only the net changes in market output. Changes in nonmarket output or in leisure activities are considered separately.

Table 1.   Expected benefits and costs of a vocational program by accounting perspective

Component	Accounting perspective		
	Social	Participant	Taxpayer
Benefits			
I. Postprogram output			
a. Increased postprogram output	+	+	o
b. Preferences for work (both in-program and postprogram)	+	+	+
c. Increased taxes	o	−	+
II. Reduced use of other programs:			
a. Sheltered workshops	+	o	+
b. Work experience programs	+	o	+
c. Work activity centers	+	o	+
d. Mainstream school	+	o	+
e. Special school	+	o	+
f. Job-training programs	+	o	+
g. Identification or case management services	+	o	+
h. Counseling services	+	o	+
i. Social/recreational services	+	o	+
j. Transportation programs	+	o	+
k. Program allowances	o	−	+
III. Residential situation			
a. Moves to residences with lower public subsidy	+	−	+
b. Greater independence	+	+	+
IV. Transfers			
a. Reduced use of Social Security programs Title XVI (SSI)			
Administrative costs	+	o	+
Transfers	o	−	+
Title II (OSADI)			
Administrative costs	+	o	+
Transfers	o	−	+
b. Other programs			
Administrative costs	+	o	+
Transfers	o	−	+
V. Other benefits			
a. Increased self-sufficiency	+	+	+
b. Quality of life	+	+	+
Costs			
I. Site operations			
a. Management	−	o	−
b. Operations	−	o	−
II. Central administration	−	o	−
III. Participant labor			
a. In-program wages	o	+	−
b. Foregone output while in program	−	−	o
c. Foregone nonmarket activity	−	−	o
IV. Value of in-program output	+	o	+

Note: The components are listed under "Benefits" or "Costs" according to whether they were expected to lead benefits or costs from the social perspective. The contrasts between the expected effects from the social perspective and those from the participant and taxpayer perspectives are shown by indicating, for each component, whether the net impact is to be a net benefit (+), net cost (−), or neither (o). Taxpayers are assumed to be all persons in society who are not participants.

is a social benefit to the extent it represents real increases in output (i.e., if it is not offset by indirect labor market effects).

One possible indirect labor market effect is that program participants displace regular workers. In the extreme, a program might simply shuffle workers among a fixed number of jobs, with no net increase in output. The participants would have higher incomes, but at the expense of other persons who are displaced. Thus, estimated social benefit-cost results would show postprogram earnings gains for participants, but those gains would be at least partially offset by the loss of output of displaced workers.

The other extreme possibility is that participants are transferred from markets with an excess supply of labor to markets where there is an excess demand. Withdrawing a worker from a market with an excess supply of labor will not affect employment or output in that market; even if the particular withdrawn worker had been employed, he or she would be immediately replaced by an unemployed worker. From the perspective of society as a whole, the opportunity cost (i.e., foregone output) of the withdrawn worker is zero. The social benefit would equal the increased earnings of the participants plus the increased earnings of the nonparticipants who filled the jobs vacated by the participants. Of course, if the participant is placed back in the *same* market, there would be displacement. In order for there to be zero opportunity costs, a program must shift participants from surplus labor markets to shortage markets where they will expand output rather than displace employed workers.

It seems clear that many education programs may have indirect effects on the employment of other workers, but it is difficult to estimate the extent of such effects. Previous benefit-cost analyses have approached indirect labor-market effects in various ways. The most common approach has been to assume that wages plus fringe benefits measure the social value of output produced—assuming either explicitly or implicitly that there is neither displacement nor free labor. The issue of indirect labor-market effects can then be assessed qualitatively in sensitivity tests.

This conventional approach has two advantages. First, there are currently no empirical bases for estimating indirect labor-market effects or even knowing their direction. Second, indirect labor-market effects depend ultimately on macroeconomic policy. As Kemper and Long (1981) have shown, the conventional assumption can be viewed as providing estimates of the potential increase in output, provided that aggregate demand is manipulated to take advantage of it.

Because estimates of program-induced earnings increases are denominated in dollars, valuing them is fairly straightforward. Typically, the only shadow prices that are needed are to estimate the value of fringe benefits (including employer-paid taxes). These values can be estimated using data collected by the U.S. Department of Labor (1980) pertaining to compensation rates. These data suggest that in recent years fringe benefits for minimum-wage workers are worth approximately 15% to 18% of gross wages. Thus, estimates of increased earnings should be increased by this amount to obtain an estimate of the increase in total compensation (i.e., the value of the increased output).

Preferences for Work Vocational education may increase participants' satisfaction to the extent that they want to work. Taxpayers may also derive psychological benefits by helping participants find and hold jobs. They may, in fact, prefer to subsidize persons in jobs rather than provide direct transfers of benefits.

These psychological benefits imply that the total value of the increased postprogram (or inprogram) output may exceed the market value of the goods produced. This excess value typically cannot be valued explicitly, but it can be qualitatively assessed in the analysis.

Taxes Associated with increased participant earnings will be increased taxes. These include income, payroll, sales, and excise taxes. Increased taxes are most easily estimated on the basis of effective tax rates applied to the estimates of increased income (earnings and transfers). Pechman and Okner (1974) estimate these effective rates to be approximately 23% of total income for low-wage workers. Any increase would represent a cost to participants and a benefit to taxpayers. Because taxes represent a transfer of resources (the costs of administering the tax system are ignored), they do not enter the social perspective.

Other Programs Participation in a vocational education program can be expected to affect students' use of other programs. It may increase their use of complementary programs—counseling or transportation—while reducing their use of programs they might have entered otherwise. These other services include direct-service programs (sheltered workshops, work experience programs, work activity centers, mainstream and special schools, and job-training programs) and support services (identification and case management, counseling, treatment, social/recreation, and transportation services).

Other programs generate benefits and costs in the same manner as the vocational educational program, using resources and providing benefits to their clients. These benefits may include all those listed for the vocational education program: increased earnings, reduced transfer program use, moves to less-subsidized and more independent residential situations, and increased self-sufficiency. Therefore, changes in the use of other programs affect all the benefit categories in the accounting framework.

Most of these effects are captured indirectly in the estimates of program effects, which are measured relative to the specified counterfactual. However, the cost implications of changes in the use of these other programs must be estimated directly. If participants reduce their use of an alternative program, resources will be freed. If they increase their use of a program, additional resources will have to be devoted to that program. In either case, the use of resources is affected and must be incorporated into the social benefit-cost calculations to avoid biasing the results. Changes in other programs' costs, to the extent that they are attributable to the vocational education program, are estimated using estimates both of the changes in participants' use of other programs and of the average costs of the other programs. Ideally, estimates of marginal costs should be employed (i.e., the change in total costs resulting from the addition or subtraction of one participant). Average costs are typically used because they are easier to measure accurately and, under plausible assumptions, should be quite close to long-run marginal costs. Average cost estimates can usually be derived from published studies of the operating costs for these other programs. For example, the costs of a broad range of education programs were estimated by Kakalik, Furry, Thomas, & Carney (1981). They indicate that in fiscal 1978 the annual per-child costs of preschool education for handicapped children ranged from $2,490 for a child with a speech handicap to $9,382 for a multiply handicapped child. For elementary school the range in per-handicapped-child annual costs is from $2,214 to $11,725 and for secondary school the range is $2,580 to $8,917. Similarly, the U.S. Department of Labor (1977) has estimated the costs of sheltered workshops and work activity centers.

Changes in program operating costs will affect the taxpayer's perspective and the social perspective (because they involve the use of resources). Changes in stipends paid by these programs to their clients will affect participants' and taxpayers' perspectives (these stipends are typically treated as transfers and therefore do not enter the social perspective). Programs that involve the production of output in exchange for a wage (e.g., sheltered workshops or on-the-job training programs) pose some difficulties in this approach. If the wages can be assumed to reflect the value of output produced, then one possibility is to treat changes in wages and output along with those associated with regular employment. The changes in program costs for special treatments (e.g., the extra costs a sheltered workshop incurs to provide services to its clients) are then treated here along with the costs of other service programs.

Residential Situation A program for mentally retarded persons may influence participants' residential situation in two ways. By increasing participants' self-sufficiency it may enable them to move to more independent living arrangements. Also, by helping participants obtain and hold regular jobs it may improve their earnings to the extent that they can move to living quarters that involve less public subsidy.

Changes in living arrangements affect both participants and taxpayers. Moves to residences that require lower subsidies would benefit taxpayers (although if such moves resulted in increased participant use of outpatient and community services, the savings in residential subsidies would be at least partially offset by increases in other program costs). At the same time, such moves may require greater expenditures by participants. The accounting framework includes the parents (or parent surrogates) of participants in the taxpayer category: participants' spouses and children would generally be included in the participant perspectives. Thus, savings accruing to participants' parents as a result of changes in participants' residential situation would be included in the taxpayer perspective. The net social effect depends on how use of resources changes, not on the fraction of housing costs borne by participants or taxpayers. In general, it appears that moves to more independent situations produce social gains as a result of shifts to arrangements that involve less daily supervision and other specialized services. Some of these costs have been estimated by Wieck and Bruininks (1980), who judge that the annual per-person cost in fiscal 1978 was approximately $19,100 for care in a public residential facility, $8,400 in a large community residential facility, and $5,800 in a small community residential facility. (Additional information would be needed, however, to properly value the total costs associated with these programs, since they likely provide different services and report expenditures in different ways.)

Any moves to more independent living arrangements would also generate psychological benefits. There is evidence that, in general, mentally retarded young adults have a preference for more independent living arrangements. Also, nonparticipants may derive psychological benefits from helping persons establish more independent residential situations. These preferences cannot be valued explicitly, but can be incorporated qualitatively in the analysis.

Transfers An analysis of participants' use of transfer programs is important for two reasons. First, if the vocational education program is successful in increasing participants' earnings, there may be corresponding reductions in transfer payments—a change that would benefit taxpayers who pay for those transfers. Second, reductions in transfer income may represent disincentives for participants to seek jobs. The magnitude of these disincentives is an important policy concern.

The biggest change in transfers for mentally retarded youths is expected to be in the Social Security disability programs: Title XVI (SSI) and Title II (Old Age, Survivors, and Disability Insurance, OASDI). In addition, there may be changes in receipt of Aid to Families with Dependent Children (AFDC), Medicaid, Food Stamps, and general assistance. Changes in the use of these programs enter the benefit-cost analysis in two ways. Reductions in the amount of transfer payments will be seen as a cost by participants and a benefit by taxpayers. The value of these transfers will cancel out from the social perspective and therefore will not enter the social benefit-cost calculation. Reductions in program *administrative* costs—the amount of resources devoted simply to making the transfers—will appear as a benefit to taxpayers. Because there is an actual resource savings, the administrative cost savings will enter the social calculation.

Changes in transfer payments and program administrative costs can be valued using estimates of average benefit amounts and average administrative costs. These estimates can often be obtained from data presented in the U.S. federal budget. Table 2 presents estimates of these costs for six transfer programs in FY 1980.

Other Benefits The last two benefit components to be considered here are increased participant self-sufficiency and the quality of participants' lives. In general, increases in either of these areas would generate benefits to both participants and taxpayers. However, these aspects of participants' behavior are extremely difficult to value. In general, benefit-cost analysis must attempt to draw general con-

Table 2.   Estimates of average monthly payment and administrative costs for transfer programs in fiscal year 1980 (in dollars)

Transfer program	Units	Average payment[a] per month	Average administrative[b] cost per month	Data source for estimates[c]
Social Security[d]				
Title XVI (SSI)	Per disabled recipient	214	13	U.S. Department of Health and
Title II (OASDI)	Per disabled recipient	393	10	Human Services (1981), tables T156 and T58
Medicaid	Per recipient	315	11	Muse & Sawyer (1982); Budget Appendix (1981)
Aid to Families	Per recipient	95	11	Budget Appendix (1981)
with Depen-	Per family	300	33	
dent Children				
General As-	Per recipient	145	15	U.S. Department of Health, Ed-
sistance	Per family	191	19	ucation and Welfare (1981)
Food Stamps	Per recipient	31	3	Budget Appendix (1981); U.S.
	Per family	94	10	Department of Agriculture (1977)

[a]Average monthly benefit was computed by dividing total benefit payments by the corresponding number of case months.

[b]For all programs except Medicaid, the estimate of average administrative cost per case month was derived by dividing total administrative cost by the total number of case months. For Medicaid an estimate of the administrative cost was estimated by multiplying the average benefit amount by the programwide ratio of administrative costs to benefit payments.

[c]Citations refer to chapter references.

[d]Figures for Title XVI are for December 1981; figures for Title II are for June 1980 to May 1981.

clusions about changes in these areas and incorporate those qualitative conclusions in the benefit-cost analysis.

Self-sufficiency can be assessed by examining the presence of personal benefactors, the ability to handle money, the ability to travel independently, and other such indicators (more independent residential situations have already been examined). The quality of life will be reflected in part by the estimated changes in earnings, residential situation, and other program use. Other qualitative assessments can also be made.

Site Operations Cost   The costs of operating the program can be estimated from the accounting records. This is usually straightforward; the major considerations are to ensure that 1) the cost estimates are in the same units and correspond to the same time period and participant group as the benefit estimates, and 2) the cost estimates incorporate the value of all resources used by the program. If benefits are estimated on an average or per-participant basis, then costs must be on the same basis. This is done by multiplying the average length of program participation (in months) by the average cost per-person month. (Average cost per-person month is estimated by dividing total costs for a defined period by total months of participation during that period.) This guarantees that the costs refer to the specific treatment being evaluated. Generally, program expenditures can be used as an accurate index of the value of the resources used. The major exceptions are: capital purchases may be treated as current expenses; goods or services may be donated to the program; goods may have been obtained but not yet paid for or payments may have been made in advance of receipt; or the costs of the specific program being evaluated may not be separated fully from the costs of other programs operated by the same management.

Central Administrative Costs   For national or multisite programs the cost of central administration must be included in the analysis. Again, these can be estimated using accounting data. They should reflect, to the extent possible, the central costs of operating only the program under study. These costs and the operating costs will be costs to taxpayers and, because they are resource costs, to society. In these instances, expenditures should be adjusted using conventional accounting practices to reflect the use of resources by the program during the time period under study.

Participant Labor Cost   The definition of these costs depends on the analytical perspective adopted. Taxpayers will view this cost as any wages and fringe benefits paid to participants while they are in the program (this is estimated using accounting data). Participants view this compensation as a benefit. As a result, from the social perspective, it can be treated as a transfer. Unlike the situation in the regular labor market, there should be no presumption that wages paid by a vocational education program measure either the value of workers' contribution to the value of output or their opportunity cost. As a result, program wages are treated as a transfer and the value of in-program output and opportunity cost of labor are estimated directly.

When participants enroll in the program, they implicitly forego the alternative employment opportunities they might have otherwise had. For participants, these foregone wages are the cost of their participation. The foregone output corresponding to these wages is the resource cost of participant labor, and so it should enter the social benefit-cost calculations. The foregone earnings included in this component would include only those associated with the time participants are enrolled in the demonstration. After they leave, the earnings they would have earned in the absence of the demonstration should be treated as an offset to the wages plus fringe benefits they actually earn. This provides the measure of increased postprogram earnings. The opportunity cost of participant labor must be estimated on the basis of the counterfactual—it is usually assumed to equal the earnings of the comparison group (including fringe benefits).

Value of In-Program Output   The value of any output participants produce while in the program is a partial offset to program costs; this offset has been very important in previous benefit-cost studies. For example, in the national

Supported Work demonstration, the value of output offset approximately 65% of the social costs.

One measure of the value of in-program output is the revenue generated by sales of participant services or participant-produced goods. This valuation method provides a reasonable lower-bound estimate of the value of in-program output, because the output was actually purchased for this amount. This value may include an altruistic component if purchasers pay more than an alternative supplier would have charged because the output is produced by program participants. However, if sites do not all pursue revenue-generating strategies, revenue may severely understate the actual value of output.

There are also several other methods for estimating the value of in-program output. Unfortunately, most of these require extensive data-collection efforts. One possible alternative is to draw on the available evidence for other programs in order to approximate the value of output. Other studies (for example, Kemper & Long, 1981; Long, 1979; Whitebread, 1982) look at the in-program productivity of workers in employment and training programs. They suggest that for a broad range of government programs covering a variety of target groups' productivity, the value of output produced per hour in work activities averages $2.75. However, there is substantial variation in actual value of in-program output, so this estimate should be used with caution. Estimates of the productivity of sheltered workshop clients (e.g., U.S. Department of Labor, 1977) may also be useful. These various estimates can be integrated in order to estimate average value of output for the program under study.

The Treatment of Time

To aggregate benefits and costs that occur at different points in time, three issues must be addressed: inflation, discounting, and extrapolation.

To adjust for the effects of inflation, all values should be denominated in dollars from a specified base period. By using the period corresponding to the cost data as the base period, the need to adjust the cost data can be eliminated. Dollar-denominated benefits can be adjusted using a price index such as the implicit price deflator for gross national product. This index is reported each quarter by the U.S. Council of Economic Advisors (1982). Use of a single index has expositional and computational advantages. Also, a broad-based index like the GNP implicit price deflator can more accurately reflect the price changes in the wide range of commodities likely to be affected by social programs. Other benefits can be valued by using shadow prices based on cost data from the base period (or based on other data and adjusted for inflation using the price index).

When summing benefits and costs that occur in different years, there is a problem in that a benefit or cost (measured as a given amount of dollars) achieved, say, in 1984 is worth more than one achieved 10 years from now, even after inflation has been taken into account. Consider a result that reduces residential costs by moving a person to an independent residential arrangement. The savings, if they occurred this year, could be reinvested and would earn a rate of return over the next 10 years. Thus, over a 10-year period the value of this residential change would equal the costs saved this year plus the return on investment over the next decade. This value would clearly exceed the value of the same change if it were to occur 10 years from now.

To reflect this, all benefits and costs must be calculated in equivalent values by discounting those that occur in the future by a factor that reflects the return that could have been earned in the interim. The resulting discounted values are termed "present values." For convenience, values are discounted to the same base period used in the inflation adjustments, the period when participants were in the program. As an example, suppose a $1,000 benefit occurs 10 years from now. What present value (PV) invested at 5% return per annum would yield $1,000 10 years from now? The PV invested today would earn 5% a year for 10 years, or $(1 + .05)^{10}$. So its value can be calculated from the equation $PV (1 + .05)^{10} =$ $1,000. Divide both sides by $(1 + .05)^{10}$ to get $PV = \$1,000 \div (1 + .05)^{10}$. This is the present value of a $1,000 benefit occurring 10 years from now (Warner & Luce [1982] discuss this in more detail, pp. 93–98).

The appropriate discount rate to use when evaluating social programs is always somewhat in dispute because, while the choice of a discount rate is very important for the evaluation and is well established theoretically, there has never been a completely satisfactory way to estimate discount rates. Baumol (1968) provides a theoretical foundation for measuring the social discount rate. He suggests that it should measure the rate of return that the resources used for the public investment would have earned otherwise in the private sector. Bradford (1975) suggests using the rate at which consumers trade off future for current consumption (the social rate-of-time preference). These approaches lead to the same rate if all markets are competitive. In the presence of markets characterized by monopoly power, inflation, taxes, and uncertainty, however, the approaches yield quite different results and are difficult to implement empirically in a correct manner. Imperfections in the markets for capital; the existence of risk, uncertainty, and inflation; and the fact that many tax-incidence questions are still unresolved have made it impossible to determine a single discount rate that is appropriate for evaluating social programs. As a result, the choice of discount rate is typically done arbitrarily. Most studies of social programs have used rates between 3% and 10% a year. Therefore, a possible procedure is to assume a middle value, 5%, and then test the sensitivity of the findings to this assumption by recomputing the values using 3% and 10% discount rates. (The 10% rate is mandated by the U.S. Office of Management and Budget, 1972, for evaluating government investments.)

In general, the social net present value will change in an opposite direction from the change in the discount rate, because social costs are generally incurred during the in-program period (i.e., the time period to which all other benefits and costs are discounted), while the benefits accrue over many time periods.

Therefore, if a higher rate is used, the present value of future benefits will fall and, because costs remain the same, estimated net present value will decline.

The extrapolation of benefits beyond the period for which data are available is difficult and controversial. It is clearly inappropriate to ignore any future unobserved benefits, but the lack of direct observations means that less confidence can be placed in these benefit estimates. One procedure for dealing with this problem is to make all extrapolations using a fairly straightforward procedure that draws on available evidence about long-term effects and can be tested easily to assess the effect of altering the extrapolation assumptions.

Such a procedure was used by Thornton et al. (1982) to extrapolate the estimates of postprogram impacts using an estimate of the long-run time pattern of effects from Manpower Development and Training Act (MDTA) employment and training programs. This time pattern was based on a study by Ashenfelter (1978) that indicated that the magnitude of effects for males decays by 50% after 5 years, while for females there was no decay over the first 5 years. These rates can be used for other programs as a crude approximation; the sensitivity of the final benefit-cost findings to the use of this rate can be assessed by calculating alternative estimates using the extreme assumptions of no extrapolation and no decay of effects after the last period of postprogram observation.

APPLICATION OF BENEFIT-COST ANALYSIS: THE JOB CORPS

The approach to benefit-cost analysis described in this chapter has been applied to several program evaluations. The results of an evaluation of Job Corps (Thornton et al., 1982) are summarized here to illustrate the use of benefit-cost analysis, particularly the analysis of sensitivity tests.

The Job Corps Program

Job Corps provides a comprehensive set of services to disadvantaged youths. These services,

primarily vocational skills training, basic education, and health care, are typically provided in residential centers and are intended to enhance the employability of participants. This is expected to lead to increased output production by Corpsmembers (and an associated increase in their earnings), as well as to several related benefits—notably, reductions in Corpsmembers' dependence on public assistance and mitigations in their antisocial behavior. It is also intended to improve Corpsmembers' health and quality of life. The counterfactual used in the analysis is what Corpsmembers would have done in the absence of Job Corps.

Overall Findings for Job Corps

The various effects of Job Corps were estimated using data collected in periodic interviews with Corpsmembers and a comparison group of similar youths who were never enrolled in Job Corps. A baseline survey of the two groups was administered in May 1977, and three follow-up interviews were subsequently administered. By the time of the third follow-up, in late 1981, the Corpsmembers had been out of Job Corps for an average of 4 years. Altogether, baseline and some follow-up data were collected for approximately 5,200 youths. Multiple regression techniques, controlling for both observed and unobserved differences between Corpsmembers and youths in the comparison sample, were used with these interview data to estimate program effects during the period covered by the interview. The resulting estimates indicate how Corpsmembers' behavior differed from what it would have been in the absence of Job Corps.

Benefits and costs are aggregated in Table 3. They suggest that the program yielded net benefits to society and to Corpsmembers under the benchmark assumptions (i.e., those with which the researchers felt most comfortable). From the social perspective, the increase in output and the reduction in crime were the most important benefits. The largest social costs were for the resources necessary to operate the program. Corpsmembers benefited principally from the increase in their postprogram earnings and from program transfers (shown as negative costs in the Corpsmember column of Table 3)

Table 3. Estimated net present values per corpsmember under the benchmark assumptions[a] (1977 dollars)

Component	Perspective ($)		
	Social	Non-Corpsmember	Corpsmember
Benefits			
I. Output produced by corpsmember			
a. In-program output	757	673	83
b. Increased postprogram output	3,276	0	3,276
c. Increased postprogram tax payments	0	596	−596
II. Reduced dependence on transfer programs			
a. Reduced transfer payments	0	791	−791
b. Reduced administrative costs	172	172	0
c. Increased utility from reduced welfare dependence	+	+	+
III. Reduced criminal activity			
a. Reduced criminal justice system costs	1,253	1,253	0
b. Reduced personal injury and property damage	1,366	1,366	0
c. Reduced stolen property	300	462	−162
d. Reduced psychological costs	+	+	+
IV. Reduced drug/alcohol abuse			
a. Reduced drug/alcohol treatment costs	31	31	0
b. Increased utility from reduced drug/alcohol dependence	+	+	+
V. Reduced utilization of alternative services			
a. Reduced costs of training and education programs other than Job Corps	244	244	0
b. Reduced training allowances	0	33	−33
VI. Other Benefits			
a. Increased utility from redistribution	+	+	+
b. Increased utility from improved well-being of Corpsmember	+	+	+
TOTAL BENEFITS	7,399	5,621	1,777
Costs			
I. Program operating expenditures			
a. Center operating expenditures, excluding transfers to Corpsmembers	2,796	2,796	0
b. Transfers to Corpsmembers	0	1,208	−1,208
c. Central administrative costs	1,347	1,347	0
II. Opportunity cost of corpsmember labor during the program			
a. Foregone output	881	0	881
b. Foregone tax payments	0	153	−153
III. Unbudgeted expenditures other than Corpsmember labor			
a. Resource costs	46	46	0
b. Transfers to Corpsmembers	0	185	−185
TOTAL COSTS	5,070	5,735	−665
Net present value (Benefits minus costs)	2,327	−115	2,442
Benefit-cost ratio[a]	1.46	0.98	1.99

Source: Thornton et al. (1982), p. 148.

Note: See the text for a review of the assumptions, estimation procedures, and their implications for the values presented in this table. For components where it was not possible to assign a dollar amount, net present value is indicated as either positive (+), negative (−), or neither (0).

[a]The numerators for the benefit-cost ratios include all of the benefits listed in this table as either positive benefits or negative costs, and the denominator includes all of the costs listed in this table as either positive costs or negative benefits.

in the form of allowances and room and board. The major costs to Corpsmembers were the foregone earnings while they were in the program, as well as the postprogram reductions in the transfer payments that accompanied their increases in earnings. Non-Corpsmembers, who had to bear the costs of both program operation and the transfer to Corpsmembers, had a slightly negative net present value.[4] They did receive substantial benefits from reductions in Corpsmembers' criminal activities, but these are not sufficient to outweigh program costs. Thus, under the benchmark assumptions, Job Corps is estimated to be a socially efficient use of resources and to cause a redistribution of resources from non-Corpsmembers to Corpsmembers.

As seen, these net present value estimates were based on several assumptions and estimates. A critical part of the analysis, therefore, was to assess the importance of these assumptions and estimates, which was done by examining the effects on the estimated net present value of changing one of the assumptions or estimates while maintaining the other benchmark assumptions and estimates.[5] Five of these sensitivity tests are summarized in Table 4.

The first alternative in Table 4 examines the extrapolation assumptions. It shows that benefits are estimated to exceed costs without any extrapolations. Thus, the specific assumptions used in the extrapolations are not crucial to the overall finding that social net present value is positive. In fact, the study found that benefits exceeded costs 3 years after Corpsmembers left the Job Corps.

The next two alternatives in the table examine the effect of changing the discount rate from the 5% benchmark assumption. Using a 3% discount rate increases the social net present value by approximately $475 per Corpsmember, compared to the benchmark estimate,

while increasing the discount rate from the 5% rate to the 10% rate decreases the net present value by almost $900 per Corpsmember. In either case, the social net present value is positive. Thus, discount rate assumptions within the plausible range do not seem crucial for this evaluation.

The last two alternatives in Table 4 deal with indirect labor market effects. The first assumes that Corpsmembers obtain jobs that would have been otherwise filled by other workers (possibly, Job Corps provides Corpsmembers with credentials that enable them to move to the head of the job queue without enabling them to leave the unskilled labor market). As seen in the table, under this assumption estimated social net present value is negative because Corpsmembers become employed only at the expense of non-Corpsmembers. The last alternative assumes that Job Corps shifts Corpsmembers from labor-surplus to labor-shortage markets. Under this assumption, all of the Corpsmembers' postprogram earnings, rather than simply the increase in their earnings, will be social benefits because other workers (non-Corpsmembers) who would have been unemployed now get the opportunity to fill the jobs vacated by Corpsmembers when they enter the labor-shortage market. If the other assumptions are not changed, estimated social and non-Corpsmember net present values per Corpsmember will rise by almost $70,000 (compared to the benchmark that assumes no indirect labor-market effects).

Thus, assumptions about the nature of the labor markets in which Corpsmembers participate have a substantial effect on estimated net present value from the social and non-Corpsmember perspectives. While the benchmark assumptions (that Job Corps increases the productivity of Corpsmembers and, thus, that the increase in their earnings represents a social

---

[4]The term *non-Corpsmember* is used rather than *taxpayer* because a specific goal of Job Corps was to increase Corpsmembers' employability and help them become taxpayers. Thus, the general term *non-Corpsmember* is used to refer to all persons who did not enroll in Job Corps including, as a small subgroup, the comparison group.

[5]Another concern is the precision with which the Job Corps effects were estimated. In this regard, it should be noted that the earnings effects and in-program crime effects (the largest benefit components) are statistically significant. In addition, the specific point estimates do not appear to be particularly sensitive to the econometric techniques used. These points are examined in Mallar (1979) and Mallar, Long, and Thornton (1982).

Table 4. Alternative estimates of net present values per corpsmembers (1977 dollars)

	Perspective ($)		
Alternative assumptions	Social	Non-Corpsmember	Corpsmember
1. Benchmark assumptions.[a]	2,327	−115	2,442
2. Effects are zero after the first 48 postprogram months (our observation period).	827	−792	1,618
3. Three percent annual real discount rate.	2,801	125	2,676
4. Ten percent annual real discount rate.	1,438	−581	2,019
5. Job Corps shuffles workers among jobs.	−1,373	−3,815	2,442
6. Job Corps shifts workers from labor-surplus to labor-shortage markets.	72,415	69,973	2,442

Source: Thornton et al. (1982).

[a]Benchmark assumptions are as follows: earnings, tax, and transfer effects fade out at a real rate of 14% per year; all other effects fade out at a real rate of 140% per year (which assumes that these other effects fade out to 25% of their base amount after 1 year and to 1 percent after 3 years); the real discount rate is 5% per annum; the expected working life of a Corpsmember is 43 years after leaving Job Corps (i.e., until age 62); Job Corps creates no displacement and there is no replacement in the labor markets Corpsmembers leave.

gain) appear to be the most reasonable that can be made in the absence of better information about indirect labor-market effects, those results suggest that the benchmark net present value estimates must be interpreted carefully in light of their sensitivity to changes in these assumptions.

Another element of uncertainty in the analysis is the importance of those generally intangible benefits and costs that have not been measured. For example, individuals may derive benefits because they prefer work over welfare. Corpsmembers may gain satisfaction and self-esteem from holding regular jobs, while non-Corpsmembers may prefer to provide employment and training opportunities rather than direct-transfer payments. Other important unmeasured benefits include the reduced psychological costs of criminal victimizations; the satisfaction of society and non-Corpsmembers from the income redistribution and increased well-being to Corpsmembers; and the value to Corpsmembers of improved health beyond what is reflected in the other measured benefits. While these benefits are not measured, there is evidence (such as public opinion to-

ward welfare and the fears of criminal victimization) that they may be important program effects.

The exclusion of these benefits from the quantitative analysis, which results from the resource-cost valuation procedures used, probably biases the results downward. There are other cases, however, where the bias was probably upward. One important case was the value of in-program output, which was estimated on the basis of the price that would be charged by an alternate supplier. This price does not measure the value society places on the output, which cannot be measured well but which economic theory suggests will usually be lower than the supply price.[6] Also, costs may be understated if the Job Corps centers cause community disruptions. In general, however, it seems that the measured benefits and costs allow accurate overall assessments to be made, particularly in view of the fact that what was not measured affects both benefits and costs. The unmeasured elements imply that the net present value estimates are only approximations, but the evaluative conclusions based on measured benefits and costs appear to be valid.

[6]If supply price—the cost of production—were below the price society was willing to pay, then the output would have presumably been supplied in the absence of Job Corps.

CONCLUSION AND RECOMMENDATIONS

This review of benefit-cost analysis has necessarily been brief, but is intended to show how the method can be used to evaluate social programs, including those related to deinstitutionalization and education of handicapped persons. It argues that benefit-cost analysis of social programs can be very useful if it is conducted and presented in a way that recognizes the information needs of decision makers and the types of information that economic analysis can provide.

The approach offered here emphasizes four features that seem to be especially important for providing necessary information to decision makers. First, if a comprehensive program assessment is to be made, as many of the important program effects as possible must be included in the analysis. In the Job Corps evaluation, for example, reduced criminal behavior—an effect rarely valued even in the analyses of programs like Job Corps, where crime effects are expected to exist—turned out to be an extremely important social benefit. However, in broadening the focus of benefit-cost evaluations to include more program effects, care must be taken to maintain analytical consistency. The resource-cost approach that focuses on those benefits and costs that are associated with using, saving, or creating resources ensures a consistent and easily interpretable analysis.

Second, since redistributing income or economic opportunities is a major policy objective of most social programs, the distributional effects must be examined by the analysis. While the evaluation of distribution must be done in the wider context of public policy, it is possible to assess the magnitude and broad implications of redistributions.

Third, an explicit accounting framework is essential in a comprehensive program evaluation as both an analytical and expositional aid. Such a framework imposes a rigor on the analysis and is a helpful tool in considering how to treat transfers between the groups of interest. In addition, the use of a single summary table, including both measured and unmeasured pro-

gram effects (by perspective), allows the user of the research to identify at a glance the benefits, costs, and distributional effects of the program, as well as what factors could not be quantified. Benefits and costs can be ranked in the order of their importance, and users can easily reweigh benefits and costs to reflect their own judgment.

Fourth, estimating the present value of benefits and costs of social programs requires numerous assumptions and approximations. Sensitivity tests examining the robustness of the conclusions with respect to changes in assumptions should be presented clearly. This will allow users to make better judgments about the program (i.e., about how much confidence can be placed in the findings).

In conclusion, this chapter has focused on the techniques specific to benefit-cost analysis, but this is only one means of interpreting evaluation findings. If the overall evaluation is to guide policy, it must include a careful documentation of the program model and how it was implemented. Also, the estimates of program effects that underlie the estimation of benefits and cost must be prepared using accepted statistical procedures. This means that attempts should be made to ensure that estimates are unbiased and as precise as possible, given programmatic and budget constraints. The preceding chapter by Heal discusses methodological considerations in assessing program effects.

To achieve the maximum effect from benefit-cost analyses of deinstitutionalization and education programs, three major changes will be required. First, programs in these areas must develop cost and outcome data bases. This will require more careful accounting of expenditures and client flows. It will also require that programs develop and implement outcome-oriented evaluations and collect more data on how their treatments affect clients. Second, administrators at all levels will need to be educated in how to use benefit-cost analysis. This tool is often unfamiliar to persons whose training has been oriented to service delivery. Before administrators can employ these analyses to their advantage, they must become familiar with the strengths and weaknesses of this approach and must be able to assess the quality of the analytical work. It is particularly important that administrators view benefit-cost analysis as an analytical tool rather than as a rigid and precise evaluation criterion. Finally, it will be necessary to develop benefit-cost paradigms that can be applied to small programs with modest levels of effort. The studies referred to in this chapter have had huge budgets and access to accurate (and expensive) estimates of a wide range of program effects. The techniques developed for these large evaluations can be applied to programs with smaller budgets, but implementation requires the development and dissemination of manuals that provide accounting frameworks, shadow prices, and even information on the probable size of hard-to-measure outcomes. The development of these manuals will go a long way toward facilitating

the use of benefit-cost analysis and educating persons about its use.

A benefit-cost analysis of a social program is a less precise and mechanical process than may be conveyed by the computations and tables of dollar values presented in this chapter. The results will always reflect judgments about what program effects are important, about how they should be measured and valued, and the assumptions about several elements of the analysis that cannot be observed directly. Awareness of these features of a benefit-cost evaluation are as important in interpreting and using the results as are the computed values themselves. By recognizing the role of the judgments and assumptions, benefit-cost analysis can help policy makers to identify important issues and program effects and to weigh the relative importance of the various effects of complex social programs.

REFERENCES

Ashenfelter, O. Estimating the effect of training programs on earnings. *Review of Economics and Statistics,* 1978, *60,* 47–57.

Baumol, W.J. On the social rate of discount. *American Economic Review,* 1968, *58,* 788–802.

Bradford, D.F. Constraints on government investment opportunities and the choice of discount rate. *American Economic Review,* 1975, *65,* 887–899.

Budget of the United States Government, Fiscal Year 1982 Appendix. Washington, DC: U.S. Government Printing Office, 1981.

Gramlich, E.M. *Benefit-cost analysis of government programs.* Englewood Cliffs, NJ: Prentice-Hall, 1981.

Hill, M., & Wehman, P. Cost benefit analysis of placing moderately and severly handicapped individuals into competitive employment. *TASH,* 1983, *8*(1), 30–38.

Kakalik, J.S., Furry, W.S., Thomas, M.A., & Carney, M.F. *The costs of special education: Summary of study findings.* Santa Monica, CA: Rand Corporation, 1981.

Kemper, P., & Long, D.A. *The supported work evaluation: Technical report on value of in-program output and costs.* Princeton: Mathematica Policy Research, 1981.

Kemper, P., Long, D.A., & Thornton, C. *The supported work evaluation: Final benefit-cost analysis.* Princeton: Mathematica Policy Research, 1981.

Long, D.A. Evaluation of the economic impacts of the Job Corps program: Value of output in work activities. Staff Paper # 79C-02. Princeton: Mathematica Policy Research, 1979.

Long, D.A., Mallar, C.D., & Thornton, C. Evaluating the benefits and costs of the Job Corps. *Journal of Policy Analysis and Management,* 1981, *1*(1), 55–76.

Mallar, C.D. Alternative econometric procedures for program evaluations: Illustrations from an evaluation of Job Corps. In: American Statistical Association, *1979 proceedings fo the Business and Economic Statistics Section.* Washington, D C : American Statistical Association, 1979.

Mallar, C.D., Long, D., & Thornton, C. *Evaluation of the economic impact of the Job Corps program: Third follow-up report.* Princeton: Mathematica Policy Research, September, 1982.

Mishan, E. *Cost-benefit analysis* (3rd ed.). Winchester, MA: Allen & Unwin, 1982.

Muse, D.N., & Sawyer, D. *The Medicare and Medicaid data book, 1981.* Washington, D C : U.S. Department of Health and Human Services, April, 1982.

Pechman, J., & Okner, B. *Who bears the tax burden?* Washington, D.C.: Brookings Institution, 1974.

Rowe, R., & Chestnut, L. *The value of visibility: Theory and application.* Cambridge, MA: Abt Books, 1982.

Thornton, C. *The benefits and costs of SW-STETS: A design overview.* Princeton: Mathematica Policy Research, 1981.

Thornton, C., Long, D., & Mallar, C. *A comparative evaluation of Job Corps after forty-eight months of postprogram observation.* Princeton: Mathematica Policy Research, 1982.

U.S. Council of Economic Advisors. *Economic indicators.* Washington DC: U.S. Government Printing Office, 1982.

U.S. Department of Agriculture. *Characteristics of Food Stamp households, September, 1976.* Washington, DC: U.S. Government Printing Office, 1977.

U.S. Department of Health and Human Services, Social

Security Administration. *Social Security Bulletin; Annual Statistical Supplement.* Washington, DC: U.S. Government Printing Office, 1981.

U.S. Department of Health, Education and Welfare (DHEW). *Public assistance statistics (October 1979 to September 1980).* Washington, DC: DHEW, 1981.

U.S. Department of Labor. *Employee compensation in the private nonfarm economy, 1977.* (Summary 80-5). Washington, DC: Bureau of Labor Statistics, 1980.

U.S. Department of Labor. *A nationwide report on sheltered workshops and their employment of handicapped individuals. Statistical appendix to Volume 1.* Washington, DC: U.S. Government Printing Office, 1977.

U.S. Office of Management and Budget (OMB). *Discount rates to be used in evaluating time—Distributed costs and benefits.* (OMB Circular No. A-94). Washington, DC: OMB, March 27, 1972.

Warner, K.E., & Luce, B.R. Cost-benefit and cost-effectiveness analysis in health care. Ann Arbor, MI: Health Administration Press, 1982.

Weisbrod, B. Distributional effects on collective goals. *Policy Analysis,* 1978.

Whitebread, C. *The value of output produced in EOPP work activities.* Princeton: Mathematica Policy Research, 1982.

Wieck, C.A., & Bruininks, R.H. *The cost of public and community residential care for the mentally retarded people in the United States.* Minneapolis: University of Minnesota, Department of Psychoeducational Studies, 1980.

Chapter 13

Community Integration and Mental Retardation

The Ecobehavioral Approach to Service Provision and Assessment

Janis G. Chadsey-Rusch

I n recent years a major emphasis in the field of mental retardation has been to integrate mentally retarded individuals into the mainstream of society. This movement has received its greatest conceptual support from the normalization principle. In 1969, Nirje defined normalization as "making available to the mentally retarded [person] patterns and conditions of everyday life which are as close as possible to the norms and patterns of the mainstream of society" (p. 181). Implied in this definition is the goal of normalizing environments (i.e., the means to achieve a normal lifestyle) and not of persons themselves. Several studies have shown, however, that a more normalized environment does not necessarily lead to more normalized behavior (Birenbaum & Re, 1979; Butler & Bjaanes, 1978; Landesman-Dwyer, Sackett, & Kleinman, 1980).

The principle of normalization has been elaborated upon by Wolfensberger (1972) who defined normalization to be the "utilization of means which are as culturally normative as possible, in order to establish and/or maintain personal behaviors and characteristics which are as culturally normative as possible" (p. 28). The twin concepts of normalizing people and environments were thus implied, with emphasis on both the process and the goal of normalization. Wolfensberger's definition implied that many mentally retarded individuals would need to learn a variety of skills (e.g., communication, social, vocational) if they were to achieve normal life-styles and be successfully integrated into communities.

The primary purpose of this chapter is to describe a rationale for approaching community integration by employing both behavioral and ecological principles, that is, by viewing normalization not only as a product of the placement decisions of service providers but as a process that focuses on the client's development within those placements. The methodological characteristics as well as strengths and weaknesses of both a behavior analytic and an ecological approach are discussed. The chapter concludes with a description of the components of an ecobehavioral approach and

The author gratefully acknowledges Bob York for his comments on an earlier draft of this chapter.

presents examples from the research literature that utilize aspects of an ecobehavioral approach in providing and evaluating community integration programs. Although much of the research that is cited here comes primarily from the literature about mentally retarded adults, implications for utilization of an ecobehavioral approach within an educational context are also noted. It can easily be argued that research with retarded adults reflecting an ecobehavioral methodology has direct relevance for educating handicapped youth. One area in which this is particularly true is in the education of severely handicapped persons, where Brown and his colleagues (Brown, Branston, Hamre-Nietupski, Pumpian, Certo, & Gruenewald, 1979) have advocated life-span planning utilizing a top-down, rather than a developmental, approach to curriculum planning.

BEHAVIOR ANALYTIC APPROACH

Baer, Wolf, and Risley (1968) described behavior analysis as the process of utilizing behavioral principles to change behavior, while concurrently evaluating which changes were the result of the application process. Applied behavior analysis (ABA) incorporates behavior analytic strategies to examine socially important behaviors in their usual social settings. The applied aspect of behavior analysis suggests that the behavior under study is not only important within the society but it is also relevant to the subject and to his or her functioning in the community. There are other unique characteristics of behavior analysis. For example, behavior selected to be changed is objectively defined so that it can be precisely measured. It is important to determine not only if and when behavior alters but also, when appropriate, whose behavior changes. Thus, it is implied that the alteration of both antecedent and consequent events may serve to modify behavior.

In applied behavior analyses, repeated measures of selected target behaviors are collected over time. Analysis of the data is ongoing and occurs during both baseline and intervention phases. The crux of the analytic process is gathering convincing evidence, via design methodology, on the effect of a specific procedure in bringing about changes in behavior.

Applied behavior analysts must describe the technological procedures they use in enough detail so that they can be replicated. This entails providing precise descriptions of the dependent and independent variables, in addition to relating the strategies used to alter behavior to the basic principles of behavior. For example, to refer to the acquisition of saying the word *ball* by first reinforcing the sound /b/ and then later requiring the production of the whole word /ball/ as shaping, allows the reader to replicate specific procedures as well as to devise similar procedures based on the basic behavioral principle of shaping.

The establishment and use of a consistent conceptual framework has been important to the development of the behavior analytic approach. Applied behavior analysts, beginning with Baer et al. (1968), have also contended that effectiveness of behavioral strategies has to be substantial enough to be of practical value. Often the value of change cannot be established scientifically but must be determined by society. In large measure then, "success" should be judged by consumers and not just by researchers.

Finally, behavior analysts look for new or modified behaviors that generalize across contexts of new people, settings, and behaviors. They also work to establish behavior that is maintained over time. Generalization and maintenance frequently do not occur automatically and must be specifically trained.

In summary, the applied behavior analytic approach can be viewed as consisting of the following components: a) objective analysis of socially important behaviors and the reasons for changing those behaviors, b) direct, repeated measurement of these target behaviors over time, c) replicable training procedures, d) visual (and where appropriate, statistical) analysis of the data to determine the variables responsible for change, e) change deemed large enough to be practical, and f) change that is durable and generalizable.

Applied Behavior Analysis in Community Integration Research

The behavior analytic approach has been demonstrated to be an effective methodology for use in the education and habilitation of mentally retarded persons. Within an educational context, this methodology has been applied to modifying a wide variety of behaviors, such as language (Guess, Sailor, Rutherford, & Baer, 1968), mealtime skills (Barton, Guess, Garcia, & Baer, 1970), and self-stimulation (Fox & Azrin, 1973). Many research studies have also utilized applied behavior analysis methodology to teach community integration skills to mentally retarded adults. Schutz, Vogelsberg, and Rusch (1980) reviewed the behavioral research area and reported on training-related studies that have been the focus of integration efforts into the community. They described studies that sought to train community mobility skills, self-care skills, money management skills, telephone skills, leisure skills, and vocational skills. In a similar vein, Martin, Rusch, and Heal (1982) reviewed research on skill acquisition problems in areas believed important for community survival. Besides looking at the same areas as Schutz et al. (1980), Martin et al. (1982) also examined research teaching social and conversational skills and self-medication.

Successful research and/or clinical practice that has utilized ABA methodology does not necessarily guarantee successful integration into the community, however. Martin et al. (1982) suggested several areas that needed to be studied to enhance knowledge in the area of community integration. These research areas included studying multiple behaviors rather than single behaviors, investigating generalization and maintenance strategies, and utilizing larger samples of subjects including individuals who may not normally be a part of the research process (e.g., coworkers, neighbors, local citizens). Many of these same areas have also been designated as important to study within an educational context (Voeltz & Evans, 1982; Wehman & Hill, 1982).

Several of these same observations had been previously made by the ecologist Willems in 1974. Although Willems lauded behavioral analysis as an effective technology, he also offered a number of reservations regarding its use. Generally, Willems stated that the emphasis of behavioral analysis on changing one behavior at a time did not answer questions of possible intervention side effects in the environment or across behaviors. For example, an intervention that is designed to change one behavior may indirectly affect other undesirable, desirable, or neutral behaviors in the subject's repertoire. Sajwaj, Twardosz, and Burke (1972) provided an example of covariation of behaviors when they applied contingencies to excessive conversation initiations of a retarded boy made to a teacher and measured the effect on that and on other behaviors. Not only did the frequency of the initiations decrease but verbal interactions to other children increased, cooperative play increased, and aggressive behavior toward adults increased. Knowing the unintended effects of interventions is often just as important as measuring their intended effects.

Other side effects in the environment can also occur as a result of the intervention process. Willems (1974) cited the example of a mother who increased child compliance by reducing the frequency of the child's nagging. The intervention was believed successful because compliance increased; however, as the study progressed the mother began to eat more, gained weight, and finally abandoned the child and left town. Willems intended these examples to serve as a rationale for collecting data on "other" behaviors. He suggested that behaviorists needed to determine which unintended effects occur frequently and why they occur. By collecting data on "other" behaviors, Willems concluded that such side effects could be reliably predicted and intervention planned around them. (For a more recent and expanded treatment of behavioral covariation, particularly in regard to intervention validity, the reader is referred to Voeltz and Evans, 1982).

Another limitation of behavioral research noted by Willems (1974) was that behaviors were usually studied for too short a time period. Willems implied that by monitoring behaviors for short periods the intervention process "might unwittingly disrupt desirable things or set undesirable things in motion that become clear over long periods of time" (p. 161). Again, Willems was primarily referring to side effects that could occur as a result of the intervention process. However, his criticism of only monitoring a behavior for a short time period has other important implications for behavior analysts. Often after a behavior is changed and an objective has been met, the monitoring of that changed behavior ceases. As Baer et al. (1968) pointed out, one of the tenets of applied behavior analysis is that a behavior should be durable or transitive over time. In a review of nearly a decade of research reported in the *Journal of Applied Behavior Analysis,* Warren (1977) reported that only 21% of the sampled articles included behavior maintenance assessment. Although this figure may have increased in articles published since 1977, Willems (1974) was clearly justified in his criticism of applied behavior analysts for monitoring behaviors for too short a time period.

Another criticism raised by Willems regarded the need for behavior analysts to be more explicit in describing their assessment and evaluation process. He felt that the ability to study complex behavior systems and select specific behaviors that would be influenced by contingencies within those systems was diagnosis at its best. According to Willems, the delineation of specific rules that emerge from studying the interaction between the behavior and environment, as well as an evaluation of the ways in which the behavior-environment relationship functions, would be helpful knowledge for both behavior analysts and ecologists.

Willems (1974) also suggested that behavior analysts should be more concerned with the influence of the physical setting on behavior— for example, the specific way that a classroom is arranged or the number of people in that classroom could increase or decrease social interactions. Willems's concern with information regarding the role of behavior-setting linkages might lead to the design of optimal environ-ments for such things as learning new information, work, and recreational activities.

In summary, although Willems (1974) contended that the applied behavioral approach had proved useful for changing a wide variety of important behaviors, he made several suggestions for improving behavior analytic study, including: a) data collection on multiple behaviors rather than single behaviors, b) data collection over longer time periods, c) more-explicit diagnostic data collection, and d) data collection on the effects of the physical environment on behavior. Willems's general concerns regarding behavioral technology were also reflected in Martin et al.'s (1982) recommendations for further research regarding training procedures for community integration. Their recommendations to study multiple behaviors rather than single behaviors, to focus on generalization and maintenance strategies, and to utilize larger samples of subjects and significant others in the subject's environment fit nicely into Willems's broader scheme for concentrating more on the ecological environment of the individual.

THE ECOLOGICAL APPROACH

The ecological approach to the study of behavior has been described by a number of psychologists (for example, Auerswald, 1969; Barker, 1968; Brunswick, 1955; Lewin, 1951; Michaels, 1974; Schoggen, 1978; Willems & Rausch, 1969). Although definitions of ecological psychology vary, several main tenets are repeated throughout the literature. Generally, an ecological approach can be thought of as the study of complex interrelationships and of the interdependence between the organism, its behavior, and the environment that occur in natural contexts. Although ecological psychology is concerned with individual (molecular) relationships in specific contexts, it is focused primarily on a broader (molar) perspective that considers interrelationships in varying contexts and at different levels.

For the ecological psychologist, the influence of setting (time and space) on the behavior of the organism is extremely important (Schoggen, 1978). For example, behavior displayed in a movie theater is, obviously, different from that displayed at a party. However, each of these environments, and the kind of controls each has over individuals, remains fairly constant across individuals. Thus, even though a number of individuals may enter into and out of various settings, the behaviors (that for the most part are setting-dependent) remain essentially the same for all members.

The fundamental methodology used by ecologists is direct observation of phenomena in natural situations (Schoggen, 1978). Generally, the data are descriptive. Research methods are used to identify the ongoing stream of behavior, and careful procedures are undertaken to minimize interruptions or interference with the natural course of events. The ecologist is interested in studying the variation, intensity, and frequency of behaviors in many different environments. Through repeated sampling of behaviors in varied situations, behavioral consistencies appear. After data are collected, they are then analyzed and sorted into taxonomies of behavior, of environment, and of behavior-environment relationships.

Two methods used by ecologists to collect data are the specimen record and the behavior-setting survey (Schoggen, 1978). The specimen record is a narrative description of one person in a natural situation over a specific time period. Observers record, in nontechnical language, everything the individual does and says and everything that is said and done to and with the individual being studied. Although the specimen record at times is inferential and interpretive, concrete and observable details are primarily expected. Specimen records may be handwritten or recorded orally.

In a description of the behavior-setting survey, Schoggen (1978) stated that the focus of observation shifts from the individual to a particular situation. Essentially, consistencies of behavior in relation to a specific time and place are noted. Thus, the approach of this method is not to study an individual or even interactions between individuals but rather to describe the behaviors of many persons associated with particular environmental settings. For example,

an ecologist may study the behaviors of many individuals eating dinner in a restaurant. From this information, ecologists would expect the patterns of behaviors associated with eating dinner in a restaurant to occur regularly and consistently and to be controlled by the restaurant setting.

In summary, ecological psychology is the study of complex interrelationships and interdependencies between the organism, its behavior, and the environment. Generally, molar phenomena are emphasized more than molecular phenomena. Behavior is studied over time, in its natural context, and efforts are made to minimize interference or interruptions during the ongoing stream of events.

Ecological Approach in Community Integration Research

Recently, a number of psychologists and educators have employed techniques of ecological methodology to study aspects of community integration and the behavior of mentally retarded persons. Although the methodology of studying retarded persons in community settings and observing what happens in their daily lives has been suggested for a number of years (Balla, Butterfield, & Zigler, 1973; Dingman, 1968), only a few studies have systematically examined the more molar effects of the environment on behavior and on the nature of social organizations (Landesman-Dwyer, Stein, & Sackett, 1978). Bjaanes and Butler (1974) used naturalistic observation to describe activities that distinguished facilities that encouraged competent and normalizing behaviors versus those that did not. Their study compared 10 individuals in two California home-care facilities with that of 54 individuals in two board-and-care facilities. They observed each subject for 2- to 3-hour sessions and coded and described ongoing activities. These data were then analyzed according to the frequency and proportion of time spent in each activity and the characteristics of the behavior. Differences in behavior characteristics were found between the facilities, leading Bjaanes and Butler to conclude that board-and-care facilities were closer to the objective of normalization and yielded more independent behavior. These authors also suggested that exposure to the community, geographic location, and caregiver involvement influenced resident activities.

In 1978, Butler and Bjaanes again used naturalistic observation to study the activities and use of time by retarded persons in community care facilities. Utilizing the concept of "life space," defined as the "physical, temporal, and social space utilized by an individual in the course of his life experience" (p. 386), Butler and Bjaanes collected information on 160 facilities in three counties in California. The facilities ranged in size from 1 to 95 residents, with the modal facility housing 3 to 6 individuals. They concluded that larger facilities used agencies, services, and programs better and had more internal normalizing activities than smaller facilities. Variation in the use of services and programs appeared to be associated with education and prior experience of service providers, the location and size of the facility, the surrounding neighborhood, and normalizing activities within the facilities. Butler and Bjaanes also emphasized that a community care facility could not be considered an "a priori normalizing environment" (p. 398) and that internal and external programs were needed to facilitate normalization.

Landesman-Dwyer et al., (1978) utilized an observation code with 10 separate behavioral or environmental categories, including 62 behavioral activities, to assess 20 group homes in Washington State. During their study, 16,000 hours of behavioral samples were compiled. After data analysis, the authors stated that the most consistent finding, even after only 2 days of coding, related retardation level and age to observed proportion of time in certain activities (i.e., mildly retarded persons spent less time in inactive behaviors and children spent more time in organized activities). They also tentatively concluded that small group homes (6–9 residents) did not maximize social behavior, that more positive social behavior was associated with homogeneous groupings of residents, that parent visitations seemed to contribute to inactive behavior, and that residents in older buildings showed more community interaction than those living in new, specially designed group homes.

In a more detailed analysis of the relationship between facility size and the behavior of staff members and residents, Landesman-Dwyer et al. (1980) reported that more social interaction among peers was found in smaller group homes. Staff behavior was not related to facility characteristics, and amount of staff-resident interaction was not related to size. A further analysis of these observational data was conducted by Landesman-Dwyer, Berkson, and Romer (1979) to investigate affiliation and friendship of mentally retarded residents in group homes. These data revealed that social interaction generally occurred within dyads rather than larger-sized groups. Also, mildly to severely retarded individuals exhibited different social behavior when they were with others versus alone. This difference was not observed with profoundly handicapped individuals. It was also observed that the amount of social interaction did not seem to be determined by sex or level of retardation but rather by group home characteristics. For example, group home size provided more opportunities for resident affiliation but did not influence the intensity of relationships, whereas the homogeneity of groupings and sex ratio seemed to affect intensity of affiliations. The 16 friendship pairs studied revealed that productive language skills, rather than intelligence, were the most important aspect of similarity among pairs.

In a series of three articles, Berkson and Romer (1980) and Romer and Berkson (1980a, 1980b) described the social relationships among mentally retarded adults in four sheltered workshops and a sheltered-care residence. Each of the 304 mentally retarded individuals were observed a minimum of 100 times, during coffee and lunch breaks, informal and structured recreation activities, on streets, in stores, in restaurants, and during some recreational outings. A behavior checklist containing 100 categories was used to code behavior. In addition, staff ratings and client interviews were conducted. Generally, these articles reported the following conclusions regarding social relationships among mentally retarded adults: a) clients who were physically attractive, who wanted to affiliate, and who had intelligent peers in the program interacted more extensively and intensively with peers; b) clients preferred same-sex peers, peers of similar attractiveness, and those to whom they had more exposure; c) opposite-sex relationships were stronger than relationships between same-sex peers; and d) clients of relatively moderate levels of intelligence interacted with both higher and lower IQ groups, thus making their presence important for social integration into a setting.

In a later series of four articles, Berkson and his colleagues (Berkson, 1981; Heller, Berkson, & Romer, 1981; Melstrom, 1982; Romer & Berkson, 1981) continued to observe the social ecology of residential and workshop facilities for mentally retarded adults. Again using naturalistic observation as the primary measurement device, the following conclusions were made: a) different residential placements (e.g., family home, independent-living arrangements, sheltered-care facilities) by themselves did not strongly correlate with work production or social skills (Berkson, 1981); b) setting variables exerted strong influence on the social behavior of mentally retarded adults when they were newly admitted to sheltered workshops (Heller et al., 1981); c) attractive physical attributes and sociability were positively related to vocational behavior (Melstrom, 1982); and d) personal characteristics (e.g., age, intelligence, sex, diagnosis, desire for affiliation) significantly predicted individual behavior and primarily accounted for the intenseness of relationships in sheltered workshops and residential settings (Romer & Berkson, 1981).

These studies can be considered ecological because they all measured the natural behavior of mentally retarded persons in different environments. Furthermore, no attempt was made to alter the ongoing stream of events. These data revealed important information regarding activities in different community facil-

ities (Bjaanes & Butler, 1974; Butler & Bjaanes, 1978), differences in behavior as a function of group home size (Landesman-Dwyer et al., 1978; Landesman-Dwyer et al., 1980), affiliation and friendship relationships in group homes (Landesman-Dwyer et al., 1979), and the social relationships among mentally retarded adults in supervised communal facilities (Berkson, 1981; Berkson & Romer, 1980; Heller et al., 1981; Melstrom, 1982; Romer & Berkson, 1980a, 1980b; Romer & Berkson, 1981).

The implications for community integration from these ecologically collected data are numerous. For example, the work of Berkson and his colleagues suggests the importance of social behavior, of setting variables, and of friendship and affiliation patterns for understanding and enhancing social and vocational integration into community settings. If one adheres to the top-down curriculum approach advocated by Brown et al. (1979), then this information collected on mentally retarded adults could have important educational implications for mentally retarded youth, as well. For example, Melstrom (1982) suggested that high sociability was positively related to vocational success in sheltered workshops. Since many severely handicapped youth may one day be employed, it behooves educational personnel in the schools to consider interpersonal skills as an important curriculum area.

Ideally, an ecological approach could be used to provide a greatly increased quantity and quality of information regarding naturalistic behavior of mentally retarded youths in a variety of settings, including educational settings. At present, little information is available regarding the ecological environment of the public school system. Although not all mentally retarded youth receive their education in the public schools, it is highly probable this will be the case in the future. For those mentally retarded children in transition between relatively highly restrictive educational settings to less-restrictive settings, prior information on behaviors used by mentally retarded and normal youth that lead to successful academic and social performance would seem to be extremely helpful. Thus, it can be argued that an ecological approach to community integration offers an evaluation strategy that has advantages to both mentally retarded adults and youths.

Although it has been demonstrated that an ecological approach can add much information to community integration efforts, the major weakness of this approach lies in the fact that it is mainly a descriptive methodology rather than an intervention methodology. The problems involved in community integration of mentally retarded individuals are numerous and varied, and, therefore, effective teaching strategies definitely will need to be formulated and tested in order to maximize successful integration. A purely descriptive methodology will not answer questions regarding teaching methods, nor will it completely resolve the issue of the most appropriate behavior(s) to teach to maximize social integration. Since one of the goals of working with mentally retarded individuals is to teach new behaviors (or eliminate problem behaviors) as quickly and as efficiently as possible, a methodological approach besides an ecological approach will need to be considered. As Risley (1977) stated, "although observation can give us . . . new conceptualizations of the world, experimental intervention gives us the methodology to change the world" (p. 161).

THE ECOBEHAVIORAL APPROACH

A number of professionals have raised concerns regarding past and future research on the behavior of mentally retarded persons (Brooks & Baumeister, 1977a, 1977b; Gaylord-Ross, 1979; House, 1977). Although House (1977) lauds the contributions of basic research to the field of mental retardation, Brooks and Baumeister (1977b) and Gaylord-Ross (1979) have argued persuasively for a different type of research methodology. In their plea for ecological validity, Brooks and Baumeister note that laboratory research has not increased our understanding of the behavior of retarded individuals. They assert that subjects should be selected based on adaptive behavior rather than IQ scores, that experimental manipulations should take place in natural settings rather than in laboratory settings, and that dependent and independent variables should be selected on the basis of relevancy for functioning in the environment rather than relevancy in functioning in artificially controlled situations.

Gaylord-Ross (1979) expanded upon this theme, advocating that research embodying ecological validity would also have direct implications for the delivery of services to retarded persons. Gaylord-Ross also suggested that research should be longitudinal and should focus on multiple behaviors and covariation of behaviors.

With these points in mind, it would seem reasonable to suggest that a combination of the ecological approach and the behavioral approach would be most likely to satisfy concerns about considering the ecology of mentally retarded individuals, while still utilizing and improving applied behavioral training methodologies. There are, in fact, several similarities between an ecological approach and a behavioral approach that make the two readily unifiable. For example, both approaches emphasize the collection of empirical data on objectively defined behavior. Thus, both methods seek to quantify how organisms behave in an environment. The importance placed on the behavior-environment interaction is also evident in the two approaches. It is accepted that behavior is largely determined by environmental stimuli or previous experience with the environment and that changing environmental variables results in the modification of behavior (Michaels, 1974; Willems, 1974).

In light of these similarities, an ecobehavioral approach to community integration can be described. It should be noted that the term *ecobehavioral* is not new. Rogers-Warren (1977), Rogers-Warren and Warren (1977), Warren (1977), and Willems (1977) have all used the term. An ecobehavioral approach can be thought of as an evaluation strategy that assesses behavior-environment relationships and behavior interrelationships in the natural environment. From an educational or habilitative standpoint, the rationale for using an ecobehavioral approach for community integration is a) to select for change the most appropriate behaviors(s) that maximize community integration, b) to evaluate the change, and c) to increase the likelihood of generalization and maintenance.

Behavior-environment relationships and behavior interrelationships can be evaluated by both direct-observation and survey methods. Direct-observation methods include naturalistic observation of behaviors and environments by the change agent. Survey methods consist of subjective evaluations of behaviors and environments by individuals other than the change agent. Direct-observation and survey methods are two procedures used in social validation. Wolf (1978) proposed the idea of social validation as a method by which society determines the focus and judges the acceptability of intervention(s). Kazdin (1977) and, later, Kazdin and Matson (1981) discussed two methods of social validation: a) social comparison and b) subjective evaluation. Social comparison involves collecting direct measures of acceptable behavior to serve as a norm for adequate functioning. Subjective evaluation is described as a method to solicit opinions from knowledgeable persons in an environment regarding specifying important behaviors for change and evaluating the outcome of training.

Direct-Observation Methods

In an ecobehavioral approach direct-observation methods begin at a molar rather than a molecular level. That is, rather than measuring only one discrete target behavior for change in only one setting, and looking at that one behavior in relation to only immediate antecedent events, an ecological perspective prevails. The first step in this process entails viewing the target behavior within the framework of more complex behavioral patterns rather than as an isolated response. Voeltz and Evans (1982) suggested that assessment of behavioral inter-

relationships (or covariation of behaviors) needs to occur not only to select the most judicious behavior for change but also to know which behaviors to monitor for intended or unintended side effects after intervention begins. These authors postulate that by measuring behavioral interrelationships, one may find that the particular target behavior that has been pinpointed for possible intervention may not be controlled completely by environmental factors but, instead, is controlled by preceding or concurrent behavioral responses within the organism. The differential reinforcement of alternative behaviors (DRA), provides a good example of a targeted behavior (e.g., handflapping) that is decreased by the reinforcement of an alternative behavior (e.g., object manipulation). In this case, the behavior that might be selected for change (e.g., toy play) might not be the behavior that was first targeted for intervention. This situation would occur if it were found that another behavior, toy play, for example, was more amenable to intervention and also had simultaneous effects on the original behavior of concern—in this example, handflapping. This is but one way that a behavior might be chosen for intervention because of larger and more positive overall effects on the mentally retarded persons's behavioral repertoire (Voeltz & Evans, 1982).

The naturalistic observation of behavior-environment relationships in different settings is the second step in the direct-observation process. Both Bronfenbrenner (1977) and Wahler and Fox (1981) have stressed the importance of examining the interdependencies of more than one setting on an individual's behavior. Conceptually, the influence of setting can be thought of in several ways: a) the overall effect of the setting, b) the influence of other people in the setting, c) the time relationships between events in the setting, d) the physical elements of the setting, and e) setting-imposed limits.

Overall Effects of Settings As stated previously, certain settings dictate behaviors. For example, the behavior displayed by most people at a football game is very different from the behavior that would be displayed at church.

Whether or not mentally retarded persons exhibit differential behaviors in the different settings in their lives is important to assess. For example, Heller et al. (1981) found that setting variables exerted a strong influence on the social behavior of mentally retarded adults when they were newly admitted to sheltered workshops. That is, newly admitted clients to a more-sociable workshop exhibited more initial social behavior than newly admitted clients to a less-sociable workshop.

Influence of Other People in Setting Assessing the influence of others in various settings can be useful in several respects. First, individuals displaying appropriate behavior can function as a norm for validating training content and can also serve as a standard to evaluate intervention (Kazdin & Matson, 1981). For example, Nutter and Reid (1978) observed over 600 nonhandicapped women in various settings in order to determine the type of clothing and color selections they chose to wear. These clothing patterns then served as a norm by which to train mentally retarded women to choose appropriate color combinations of clothing. Similarly, O'Brien and Azrin (1972) used the mean number of mealtime errors made by nonhandicapped patrons in a restaurant to serve as a standard to evaluate mealtime instruction with mentally retarded persons in an institution. Both of these studies (Nutter & Reid, 1978; O'Brien & Azrin, 1972) suggest the usefulness of assessing representative others in natural environments. This same strategy, referred to as an ecological inventory strategy (Falvey, Brown, Lyon, Baumgart, & Schroeder, 1981), has also been suggested by Falvey et al. (1981) as a method to provide critical information regarding present and future school and community settings.

Individuals in different settings can also be observed to discover naturally occurring antecedent and consequent events. This information can be obtained by observing the interactions between nonhandicapped persons, between nonhandicapped and handicapped persons, and between handicapped persons— all in relation to target behavior selected for change. By viewing these relationships and describing the occurrence of specific antecedent and consequent events, the natural contingencies maintaining the target behavior can be discovered (Rogers-Warren, 1977). Stokes and Baer (1977) suggested this as one strategy to use to promote generalization. This concept has been further expanded through the addition of a decision-making strategy for the selection of cues and correction procedures to use when teaching severely handicapped students (Falvey et al., 1981).

Time Relationships Between Events in Setting In their discussion of setting events, Wahler and Fox (1981) suggested that there should be "no a priori assumptions concerning ideal or even necessary time spans between a suspected setting event and a particular target behavior" (p. 322). That is, behavior is not necessarily controlled only by immediate antecedents or consequences. To illustrate their point, Wahler and Fox cited a study conducted by Krantz and Risley (1977) in which a quiet play period that was scheduled prior to a group activity was found to increase attention. The temporally distant play period functioned as the stimulus controlling children's attention. Although the influence of the time of setting events has not been investigated extensively with mentally retarded persons, it is conceivable that setting events occurring minutes or even hours prior to a particular target behavior can function to control that behavior. For example, a physically or psychologically unpleasant bus ride for a mentally retarded student may be associated with an increase in noncompliance throughout the school day. Thus, it is worthwhile to consider the assessment of a range of prior setting events as being possible controlling stimuli for targeted behavioral patterns.

Physical Elements of Setting The physical environment (e.g., furniture, room arrangement, space available) can also potentially influence the target behavior (see, for example, Minuchin & Shapiro, 1982, for a review). For instance, furniture arrangement at a school party can increase or decrease social interactions, or small amounts of living space may increase aggressive acts. Thus, consideration should be given to the assessment of the physical elements of a setting and of their possible influence on behavior.

Setting-Imposed Limits Rogers-Warren (1977) has suggested that setting-imposed limits should be another facet of the ecobehavioral evaluation process. For example, if parents wanted their child to learn to climb stairs but there were no stairs in the school environment to practice on, then a stair-climbing program would need to be taught in a different environment. Thus, the lack of stairs in the school environment would be considered a setting-imposed limit for the acquisition of those behaviors needed for climbing stairs. Thoroughly assessing the setting prior to intervention procedures would possibly reveal potential barriers that could be altered, or at least recognized, before implementing the intervention.

Summary Directly observing the ecological environment of mentally retarded persons involves thoroughly assessing behavioral interrelationships and behavior-environment relationships in natural settings. Assessment of behavior interrelationships includes specification of a behavior or behavior patterns that either preceded, occurred concurrently with, or occurred after the target behavior. Evaluating such behavior interrelationships is suggested as a means to a more careful selection of the most appropriate behavior for change and to a determination of which other covarying behaviors to monitor for intended or unintended side effects after intervention.

The evaluation of the environment and its relationship and influence on behavior is conceptualized as a five-step process, including an assessment of: a) the overall effect of the setting, b) the influence of other people in the setting, c) the time sequences of events in the setting, d) the physical elements of the setting, and e) setting-imposed limits. The evaluation of the interdependencies between settings and behavior is viewed as an assessment strategy for selecting appropriate target behaviors for change that maximize integration, as a process for determining naturally occurring antecedents and consequences that maintain the target behavior, as a standard by which to evaluate

intervention procedures based upon normative values, and as a method for promoting generalization. Admittedly, this five-step process should only be considered a starting point for the direct observation of an environment.

Survey Methods

Both direct-observation and survey strategies can be used for similar purposes. That is, both can be used to select appropriate target behaviors and to evaluate the target behavior after intervention. They differ, however, in their methodology; direct observation involves naturalistic observation procedures, whereas survey methodology involves soliciting opinions from members of society. The use of survey methods, or subjective evaluation (Kazdin, 1977), to select the focus of intervention and to judge intervention effects has been particularly evident in the vocational training research with mentally retarded adults (Rusch & Schutz, 1981; White & Rusch, 1983).

Selecting the Focus of Intervention Instead of observing others (either nonhandicapped or handicapped persons) to determine the behaviors naturally displayed in varying settings, opinions from nonhandicapped or handicapped persons regarding important behaviors and the standards needed for successful functioning can be solicited. For example, Johnson and Mithaug (1978) and Mithaug and Hagmeier (1978) surveyed supervisors from five northwestern states and from Kansas to determine essential social and vocational skills needed for entry into sheltered employment. Supervisors were asked to rate behaviors in terms of importance for a variety of curricular areas (e.g., self-help/grooming skills, worker behavior skills, social/communication skills) so that a general list of instructional objectives could be identified for assessment and training purposes. In a similar manner, Rusch, Schutz, and Agran (1982) surveyed supervisors from light industrial occupations (e.g., packaging industries, electronics industries) and service occupations (e.g., janitorial service, food service, maid service) to determine social and vocational skills believed important for competitive employment.

Bates (1980) provided another example of seeking the opinions of others to validate training content. Bates asked significant others (e.g., house parents and work supervisors) to validate the content of a social skills, role-play assessment instrument for use with mentally retarded adults living in a group residential facility. First, individuals in the resident's environment were surveyed to determine commonly encountered situations involving interpersonal relationships. From the survey, two problematic situations were generated for each skill area. Then, for each problem, two parallel role-play activities were constructed. Sample responses to these situations were solicited from group home parents, other retarded adults, and experimenters. The responses were categorized into five content areas and subsequently rank ordered. The scenes from this role-play assessment, having been socially validated, were then used for training and measurement. Although new social skills were acquired and generalized to untrained role-play situations, these skills were not used in a more natural setting (e.g., grocery store).

In addition to using survey methods to validate the content of interventions, Menchetti, Rusch, and Lamson (1981) surveyed college and university food-service professionals regarding the acceptability of certain behavioral procedures used to train mentally retarded employees in a nonsheltered employment setting. These authors measured treatment acceptability in regard to data-collection procedures, error-correction techniques, behavior-management strategies, types and schedules of reinforcement, levels of instructional assistance, modification of work environment, and selection of social skills to be trained on the job.

Evaluating Intervention   Although objective data may reveal that a target behavior was successfully changed, change also must be judged meaningful by significant others. Significant others represent important persons who interact with mentally retarded persons on a daily basis and/or are believed particularly knowledgeable in a curricular area (e.g., workshop supervisors). For example, Kelly, Wildman, and Berler (1980) used restaurant managers from McDonald's Restaurants to rate pre-

and posttreatment interviews with mentally retarded adolescents. These authors also tape-recorded the job interviews and had other experienced personnel managers, who were naive to the purpose of the research, rate the tapes on a global criterion of effectiveness. These results, which were empirically and socially validated, showed that job-interview performance increased substantially over baseline levels after training.

"Consumer" satisfaction questionnaires were given to a variety of individuals (e.g., living unit staff, administrators, members of the local National Association for Retarded Citizens) in a study by Van Biervliet, Spangler, and Marshall (1981). These significant others watched videotapes of mentally retarded persons being served family style (i.e., passing food around a table) versus institutional style (i.e., picking up food-filled trays). In this study, mealtime language was found to increase as a result of the meals being served in family style. Social-validation measures also suggested that family-style procedures were preferred by consumers.

In another study, Rusch, Weithers, Menchetti, and Schutz (1980) asked coworkers to judge the effectiveness of a training protocol on the reduction of topic repetitions in one mentally retarded adult. At the end of the study, coworkers rated the number of topic repetitions higher than at any other previous point in the study, even though objective measures indicated repetitions were at an all-time low level. In this case, intervention procedures may not have been strong enough to alter the ratings of coworkers. The authors suggested several other possible reasons for the discrepancy between the objective and subjective measures of topic repetitions, including differing conceptualizations of the behavior being assessed and the time period in which the assessment was to take place. Thus, while surveys may provide relevant information, they may also provide biased and incorrect data.

Summary

An ecobehavioral approach assesses behavior interrelationships and behavior-environment relationships in natural environments via direct-observation or survey methods. A direct-observation measure is important to provide empirical evidence, while survey methods can subjectively document societal standards. Although Baer et al. (1968) suggested that these measures ought to hold equal weight as components of applied behavior analysis, it has been only recently, with the advent of social-validation methodology, that behavior analysts have begun to emphasize both measures. While both procedures are suited to assessing the ecological environment of mentally retarded and other handicapped persons, the social-validation component of each deserves further methodological, philosophical, and practical expansion (Kazdin & Matson, 1981).

IMPLICATIONS FOR TEACHING

Few mentally retarded persons, particularly those with moderate and severe handicaps, acquire and generalize skills as rapidly as non-handicapped persons. This does not mean, however, that moderately and severely handicapped persons cannot learn to function successfully in a variety of environments. In this chapter, an ecobehavioral approach was suggested as a way to evaluate training for mentally retarded persons to enable them to be integrated more successfully into community settings. Such an approach, which studies behavior interrelationships and behavior-environment relationships in natural contexts, provides important information regarding the essential behaviors necessary to function in community settings. Thus, when community integration skills are taught, information should be compiled regarding these essential community behaviors.

Empirically, little is known about those settings in which mentally retarded persons are being placed. For example, consider the case of a moderately mentally retarded girl who is going to receive the remainder of her educational experiences in a public high schoool. What are the skills she will need to function successfully in a gym class, in the lunchroom, or during assembly periods? What behaviors are needed to maximize interactions with other high school students? How do nonhandicapped

high school students behave? If these questions are not answered, school and community integration may result in placing unnecessarily rigid and/or expansive standards upon success.

A number of recent studies have incorporated ecobehavioral strategies to address questions regarding the environments that deinstitutionalized adults experience. These studies have provided information regarding behaviors and standards necessary for ultimate functioning (Brown, Nietupski, & Hamre-Nietupski, 1976) in these specified settings. Although the focus of this information has specific implications for community integration, it also has educational implications. Among them is the notion of life-span planning utilizing a top-down curriculum approach to educate severely handicapped students (Brown et al., 1979) and the related formation of individualized transition plans (Brown, Pumpian, Baumgart, Vandeventer, Ford, Nisbet, Schroeder, & Gruenewald, 1981). An individualized transition plan includes provisions for the acquisition of behaviors needed to function in a succession of environments. For example, certain skills would be taught in junior high school so that performance in high school would be as independent and productive as possible. Although this idea has logical appeal, it has not been sufficiently validated yet. As this approach is implemented, more will need to be learned about the essential behaviors required to function in different environments. One area in which this process has begun is that of employment education. Since many of the necessary social and vocational behaviors needed for successful employment have been identified, high school students (and younger) can be specifically trained in these areas of validated importance. This curricular approach is expanded upon by Rusch (1983), Wehman and McLaughlin (1980), and Wilcox and Bellamy (1982).

Clearly, an ecobehavioral approach has direct implications for the development and community integration of mentally retarded persons. The method is highly complementary to the principle of normalization, in that it recognizes the interrelatedness and mutual influences of the individual, the individual's behavior, and his or her environment. The ecobehavioral approach furthermore has intuitive validity as a methodology readily adaptable to the problems of training and integrating

mentally retarded persons into community settings. The near future should see considerable expansion of its empirical validation.

REFERENCES

Auerswald, E.H. Interdisciplinary versus ecological approach. In: W. Gray, F.J. Duhl, & N.D. Rizzo (eds.), *General systems theory and psychiatry*. Boston: Little, Brown & Co., 1969.

Baer, D.M., Wolf, M.M., & Risley, T.R. Some current dimensions of applied behavior analysis. *Journal of Applied Behavior Analysis*, 1968, *1*, 91–97.

Balla, D.A., Butterfield, E., & Zigler, E. Effects of institutionalization on retarded children: A longitudinal cross-institutional investigation. *American Journal of Mental Deficiency*, 1973, *77*, 654–669.

Barker, R.G. *Ecological Psychology*. Stanford: Stanford University Press, 1968.

Barton, E.S., Guess, D., Garcia, E., & Baer, D. Improvement of retardate's mealtime behaviors by timeout procedures using multiple baseline techniques. *Journal of Applied Behavior Analysis*, 1970, *3*, 77–84.

Bates, P. The effectiveness of interpersonal skills training on social skills: Acquisition of moderately and mildly retarded adults. *Journal of Applied Behavioral Analysis*, 1980, *13*, 237–248.

Berkson, G. Social ecology of supervised communal facilities for mentally disabled adults: V. Residence as a predictor of social and work adjustment. *American Journal of Mental Deficiency*, 1981, *86*, 39–42.

Berkson, G., & Romer, D. Social ecology of supervised communal facilities for mentally disabled adults: An Introduction. *American Journal of Mental Deficiency*, 1980, *85*(3), 219–228.

Birenbaum, A., & Re, M.A. Resettling mentally retarded adults in the community—almost four years later. *American Journal of Mental Deficiency*, 1979, *3*, 323–329.

Bjaanes, A.T., & Butler, E.W. Environmental variation in community care facilities for mentally retarded persons. *American Journal of Mental Deficiency*, 1974, *78*(4), 429–439.

Bronfenbrenner, U. Toward an experimental ecology of human development. *American Psychologist*, 1977, *32*, 513–531.

Brooks, P.H., & Baumeister, A.A. A plea for consideration of ecological validity in experimental psychology of mental retardation: A guest editorial. *American Journal of Mental Deficiency*, 1977a, *81*, 407–416.

Brooks, P.H., & Baumeister, A.A. Are we making a science of missing the point? *American Journal of Mental Deficiency*, 1977b, *81*, 543–546.

Brown, L., Branston, M.B., Hamre-Nietupski, S., Pumpian, I., Certo, N., & Gruenewald, L. A strategy for developing chronological age appropriate and functional curricular content for severely handicapped adolescents and young adults. *Journal of Special Education*, 1979, *13*, 81–90.

Brown, L., Nietupski, J., & Hamre-Nieptupski, S. The criterion of ultimate functioning and public school services for severely handicapped students. In: M.A.

Thomas (ed.), *Hey, don't forget about me: Education's investment in the severely, profoundly, and multiply handicapped*. Reston: VA: Council for Exceptional Children, 1976.

Brown, L., Pumpian, I., Baumgart, D., Vandeventer, P., Ford, A., Nisbet, J., Schroeder, J., & Gruenewald, L. Longitudinal transition plans in programs for severely handicapped students. *Exceptional Children*, 1981, *47*, 624–630.

Brunswik, E. Representative design and probabilistic theory in a functional psychology. *Psychological Review*, 1955, *62*, 193–217.

Butler, E.W., & Bjaanes, A.T. Activities and the use of time by retarded persons in community care facilities. In: G.P. Sackett (ed.), *Observing behavior*, Vol. 1: *Theory and applications in mental retardation*. Baltimore: University Park Press, 1978.

Dingman, H.F. A plea for social research in mental retardation. *American Journal of Mental Deficiency*, 1968, *72*, 2–4.

Falvey, M., Brown, L., Lyon, S., Baumgart, D., & Schroeder, J. Strategies for using cues and correction procedures. In: W. Sailor, B. Wilcox, & L. Brown (eds.), *Methods of instruction for severely handicapped students*. Baltimore: Paul H. Brookes Publishing Co., 1981.

Fox, R.M., & Azrin, N.H. The elimination of autistic self-stimulatory behavior by overcorrection. *Journal of Applied Behavior Analysis*, 1973, *6*, 1–14.

Gaylord-Ross, R. Mental retardation, ecological validity, and the delivery of longitudinal education programs. *Journal of Special Education*, 1979, *13*, 69–80.

Guess, D., Sailor, W., Rutherford, G., & Baer, D. An experimental analysis of linguistic development: The productive use of the plural morpheme. *Journal of Applied Behavior Analysis*, 1968, *1*, 294–306.

Heller, T., Berkson, G., & Romer, D. Social ecology of supervised communal facilities for mentally disabled adults: VI. Initial social adaptation. *American Journal of Mental Deficiency*, 1981, *86*, 43–49.

House, B.I. Scientific explanation and ecological validity: A reply to Brooks and Baumeister. *American Journal of Mental Deficiency*, 1977, *81*, 534–542.

Johnson, J.L., & Mithaug, D.E. A replication of sheltered workshop entry requirements. *AAESPH Review*, 1978, *3*, 116–122.

Kazdin, A.E. Assessing the clinical or applied importance of behavior change through social validation. *Behavior Modification*, 1977, *1*, 427–452.

Kazdin, A.E., & Matson, J.L. Social validation in mental retardation. *Applied Research in Mental Retardation*, 1981, *2*, 39–53.

Kelly, J.A., Wildman, B.G., & Berler, E.S. Small group behavioral training to improve the job interview skills repertoire of mildly retarded adolescents. *Journal of Applied Behavior Analysis*, 1980, *13*, 461–471.

Krantz, P.J., & Risley, T.R. Behavioral ecology in the classroom. In: S.G. O'Leary & K.D. O'Leary (eds.), *Classroom management: The successful use of behavior modification.* New York: Pergamon Press, 1977.

Landesman-Dwyer, S., Berkson, G., & Romer, D. Affiliation and friendship of mentally retarded residents in group homes. *American Journal of Mental Deficiency,* 1979, *83,*(6), 571–580.

Landesman-Dwyer, S., Sackett, G.P., & Kleinman, J.S. Relationship of size to resident and staff behavior in small community residences. *American Journal of Mental Deficiency,* 1980, *85*(1), 6–17.

Landesman-Dwyer, S., Stein, J., & Sackett, G. A behavioral and ecological study of group homes. In: G.P. Sackett (ed.), *Observing behavior,* Vol. 1: *Theory and applications in mental retardation.* Baltimore: University Park Press, 1978.

Lewin, K. Psychological ecology. In: D. Cartwright (ed.), *Field theory in social science.* New York: Harper & Brothers, 1951.

Martin, J.E., Rusch, F.R., & Heal, L.W. Teaching community survival skills to mentally retarded adults: A review and analysis. *Journal of Special Education,* 1982, *17,* 243–268.

Melstrom, M. Social ecology of supervised communal facilities for mentally disabled adults: VII. Productivity and turnover rate in sheltered workshops. *American Journal of Mental Deficiency,* 1982, *87,* 40–47.

Menchetti, B.M., Rusch, F.R., & Lamson, D.S. Social validation of behavioral training techniques: Assessing the normalizing qualities of competitive employment training procedures. *Journal of the Association for the Severely Handicapped,* 1981, *6,* 6–16.

Michaels, J.W. On the relation between human ecology and behavior social psychology. *Social Forces,* 1974, *57,* 313–321.

Minuchin, P.O., & Shapiro, E.K. The school as a context for social development. In: P.H. Mussen (ed.), *Handbook of Child Psychology* (4th ed.) Vol. 3 of *Social Development,* ed. E.M. Hetherington. New York: John Wiley & Sons, 1982.

Mithaug, D.E., & Hagmeier, L.D. The development of procedures to assess prevocational competencies of severely handicapped young adults. *AAESPH Review,* 1978, *3,* 94–115.

Nirje, B. The normalization principle and its human management implication. In: R. Kugel & W. Wolfensberger (eds.), *Changing patterns in residential services for the mentally retarded.* Washington, D C : President's Committee on Mental Retardation, 1969.

Nutter, D., & Reid, D.H. Teaching retarded women a clothing selection skill using community norms. *Journal of Applied Behavioral Analysis,* 1978, *11,* 475–487.

O'Brien, F., & Azrin, N.H. Developing proper mealtime behaviors of the institutionalized retarded. *Journal of Applied Behavioral Analysis,* 1972, *5,* 289–399.

Risley, T. The ecology of applied behavior analysis. In: A. Rogers-Warren & S.F. Warren (eds.), *Ecological perspectives in behavior analysis.* Baltimore: University Park Press, 1977.

Rogers-Warren, A. Planned change: Ecobehaviorally based interventions. In: A. Rogers-Warren & S.F. Warren (eds.), *Ecological perspectives in behavior analysis.* Baltimore: University Park Press, 1977.

Rogers-Warren, A., & Warren, S.F. The developing eco-

behavioral psychology. In: A. Rogers-Warren & S.F. Warren (eds.), *Ecological perspectives in behavior analysis.* Baltimore: University Park Press, 1977.

Romer, D., & Berkson, G. Social ecology of supervised communal faciliaties for mentally disabled adults: II. Predictors of affiliation. *American Journal of Mental Deficiency,* 1980a, *85*(3), 229–242.

Romer, D., & Berkson, G. Social ecology of supervised communal facilities for mentally disabled adults: III. Predictors of social choice. *American Journal of Mental Deficiency,* 1980b, *85*(3), 243–252.

Romer, D., & Berkson, G. Social ecology of supervised communal facilities for mentally retarded disabled adults: IV. Characteristics of social behavior. *American Journal of Mental Deficiency,* 1981, *86,* 28–38.

Rusch, F.R. Competitive employment. In: M. Snell (ed.), *Systematic instruction for the moderately and severely handicapped* (2d ed.). Columbus, OH: Charles E. Merrill Publishing Co., 1983.

Rusch, F.R., & Schutz, R.P. Vocational and social work behavior: An evaluative review. In: J.L. Matson & J.R. McCartney (eds.), *Handbook of behavior modification with the mentally retarded.* New York: Plenum Publishing Corp., 1981.

Rusch, F.R., Schutz, R.P., & Agran, M. Validating entry level survival skills for service occupations: Implications for curriculum development. *Journal of the Association for the Severely Handicapped,* 1982, *7,* 32–41.

Rusch, F.R., Weithers, J.A., Menchetti, B.M., & Schutz, R.P. *Education and Training of the Mentally Retarded,* 1980, *15,* 208–215.

Sajwaj, T., Twardosz, S., & Burke, M. Side effects of extinction procedures in a remedial preschool. *Journal of Applied Behavior Analysis,* 1972, *5,* 163–175.

Schoggen, P. Ecological psychology and mental retardation. In: G.P. Sackett (ed.), *Observing behavior* Vol. 1: *Theory and applications in mental retardation.* Baltimore: University Park Press, 1978.

Schutz, R.P., Vogelsberg, R.T., & Rusch, F.R. A behavioral approach to integrating individuals into the community. In: A.R. Novak & L.W. Heal (eds.), *Integration of developmentally disabled individauls into the community.* Baltimore: Paul H. Brookes Publishing Co., 1980.

Stokes, T.F., & Baer, D.M. An implicit technology of generalization. *Journal of Applied Behavior Analysis,* 1977, *10,* 349–367.

Van Biervliet, A., Spangler, P.F., & Marshall, A. An ecobehavioral examination of a simple strategy for increasing mealtime language in residential facilities. *Journal of Applied Behavior Analysis,* 1981, *14,* 295–305.

Voeltz, L.M., & Evans, I. The assessment of behavioral interrelationships in child behavior therapy. *Behavioral Assessment,* 1982, *4,* 131–165.

Wahler, R.G., & Fox, J.J. Setting events in applied behavior analysis: Toward a conceptual and methodological expansion. *Journal of Applied Behavior Analysis,* 1981, *14,* 327–338.

Warren, S.F., A useful ecobehavioral perspective for applied behavior analysis. In: A. Rogers-Warren & S.F. Warren (eds.), *Ecological perspectives in behavior analysis.* Baltimore: University Park Press, 1977.

Wehman, P., & Hill, J. Preparing severely handicapped youth for less restrictive environments. *Journal of the*

Association for the Severely Handicapped, 1982, *1,* 33–39.

Wehman, P., & McLaughlin, P.J. *Vocational curriculum for developmentally disabled persons.* Baltimore: University Park Press, 1980.

White, D., & Rusch, F.R. Issues in social validation: Evaluating work performance. *Applied Research in Mental Retardation,* 1983.

Wilcox, B., & Bellamy, G.T. *Design of high school programs for severely handicapped students.* Baltimore: Paul H. Brookes Publishing Co., 1982.

Willems, E.P. Behavioral technology and behavioral ecology. *Journal of Applied Behavior Analysis,* 1974, *7,* 151–165.

Willems, E.P. Steps toward an ecobehavioral technology. In: A. Rogers-Warren & S.F. Warren (eds.), *Ecological perspectives in behavior analysis.* Baltimore: University Park Press, 1977.

Willems, E.P., & Raush, H.L. *Naturalistic viewpoints in psychological research.* New York: Holt, Rinehart & Winston, 1969.

Wolf, M. Social validity: The case for subjective measurement or how applied behavior analysis is finding its heart. *Journal of Applied Behavior Analysis,* 1978, *11,* 203–214.

Wolfensberger, W. *The principle of normalization in human services.* Toronto: National Institute of Mental Retardation, 1972.

Part VI

_____

SUMMARY

Chapter 14

Perspectives and Prospects for Social and Educational Integration

Robert H. Bruininks and K. Charlie Lakin

O nly a few years ago persons who had worked hard through the 1970s to institute programs for handicapped persons were justifiably concerned. It was the International Year of the Disabled Person (1981) and America was celebrating it by watching the federal government attempt to cut the funding for or reduce the scope of much of the legislation and judicial decisions that had served as the basis for improved programs for handicapped persons in the previous decade. In time it became clearer that concerns about the impact of these efforts reflected an inadequate appreciation of the depth of social commitment that had served as a foundation for the earlier gains of handicapped persons. To be sure, there have been some negative shifts in public policy toward handicapped persons at all governmental levels since 1980, but is is perhaps now better understood that uphill marches have their occasional steps backward, and that—whatever the motive for the attempted reductions—such steps back have value in compelling reevaluation of what existing programs have accomplished. In recent months, some funding has been restored in federal and state programs, and the Reagen administration has proclaimed the 1980s the "Decade of the Disabled."

Much of the concern over whether the major social advances in behalf of handicapped persons in the 1970s would survive the 1980s has now dissipated.

The uncertainties of the first years of the "Decade of the Disabled" have impressed upon many the frequent need to reexamine and provide renewed commitment for the principles and goals of social programs for handicapped citizens. The recent challenges to these programs were met by coalitions of parents, advocates, professionals, and allies of handicapped persons that were unprecedented in their size and resolve, thus helping to assure that society's commitment to handicapped persons and their families will remain firm for the rest of the decade. But continued support, particularly when other needful groups have fared less well, places greater responsibility on service institutions—whether federal, state, or local—to provide services that reflect the contemporary vision of what social programs should be accomplishing with severely handicapped persons.

For the remainder of the 1980s, services will be judged on their effectiveness in continuing to promote deinstitutionalization and integration of severely handicapped persons in our society. While it is now generally accepted, even by those who initially opposed it, that the desegregation of educational, residential, and other activities for mildly and moderately handicapped persons has been a successful social policy, many still maintain that segregated schools, isolated residential institutions, and other forms of separation remain justifiable for severely and profoundly impaired persons. These people claim that protective care is a valid social response to human limitations, since without it thousands of handicapped individuals would be or could be "dumped" into community settings with inadequate support or concern for their welfare. It is further contended that there is no way to prove that severely handicapped persons are better off when integrated into the society than when segregated from it. Although a growing body of research disputes such assertions (see Rotegard, Bruininks, Gorder, & Lakin in this volume), perhaps the most relevant counterclaim is the one contained in the United Nations General Assembly 1975 Declaration on the Rights of Mentally Retarded Persons and the Rights of Disabled Persons:

> Disabled persons have the inherent right to respect for their human dignity. Disabled persons, whatever the origin, nature and seriousness of their handicaps and disabilities, have the same fundamental rights as their fellow citizens of the same age, which implies first and foremost the right to enjoy a decent life, as normal and full as possible (in United Nations General Assembly, 1977, p. 411).

Professional practices in regard to handicapped persons, and the social and fiscal policies that sustain those practices, are justifiable only insofar as they preserve rights to dignity and normality in life experiences. This volume has sought to outline social, philosophical, and research bases of evolving standards of care and treatment of handicapped children and youth and to identify means of determining whether contemporary services are meeting these standards. Also discussed, but with somewhat less emphasis, are social policies that can be instituted at various levels of government to promote the implementation of the best contemporary standards and practices in service of these rights. These social policies are more directly the focus of this chapter.

IDEOLOGICAL BASES OF POLICY

Changes in human services provisions for severely handicapped persons in the past two decades have occurred largely as the result of a significant civil rights movement and concomitant changes in social perceptions of the rights and potential of persons with disabilities. It often appears from casual observation that current human services provisions primarily reflect the purposes and expertise of professionals responding to people whose needs they are trained to know. However, the history of response to handicapped citizens shows clearly that the goals and objectives of care and treatment have derived more from prevailing political and social perceptions than from a rational response to human needs. When such perceptions have been progressive, handicapped persons have generally benefited through improved and expanded services. When conservative or regressive orientations have prevailed, responses to disabilities and handicaps have generally led to neglect, isolation, and deprivation of basic civil liberties. Appreciating the power of social and political forces over the lives of handicapped persons is essential. Only the most naive can continue to believe that program quality can be improved without forward-looking changes in the social attitudes and fiscal policies that determine the purpose, locus, nature, and intensity of programs.

As noted in the first chapter in this book, the policies of deinsititutionalization and of mainstreaming must be perceived within the larger context of the civil rights and equal rights movements in the United States. It is also true that these broad social movements have been aided by specific philosophical and policy orientations of programs for handicapped subpopulations within the larger group of people against whom society has traditionally discriminated, as reflected in the concepts of *normalization* and placement in the *least restrictive environment* (mainstreaming). Although these concepts increasingly are evolving into ongoing national social policy and are providing direction to considerable changes in services to handicapped persons, they are not always consistently applied nor, for that matter, are they uniformly understood in educational and human service programs.

In Chapter 2 in this volume, Bachrach emphasized that in the tradition of early general semanticists, ambiguity often accompanies the terms *normalization* and *least restrictive environment*. Critics questioning the viability of these concepts for handicapped persons have pointed to the absence of irrefutable evidence for the developmental benefits of deinstitutionalization, of placement in community-based living arrangements, or of educational integration. Such questioning, while stimulating profitable debate, often misses the essential point that such concepts do not refer to static states. Rather, the primary force of these concepts is in their recognition of handicapped citizens' common rights to standard social opportunities that cannot justifiably be superceded by responses to their particular disabilities (Nirje, 1976; Wolfensberger, 1980). These concepts refer to the contexts, goals, and processes that should guide service programs that recognize that the society into which handicappped children are born is the same as that of their nonhandicapped peers. Such an orientation directs people to ask not whether placements in integrated settings ''work'' but how they can be made to work. At issue, after all, is which agency managers and service providers, providing what services, to clients of what kinds of specific needs, in what kinds of integrated settings, and under what kind of administrative and fiscal arrangements can make them work better. Indeed, it is fair to ask why those professionals and program administrators who claim that such placements will not be successful are not challenged to embrace a philosophy that includes concepts of *normalization* and *least restrictive environment*. Certainly among the most crucial decisions affecting the integration of handicapped persons are the ones that place or fail to place in positions of leadership persons with a high enough

commitment to integration to make federal, state, local, and neighborhood programs work to that end.

However, commitment to integration need not be built only on appeals to human values. It can also be developed through professional values—through expectations that professional practices conform to the knowledge base of the profession, a knowledge base that increasingly indicates that the most effective teaching of skills of daily living is that which occurs in the environment in which the skills must be used. Habilitation and education are professional concepts, and it is clear that minimal standards of professional activity include valuing the importance of environmental conditions in which activities of education and habilitation are being carried out. In a general sense, failure to maximize training opportunities for handicapped persons in integrated settings represents professional failure to adequately prepare people for integrated settings. In assessing the efforts of state and local agency professionals, it seems reasonable to hold such professionals accountable for professional practices that are roughly equivalent to expecting that medical training should take place in hospitals or clinics, that driver training should take place in a motor vehicle, or that television-repair training should take place in an electrical repair shop.

To improve the knowledge base supporting integration efforts, there is clearly a need for more precise definitional and measurement practices to assess the environmental qualities of service programs. Much of the knowledge to date has emphasized simple physical features of environments, such as size and extent of privacy with relatively little attention given to the identifiable qualities of environments that facilitate acquisition, maintenance, and generalization of skills that are essential to development, to adjustment, and to increased reciprocity with other society members. Researching these other factors would include examining environmental aspects associated with the qualities of interaction of severely handicapped persons with one another and with nonhandicapped people, the organization and use of available natural reinforcements, arrangement of space and other physical features, the amount and types of community participation, and types of natural and planned interventions to increase daily living skills. Several chapters in this volume (e.g., those by Landesman-Dwyer, Chadsey-Rusch, and Rotegard et al.) stressed the importance of considering the total ecology of environments as important, complex, and multivariate aspects of facilitating the adjustment of severely handicapped persons to less-restrictive settings. Research on the treatment practices and other events that affect the daily lives and living skills of handicapped persons must likewise share this consideration. Progress in this area can occur much more rapidly given increased precision both in the concepts and contexts studied and in the practices for measuring them, as pointed out by Heal in Chapter 11.

Another major problem regarding the development of the knowledge base is a continuing tendency to dwell on issues irrelevant to handicapped persons' present status and needs. For example, in reviewing current studies and arguments, one notes considerable emphasis applied to attempting to determine whether normalization "works," rather than to discovering effective means of enhancing the capabilities and opportunities of handicapped citizens to live in culturally normal environments. A curious fact and one that is perhaps largely symptomatic of today's conservative trend is that efforts to reform practices to better reflect egalitarian values toward handicapped persons are requested to provide evidence demonstrating efficacy, while both the *lack* of evidence supporting the efficacy for *prevailing* practices and the wealth of evidence demonstrating numerous generalizable negative effects are ignored. Although the need to examine the efficacy of programs ostensibly promoting integration is crucial, this cannot be done without a simultaneous appreciation both of what has already been learned about the alternatives (that have made the development of integrated, community-based programs so imperative), and of the need to focus our energies more fully to discover means for improving current practice.

The philosophical principles of *normalization, least restrictive environment,* and *mainstreaming* reflect social and professional values rather than concrete standards. Assessing their efficacy, to paraphrase Ian Mitroff (cited in Zaltman & Duncan, 1977), is akin to creating the statistical "error of the third kind"— the probability of solving the wrong problem. It bears reemphasizing that the issue is no longer one of whether these principles can be operationalized to work but of how they can be made to work better. The changing focus of researchers toward assessing the effect of multivariate and dynamic environmental qualities upon behavior and upon the acquisition and maintenance of skills in normalized settings reflects a promising direction for expanding knowledge that can improve the state of contemporary and future practices.

Noninstitutionalization

Kiesler (1982) notes with regard to the care and treatment of mentally ill patients that deinsitituionalization as social policy has only partially reflected the proposition that large, physically isolated institutions are ineffective and inappropriate settings for providing habilitative services. The stark and counterproductive realities of such institutional settings have for years been richly documented and widely publicized (e.g., Blatt, 1970, 1973; Goffman, 1961), with the result that a dramatic social and professional shift has occurred away from institutional care and toward care models that emphasize community-based programs with a focus on normalized living patterns, community participation, purposeful daytime activities, and expanded use of nonprofessionalized services. But in large measure the social policy formulation of deinstitutionalization has not served the ideology well. It has somehow been found semantically tolerable to define deinstitutionalization as a process involving three components: 1) preventing institutional admissions, 2) returning institutionalized residents to community settings, and 3) improving the conditions of residence and habilitation for those persons who remain institutionalized (NASPRFMR, 1974). Accepting the final component of the definition as part of the general social policy has created a vacuum of meaning in which keeping people in improved institutional settings is part of the same process as getting them out into less restrictive settings. Such nonpurposeful social policy has led to states spending nearly $2 billion in the last few years on the physical plants of state institutions (NASMRPD, 1980; Scheerenberger, 1982, 1983), when such funds would have tremendously aided efforts at undertaking a policy of noninstitutionalization. In the meantime, barring the passage of legislation directly affecting the reimbursement system for institutional services, thousands of persons can be expected to remain institutionalized as states recoup their capital improvement costs through years of Medicaid reimbursements for institutional care. The situation is particularly tragic in that efforts to affect legislation that would decrease federal funding of institutions and make those funds available for community-based settings face sizable opposition from those same states. There is every reason to question the values of legislators who are more concerned about bond amortization than about their responsibility to provide care that meets contemporary standards of appropriateness and habilitative potential.

The negative long-term effects of institutional placement have been empirically established for mental hospital patients (see Kiesler, 1982) and for residents of state institutions for mentally retarded persons (see Pilewski & Heal, 1980). In both types of institutions, the single best predictor of future institutional placement is whether people have previously been residents of these same institutions (Kiesler, 1982; Rotegard & Bruininks, 1983). Recognizing that institutional placements are incongruous with the sentiments, if not of all the definitions, of deinstitutionalization, several states (e.g., New Hampshire, Rhode Island, Vermont, as well as the District of Columbia) have completely or virtually eliminated placements into such facilities. But a number of federal and state policies continue to promote institutional placements under an incomprehensibly broad conceptualization of deinstitutionalization. It should be obvious, however, that it is simply no longer tolerable to

conduct deinstitutionalization linguistically. Improved institutions are still institutions; calling them "public residential facilities" or bringing them into compliance with minimum standards for Medicaid participation does not alter that reality, as numerous recent court decisions have shown (see chapters by Laski and by Bradley in this volume for discussions of these cases). A concerted effort toward sharply focused federal and state policies of noninstitutionalization is now needed.

Those concerned both with the right of severely handicapped persons to nonconfinement in the absence of committed social ill and with the related development of community-based care have begun to insist on government's use of reimbursement to promote noninstitutional care. For example, national legislation supported by the Association for Retarded Citizens and introduced in November, 1983, by Senator John Chaffee as the "Community Living Amendments of 1983" would phase out Medicaid funding for larger institutions (16 or more residents) over a fixed time period. At the same time the legislation would require maintenance of current federal Medicaid standards of care in state institutions and increase the federal match of state funds during the first years of an extra-institutional placement. The impact of such legislation would be enormous. For example, of the 143,150 Medicaid-reimbursed beds in residential facilities for mentally retarded persons as of June 30, 1982, fewer than 10,000 were in facilities of 1–15 residents (unpublished data of the Center for Residential and Community Services, University of Minnesota, 1983). The scope of this legislation, which proposes to move over 100,000 Medicaid recipients from their present placements, as well as to eliminate Medicaid funding for state institutions and to open eligibility for a Medicaid benefit to hundreds of thousands of severely handicapped persons not now served under Medicaid, will probably generate significant opposition and amendments. However, even if not as successful as many now hope, the proposed legislation has served to refocus public attention on the need to examine the ways that institutionalization has been propagated by federal policy. It furthermore emphasizes the need to formulate policies of noninstitutionalization—for example, by not allowing Medicaid eligibility for any person moving from a community-based facility (family or small extrafamilial setting) to a state or private facility with more than 15 residents, or by requiring that parents' income be taken into account in institutional settings in determining Medicaid eligibility so that institutional placements do not become preferable to parents for financial reasons. All such proposals share the sense that, as a major shaper of how and where handicapped persons are served in this society, the federal government should maintain policies that enhance, rather than reduce, the probability that individuals will be placed in settings that recognize and protect their best interests. When disincentives for institutional care are used in concert with more value-neutral opportunities for states to initiate their own efforts to better serve present populations with existing funding—such as that available through the Medicaid Home and Community Based Services waiver program (Greenberg, Schmitz, & Lakin, 1983)—the federal government can provide both mechanisms and inducements for states to improve their services systems.

As the populations of state and private institutions continue to become more severely handicapped, the claim that reasonable goals for the policy of deinstitutionalization have been largely attained will continue. Such "realistic" appraisals of the natural limits of efforts to depopulate state institutions can be documented from the middle of this century on. In 1946 A. W. Pense noted in New York that

> there has been a decrease in the proportion of patients with higher intellectual endowment in the institutional population. . . . For obvious reasons efforts to adjust the feeble-minded to the community have been more successful with the higher mentality patients. This tends to increase the institutional residue of low grade cases (p. 455).

Pense's "residue," and the "residual populations" of institutions spoken of in more recent years differ only in the fact that, as years

have passed, more and more members of the "residual population" of previous eras now live outside of institutions. Nevertheless, many program planners and evaluators continue to suggest that there be

> simple acknowledgement that successful deinstitutionalization is becoming more difficult to realize and that deinstitutionalization rates are likely to decline . . . [and] that deinstitutionalization goals should be reevaluated based on a consideration of the characteristics of the clients available for placement and on the capabilities of the community to provide the services they need (Mayeda & Sutter, 1981, pp. 379–380).

Two major shortcomings can be seen in the recurrent observation that the depopulation of institutional settings will eventually dwindle to a trickle, leaving behind those for whom only an institution can provide the needed level of care. First, had it ever been fully accepted in one of its past variations, the movement to depopulate state institutions would never have attained anywhere near its present level of success. Second, such a perspective continues to approach community-setting placements of handicapped persons in terms of a responsibility on the part of the client to successfully adjust to available community settings. Such a perspective is a vestige of the days when handicapped citizens bore the burden of proving themselves worthy of living in the community, with few people asking how well the same persons were "adjusting" to institutions. Today, after more than half a century of research, it is increasingly recognized that successful adjustment to any placement is better predicted by the ability of the service setting and its care providers to adjust the demands of that setting to the needs and abilities of their clients than it is by assessed capabilities of those clients (Cobb, 1972; Lakin, Bruininks, & Sigford, 1981; McCarver & Craig, 1974). Institutionalized populations reflect more the extent of failure of the services systems to adapt than they do deficiencies in their own adaptive potential. Nothing demonstrates this better than the wide variability among states in the proportions of their severely/profoundly retarded residential population living in community-based settings.

As persons with greater needs are placed in community-based settings, the evidence is more unequivocal that few if any client conditions are not amenable to some form of community-based care. Yet, it also appears clear that where national and state policies fail to specifically promote community-based care through an explicit policy of noninstitutionalization, inertia is difficult to overcome. A specifically formulated policy of noninstitutionalization, with incentives that promote alternative forms of care, could greatly assist the continued promotion of practices that bring about meaningful integration of severely handicapped citizens and, through their integration, improved opportunities for habilitation. Thompson and Wray (in Lakin & Bruininks, in press) point out well that efforts focused at this "policy level" must be viewed by those concerned with the well-being of handicapped persons as equally essential and worthy of planned intervention as are efforts to meet the individual needs of clients.

Nonsegregation in Education

Closely related to the issues of deinstitutionalization and noninstitutionalization is the issue of educational integration. Not unlike the "top-down" implementation of the least restrictive alternative in residential programs (in which least-impaired persons are integrated first and most severely impaired persons last), educational integration efforts have been viewed largely as programs for relatively mild and moderately impaired students. Virtually all of the 68% of handicapped students participating in regular education classes in the United States in 1979–1980 were from this group (Pyecha, 1980). However, even though no data exist on the extent of regular class participation of severely handicapped children and youth, there are indications that educational programs for these students are being brought closer to the mainstream. For example, the percentage of all handicapped students of school age (6–17 years) educated in separate schools and other noneducational settings (e.g., hospitals) decreased from 7.9% (313,000) to 6.0% (233,371) between the 1976–1977 and 1980–

1981 school years (U.S. Department of Education, 1983, p. 136). These have traditionally been the placements of the most severely handicapped children and youth.

Severely handicapped children and youth not only share rights to education with their nonhandicapped peers, they also share the need to learn how to function in their community. As has been shown with nonhandicapped learners, direct instruction is the most consistently effective teaching strategy (Becker, 1977; Rosenshine, 1977; Stallings, 1979). Direct training and experience with a specific skill in the actual setting in which it is to be performed enhance acquisition (see Rusch & Mithaug in Lakin & Bruininks, in press). But as Liberty (in Lakin & Bruininks, in press) has thoroughly discussed, educating severely handicapped students requires particular concern for teaching and assessing students' abilities to maintain, to generalize, and to adapt what they have been taught to other settings and other times. Efficiency is demanded in the education and training of severely handicapped students, and it is well validated that the required levels of efficiency of instruction can be provided most effectively at the intersection of important life functions and the social settings in which those functions are to be demonstrated.

The developmental model of instruction in areas such as self-help, motor, and communication delivered within segregated settings is increasingly recognized as not only an unwarranted deprivation of normal social opportunity but also an inefficient means of promoting the maximum independence of severely handicapped people. The more effective curricula for individuals are less often based on the presumption that there is a general path of development through which all children should be led and more often predicated on the view that priorities should be established from each individual's specific immediate- and future-needed behavioral repertoire in order for the individual to function as well as possible in his or her natural community. This modern understanding of the role of the environment in developing the abilities of handicapped persons continues to place high importance on teaching, but also increasingly looks to the setting in which that education is delivered as a mutual condition of effective instruction. Today the need for an education that is not confined to experiences within a special school or a particular room of a school—where the experiences and models of behavior are almost exclusively abnormal—is becoming much more widely recognized. Appropriate educational experiences for severely handicapped students are increasingly defined as ones that take place in a variety of normal school and community environments with the most normal support services possible (e.g., travel to school in regular school buses, use of school resources such as libraries and gymnasiums); that teach students the specific skills needed to function as competently as they are able in typical community settings; that provide opportunities for interaction with nonhandicapped peers in environments where culturally normal, age-appropriate behavior predominates; and that emphasize the use of acquired skills in culturally normal environments of daily living where these skills can be more meaningfully practiced and reinforced. When such standards are applied to educational programs, students not only are able to improve their general rates of acquisition, maintenance, and generalization of skills, but they do so while acquiring skills that have clear value in their present and future daily lives.

Like noninstitutionalization, nonsegregation in education and training programs is an easily justified goal for social policy. The related-services provision of Public Law 94-142, requiring "transportation, and such developmental, corrective, and other supportive services . . . as may be required to benefit from special education" (Section 602.17) and by implication education in the least restrictive alternative, are an example of federal policy supporting integration of severely handicapped persons. However, this provision has been seen by many school districts as a virtual Pandora's box of potentially costly services. In theory the educational plans developed by school personnel in cooperation with parents should be constructed around the educational and related services needed to provide the most

highly integrated, appropriate education possible without consideration of their costs, whereas in reality costs appear often to be the primary consideration (Sterns, Green, & David, 1980, 1981). For example, commenting on the related services provision in Public Law 94-142, one school psychologist is reported to have remarked: "Laws like this pervade the atmosphere with 'let's be careful.' I no longer tell parents what I think is best for the child" (Sterns et al., 1980, p. 96). Of course, restricted interpretation of federally legislated services when the burden of paying for those services is predominantly borne at the local and state level should not be unexpected. Such an interpretation has been reinforced in the past in that during the period in which the domain of related services was being expanded, in each fiscal year the ratio of federal dollars appropriated to the dollars originally authorized in Public Law 94-142 decreased, to a level of less than one-third in fiscal year 1981 (General Accounting Office, 1981). Further caution in this area has been created by various court interpretations of the related-services provision to include summer programs, physical therapy, psychotherapy, and other services that are often questionably related to educational attainment and/or that are outside the traditionally mandated responsibilities of local schools. In an effort to realize the intent of the related services provision, the U.S. Department of Education should be encouraged to provide means of supplementing local and state expenditures for related services and to specify more clearly the types of services that are allowable under this provision. In so doing, careful attention should be given to alternatives such as those developed by states under the Medicaid Home and Community Based Services waiver program. For example, the waiver program permits states to use Medicaid funds for one-time, one-client, annual capitated expenditure for renting, buying, or building a specific apparatus or structural modification to maintain clients in a less-restrictive and, over the long run, less-costly setting. If special education amendments would permit a much more generous federal share of the payment for the relatively uncommon but often significant costs for special apparatus or modification of settings, the related-services intent of Public Law 94-142 would have a much greater likelihood of being carried out in spirit and in reality. Nothing detracts more from the accomplishments of Public Law 94-142 than the vision of a school superintendent and school board fighting with all the resources available to them a request by parents and advocates of a handicapped child that he or she be able to attend a school that is fully accessible in a wheelchair. Neither is it reasonable to maintain the related-services provision as an ambiguous cornucopia under which virtually any service can be sought with an argument that it in some way enhances the ability to benefit from special education.

The related-services provision was one of the most creative aspects of Public Law 94-142. With it, extraordinary services could be provided to individual students who but for those services would experience a considerably more restrictive educational experience. However, there is little support for the benefits of many related services, and current funding for these services is simply too low to encourage the creative use that this provision deserves. One direct way that federal and/or state governments should address the related-services problem in order to better serve the process of integration is to authorize and reimburse related services through an independent administrative program and at a substantially higher funding rate. In the meantime state and local agencies must seek ways to innovatively combine federal, state, and local funding systems to provide sufficient funding to ensure that the critical concept underlying related services is not lost in the difficulty of finding an agency eager to foot the bill (see Copeland and Iversen, in Lakin & Bruininks, in press, for a detailed description of strategies for pooling funds).

An example of a policy that supports integrated experiences for handicapped children and youth is the 1975 amendment (Public Law 93-380) of Public Law 89-313. This amendment allows the federal funds available for edu-

cational programs in state institutions to follow deinstitutionalized children and youth into local school districts. In 1979 about 25,000 students (most of whom were mentally retarded persons) were served in over 3,000 local school districts under this authorization at an average federal supplement of $578 per student (Bureau of Education for the Handicapped, 1979). Although no data are available on the nature of the education programs these students received, it is hard to imagine how they could have failed to be considerably more integrated than students in the state institutions.

In addition to the related-services provision and funds for schooling of deinstitutionalized students, another example of a national commitment to integrate severely handicapped children and youth is the Severely Handicapped Children and Youth Program of the Special Education Programs office. This program supports the development of models to integrate severely handicapped children and youth in normal school settings and to disseminate information about effective services. Many of these programs have been instrumental in demonstrating that effective integration of severely handicapped children and youth can be accomplished with benefits to all (see Brown, Branston, Hamre-Nietupski, Johnson, Wilcox, & Gruenwald, 1979). Still, despite these provisions, there are neither direct federal incentives in Public Law 89-313 and Public Law 94-142 for utilizing the state-of-the-art practices identified, developed, and/or demonstrated by these projects, nor any disincentives for maintaining unnecessarily segregated programs. The formulation of such incentives and disincentives would be a ready means of promoting cost-effective, socially desirable educational practices.

IMPLEMENTATION ISSUES

It appears likely that in the future the role of federal and state courts in prompting the integration of severely handicapped persons will be considerably diminished (see chapters by Laski and Bradley in this volume). Correspondingly greater responsibility will be placed on policy making and on implementing agencies to effect goals maintained for severely handicapped persons. Currently, the realization of deinstitutionalization and of least restrictive placement goals is beset by a number of problems. According to one viewpoint, the record of residential services in the past several years is one of decreasing institution populations, reduced size of facilities, and dramatic increases in foster home and other small community-centered placements. Yet, despite such apparent progress, slightly over half of the severely/profoundly retarded persons in supervised residential placements live in government-operated facilities of 64 or more residents (Center for Residential and Community Services, 1983). While the trends are favorable, there remains a failure to develop social policy sufficiently robust to fully realize desired social ends. This failure is not centered solely on the issues of physically depopulating the larger state and private facilities and of creating correspondingly more community-based placements. The problems evident in providing community-based residential and human services care to severely handicapped persons are also related to such areas as personnel preparation and retention, adequacy and stability of funding, coordination of resident programs among service agencies, identification of needed services, monitoring and regulatory practices, client and program evaluation, and the interrelationships among all of these important program aspects (Bradley, 1978; Bruininks, Hauber, & Kudla, 1979; Bruininks, Thurlow, Thurman, & Fiorelli, 1980; Gettings, 1977; Lakin et al., 1981; Muzzio, Koshel, & Bradley, 1981). Without substantial improvement in solving many of these problems, public policies of integration stand little chance of being as successful as has been desired. The major issues comprising an effective, full-scale policy of social integration of severely handicapped persons are highly interrelated and can only be resolved properly if approached in concert. These issues are discussed extensively in Lakin and Bruininks (in press).

Barriers to Implementation: A View from the Field

Many of the important barriers to implementing progressive policies and effective practices for severely handicapped children and youth were addressed by 25 participants at a three-day working conference on Deinstitutionalization and Education of Handicapped Children and Youth, held in Minneapolis in November, 1982 (Bruininks & Putnam, 1983). The participants included parents and professionals, researchers, and administrators from a variety of fields including education, law, social work, mental health, psychology, and economics. Through a carefully structured format, participants generated conclusions and recommendations regarding *status and trends in services, priorities for research and development,* and *recommendations for improving policies and practices*. Separate working groups considered these issues within one of three areas: *government policy, management of services,* and *interventions* provided handicapped individuals and their families.

Throughout the conference, technical papers and discussions were devoted to the issues of providing more effective living and learning opportunities for severely handicapped persons. Approximately 60 conclusions and recommendations were generated through this process (see, for example, Bruininks & Putnam, 1983, for a more complete summary). These conclusions identified some of the following ideas for improving service effectiveness.

1. The social and ecological conditions of training program sites must continually be made more similar to the conditions of daily living to enhance the acquisition and transfer of skills by severely handicapped individuals to natural settings.

2. Substantial improvements are needed in the assessment of clients and evaluation of programs. Monitoring and reimbursement systems should assess client outcomes as

well as input and process characteristics of service programs.

3. Significant changes are needed in public management to reduce disincentives and increase incentives for adopting state-of-the-art service practices. Funding should be tied to clients rather than agencies, and flexibility should be increased for agencies to combine resources across categorically organized service programs. Service integration at the service agency and client levels must be improved.

4. The current research agenda with respect to deinstitutionalization and education of handicapped persons must be improved through more careful study of alternative service programs and treatment strategies. The state of research on the implementation of public policies is also inadequate, and management information systems to inform and improve decisions and for researching and disseminating needed information on successful practices should be strengthened at all levels.

Consistently throughout these discussions, the view was expressed that policy development, organizational changes, management practices, treatment strategies, and funding approaches had not kept pace with the growing adherence to integration implicit in the concepts of normalization, mainstreaming, and placement in the least restrictive environment. The ideas generated reflected an uncertain prognosis regarding the prospects for truly coordinating services and integrating handicapped citizens into society. Conference members consistently identified the same problems as endemic to current service programs and also displayed remarkable agreement on the solutions they proposed. To improve the implementation of policies, changes were recommended throughout the service delivery system. Participants did not cite isolated problems but identified broader relationships among policies, regulations, public management, and service provision. Starting with a recommendation to reaffirm principles currently articulated in national and state policies, as a needed foundation, other recommendations pointed to a desire to identify and adopt straightforward and currently feasible strategies to improve services and opportunities for handicapped citizens.

THE FUTURE

There is little question that the past 20 years have produced much progress in expanding integration of handicapped persons into more normal settings through significant changes in policies and practices of educational, residential, and other human service programs. Throughout this volume progress has been noted, along with reference to problems that remain in providing effective and more integrated service programs. The importance of understanding the present context of services assumes special meaning when juxtaposed against future scenarios for the evolution of human services. With all major social movements, initial bursts of energy and dramatic changes are often succeeded by later periods of consolidation, bureaucratization of gains, surfacing of active resistance to innovation, and even inertia. Through careful assessment of current issues and informed anticipation of future trends, it is hoped that the prospects for future improvements in the social and educational integration of handicapped persons can be enhanced.

Predicting the future in any area is, at best, an uncertain undertaking. However, systematic attempts to project the future can often assist in improving policy formation and management of service programs. Putnam and Bruininks (1984) recently completed a Delphi forecasting survey to assess trends related to the future of deinstitutionalization and educational services for handicapped persons. The survey was designed to analyze the views of well-informed individuals through two rounds of mailed questionnaires that asked participants to clarify issues, set goals, and forecast future events (Dalkey & Helmer, 1963; Delbecq, Van de Ven, & Gustafson, 1974). This procedure is useful because it provides participation of diverse groups without the biasing influence of strong personalities or judgments of others; controlled feedback to participants; inclusion of participants in different locations; and statistical analysis of responses. A total of 33 people from several different states and with strong reputations, responsibilities, and interest in educational and human services for handicapped individuals participated in the study. They represented state and federal policy makers and managers, local directors and managers, advocacy organizations, parents, and university researchers.

The initial questionnaire contained 73 statements divided into one of eight categories: 1) philosophical and conceptual trends, 2) legal trends, 3) residential and educational services, 4) service system perspectives, 5) financial considerations, 6) intervention strategies, 7) personnel preparation and program staffing, and 8) attitudes. Ratings were solicited from the respondents on the two dimensions of *likelihood of occurrence* and *desirability*. The likelihood ratings were projected in specific time intervals, generally in periods of 5 years, between 1983 and the year 2000. Desirability ratings ranged on a five-point scale from *extremely undesirable* to *extremely desirable*. Two separate rounds were conducted of the Delphi survey. In the survey, consensus on occurrence of a trend was considered to be achieved when 70% or more of the respondents had predicted its implementation. Only a few projected trends are highlighted in this chapter.

First, panel members strongly affirmed the desirability of programming in the least restrictive environment for all handicapped (including severely and profoundly handicapped) persons, but they did not expect the goal to be substantially realized for more than a decade (over 70% said not before 1996). They did not, however, predict loss of momentum for the deinstitutionalization movement, and felt that in the future large-scale institutions would be considered unacceptable for people who represented no physical threat to others.

Second, although respondents considered the trend undesirable, they predicted a sharp decrease in assistance to reform institutions through litigation. Interestingly, respondents felt the federal role in policy making and regulations would not materially change, but there was strong support for shifting regulatory practices from monitoring processes to monitoring outcomes of services for clients.

Regarding service programs, respondents foresaw increased integration for severely handicapped children and youth, but not substantially before the 1991–1995 interval. A large number of trends that reflected greater coordination of services across disciplines, agencies, and settings were considered highly desirable, but respondents were pessimistic regarding realization of the goals inherent in these trends before the late 1990s. There was more optimism, however, regarding prospects for maintaining financial commitments for services, but little consensus regarding the probability of integrating funding across designated categorical reimbursement programs. A number of innovations in the technology of assessment and integration of training into natural environments were given highly desirable ratings, but were not projected for general implementation until the 1990s.

Based upon only a cursory review of trends from this study, it seems reasonable to conclude that the respondents were relatively optimistic that deinstitutionalization and service within less restrictive environments would continue as national policies toward handicapped persons. They were far less sanguine regarding an acceleration in the pace of adopting needed changes to fully implement current state-of-the-art policies. Many of the practices considered as necessary ingredients of the infrastructure for these policies were projected to occur late in the 1990s. Although this survey is more detailed than earlier ones (such as that by Roos, 1978, conducted in the 1970s), the pattern of findings reflects greater concern with the projected rate of change and the systemic problems of effectively integrating services and professional practices than was reported in the Roos (1978) survey.

The general consensus of respondents regarding the desirability of continued movement of severely handicapped children and youth and of programs for them into community settings, but at the same time, the wide variance of opinion with respect to how well or how soon this might be realized, suggests that substantial obstacles to integration still exist. In Zaltman and Duncan's (1977) list of strategies for promoting adoption of change discussed earlier, it would appear that reeducative strategies may be relatively poorly supported by facilitative, persuasive, and power strategies. Increasing the use of these latter approaches may well be critical at this time.

Chapters in this book have described data-collection and analysis methodologies ranging from those used with multiple programs to those for specific programs with one major goal, from those measuring the effects of a single service on a group of clients to those assessing behavioral change in an individual client. The stress on interpreting accurate data has become more crucial to the continuing development of programs providing services in the least restrictive setting. Because the extent of integration of severely handicapped children and youth into neighborhood schools and community-based residences remains limited, it is important to develop a data base on the effectiveness of available placements to guide future development policies. Such research should examine not only program effectiveness but cost-effectiveness; it should not only compare integrated settings with nonintegrated settings but should also attempt to identify the program-

matic and environmental features most conducive to client development and social participation. This research must, in addition, involve careful fiscal and systems analyses. Far too little is known about the processes and procedures by which some states, regions, and/or localities have developed exemplary systems of services for severely handicapped children and youth while others maintain archaic systems of segregated education, residential, and support services. Finally, the knowledge gained from these analyses must be presented to the public and its representatives not only to show what can be accomplished for and by severely handicapped persons in community settings but to aid policy development.

Providing services to severely handicapped persons in least restrictive environments seems securely rooted as a national commitment and is increasingly accepted as state-of-the-art practice. The last few decades have witnessed widespread approval of this ideal and considerable movement toward implementing integrated service programs. More extensive adoption of such state-of-the-art practices is still required, however, and changes will need to be implemented on the basis of improved program models that are more firmly based on valid findings of research and development efforts. Notwithstanding many remaining problems, through application of currently available methods for improving programs and policies, future opportunities for enhanced development and greater social integration of severely handicapped citizens can be more fully assured.

REFERENCES

Ackoff, R. Towards a system of systems concepts. *Management Science*, 1971, *17*, 661–671.

Baker, B.L. Parent involvement in programming for developmentally disabled children and youth. In: L.L. Lloyd (ed.), *Communication assessment and intervention strategies*. Baltimore: University Park Press, 1976.

Bardach, E. *The implementation game: What happens after a bill becomes a law*. Cambridge, MA: MIT Press, 1977.

Becker, W. Teaching reading and language to the disadvantaged: What we have learned from field research. *Harvard Education Review*, 1977, *47*(4), 518–543.

Blatt, B. *Exodus from pandemonium: Human abuse and a*

reformation of public policy. Boston: Allyn & Bacon, 1970.

Blatt, B. *Souls in extremis*. Boston: Allyn & Bacon, 1973.

Bradley, V.J. *Deinstitutionalization of developmentally disabled persons*. Baltimore: University Park Press, 1978.

Brown, L., Branston, M., Hamre-Nietupski, S., Johnson, F., Wilcox, B., & Gruenwald, L. A rationale for comprehensive longitudinal interactions between severely handicapped students and nonhandicapped students and other citizens. *AAESPH Review*, 1979, *4*(1), 3–14.

Bruininks, R.H., Hauber, F.A., & Kudla, M.J. *National survey of community residential facilities: A profile of facilities and residents in 1977.* Minneapolis: University of Minnesota, Department of Educational Psychology, 1979.

Bruininks, R.H., & Putnam, J. *Working conference on deinstitutionalization and education of handicapped children and youth: Results of group work activities.* Unpublished report, University of Minnesota, Department of Educational Psychology, 1983.

Bruininks, R.H., Thurlow, M.L, Thurman, S.K., & Fiorelli, J.S. Deinstitutionalization and community services. In: J. Wortis (ed.), *Mental retardation and developmental disabilities,* Vol. 11. New York: Brunner/Mazel, 1980.

Bureau of Education for the Handicapped (BEH). *States to receive $134 million in Public Law 89-313 allocations for FY 1979* (BEH Data Notes). Washington, DC: U.S. Department of Education, 1979.

Center for Residential and Community Services. *1982 national census of residential facilities: Summary report.* Minneapolis: University of Minnesota, Department of Educational Psychology, 1983.

Chaffee, J.H. Community and Family Living Amendments Act, *Congressional Record,* 1983 (November 4), 98–150, 515480–515485.

Cobb, H.V. *The forecast of fulfillment.* New York: Teachers College Press, 1972.

Cox, W.D., & Matthews, C.O. Parent group education: What does it do for children? *Journal of School Psychology,* 1977, *15,* 358–361.

Dalkey, N.C., & Helmer, O. An experimental application of the Delphi method to the use of experts. *Management Science,* 1963, *9,* 458–467.

Delbecq, A., Van de Ven, A., & Gustafson, D. *Group techniques for program planning.* Glenview, IL: Scott, Foresman & Co., 1974.

Delp, P., Thesen, A., Motwalla, J., & Seshardi, N. *Systems tools for project planning.* Bloomington, IN: International Development Institute, Indiana University, 1977.

Flynn, R.J., & Nitsch, K.E. Introduction. In: R.J. Flynn & K.E. Nitsch (eds.), *Normalization, social integration, and community services.* Baltimore: University Park Press, 1980.

Freeman, H. Fostercare for mentally retarded children: Can it work? *Child Welfare,* 1978, *57,* 113–121.

Gans, S.P., & Horton, G.T. *Integration of human services: The state and municipal levels.* New York: Praeger Publishers, 1975.

General Accounting Office. *Disparities still exist in who gets special education* (Pub. # 0-361-843/794). Washington, D C : U.S. Government Printing Office, 1981.

Gettings, R. Hidden impediments to deinstitutionalization. *State Government,* 1977, *50,* 214–219.

Goffman, E. *Asylums: Essays on the social situation of mental patients and other inmates.* Garden City, NY: Doubleday & Co., 1961.

Greenberg, J.N., Schmitz, M.A., & Lakin, K.C. *An analysis of responses to the Medicaid home- and community-based long-term care waiver program (Section 2176 of Public Law 97-35).* Washington, D C : National Governor's Association, 1983.

Halderman v. Pennhurst State School and Hospital, 446 F. Supp. 1295 (E.D. Pa. 1977).

Henderson, A.T. *Parent participation/student involvement: The evidence grows.* Columbia, MD: National Committee for Citizens in Education, 1982.

Kiesler, C.A. Mental hospitals and alternative care. *American Psychologist,* 1982, *37*(4), 349–360.

Lakin, K.C. *Demographic studies of residential facilities for the mentally retarded.* Minneapolis, MN: University of Minnesota, Department of Educational Psychology, 1979.

Lakin, K.C., & Bruininks, R.H. (eds.) *Strategies for achieving community integration of developmentally disabled citizens.* Baltimore: Paul H. Brookes Publishing Co., in press.

Lakin, K.C., Bruininks, R.H., & Sigford, B.B. Early perspectives on the community adjustment of mentally retarded people. In: R.H. Bruinks, C.E. Meyers, B.B. Sigford, & K.C. Lakin (eds.), *Deinstitutionalization and community adjustment of mentally retarded people.* Washington, DC: American Association on Mental Deficiency, 1981.

Lakin, K.C., Hill, B.K., Hauber, F.A., & Bruininks, R.H. A response to the GAO report: "Disparities still exist in who gets special education." *Exceptional Children,* 1983, *50*(1), 30–36.

McCarver, R.B., & Craig, E.M. Placement of the retarded in the community: Prognosis and outcome. In: N.R. Ellis (ed.), *International review of research in mental retardation,* Vol. 7. New York: Academic Press, 1974.

Mayeda, T., & Sutter, P. Deinstitutionalization: Phase II. In: R.H. Bruininks, C.E. Meyers, B.B. Sigford, and K.C. Lakin (eds.), *Deinstitutionalization and community adjustment of mentally retarded people.* Washington, D C : American Association on Mental Deficiency, 1981.

Muzzio, T.C., Koshel, J.J., & Bradley, V. (eds.). *Alternative community living arrangements and non-vocational social service for developmentally disabled people.* Washington, D C : Urban Institute, 1981.

NASMRPD. *See under* National Association of State Mental Retardation Program Directors.

NASPRFMR. *See under* National Association of Superintendents of Public Residential Facilities for the Mentally Retarded.

National Association of State Mental Retardation Program Directors (NASMRPD). *Trends in capital expenditures for mental retardation facilities: A state-by-state survey.* Arlington, VA: NASMRPD, 1980.

National Association of Superintendents of Public Residential Facilities for the Mentally Retraded (NASPRFMR). *Contemporary issues in residential programming.* Washington, D C : President's Committee on Mental Retardation, 1974.

National Council on the Handicapped. *A national policy for persons with disabilities.* Washington, D C : National Council on the Handicapped, 1983.

Nirje, B. The normalization principle. In: R. Kugel & A. Shearer (eds.), *Changing patterns in residential services for the mentally retarded.* Washington, D C : President's Committee on Mental Retardation, 1976.

Pense, A.W. Trends in institutional care for the mentally defective. *American Journal of Mental Deficiency,* 1946, *50,* 453–457.

Pilewski, M.E., & Heal, L.W. Empirical support for deinstitutionalization. In: A.R. Novak & L.W. Heal (eds.), *Integration of developmentally disabled individuals into the community.* Baltimore: Paul H. Brookes Publishing Co., 1980.

Putnam, J.W., & Bruininks, R.H. *Deinstitutionalization and education of handicapped children and youth: A*

Delphi forecasting survey. Minneapolis, MN: University of Minnesota, 1984.

Pyecha, J.N. *A national survey of individualized education programs for handicapped children.* Research Triangle Park, NC: Research Triangle Institute, Center for Educational Research and Evaluation, 1980.

Roos, S. The future of residential services for the mentally retarded in the United States: A Delphi study. *Mental Retardation,* 1978, *16,* 355–356.

Rosenshine, B.V. Academic engaged time, content covered, and direct instruction. *Journal of Education,* 1977, *159,* 38–66.

Rotegard, L.L., & Bruininks, R.H. *Mentally retarded people in state-operated residential facilities: Years ending June 30, 1981 and 1982.* Minneapolis, MN: University of Minnesota, Department of Educational Psychology, 1983.

Scheerenberger, R.C. *Public residential services for the mentally retarded, 1981.* Minneapolis, MN: University of Minnesota, Department of Educational Psychology, 1982.

Scheerenberger, R.C. *Public residential services for the mentally retarded, 1982.* Minneapolis, MN: University of Minnesota, Department of Educational Psychology, 1983.

Schumacher, E.F. *Small is beautiful.* New York: Harper & Row, 1973.

Stallings, J.A. *How to change the process of reading in secondary schools.* Menlo Park, CA: SRI International, 1979.

Sterns, M., Green, D., & David, J. *Local implementation of Public Law 94-142: Report on a longitudinal study.* Menlo Park, CA: SRI International, 1980.

Sterns, M., Green, D., & David, J. *Local implementation of Public Law 94-142: Report on a longitudinal study.* Menlo Park, CA: SRI International, 1981.

United Nations General Assembly. Declaration on the rights of disabled persons. Reprinted in: *The White House Conference on Handicapped Individuals (Vol. 1): Awareness papers.* Washington, D C : U.S. Government Printing Office, 1977.

U.S. Department of Education. *Fifth annual report to Congress on the implementation of Public Law 94-142: The Education for All Handicapped Children Act.* Washington, D C : U.S. Government Printing Office, 1983.

Wolfensberger, W. Research, empiricism, and the principle of normalization. In: R. Flynn and K. Nitsch (eds.), *Normalization, social integration and community services.* Baltimore: University Park Press, 1980.

Zaltman, G., & Duncan, R. *Strategies for planned change.* New York: John Wiley & Sons, 1977.

Index

New directions for improving the quality of life of citizens with handicaps...

Living and Learning in the Least Restrictive Environment

**Edited by Robert H. Bruininks, Ph.D.,
& K. Charlie Lakin, Ph.D.,
Department of Educational Psychology,
University of Minnesota**

This penetrating book evaluates the current status of the integration effort, explains the issues still to be overcome, and projects the future needs and developments in the care of severely handicapped children and young adults. Providing a comprehensive analysis of the concepts of *normalization, deinstitutionalization,* and the *least restrictive environment,* the book examines the impact they have had in the courts, in the community, in the school system, in the service delivery systems, in the family, in the government and economy, and in the lives of handicapped persons themselves.

For those who have sometimes witnessed disabled persons being adversely affected by the inappropriate implementation of these principles, this book will be valued for its recommendations to redefine, reorganize, and better utilize living and learning opportunities in order to improve the quality of life for severely handicapped persons.

And the companion volume...

Strategies for Achieving Community Integration of Developmentally Disabled Citizens

**Edited by K. Charlie Lakin, Ph.D.,
& Robert H. Bruininks, Ph.D.**

Complementing the chapters of *Living and Learning in the Least Restrictive Environment,* this book presents successful strategies for developing the independent skills of severely handicapped persons from early childhood through adulthood. Included are strategies for assessment, intervention, social skill development, and vocational preparation, as well as organizational and fiscal planning.

ISBN 0-933716-42-7